A Step-by-Step Guide to Qualitative Data Coding

A Step-by-Step Guide to Qualitative Data Coding is a comprehensive qualitative data analysis guide. It is designed to help readers to systematically analyze qualitative data in a transparent and consistent manner, thus promoting the credibility of their findings.

The book examines the art of coding data, categorizing codes, and synthesizing categories and themes. Using real data for demonstrations, it provides step-by-step instructions and illustrations for analyzing qualitative data. Some of the demonstrations include conducting manual coding using Microsoft Word and how to use qualitative data analysis software such as Dedoose, NVivo and QDA Miner Lite to analyze data. It also contains creative ways of presenting qualitative findings and provides practical examples.

After reading this book, readers will be able to:

- Analyze qualitative data and present their findings
- Select an appropriate qualitative analysis tool
- Decide on the right qualitative coding and categorization strategies for their analysis
- Develop relationships among categories/themes
- Choose a suitable format for the presentation of the findings

It is a great resource for qualitative research instructors and undergraduate and graduate students who want to gain skills in analyzing qualitative data or who plan to conduct a qualitative study. It is also useful for researchers and practitioners in the social and health sciences fields.

Philip Adu is a Methodology Expert at The Chicago School of Professional Psychology (TCSPP). He has spent over six years at TCSPP providing methodology support to doctoral students. He has designed and taught numerous research method courses. He is skilled in demystifying the qualitative analysis process, including how to use qualitative data analysis software (QDAS).

A Step-by-Step Guide to Qualitative Data Coding

Philip Adu

Routledge
Taylor & Francis Group

LONDON AND NEW YORK

First published 2019
by Routledge
2 Park Square, Milton Park, Abingdon, Oxon OX14 4RN

and by Routledge
52 Vanderbilt Avenue, New York, NY 10017

Routledge is an imprint of the Taylor & Francis Group, an informa business

© 2019 Philip Adu

The right of Philip Adu to be identified as author of this work has been asserted by him in accordance with sections 77 and 78 of the Copyright, Designs and Patents Act 1988.

Trademark notice: Product or corporate names may be trademarks or registered trademarks, and are used only for identification and explanation without intent to infringe.

British Library Cataloguing in Publication Data
A catalogue record for this book is available from the British Library

Library of Congress Cataloging in Publication Data
Names: Adu, Philip, author.
Title: A step-by-step guide to qualitative data coding / Philip Adu.
Description: New York : Routledge, 2019.
Identifiers: LCCN 2018057100 | ISBN 9781138486850 (hardback) |
ISBN 9781138486874 (pbk.) | ISBN 9781351044516 (ebook)
Subjects: LCSH: Psychology–Qualitative research.
Classification: LCC BF76.5 .A228 2019 | DDC 150.72–dc23
LC record available at https://lccn.loc.gov/2018057100

ISBN: 978-1-138-48685-0 (hbk)
ISBN: 978-1-138-48687-4 (pbk)
ISBN: 978-1-351-04451-6 (ebk)

Typeset in Frutiger Light
by Newgen Publishing UK

Visit the eResources: www.routledge.com/9781138486874

I dedicate this book to my lovely wife Monique and three wonderful children Miriam, Olivia and Evan.

Brief contents

Detailed contents

Exhibits

Figures

Tables

Boxes

Acknowledgment

I want to thank my wife Monique Adu, DO, FAAP, for her valuable support in putting this book together. I would not have been able to successfully complete the book without her continuous encouragement, critique and feedback.

Introduction to qualitative data analysis

OBJECTIVES

Readers will be able to:

1. Understand how qualitative research and methods emerged
2. Recognize different types of paradigms and their assumptions
3. Determine which of the paradigms best fits their beliefs and research approach

EMERGENCE OF QUALITATIVE RESEARCH AS AN ACCEPTABLE RESEARCH INQUIRY

The acceptance or popularity of qualitative methods as an alternative tool for research inquiry wasn't linear. However, Kuhn's (1996) assertion regarding how a paradigm (i.e. set of beliefs and procedures held by a particular discipline or research community) is maintained, adjusted and rejected could help us to better understand how qualitative methods became widely used in the health and social sciences. According to Kuhn (1996), paradigms are continuously being challenged or tested by new ideas, findings and theories. Crisis occurs when a discipline is unable to resolve inconsistencies in its paradigm. An unresolved crisis in the paradigm could lead to its abandonment – giving way to the formation of a new paradigm. Sometimes, a crisis is resolved by adjusting the existing paradigm.

Positivism was a dominant paradigm during the 19th century (Bentz & Shapiro, 2001). Positivists believed that there is a single 'Truth' and that there can be a universal knowledge that transcends time and context (Patton, 2015). They mainly use quantitative methods to conduct research inquiry. To them, qualitative methods lack the strength to attain the 'Truth' and they do not require the rigor and objectivity associated with obtaining generalizable findings. As social sciences began to grow, researchers in this discipline started critiquing positivism – revealing inconsistencies and questioning their ontological (about reality), epistemological (about knowledge), axiological (about value) and methodological (about the research process) assumptions associated with positivism (Patton, 2015).

The postpositivism paradigm emerged out of the positivism crisis to address most of the criticisms leveled against the positivists (Patton, 2015). The postpositivists argue that there are multiple truths, which could be investigated utilizing "multiple methods, both quantitative and qualitative [methods]" (Patton, 2015, p. 105). These truths (in the form of hypotheses and theories) can be accepted, rejected or refined based on new discoveries. In addition, they can change based on time and context – debunking positivists' assertion of a time-free and context-free 'Truth' or knowledge. Postpositivists mainly use quantitative methods to conduct research but sometimes utilize qualitative approaches to play supporting roles in their studies.

The emergence of the worldview of postpositivism in response to the critics of positivism couldn't stop the rise of a naturalistic/interpretive paradigm with qualitative approaches as the main alternative methods of inquiry. Briefly, researchers and scholars with a naturalistic or an interpretive worldview are of the view that:

- There are multiple ways of looking at or interpreting an issue (i.e. multiple realities)
- Individuals' characteristics influence how they see the world or interpret their experience
- All truth or knowledge is linked to a context (i.e. context-bound knowledge)

Under this paradigm, the main worldviews are constructivist, social constructivist and transformative positions. There is not much difference among these worldviews in terms of their philosophical assumptions in relation to ontology (i.e. there is more than one reality), epistemology (i.e. there is a researcher–phenomenon of study link), axiology (i.e. research results are based on the context) and methodology (i.e. conducting an inquiry using qualitative methods) (Creswell & Poth, 2018; Yilmaz, 2013). However, constructivists contend that we individually construct ideas (i.e. knowledge or reality), making sense of our environment as we interact with people, places, objects and situations. Taking a step further, social constructivists believe that, yes, we build knowledge through interactions but it is socially constructed. As we interact with our society, receiving and sharing ideas, we end up building knowledge which is shared by all members (including us) of the society. I must emphasize that the social construction of knowledge is a continuous process. Members constantly create, refine and maintain ideas.

Researchers and practitioners who hold the transformative worldview believe that socially constructed knowledge could be oppressive, pushing people with less power to a disadvantaged position (Mertens, 2003). As you may know, there are socially constructed rules and norms that could be discriminatory and disempowering. These norms and regulations prevent certain groups of people from meeting their goals in life. In response, researchers with a transformative worldview are concerned about helping people to remove obstacles in their lives and working with them to come up with solutions to address their oppressive situation. Their research is not only about contributing to the knowledge in their discipline but about improving participants' conditions.

There are paradigms that have some similarities with the transformative worldview. They include: critical, feminism, queer and disability theories (Creswell & Poth, 2018). These theories have one thing in common, which is pointing out injustice, unfairness and discrimination, and advocating for empowerment and equality. Creswell and Poth (2018) discuss these theories in detail in their book, *Qualitative Inquiry and Research Design: Choosing among Five Approaches.*

Pragmatism is another paradigm which has recently gained popularity, especially among researchers who advocate for the use of the mixed methods approach. Pragmatists focus on evaluating existing models, theories, paradigms and research methods, and selecting appropriate ones for their inquiry. They are not associated with any particular paradigm, but are concerned with using any suitable research tool that could aid in solving their research problem, explaining a phenomenon of study or addressing a research question (Hanson, Creswell, Plano Clark, Petska, & Creswell, 2005). In others words, if a paradigm works, they adopt and use it to achieve their goal (Creswell & Poth, 2018).

WHAT IS YOUR PARADIGM?

Which one of the paradigms best suits your beliefs about knowledge in terms of how it should be researched? Do you believe that there is one ultimate 'Truth' out there? Do you believe there are multiple realities? You could think about these and similar questions to help you choose a paradigm which is closely related to your philosophical beliefs. You may see yourself being a part of one or more of the worldviews, or you are not sure where you belong. Irrespective of the paradigm you identify with, you should be aware of their philosophical assumptions (*explained above*), strengths (*expressed by their gatekeepers*), weaknesses (*raised by their critics*) and concerns (*brought forward by their skeptics*).

Similar to Kuhn's (1996) submission about the emergence and extinction of paradigms, I see four main roles that researchers and scholars could play to sustain or reject existing paradigms, or create new ones. Within a paradigm, there are gatekeepers and skeptics (see Figure 1.1).

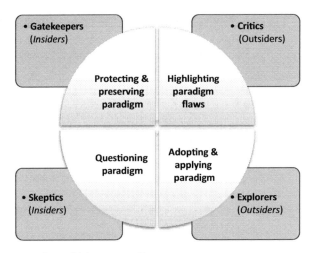

Figure 1.1. Four roles within a paradigm

Gatekeepers see themselves as guardians of the elements of the para-digm – ready to explain their worldview, respond to critics, and initiate new members. However, skeptics within the paradigm don't take things for granted; they question aspects of the paradigm as they determine its consistency compared to evidence, findings and/or new ideas. If they are not satisfied (for example, due to the inability of the paradigm/gatekeepers to address their questions), they reject the paradigm and join an existing worldview or create a new one.

Conversely, there are two main groups of scholars (outside a paradigm) whose role is to critically examine the worldview: critics and explorers. The role of the critics is to point out the weaknesses of the paradigm and sometimes make recommendations. However, the explorers' focus is to identify and utilize applicable and result-oriented aspects of a paradigm to address a research problem. Their role is quite similar to that of the pragmatists (see Creswell & Poth, 2018). All of these roles are essential to the advancement of knowledge.

Whether you are a part of an existing paradigm or not, there is a role you could play to help advance knowledge in your field. You could be:

- A *paradigm gatekeeper* – fortifying your paradigm boundaries with a strong scholarly response to issues raised by critics (Phillips, 1979)
- A *paradigm skeptic* – questioning issues in the paradigm you are affiliated with (Patton, 2015)
- A *paradigm critic* – bringing to light the weakness of a paradigm, and explaining new ideas or research findings (Kuhn, 1996)
- A *paradigm explorer* – examining, adopting and applying paradigms to carry out your research (Creswell & Poth, 2018)

Irrespective of our role in paradigm development and maintenance, when conducting a study we need to be aware of the characteristics of the research methods we use and their respective philosophical assumptions. Every paradigm is regulated by its philosophical assumptions, which in turn inform the research methods being used. In other words, every worldview held by a research community or discipline (i.e. paradigm) has conditions that should be met or rules which need to be followed (i.e. philosophical assumptions) when using recommended research tools/ methods to conduct research.

Whenever we select a methodology for your study, we need to learn more about its philosophical assumptions so as to conduct a study that is credible. For instance, if you choose and use a quasi-experimental design as your quantitative research method for your study, the decisions and actions you take (in relation to data collection and analysis, and presentation and interpretation of results) should reflect the philosophical assumptions associated with positivist or postpositivist worldviews. This includes but is not limited to the following:

- The research environment should be free from the 'researcher-participant influence' and/or 'researcher–phenomenon of study influence'. The study should be free from the researcher's biases.
- The study should be consistent with a deductive reasoning process where data is collected to test hypotheses.
- There should be testable hypotheses. The hypotheses should contain measurable variables.
- Findings could be generalizable if participants were selected using a probability sampling technique.
- There is a possibility of establishing a cause-and-effect relationship if experimental-related procedures are followed.

ASSUMPTIONS ASSOCIATED WITH THE INTERPRETATIVE PARADIGMS

Let's limit our discussion to the interpretative paradigms (such as constructivism, social constructivism, and transformative worldviews) since this book is about conducting qualitative analysis. All of these paradigms mainly use qualitative methods to explore a research phenomenon, examine a complex experience, and highlight unnoticed and sensitive issues – getting to the depth of an experience, a situation or a process. Whenever we choose a qualitative method as our research approach for a study, it is implied that we accept the following assumptions:

- **Multiple realities:** We and potential participants for our study have history (which includes our background, past experiences, beliefs and education) and a present situation. Since past and present experiences differ from one person to another, the way we see the world and interpret our experiences is different. So, in using a qualitative method, it is expected that participants may provide varied descriptions about their experiences and the meaning they make out of them. This supports the assumption that there are multiple interpretations of the world, which are influenced by our history and present situation (Creswell & Poth, 2018).

- **Reciprocal influence among researcher, participants and phenomenon of study:** Conducting a qualitative study is a subjective experience with the researcher deciding on what to study, who to talk to, what kind of questions to ask participants, what documents/artifacts to look for, how data should be analyzed and how participants' stories should be told. Our history and present situation influence the decisions we make and actions we take in the qualitative study. Within this subjective experience, we are able to get closer to participants – getting to know each other and building trust. Out of this harmonious environment of mutual respect and trust comes rich data from willing participants. Our knowledge about participants and their situation influences how we make sense of the data (Adu, 2016). During the data analysis process, we sometimes allow the data to guide our curious eyes to an unexplored and intriguing portion of the phenomenon of study. Here is how reciprocal influence works in qualitative research: Think about two researchers who plan to conduct qualitative research on domestic violence – examining the experience of domestic violence victims who left their abusive partners. Imagine one of them has experienced abuse in his/her marriage and the other has not; there is a likelihood that their decisions on a specific focus, qualitative method, data collection and analysis, and presentation of the findings will differ.

- **Context-based qualitative findings:** Context in qualitative research includes but is not limited to research location, situation, participants' history, and characteristics. Qualitative data is not complete without gathering information about the context. The context not only helps us to make sense of individual participants' views and experiences when analyzing data, but also assists our audience to understand the circumstances in which the findings are applied. For instance, we can collect demographic information about participants such as age, gender, educational level, work experience, marital status, and race to share with our audience when presenting our findings. The audience will better comprehend the themes presented if they are supported with quotes from participants, together with a brief description of their background and the situation they are in. This helps in attaining transferability of the findings. Ensuring transferability involves describing the context (when presenting the findings) in such a way that future researchers can easily transfer the findings or apply the interpretation of the results to a similar context (Trochim, 2006).

CONCLUSION

You may ask, should I select the methodology first before the paradigm or vice versa? Either option is okay. The most important thing is to make sure the methodology is appropriate considering your research problem, purpose and question(s). After selecting a specific qualitative research method, ensure that you know the paradigm that informs the approach – familiarizing yourself with the philosophical assumptions associated with the method. It is all about ensuring consistency among the paradigm, its assumptions and qualitative method, data collection strategies, data analysis strategies and presentation of the findings format (see Figure 1.2).

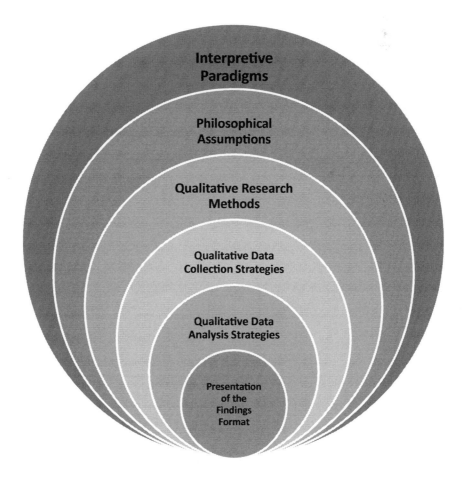

Figure 1.2. How interpretative paradigms inform the qualitative research process

REFERENCES

Adu, P. (2016). Writing the methodology chapter of a qualitative study [PowerPoint slides]. SlideShare. Retrieved from www.slideshare.net/kontorphilip/writing-the-methodology-chapter-of-a-qualitative-study

Bentz, V. M., & Shapiro, J. J. (2001). *Mindful inquiry in social research.* Thousand Oaks, CA: Sage.

Creswell, J. W., & Poth, C. N. (2018). *Qualitative inquiry & research design: Choosing among five approaches.* Los Angeles, CA: Sage.

Hanson, W. E., Creswell, J. W., Plano Clark, V. L., Petska, K. S., & Creswell, D. J. (2005). Mixed methods research designs in counseling psychology. *Journal of Counseling Psychology, 2*(55), 224–235. doi:10.1037/0022-0167.52.2.224

Kuhn, T. S. (1996). *The structure of scientific revolutions.* Chicago, IL: University of Chicago Press.

Mertens, D. M. (2003). Mixed methods and the politics of human research: The transformative-emancipatory perspective. In A. Tashakkori & C. Teddlie (Eds.), *Handbook of mixed methods in social and behavioral research* (pp. 135–164). Thousand Oaks, CA: Sage.

Patton, M. Q. (2015). *Qualitative research & evaluation methods: Integrating theory and practice.* Los Angeles, CA: Sage.

Phillips, G. M. (1979). The peculiar intimacy of graduate study: A conservative view. *Communication Education, 28*, 339–345.

Trochim, W. M. K. (2006, October 20). Qualitative validity. Retrieved from www.socialresearchmethods.net/kb/qualval.php

Yilmaz, K. (2013). Comparison of quantitative and qualitative research traditions: Epistemological, theoretical, and methodological differences. *European Journal of Education, 48*(2), 311–325.

Review of qualitative approaches and their data analysis methods

OBJECTIVES

Readers will be able to:

1. Decide on an appropriate qualitative approach for their study
2. Determine an appropriate data analysis method for their qualitative study

QUALITATIVE APPROACHES AND THEIR RESPECTIVE DATA ANALYSIS PROCESSES

There are many types and varieties of qualitative approaches. The following are commonly used types: phenomenological approach, hermeneutic phenomenological approach, interpretative phenomenological analysis, transcendental phenomenological approach, ethnography, narrative approach, case study and grounded theory approach. Below is a brief description of each qualitative approach and associated qualitative analysis method.

Phenomenological approach

Imagine you're interested in studying a phenomenon such as homelessness or mental health illness and you want to examine the views and stories of people who have directly or indirectly experienced the phenomenon. The phenomenological approach could be used to conduct this kind of study (Creswell & Poth, 2018; Moustakas, 1994). With this approach, you recruit participants (who have experienced the phenomenon of interest) and ask them mostly open-ended questions. These questions could elicit rich responses about the experiences. You then analyze the data to produce themes that represent the multiple perspectives of the experiences.

When to use the phenomenological approach

✓ When studying a phenomenon directly or indirectly experienced by a group of people
✓ When potential participants have experienced or are currently experiencing the phenomenon
✓ When you are expecting participants to share their experience and/ or their thoughts about the experience

Giorgi's (1975) approach towards analyzing phenomenological data

Whiting (2001) discusses Giorgi's (1975) structured way of analyzing phenomenological data in her article, "Analysis of Phenomenological Data: Personal Reflections on Giorgi's Method". As described by Whiting (2001), here are the five main steps:

1. Put aside your preconceived ideas
2. Review the interview transcripts
3. Group the transcripts into units (such as having chunks of relevant information)
4. Create themes based on the relevant units created
5. With the phenomenon of study, purpose of the study and research question(s) in mind, present descriptions of the themes

Hermeneutic phenomenological approach

The hermeneutic phenomenological approach (HPA) is a type of phenomenological approach used to critically analyze mainly written documents (i.e. text) – extracting underlying meaning to address a research problem, purpose or question. This method is popular among biblical scholars, who use it to interpret portions of the Bible, and to formulate meanings and principles that could be applied to current situations (Vandermause & Fleming, 2011). When using HPA, we need to make sure our beliefs, past experiences and biases don't influence how we interpret the text (Kafle, 2013). It is an undeniable fact that our history could affect the meaning we derive from the data, but we can definitely minimize its impact by first acknowledging our preconceptions and making sure we distance them from the text analysis process (see Chapter 5). To attain a deeper understanding of the text, we need to examine the characteristics, history and intent of the author, the context in which the text was written, recipients of the message, and recipients' characteristics and history. Although most of the written documents used in the analysis are written before a study is conducted, some are written by participants (such as personal journals) during the data collection stage.

When to use the hermeneutic phenomenological approach

✓ When written documents are your main data
✓ When you are planning to bring to light the underlying meaning of text
✓ When you want to describe or examine people's experiences by interpreting documents they have written
✓ When exploring a phenomenon by critically analyzing text

Conducting hermeneutic phenomenological analysis

In my presentation, *Analyzing Social Media Data Using NVivo 11: A Hermeneutic Phenomenological Approach*, I discuss Kafle's (2013) description on conducting hermeneutic phenomenological analysis (see Adu, 2016a). Here are the data analysis steps based on the presentation:

1. Reflecting on your background and biases and putting them aside – preventing them from impacting your interpretation of the text
2. Cleaning the data for analysis
3. Documenting your thoughts and ideas that come into mind during the analysis process
4. Reviewing the data as you address the following questions:
    a. When was the document written and for what purpose?
    b. Who wrote the text and what was his/her intent?
    c. What was happening at that time that may be relevant to the intent of the author?
    d. Who were the audience?
    e. What was the author trying to communicate?
5. Identify areas in the text that are relevant to the purpose of the study or research question(s)
6. Determine the meanings of the relevant portions of the data
7. Develop codes to represent the relevant excerpts in the data
8. Generate themes based on the codes created

Interpretative phenomenological analysis

Interpretative phenomenological analysis (IPA) is quite similar to the phenomenological approach since both focus on collecting and analyzing participants' lived experience. What makes IPA uniquely different from the phenomenological approach is its hermeneutic characteristic – emphasizing the interpretation of participants' views about what they have experienced. With this approach, participants present their perspectives of their experience while the researcher interprets those accounts, including their history and circumstances (Smith, Flowers, & Larkin, 2012). As Smith et al. (2012) put it, "in choosing IPA for a research project, we commit ourselves to exploring, describing and situating the means by which our participants make sense of their experiences" (p. 40).

When using IPA, we need to acknowledge the complexity of the data collected from participants. There are multiple layers we should unravel when analyzing the data. First, we should be aware that participants experience a phenomenon (such as substance abuse or homelessness) differently due to the variances in their history and situation. Second, when interviewing participants, their history and the situation in which they find themselves could influence how they talk about their lived experiences. Last, as researchers, we have our own history and biases which may affect how we interpret participants' stories. All these factors should be taken into consideration when using IPA to analyze data.

When to use interpretative phenomenological analysis

✓ When assessing how participants make sense of their experience
✓ When you want to understand why people do what they do – going beyond just describing their experience to examine the rationale behind their decisions and actions
✓ When exploring the core components of participants' experience and its essence

Conducting interpretative phenomenological analysis at the data analysis stage

IPA can be seen as both a research approach and data analysis method. Smith et al. (2012) discuss a step-by-step process for analyzing IPA data. Here are five IPA steps:

1. Review the transcripts to learn more about participants' responses to the interview questions
2. With the purpose of the study and research question(s) in mind, go through the data – identifying relevant information
3. For the relevant information selected, write down your interpretations by addressing some of the following questions:
   a. What does this information mean?
   b. What is the participant trying to say or imply?
   c. What is the intent of the participant based on this information?
4. Develop themes based on the interpretations
5. Determine the relationship between the themes by comparing and contrasting them

Transcendental phenomenological approach

One of the critiques of qualitative research is a lack of objective findings due to the researcher's close connection with the phenomenon of study and the potential influence of their history on how they make sense of data and interpret the findings. What if you have a qualitative approach that could lead you to 'objective' qualitative findings – obtaining results that have no or little influence from your prior knowledge and experience (Moustakas, 1994)? The transcendental phenomenological approach (TPA) is a type of a phenomenological method that could be used to achieve a researcher's personal-history-free results. One unique characteristic of TPA is a continuous practice of reaching a level of consciousness where the researchers block all the past experience and preconceptions from affecting how they collect and analyze data, and interpret findings (Moustakas, 1994). Moustakas (1994) refers to this activity as "reflective-meditation" (p. 88).

When to use the transcendental phenomenological approach

- ✓ When you want to access the underlying meaning behind participants' experience
- ✓ When you want to prevent your past knowledge and experience from influencing how you:
  - Interview participants
  - Observe objects, behaviors, events or processes
  - Make sense of data – determining the essence of what participants have experienced
- ✓ When bracketing your background and biases to attain close to 'objective' results (Moustakas, 1994)
- ✓ When interviewing participants to talk about what they have experienced
- ✓ When analyzing participants' experience to produce "…a textural description of the experiences of the persons (what participants experienced), a structural description of their experiences (how they experienced it in terms of the conditions, situations, or context)…" (Creswell & Poth, 2018, p. 78).

Conducting transcendental phenomenological analysis

According to Moustakas (1994), there are four main stages of TPA: epoché, phenomenological reduction, imaginative variation and meaning synthesizing. Epoché involves engaging in self-reflection to identify and "set aside" your history and preconceived ideas (Moustakas, 1994, p. 84). It is "…a Greek word meaning to stay away from or abstain" (Moustakas, 1994, p. 33). The essence of conducting epoché is to review the data from fresh perspectives and be open to multiple interpretations. The second stage involves conducting a phenomenological reduction, which is about engaging in data reduction – extracting essential excerpts from the data. Based on the selected relevant information, you develop themes leading to the formation of textual descriptions. The third stage, imaginative variation, includes developing multiple meanings or interpretations based on potential connections among the themes and selecting the one that best represents the data (Moustakas, 1994). The selected meaning is called structural descriptions (Moustakas, 1994). This leads us to the final stage, meaning synthesizing, which consists of developing the essence of participants' experience by combining the structural descriptions with the textual descriptions and comparing them with the relevant data (Moerer-Urdahl & Creswell, 2004; Moustakas, 1994).

In my presentation, *Using NVivo to Conduct Transcendental Phenomenological Analysis*, I discuss Moustakas' (1994) guide on conducting TPA (see Adu, 2016b). Here are the data analysis steps based on the presentation:

1. Practicing *epoché* so as to reach a mental state where your background and biases have been blocked from influencing the data analysis process
   a. Think about your past experience and biases, and document them
   b. Imagine being a researcher with no biases who is open to examining issues from multiple perspectives
2. Engaging in *phenomenological reduction* leading to the development of textual description
   a. With the research purpose or question(s) in mind, go through the data and select significant statements
   b. Compile all the significant statements and group them based on similarity of participants' experience
   c. For each group of experience, select one or a few statements which represent the group
   d. Create themes based on the selected statements by thinking about the following questions:
      i. What was the participant trying to say?
      ii. What does the statement mean?
      iii. What assumptions did the participant want to make?
      iv. What is the underlying meaning of the statement?
   e. Categorize the themes if needed to reduce them to a manageable size
   f. Develop textual descriptions by describing each theme to depict what has been experienced
3. Developing imaginative variation leading to the creation of structural descriptions
   a. Examine the features of each theme and potential relationships
   b. Bring the themes together to create possible meanings of participants' experience
   c. Generate structural descriptions by selecting the meanings which best represent their experience

4. Synthesizing the meanings to form the essence of participants' experience
   a. Examine the meanings generated by addressing the following questions:
      i. What underlying meaning can be drawn from the meanings?
      ii. In what context does the underlying meaning exist or how could it be applied?
   b. Compare the essence of the experience (i.e. underlying meaning) with the relevant data to make sure they adequately represent participants' experience, thoughts or emotions
      i. Make the adjustments to the essence of the experience if necessary

Ethnography

Sometimes in our research exploration, we want to not only collect participants' narration about what they have experienced, but to directly witness and document their interactions with their "natural setting" (Murtagh, 2007, p. 194). Ethnography is an appropriate qualitative method for such an inquiry. It is used to examine a phenomenon as it happens in its natural environment (Creswell & Poth, 2018; Maanen, 2011). Ethnographers are always interested in getting 'closer to the action', which may include participating in an event of interest. By doing this, they acquire a rich account of the event from primary sources, get firsthand experience of the happenings and gather relevant data to help address their research problem, purpose or question(s). A researcher using the ethnographic approach is expected to:

- Be present at the research location
- Spend a considerable amount of time building trust and collecting data
- Observe, question and document what is seen
- Interact with participants who are directly or indirectly participating in the event
- Collect multiple data using data collection strategies such as observations, interviews, focus groups and document/artifact collection

When to use ethnography

✓ When spending a lot of time with participants in their natural setting
✓ When observing participants' interactions in their natural setting
✓ When documenting an event or a practice as it occurs
✓ When actively involving participants in the research process

✓ When interacting with participants as they experience a phenomenon or participate in an event

✓ When describing an event or activity with a rich depiction of the
context

✓ When working with participants to examine and explain a
phenomenon

✓ When you want to understand the culture of a group – examining
'why they do what they do'

Conducting analysis of ethnographic data

Since ethnographers focus on examining events, processes or behaviors,
the data analysis process is mainly informed by a grounded theory
approach. They use grounded theory data analysis techniques (namely,
open coding and focused coding) to look for patterns in the data, identify relevant themes and determine the relationship between the themes
(Charmaz, 2014). Similar to grounded theory, analysis of field notes could
lead to the generation of a theory, and memo writing during the analysis
process is encouraged. In their book, *Writing Ethnographic Fieldnotes*,
Emerson, Fretz, and Shaw (2011) discuss four main steps of analyzing
field notes. Here are the steps:

1. Taking a fresh look at the data collected (i.e. field notes) – reviewing
   the entire data before creating codes
2. Conducting open coding by going through the data to develop
   codes and themes, and selecting relevant themes for further
   examination
3. Utilizing the focus coding technique to compare and contrast
   significant themes and the data, refine the themes, and create
   sub-themes
4. Integrating themes and sub-themes to form a theory to explain an
   event, a behavior or a process

Narrative approach

Do you want to conduct a study to tell your story or the story of others? Do
you want to describe the experience of one person or a group of people
in a narrative form? Do you want to observe an event or participants'
behavior, or review documents to help tell a story? If your response to
any of these questions is yes, then the narrative approach could be an
appropriate qualitative method for your study. Storytelling is a powerful
means of communicating participants' experiences or describing events.
The narrative approach is used when you want to collect participants'
stories, analyze and restructure the stories, and present them in a

specified pattern (Creswell & Poth, 2018). The narrative (which include participants' situation, action and reactions) could be presented in a chronological order, via themes, or both. A good narrative report should have character(s), setting, sequence of events, crisis or problem, and resolution (Patterson, 2013). Narrative research includes helping to recount participants' stories – containing the above narrative components. The narrative researcher then looks for common experiences and themes in the stories and arrives at results which represent those stories.

When to use the narrative approach

✓ When telling a story based on participants' narration of their experience
✓ When describing an event or experience in a story form
✓ When bringing to light a unique experience of a person or a group of people
✓ When describing your own experience in a narrative form

Conducting narrative analysis

In her book chapter, "Narratives of Events: Labovian Narrative Analysis and its Limitations", Patterson (2013) describes the Labovian approach to narrative analysis. The approach focuses on categorizing participants' stories based on the six components of a narrative, namely: "abstract (A), orientation (O), complicating action (CA), result (R), evaluation (E), coda (C)" (Patterson, 2013, p. 29). When analyzing narrative data, we look for: what the story is about (*abstract*), characters in the story, time and setting (*orientation*), "series of events" including actions and reactions (*complication action*), end of the story (*results*), participant's thoughts and reactions about the story (*evaluation*), and the concluding part of the story that makes reference to the current situation (*coda*) (Patterson, 2013, p. 30). Using this approach, here are seven steps you could follow:

1. Reading through all the transcripts before coding the data
2. Identifying significant information and assigning a word or phrase (i.e. code) to represent them
3. Examining the characteristics of each code to determine which of the six narrative components they are connected to
4. Compiling the codes under their respective narrative components
5. Creating categories under each component based on similarities among the codes
6. Examining categories across the narrative components to develop a story (narrative)
7. Comparing the proposed narrative with the data and making adjustments when needed to better represent participants' stories

Case study approach

Cases include but are not limited to events, processes, conditions and phenomena. The main characteristic of a researchable case is its defined boundary, which could be based on the time, duration and/or location in which it happened (e.g. Hurricane Irma in Florida) or the demographics of the people connected to it (e.g. severe depression among working adults in the U.S. between 25 and 40 years old) (Creswell & Poth, 2018; Stake, 1995; Yin, 2014). I see the case study approach as a method of examining a case or a group of cases by collecting and analyzing more than one kind of data for a descriptive or explanatory purpose (Creswell & Poth, 2018). There are two main types of case study based on the purpose of the study. If you plan to describe or bring to light the distinctiveness of a case, then you will be doing an intrinsic case study (Stake, 1995). Another type is an instrumental case study, which focuses on "understanding" a case (Stake, 1995, p. 3).

When to use the case study approach

- ✓ When examining a well-defined but complex issue
- ✓ When using more than one data collection strategy (such as interviews, focus groups, observations, document collection and surveys) to generate data about the case(s)
- ✓ When describing a unique or overlooked case
- ✓ When comparing cases

Conducting case study analysis

There isn't an agreed single way of analyzing case study data. This is because every case is unique and the researcher works on data from multiple sources, making it nearly impossible to have a consensus among qualitative researchers on one appropriate qualitative analysis strategy for case study data. This means that you could adopt data analysis strategies from other qualitative methods. When searching for appropriate data analysis strategies, I would address the following question: which of the strategies will help me to meet my research goal (which could be to explain, compare or describe case(s))? Sometimes, statistical analysis will be needed to analyze quantitative data collected. In Yin's (2014) book, *Case Study Research: Design and Methods*, he suggests the following steps and strategies:

- Exploring the data – "searching for promising patterns, insights, or concepts—the goal being to define your priorities for what to analyze and why" (Yin, 2014, p. 135)
- Writing memos – documenting the analytical process and your thoughts

- Using any of the following data analysis strategies:
  - Coding data using your conceptual/theoretical framework (*similar to the content analysis process*)
  - Developing codes, themes, models or theory to explain the case(s) (*similar to the grounded theory data analysis process*)
  - Using a logic model framework to analysis the data – working on its basic components, namely: conditions, situations or resources which contributed to an incident or event (input); the incident or event itself (activity/process); and the result based on the activity (output/outcome)
  - Comparing competing or alternative explanations of a case (*similar to transcendental phenomenological analysis*)

Grounded theory approach

Grounded theory is one of the most powerful qualitative research methods used to develop a data-driven theory to explain a process (e.g. how to reduce homelessness among veterans), a behavior (e.g. learned helplessness among domestic violence victims), an experience (e.g. lived experience after winning a lottery) or a phenomenon (e.g. childhood obesity) (Adu, 2017; Charmaz, 2014). From an interpretative perspective, the theory developed under this approach entails relationships among concepts generated from the data (Charmaz, 2014). The most important thing is that the grounded theory analysis outcome (e.g. model or theory created) should represent the data collected and explain the phenomenon of study. According to Charmaz (2014), to attain the goal of creating a data-driven theory during the analysis stage, you must:

- Prevent your preconceptions and prior knowledge of the phenomenon from influencing your interpretation of the data
- Use gerund (i.e. a verb plus 'ing') codes (e.g. '*accepting* her current situation') to facilitate the generation of themes and theory
- Start analyzing the initial data as subsequent data is being collected
- Code data on each line of the document (i.e. conducting line-by-line coding)
- Constantly compare themes and proposed theory to data (i.e. using the constant comparative method)
- Document your thoughts and the analysis steps (i.e. writing memos)
- Sample participants who you think could help address questions which emerged when developing an initial theory (i.e. conducting theoretical sampling)
- Revise the proposed theory until it can adequately represent new data collected (i.e. reaching saturation during data analysis)

Table 2.1 Qualitative research methods and their respective purpose and data analysis goal

Research method	Main purpose of the method	Main goal of the data analysis
Phenomenological approach	Examine participants' experience	Develop themes or concepts which represent participants' experience
Hermeneutic phenomenological approach	Examine and interpret documents to capture their underlying meaning (i.e. making sense of text)	Provide the meaning of the text in a condensed form
Interpretative phenomenological analysis	Explore participants' thoughts about a phenomenon experienced	Assess participants' perspectives of their experience and interpret their views
Transcendental phenomenological approach	Examine participants' experience and make sense of the experience from a bias-free perspective	In a bias-free state, develop themes which reflect participants' experience and determine the essence of the experience
Ethnography	Explore a phenomenon or an event as it happens in its natural setting	Develop themes to describe or generate a theory to explain a process, phenomenon or event which occurred in its natural environment
Narrative approach	Gather participants' stories with the aim of restating those narratives	Combine participants' stories and narrate them in a chronological order and/or specified themes
Case study	Understand a case or bring to light a unique case – collecting multiple kinds of data	Develop themes, models or theories to explain a case, describe a unique case or compare cases
Grounded theory	Explain a process, behavior, event or phenomenon	Develop a statement, model or theory to explain a process, behavior, event or phenomenon

When to use the grounded theory approach

✓ When examining a process, behavior, experience or phenomenon
✓ When developing a model or theory based on the data collected

Conducting grounded theory analysis

In my presentation, *Using Grounded Theory Approach: From Start to Finish,* I discuss Charmaz's (2014) procedure of conducting grounded theory analysis (see Adu, 2017). According to Charmaz, there are three main steps involved:

- *Initial coding:* Going through each participant's statement, determining what they mean, and assigning codes to them
- *Focused coding:* Developing categories by identifying dominant code(s) and examining their relationship with remaining codes
- *Theoretical coding:* Building a theory (based on the relationship between the categories/themes) and assessing its representativeness by comparing it with new data to reach saturation

CONCLUSION

In this chapter, I presented eight main qualitative methods – describing what they are, when to use them and what data analysis steps should be followed. Each of the approaches are differentiated based on the main rationale of the method and goal of its data analysis procedure (see Table 2.1). However, when it comes to the data analysis process, there are similarities. Almost all the qualitative approaches discussed include the need to: bracket your background and biases (see Chapter 5), document your reflections and analytical process (see Chapter 6), create codes to represent significant information captured in the data (see Chapter 7), and group codes to develop categories and themes (see Chapter 8).

REFERENCES

Adu, P. (2016a). Analyzing social media data using NVivo 11: A hermeneutic phenomenological approach [PowerPoint slides]. SlideShare. Retrieved from www.slideshare.net/kontorphilip/analyzing-social-media-data-using-nvivo

Adu, P. (2016b). Using NVivo to conduct transcendental phenomenological analysis [PowerPoint slides]. SlideShare. Retrieved from www.slideshare.net/kontorphilip/using-nvivo-to-conduct-transcendental-phenomenological-analysis

Adu, P. (2017). Using grounded theory approach: From start to finish [PowerPoint slides]. SlideShare. Retrieved from www.slideshare.net/kontorphilip/using-grounded-theory-approach-from-start-to-finish

Charmaz, K. (2014). *Constructing grounded theory.* London, England: Sage.

Creswell, J. W., & Poth, C. N. (2018). *Qualitative inquiry & research design: Choosing among five approaches.* Los Angeles, CA: Sage.

Emerson, R. M., Fretz, R. I., & Shaw, L. L. (2011). *Writing ethnographic field notes* (2nd ed.). Chicago, IL: University of Chicago Press.

Giorgi, A (1975) An application of phenomenological method in psychology. *Duqesne Studies in Phenomenological Psychology*, *2*, 82–103. doi:10.5840/dspp197529

Kafle, N. P. (2013). Hermeneutic phenomenological research method simplified. *Bodhi: An Interdisciplinary Journal*, *5*(1), 181–200. doi:10.3126/bodhi.v5i1.8053

Maanen, J. V. (2011). *Tales of the field: On writing ethnography*. Chicago, IL: University of Chicago Press.

Moerer-Urdahl, T., & Creswell, J. (2004). Using transcendental phenomenology to explore the "ripple effect" in a leadership mentoring program. *International Journal of Qualitative Methods*, *3*(2), Article 2. Retrieved from https://sites.ualberta.ca/~iiqm/backissues/3_2/pdf/moerer.pdf

Moustakas, C. (1994). *Phenomenological research methods*. Thousand Oaks, CA: Sage.

Murtagh, L. (2007). Implementing a critically quasi-ethnographic approach. *The Qualitative Report*, *12*(2), 193–215. Retrieved from https://nsuworks.nova.edu/tqr/vol12/iss2/5/

Patterson, W. (2013). Narratives of events: Labovian narrative analysis and its limitations. In M. Andrews, C. Squire, & M. Tamboukou (Eds.), *Doing narrative research* (pp. 27–46). Los Angeles, CA: Sage.

Smith, J. A., Flowers, P., & Larkin, M. (2012). *Interpretative phenomenological analysis: theory, method and research*. London, England: Sage.

Stake, R. E. (1995). *The art of case study research*. Thousand Oaks, CA: Sage.

Vandermause, R. K., & Fleming, S. E. (2011). Philosophical hermeneutic interviewing. *International Journal of Qualitative Methods*, *10*(4), 367–377. https://doi.org/10.1177/160940691101000405

Whiting, L. S. (2001). Analysis of phenomenological data: Personal reflections on Giorgi's method. *Nurse Researcher*, *9*(2), 60–74. doi:10.7748/nr.9.2.60.s6

Yin, R. K. (2014). *Case study research: Design and methods* (5th ed.). Los Angeles, CA: Sage.

Understanding the art of coding qualitative data

OBJECTIVES

Readers will be able to:

1. Understand the qualitative data analysis process
2. Identify which coding strategy is appropriate for their analysis
3. Engage in the art of qualitative coding

WHAT IS QUALITATIVE CODING?

When thinking about the meaning of qualitative coding or qualitative analysis, the following phrases come to mind: data reduction, subjective process, credibility of the findings, transparency of the data analysis process, and generation of concepts, logical statements, models and theories (Adu, 2017a). Bazeley (2013) characterizes qualitative coding as a rigorous process which involves making meaning of the data collected. He adds, "it involves seeing and interpreting what has been said, written, or done; reflecting on evolving categories; deciding [on] what is important to follow up" (p. 15). As mentioned in Chapter 2, although there are differences in the data analysis procedure among qualitative methods, the coding steps (i.e. qualitative coding process) such as generating codes based on the significant information in the data and developing categories and themes are generally similar. In this chapter, greater emphasis is placed on conducting qualitative coding to help you use any of the three coding strategies irrespective of the qualitative analysis method you adopt. Qualitative coding, which is a sub-category of qualitative analysis, is a systematic, subjective and trans-parent process of reducing data to meaningful and credible concepts which adequately represent the data and address the research problem, purpose or question(s) (Adu, 2013).

WHAT COMPRISES THE ART OF CODING?

Let me explain further the concepts mentioned or implied in the qualitative coding definition. They are: systematic process, data reduction, subjectivity and transparency.

Systematic process

Attaining qualitative findings that best represent the data analyzed mostly depends on an orderly series of actions a qualitative coder takes. It is similar to engaging in gold mining, where there are specific required steps gold miners take to obtain pure gold from the ore. In basic generic steps, after the miners have located and mined land rich with gold ore, they grind the ore and put it in a solution to separate the rock dust and other minerals from the raw gold. The raw gold is melted to further separate the real gold from unwanted materials. With the help of mercury, a pure and refined gold is produced (see Hoffmann, 2008).

Generally speaking, the basic steps, between collecting raw qualitative data and attaining refined themes are choosing relevant information from the data, labeling the selected information, and grouping the labels (i.e. codes) into mostly abstract concepts – generating categories and themes (Saldaña, 2016). So why should we engage in a systematic process when conducting qualitative coding? The reasons are:

- To maintain consistency in the qualitative analysis process
- To promote repeatability of the qualitative coding steps
- To ensure believability of the qualitative findings

Maintaining consistency

To put it in basic terms, there are principles and beliefs that govern the qualitative researcher's decisions and actions when conducting their study. These are called philosophical assumptions[1] (Creswell & Poth, 2018). It is expected that we follow clear steps consistent with the assumptions associated with conducting a qualitative study.

One may ask, *how do I make sure the qualitative analysis process is consistent with the philosophical assumptions of qualitative research?* One way is to follow the qualitative analysis steps taken or suggested by previous qualitative researchers. Some of the qualitative coding guidelines are based on the specific research method you choose for your study (as discussed in Chapter 1). For instance, just to mention a few, you could select Moustakas' (1994) qualitative analysis strategy if you plan to conduct transcendental phenomenological research. Also, if you plan to conduct a grounded theory study, Charmaz's (2014) qualitative analysis approach would be appropriate (see Table 2.1).

Promoting repeatability

As part of a research community, we are encouraged to provide a clear description of actions and decisions taken in our study – including our data analysis procedure. Providing well-organized qualitative coding steps helps readers, including future researchers, to easily follow and utilize the procedure – leading to the attainment of similar results. I can see the ripple beneficial effect of following a well-presented qualitative coding process in a methodological manner. It promotes continuous use, reuse and adaptation of the coding techniques, which may promote the never-ending building, sharing, acknowledgement and application of knowledge.

Ensuring believability

For your research findings to have a great influence in the research community (in terms of utilization of the results), you need to systematically demonstrate how you collected and analyzed your data. By so doing, people will trust the codes, categories, themes and theories developed, and accept the data and results-driven conclusions made. For our audience to believe what we found in the data, we need to provide satisfactory answers to the following questions:

- How did we identify relevant information in the data?
- What specific codes were generated to represent the information identified?
- What were the meanings of the codes?
- How did we move from codes to categories?
- What did the categories mean?
- How were the themes generated?
- What specific research problem, purpose or question was the themes addressing?

Since the audience (in most circumstances) were not there when the data were being analyzed, it is important to chronologically show them the analysis procedure by adequately addressing the above questions (Adu, 2018).

Data reduction

Data reduction is all about summarizing data to the extent that the condensed form adequately represents: participants' responses to the interview questions; relevant document collected; event, behavior or process observed; and/or field notes compiled. It involves transforming specific information to more "general" concepts (Saldaña, 2016, p. 15). During the transformation process, relevant data (i.e. information which could help in addressing the research problem, purpose or question) is

Figure 3.1. Qualitative data reduction process

Source: Adu, 2017b, Slide 1

separated from the raw data. Based on how the researcher understands the relevant information, a word or phrase is used to label each of the chunks of the information (Auerbach & Silverstein, 2003). These labels, which are normally called codes, are further examined to develop categories and themes (see Figure 3.1).

Subjectivity

As qualitative researchers, the main instrument we use to produce codes, categories, themes and even theory is ourselves. In a process of transforming the data into concise and representative outcomes, we decide which parts of the data are relevant, what meaning should be ascribed to the selected portions of the data and how the findings should be presented to our audience. All these decisions could differ from one researcher to another. This is because we have unique and diverse experiences, backgrounds, biases and lenses. These personal characteristics influence how we see things, and how we interpret and communicate them. As qualitative researchers, we are: vessels used to collect and make sense of data, filters through which relevant information is extracted from the raw data, and a liaison between participants and audiences – helping them to make their experiences and thoughts known. Although conducting an inquiry which is subjective in nature could be viewed as a methodological weakness, it is the best way of examining complex and unique issues that are difficult to quantify.

Transparency

Imagine working in a research environment where detailed data collection and analysis procedures are clearly presented and widely shared. You would be able to replicate a study and examine how its results are similar or different from your findings. Also, you could easily transfer the qualitative results to a similar context. Due to the subjective nature of the qualitative coding process, to help the audience believe what you found, it is important to be open about how you analyzed your data. The audience are inclined to better understand and trust the findings if you provide a detailed step-by-step overview of the analysis process – from the time you bracketed your background and biases to the time you arrived at your results. Bringing to light a subjective data analysis experience would help future researchers to follow the same data analysis process and compare their findings to yours, leading to the advancement of knowledge.

ORIENTATION TO THE ART OF QUALITATIVE CODING

To make sure we are on the same page with respect to the meaning of the qualitative analysis terms I will frequently be using in this and subsequent chapters, I have defined the terms below:

- **Empirical indicators:** These are relevant portions of the data selected to help address the research problem, purpose or question (Strauss, 1989). There are two main empirical indicators.
  - *Explicit empirical indicators:* These constitute significant information that is easy to identify in the data. They can be used to directly address the research problem or question without determining what they mean. With these indicators, codes can be easily developed without having to interpret them. The codes are developed out of description of the relevant information.
  - *Implicit empirical indicators:* These constitute significant information hidden in the data. They need to be further analyzed to determine whether they can address the research problem or question. Under this type, codes are generated after an intensive "interaction with" the potential relevant information in the data (Charmaz, 2014, p. 252). Codes are developed based on how the researcher interprets the information identified.
- **Codes:** Codes can be called *concepts* (Strauss, 1989). They are labels given to relevant information identified in the data (Saldaña, 2016).

QUALITATIVE CODING STRATEGIES

After an extensive review of existing qualitative analysis methods and coding strategies, I have produced a coding method which would help researchers (especially those who are new to qualitative analysis) to systematically code their data. This method is compatible with most of the qualitative-method-specific data analysis techniques discussed in Chapter 2, since this method focuses mainly on the coding aspect of the qualitative analysis. It is called the **DIP** coding method, which is an acronym representing the three main coding strategies: **D**escription-focused coding, **I**nterpretation-focused coding, and **P**resumption-focused coding. With these new coding strategies, you could still use the qualitative-method-specific data analysis steps or utilize the generic coding methods Saldaña (2016) discusses. The most important thing is to select a coding strategy which is consistent with the purpose of the study and research question(s), and will help to create uniform codes. By so doing, it becomes easier to smoothly transition

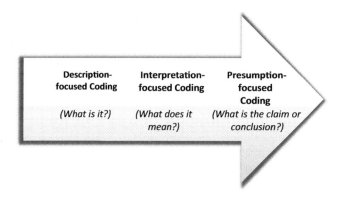

Figure 3.2. The three coding strategies under the DIP coding method

from generating codes to developing categories, themes and even creating theories. The DIP coding method starts from a basic level of coding
(i.e. description-focused coding) to an advanced level of coding, which
is presumption-focused coding. Between these two coding strategies is
interpretation-focused coding (see Figure 3.2).

Description-focused coding strategy

Description-focused coding involves describing events, settings, behaviors,
experiences or stories. This strategy is similar to descriptive coding, which
"summarizes in a word or short phrase – most often a noun – the basic
topic of a passage of qualitative data" (Saldaña, 2016, p. 102). However,
with the description-focused coding strategy, you allow the data to speak
for itself – summarizing the relevant information (i.e. empirical indicators)
in the data without introducing your interpretation into the construction
of the codes. The purpose of using this coding strategy is to generate
codes that are closely connected to the empirical indicators. Analogically
speaking, your role is similar to that of a journalist – mainly responsible
for reporting what he/she sees and leaving it up to the readers/viewers
to make sense of the report. Because this strategy focuses on presenting
what you find rather than what you think about the data, your background and biases have less impact on the findings. Description-focused
coding will be helpful for researchers conducting a narrative study and
intrinsic case study (focusing on describing a unique case). If you are new
to qualitative coding, I recommend that you start with this coding strategy
before using more advanced and intensive levels of coding strategies such
as interpretation-focused and presumption-focused coding.

Characteristics of description-focused coding

- **No interpretation or inference:** One of the unique features of
  description-focused coding is that it offers the opportunity for the

data to speak to you without bringing in your interpretation or making conclusions based on what you find.

- **Utilizing In Vivo coding:** Sometimes, the best way of capturing what empirical indicators portray is to use the words and phrases in the data to create codes. This coding strategy is called In Vivo coding (Saldaña, 2016). Description-focused coding allows the use of other descriptive-oriented coding strategies which include In Vivo coding to better summarize relevant information found in the data.
- **Codes generated are more concrete:** In description-focused coding, you want your codes to be as close as possible to the empirical indicators. Your aim is to create less abstract ideas compared to interpretation-focused and presumption-focused coding strategies.

When to use description-focused coding

- *When there is a description-focused purpose of a study:* Description-focused coding is appropriate for studies with the main purpose of identifying or describing specific behaviors, settings, phenomena, experiences or events.
- *When you have a description-focused research question:* Description-focused coding is normally used for research questions that start with 'what', 'where', 'when', or 'who'.
- *When you have less complex data (i.e. data with explicit empirical indicators):* This coding strategy is appropriate when working with data in which the information you plan to code is easy to find without engaging in a critical and intensive review.

Demonstration 3.1

To help you better understand how description-focused coding is used, I have analyzed five transcripts. These structured interview responses were created for qualitative coding demonstration purposes. Let's assume you are conducting a study on mental health stigma with the purpose of describing the views of mental health providers on factors contributing to mental health stigma and what can be done to address it. One of the research questions is: *"From the perspective of mental health providers, what factors promote mental health stigma?"* Table 3.1 shows the demographic information of five participants interviewed. In all, participants were asked eleven questions. The first five were demographic questions. Exhibits 3.1 to 3.5 show participants' responses to the interview questions and codes created using description-focused coding.

Considering the purpose of the study and research question, your role is to simply identify significant information (i.e. empirical indicators) in the data, related to mental health stigma contributing factors, and assign codes to them. You start with reviewing all participants' responses

Table 3.1 Demographics of participants (mental health providers)

Participant ID	Age	Gender	Level of education	Years of experience	Kinds of patients they often see
P1	25	Male	Master's degree	5	Substance abuse patients
P2	57	Female	Master's degree	25	Mainly children
P3	33	Male	Associate's degree	0.5	People of all ages
P4	29	Female	Associate's degree	3	Mainly children
P5	60	Female	Doctorate degree	27	Adults

and identifying those that are potentially indicative of factors promoting mental health stigma. You then use a word or phrase to represent the relevant information. With the description-focused coding, you are expected to just state what the empirical indicators stand for, but not what you think they mean. For instance, imagine you identify the following empirical indicator:

> Once one hears that someone has struggled with a mental health issue, more often times, than not, certain stereotypes and negative assumptions are made.
>
> *(From Participant 'P1' response to interview question 6; see Exhibit 3.1)*

Using description-focused coding and with the research question in mind, you could ask: *what word or phrase should I use to depict the above empirical indicator?* Asking such a question would help you to generate a list of words and phrases which could represent the statement. The following phrases may come to mind: *'Hearing about someone's mental illness', 'Finding out mental illness', 'Noticing someone with mental illness', 'Hearing about someone's unresolved mental issues'* and *'Knowing someone's mental health struggles'*. From the list, you could choose the one which you think best represents the participant's statement. At the end, I selected *'Hearing about someone's mental illness'* as a code for the empirical indictor (see Exhibit 3.1). Your choice doesn't have to be perfect when coding. You can always go back and make revisions to the initial codes generated if new ideas come to mind. You just need to make sure the phrase is not too long. Having no more than five words in a phrase for your code would be ideal.

P1 *(Mental Health Provider)*

1. *How old are you?* 25
2. *What is your gender?* Male
3. *What is your highest level of education?* Masters
4. *How long have you worked as a mental health provider?* 5 years
5. *What kinds of patients do you frequently see?* Substance abuse patients
6. *What are your thoughts about mental health stigma?* Once one hears that someone has struggled with a mental health issue, more often times, than not, certain stereotypes and negative assumptions are made. This then prevents us from getting to know people fully, because we often have our own unfounded biases early on.

   PA
   Hearing about someone's mental illness

7. *How concerned are your patients in terms of fear of being discriminated against due to their mental health issues?* They are very worried, and often times ask us to ensure confidentiality for their visit, which is a must anyway for health care providers.
8. *What do you think may be the causes of mental health stigma?* Our culture often supports the negative notions of others that have been affected by mental health, by the media we see, the conversations we grow up hearing.

   PA
   Cultural influence

   PA
   Educational background

9. *What may be some of the factors fueling the prevalence of mental health stigma?* Educational background, culture, financial status, income.

   PA
   Cultural influence

10. *What is currently being done to address this problem?*

    PA
    Socio-economic status

    a. *Personally:* I educate those that I come across as much as I can, so that we can be supportive of those with mental health issues.
    b. *Your organization:* Educational pamphlets
    c. *Community:* Educational outreach
    d. *Country:* We still need to have a lot more work done, but there are programs; such as through social workers, and case managers, that may be able to provide support for those with mental health issues.
11. *What can be done to address mental health stigma?* Teach our youth, teachers, health care providers early on about mental health issues, and how we can support each other.

Exhibit 3.1. Participant 'P1' transcript with codes generated using description-focused coding

Sometimes you may be tempted to bring your own interpretation into the coding process when using description-focused coding. It happens to me too. One way to overcome this temptation is to take advantage of participants rich responses to the interview question – by using or modifying their own words to create codes. This coding method is termed "In Vivo coding" (Saldaña, 2016, p. 67). I used Participant P2's own words to create phrases such as *'Ignorance'*, *'Lack of empathy'* and *'Lack of education'* (see Exhibit 3.2).

Interpretation-focused coding strategy

With interpretation-focused coding, we go beyond just describing the empirical indicators. We examine the indicators to bring to live what they mean. Meaning making is the main characteristic of this coding strategy. It involves identifying significant information in the data and coming up with a code that represents our understanding of the information. Since a researcher's background and biases could influence his or her interpretation when unwrapping the underlying meaning of an empirical indicator, it is important to bracket them (Charmaz, 2014; Moustakas, 1994). In addition, to better interpret relevant information in the data, the following factors should be considered: the intent, background and demographics of participants, and the question that elicited such a response from them. Similarly, when analyzing documents, the following should be taken into consideration: the characteristics of the author(s) of the documents, the circumstance that led to the writing of the documents, and their purpose and intended audience. Also, when implementing the interpretation-focused coding strategy, we treat each significant piece of information in the data as part of a network of empirical indicators. In effect, when producing a code for an empirical indicator, consider how it is related to other indicators.

The interpretation-focused coding strategy is informed by the hermeneutic approach, which involves "the interpretation of texts and in general the theory of interpretation and understanding" (Bentz & Shapiro, 2001, p. 40). This coding strategy can be used with description-focused coding when coding your qualitative data. After selecting an empirical indicator, you could first find out what it is (with the description-focused coding) and then determine what it means (with the interpretation-focused coding).

Characteristics of interpretation-focused coding

- There is the tendency for the researcher's background and biases to influence how he/she interprets the data
- There is the possibility of producing multiple meanings for an empirical indicator

P2 *(Mental Health Provider)*

1. *How old are you?* 57
2. *What is your gender?* Female
3. *What is your highest level of education?* Masters
4. *How long have you worked as a mental health provider?*
   25 years
5. *What kinds of patients do you frequently see?* Mainly
   pediatric patients
6. *What are your thoughts about mental health stigma?* It is
   a big problem in our society today: many people are labeled
   unfavorably due to their mental health background

   PA
   Giving unfavorable
   labels

7. *How concerned are your patients in terms of fear of being
   discriminated against due to their mental health issues?*
   Very concerned, especially as young children/teens that
   may face cruel bullying if anyone was to find out about their
   mental health background.

   PA
   Finding out a person's
   mental health
   condition

   PA
   Ignorance

8. *What do you think may be the causes of mental health
   stigma?* Ignorance, lack of empathy and understanding that
   mental health issues are not self-inflicted.

   PA
   Lack of empathy

9. *What may be some of the factors fueling the prevalence of
   mental health stigma?* Lack of education

   PA
   Lack of education

10. *What is currently being done to address this problem?*
    a. *Personally:* As a health care provider for the young
       it is my mission to assist them in finding a place of
       trust, and empathy regarding their mental health,
       and social concerns.
    b. *Your organization:* My organization is committed to
       provide a safe haven for the young as well.
    c. *Community:* Community outreach programs
    d. *Country:* Federally funded agencies that assist those
       with mental health issues.
11. *What can be done to address mental health stigma?* Each
    of us one by one can make a difference by being open to
    others' differences, and not judging before knowing and
    understanding each other.

Exhibit 3.2. Participant 'P2' transcript with codes generated using description-focused coding

- Codes created are more abstract in nature compared to the description-focused codes

When to use interpretation-focused coding

- *When a study has an interpretation-focused purpose:* Interpretation-focused coding is appropriate for studies with the main purpose of

P3 *(Mental Health Provider)*

1. *How old are you?* 33
2. *What is your gender?* Male
3. *What is your highest level of education?* Associates
4. *How long have you worked as a mental health provider?* 6 months
5. *What kinds of patients do you frequently see?* I see people of all ages
6. *What are your thoughts about mental health stigma?* It is a big problem in our world today, from the U.S. to abroad people are often stigmatized when others find out they have mental illnesses.

    PA
    Finding out a person's mental health condition

7. *How concerned are your patients in terms of fear of being discriminated against due to their mental health issues?* They are very fearful and concerned.
8. *What do you think may be the causes of mental health stigma?* Fear of the unknown, not understanding the complexities of the human mind and behaviors.

    PA
    Fear of the unknown

    PA
    Lack of understanding about mental illness

9. *What may be some of the factors fueling the prevalence of mental health stigma?* Fear, unwillingness to learn about other people's differences.

    PA
    Not willing 'to learn about other[s]'

10. *What is currently being done to address this problem?*
    a. *Personally:* As a social worker I work closely with helping patients find resources that they can use to obtain mental health support: i.e. physicians, school programs, medical insurance.
    b. *Your organization:* Provides resources, and information on providers, and programs that can be of benefit to patients with mental health issues.
    c. *Community:* We run community health fairs, and programs every year to encourage acceptance, and provide resources for families.
    d. *Country:* Programs within hospitals/outpatient centers are federally funded to provide assistance to those that need it.
11. *What can be done to address mental health stigma?* Increase programs that can help provide assistance to patients and families; as there is a lack thereof of programs in relation to the number of patients.

Exhibit 3.3. Participant 'P3' transcript with codes generated using description-focused coding

P4 *(Mental Health Provider)*

1. *How old are you?* 29
2. *What is your gender?* Female
3. *What is your highest level of education?* Associates
4. *How long have you worked as a mental health provider?* 3 years
5. *What kinds of patients do you frequently see?* I see mainly children
6. *What are your thoughts about mental health stigma?* It is a big problem in our nation and abroad: especially in cultures that shun mental health illnesses.
7. *How concerned are your patients in terms of fear of being discriminated against due to their mental health issues?* They are almost always fearful because they do not want to be treated differently due to something they are not able to control.
8. *What do you think may be the causes of mental health stigma?* Misunderstanding of how mental health issues originate, and how people are personally affected by them.
9. *What may be some of the factors fueling the prevalence of mental health stigma?* Cultural beliefs, and pre-conceived practices
10. *What is currently being done to address this problem?*
    a. *Personally:* As a case manager for a private practice, I interact with many families and patients to help coordinate and provide resources
    b. *Your organization:* Outreach programs
    c. *Community:* Very limited resources for those with mental health stigma. I work in a small town and we are the main mental health resource for the community.
    d. *Country:* There are some federally and government funded programs that help those with mental health illnesses.
11. *What can be done to address the promote metal health stigma?* Increase awareness nationwide

PA
Misunderstanding of mental illness

PA
Cultural beliefs

PA
Prejudiced behaviors

Exhibit 3.4. Participant 'P4' transcript with codes generated using description-focused coding

P5 *(Mental Health Provider)*

1. ***How old are you?*** 60
2. ***What is your gender?*** Female
3. ***What is your highest level of education?*** Doctorate
4. How long have you worked as a mental health provider? 27 years
5. ***What kinds of patients do you frequently see?*** Adults
6. ***What are your thoughts about mental health stigma?*** It is a big hurdle that we face; and affects people from every background, race, culture, and ethnicity. It is something that we have to overcome in order to be able to effectively treat and help those that are afflicted.
7. ***How concerned are your patients in terms of fear of being discriminated against due to their mental health issues?*** They are very fearful, especially for those that would like to maintain a job in order to secure income. They fear that with a background check, many past factors such as imprisonment or institutionalization may be uncovered.
8. ***What do you think may be the causes of mental health stigma?*** Fear of being harmed; based on how our media portrays persons with mental health issues.
9. ***What may be some of the factors fueling the prevalence of mental health stigma?*** Fear, misunderstanding
10. ***What is currently being done to address this problem?***
    a. *Personally:* Dedication to provide care, resources, and help to those with mental health concerns
    b. *Your organization:* Commitment to care for those that come through our doors
    c. *Community:* Outreach programs
    d. *Country:* Federally funded programs geared to providing resources
11. ***What can be done to address mental health stigma?*** Educational programs for health care providers, teachers, social workers, case managers, any persons involved in health care; because if they are educated, then they can promote tolerance and understanding in the platform they have.

PA
Fear of being harmed

PA
Media's unfavorable view of people with mental illness

PA
Fear

PA
Misunderstanding of mental illness

Exhibit 3.5. Participant 'P5' transcript with codes generated using description-focused coding

Table 3.2 Demographics of participants (African American physicians)

Participant	Age	Gender	Years of experience	Specialty	Kinds of patients they treat
Mary	35	Female	3	Pediatrics	Infants, children, teens, and young adults
Mike	65	Male	30	Family medicine	Infants through adulthood
Emily	50	Female	12	Surgery	Surgical trauma patients of all ages
Stephen	47	Male	13	Hematology/ oncology	Pediatric cancer patients
John	43	Male	10	Internal medicine	Hospitalized adult patients

exploring, explaining or understanding specific behaviors, settings, phenomena, experiences or events.

- *When you have an interpretation-focused research question:* Interpretation-focused coding is normally used for research questions that start with 'what' or 'how'.
- *When you have complex data (i.e. data with implicit empirical indicators):* This coding strategy is appropriate when working with data with less obvious empirical indicators – requiring critical and intensive review of the data to locate indicators and create codes.

Demonstration 3.2

Let's use five interview transcripts (not from real participants) generated for the purpose of this interpretation-focused coding demonstration. The structured interviews were about the experience of African American physicians. The purpose was to examine their experience and the challenges they face as physicians. One of the research questions was: *What is it like to be an African American physician?* Regarding participants' demographics, most of them were males. The age range was 35 to 65 years with work experience between 3 and 30 years. They had diverse specialties and served a diverse range of patients (see Table 3.2).

To determine the appropriate coding strategy, there are three actions you could take:

- *Identify the operative word used in the purpose statement:* Based on the purpose stated above, the operative word is *'examine'*, which is compatible with the interpretation-focused coding strategy.

Figure 3.3. Connection between harvesting apples and using description-focused and interpretation-focused coding

- *Examine the research question to help determine the kind of significant information (i.e. empirical indicators) you will be looking for:* With the research question, *What is it like to be an African American physician?* you search (in the data) for their day-to-day experience of caring for patients and for their thoughts about what they experience. With this kind of question, you need a high level of engagement with the data to capture participants' perspectives on their experience – making interpretation-focused coding a better choice compared to description-focused coding.
- *Review all of the transcripts to determine whether the potential empirical indicators are more implicit than explicit:* You could use interpretation-focused coding if the indicators are predominately hidden in the data and it requires an extensive examination to determine what they mean and what codes to generate. It is just like reaping a yield of apples; you need less effort to harvest them if you plan to focus on the ones which have fallen on the ground already, compared to targeting those which are still attached to the tree (see Figure 3.3).

With the research question in mind and using interpretation-focused coding, you go through the participant's response to each interview question. When a significant word, phrase or statement is identified, you ask yourself, what does it mean? What does the participant mean, considering his/her background and demographic information? What does the participant want to communicate? What does he/she want us to know? The essence of considering these questions is to get to the core meaning of the empirical indicator identified.

For some of the empirical indicators I selected, it was easy to create codes since the meaning was not fully hidden. For instance, I coded Mary's response to question 6, *"I see myself as one of very few among my own peers"* and Stephen's response to the same question, *"I see myself as one of a rare minority of persons in health care. I am the only one in my family ever to achieve such a high degree of education"* as *'Being part of a few'* (see Exhibit 3.6 and Exhibit 3.9). Looking at their responses, both participants were aware that a small number of their kind (in terms of their race) were in the health sector as physicians and they were proud to be able to provide care to patients in this capacity.

In Vivo coding could sometimes be used to generate interpretation-focused codes (Saldaña, 2016). The most important aspect is to make sure the codes created represent the empirical indicators, portray your interpretation of the indicators and address the research question. On a few occasions I used participants' own words to create codes. For example, I coded Mike's response to question 9, *"Mistrust by those that may not take the time to know and understand me as their physician, and just human being"* as *' "Mistrust" due to race'* (see Exhibit 3.7). Also, I coded part of John's response to question 7, *"Day to day I see myself as well-respected for the most part"* as *' "Well-respected" physician'* (see Exhibit 3.10).

You could also utilize the gerund form (i.e. adding 'ing' to a verb to turn it into a noun) to create codes specifically for interpreting a situation, process or participant's behavior (Charmaz, 2014). Coming up with a code to represent part of Emily's response to question 6, *"I focus on what my skills are, and what I can do to help provide good surgical care to those that need it"*, I stated *'Focusing on providing care'* (see Exhibit 3.8). Similarly, a portion of Mary's response to question 7, *"I take my position as a blessing and privilege"* was coded as *'Seeing job as a great opportunity'* (see Exhibit 3.6).

Another strategy I used under interpretation-focused coding was to brainstorm potential codes for the empirical indicators and choose the codes that best reflect the empirical indicators, depict my interpretation of the indicators and address the research question. To illustrate, I generated *'Demonstrate ability'*, *'Having to constantly prove capability'*, *'Questioning capability due to race'*, and *'Showing capability due to race'* as potential codes to represent the empirical indicator, *"I always have to prove myself over and beyond that of some of my non-African American colleagues, just because of the skin I am in"* (see Exhibit 3.7; Mike's response to question 7). I finally selected *'Questioning capability due to race'* as the code best suited to the meaning of Mike's response.

Mary (African American Physician)

1. **How old are you?** 35
2. **How long have you worked as a physician?** 3 years
3. **What is your gender?** Female
4. **What is your area of specialty?** Pediatrics
5. **What kind of patients do you treat?** Infants, children, teens, and young adults

6. **How do you see yourself as an African American physician?** I see myself as one of very few among my own peers. I take my position as a blessing and privilege.

7. **What is your day-to-day experience as an African American physician?** I see myself no differently than my peers, as I have worked just as hard, or even harder than my counterparts to become a physician. However, it is apparent at times due to my race, that the way I am seen by colleagues, parents, or patients may be quite different than someone of another race.

8. **How do most patients/parents see you?** Most parents see me as qualified and able to care for their children.

9. **What are challenges you face when providing treatment to patients?** Some challenges I face are parents building trust in me, and being willing to work together to provide the best care for their children. This may in part also be because I do appear younger than my stated age. Of note, when I was in training as a resident physician, parents would often refer to me as being a nurse, or mistake me for another provider, other than that of a physician, even if I stated my status as that of a physician. It seems, some people just don't want to accept that you are what you say you are.

10. **How is your relationship with other non- African American physicians?** My relationship is very good. I am of a limited few, and that automatically builds a bond with my fellow colleagues, that we will always have.

11. **How do non- African American physicians see you?** It is hard to say because I cannot read their mind; and I have never asked. However, I can feel how I am treated at times, when in comparison to others of a different color, with equal credentials. It is different; and is one of a lower degree of acknowledgement.

PA
Being part of a few

PA
Seeing job as a great opportunity

PA
Perceived differently due to race

PA
Perceived as a competent physician

PA
Not being trusted by patients

PA
Not being accepted as physician

PA
Cordial relationship with colleagues

PA
Treated differently due to race

Exhibit 3.6. Mary's transcript with codes generated using interpretation-focused coding

Mike (African American Physician)

1. **How old are you?** 65
2. **How long have you worked as a physician?** 30 years
3. **What is your gender?** Male
4. **What is your area of specialty?** Family medicine
5. **What kind of patients do you treat?** Infants through adulthood
6. **How do you see yourself as an African American physician?** I see myself as a person of accomplishment, as I know those that were before me had gone through much challenges in order to reach the level I have gotten to.

   PA
   Having a sense of fulfillment

7. **What is your day-to-day experience as an African American physician?** I have been in this field for many years, and I have seen things change for the better, and some things are still the same. As an African American physician, I always have to prove myself over and beyond that of some of my non-African American colleagues, just because of the skin I am in. It can be frustrating and bewildering, but I have grown strong from it; as I push myself even more to be as knowledgeable as I can be.

   PA
   Questioning capability due to race

   PA
   Frustration due to unfavorable treatment

   PA
   Gained strength despite unfavorable treatment

8. **How do most patients/parents see you?** They see me as a respected physician, and even make me feel that I am a part of their family; as I have cared for patients, and even the children of my patients as they grow up.

   PA
   Being accepted by patients

9. **What are challenges you face when providing treatment to patients?** Mistrust by those that may not take the time to know and understand me as their physician, and just human being.

   PA
   'Mistrust' due to race

10. **How is your relationship with other non- African American physicians?** It is very good.

    PA
    Cordial relationship with colleagues

11. **How do non- African American physicians see you?** Unfortunately, there are times when one can see there is an obvious divide. However, I have been in this field for so many years, and I am most often than not, well-respected.

    PA
    'Well-respected' by colleagues

Exhibit 3.7. Mike's transcript with codes generated using interpretation-focused coding

Emily (African American Physician)

1. **How old are you?** 50
2. **How long have you worked as a physician?** 12 years
3. **What is your gender?** Female
4. **What is your area of specialty?** Surgery
5. **What kind of patients do you treat?** Surgical trauma patients of all ages
6. **How do you see yourself as an African American physician?** I see myself as a human being; I make no distinction that I am African American in comparison to others. I focus on what my skills are, and what I can do to help provide good surgical care to those that need it. My background is honestly secondary to me.

   PA
   Not focusing on race

   PA
   Focusing on providing care

7. **What is your day-to-day experience as an African American physician?** I do notice that there is a difference if I were to think about it, and compare myself to other non-African American physicians in my distinctive field. Unfortunately, racism still exists, but I try to push beyond it, and focus on what matters the most, and that is saving a life.

   PA
   Acknowledging the existence of racism

   PA
   Looking beyond racial differences

8. **How do most patients/parents see you?** Most patients/parents when they first see me are taken aback that I will be the surgeon working on their loved ones. I am a small woman, and I know it is admittedly rare to have an African American surgeon. However, after I explain to them what they or their child will need to have the best survival outcomes, and build a relationship, they welcome that I am their physician.

   PA
   Building trust and credibility

9. **What are challenges you face when providing treatment to patients?** Growing up in the 50's and 60's I faced racism, and prejudice first hand, and some of those thoughts still linger in our society, and especially so when I present myself to families as their surgeon. No matter how high of a degree, or skill you have obtained, discrimination still exists.

   PA
   Acknowledging the existence of racism

10. **How is your relationship with other non- African American physicians?** It is one that is sometimes great, and at other times limited. Sometimes, unfortunately our peers do not support each other, as we should.

    PA
    Feels less supported

11. **How do non-African American physicians see you?** Usually, I often have to prove myself over and beyond what others with similar skill and background would have to do. However, after people understand that I am just as qualified as they are, we usually have a solid relationship.

    PA
    Having to prove competency

Exhibit 3.8. Emily's transcript with codes generated using interpretation-focused coding

Stephen (African American Physician)

1. **How old are you?** 47
2. **How long have you worked as a physician?** 13 years
3. **What is your gender?** Male
4. **What is your area of specialty?** Hematology/Oncology
5. **What kind of patients do you treat?** Pediatric cancer patients
6. **How do you see yourself as an African American physician?** I see myself as one of a rare minority of persons in health care. I am the only one in my family ever to achieve such a high degree of education. | — **PA** Being part of a few
7. **What is your day-to-day experience as an African American physician?** It is grueling, challenging, rewarding, and inspiring. I am at the forefront of care for some of the sickest people that health care providers may come across; and I am honored to be able to serve in this capacity. | — **PA** Having a 'challenging' and 'rewarding' job
8. **How do most patients/parents see you?** Most parents/patients dealing with cancer are often very worried, and fearful of the unknown; and when they meet me they are honestly looking for hope and answers; so most of the time I am met with an open heart. There are occasions however, when some patients/parents may ask to have another physician see them who is non-African American; and in those cases I can only do the best I can do to reassure and build a relationship with those I care for; and usually they are ok with me caring for them, and are satisfied with the care I give. | — **PA** Being accepted by patients / **PA** Building trust and credibility
9. **What are challenges you face when providing treatment to patients?** Prejudice due to my race. | — **PA** Experiencing 'prejudice'
10. **How is your relationship with other non- African American Physicians?** It is usually very good; as we are one of very few. | — **PA** Cordial relationship with colleagues
11. **How do non- African American physicians see you?** As some of the parents and patients often need time to feel comfortable when we first meet, and understand that I am just as qualified as any other non-African American physician; my colleagues are likewise the same. After coming to this realization of equal professional status, they are often very receptive. | — **PA** Having to prove competency

Exhibit 3.9. Stephen's transcript with codes generated using interpretation-focused coding

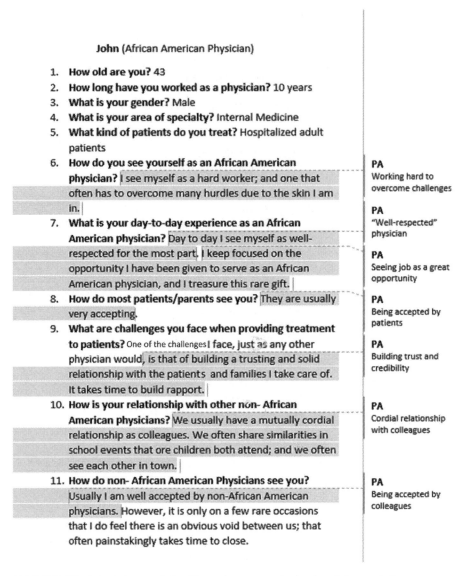

John (African American Physician)

1. **How old are you?** 43
2. **How long have you worked as a physician?** 10 years
3. **What is your gender?** Male
4. **What is your area of specialty?** Internal Medicine
5. **What kind of patients do you treat?** Hospitalized adult patients
6. **How do you see yourself as an African American physician?** I see myself as a hard worker; and one that often has to overcome many hurdles due to the skin I am in. — PA Working hard to overcome challenges
7. **What is your day-to-day experience as an African American physician?** Day to day I see myself as well-respected for the most part. I keep focused on the opportunity I have been given to serve as an African American physician, and I treasure this rare gift. — PA "Well-respected" physician / PA Seeing job as a great opportunity
8. **How do most patients/parents see you?** They are usually very accepting. — PA Being accepted by patients
9. **What are challenges you face when providing treatment to patients?** One of the challenges I face, just as any other physician would, is that of building a trusting and solid relationship with the patients and families I take care of. It takes time to build rapport. — PA Building trust and credibility
10. **How is your relationship with other non- African American physicians?** We usually have a mutually cordial relationship as colleagues. We often share similarities in school events that ore children both attend; and we often see each other in town. — PA Cordial relationship with colleagues
11. **How do non- African American Physicians see you?** Usually I am well accepted by non-African American physicians. However, it is only on a few rare occasions that I do feel there is an obvious void between us; that often painstakingly takes time to close. — PA Being accepted by colleagues

Exhibit 3.10. John's transcript with codes generated using interpretation-focused coding

Presumption-focused coding strategy

Throughout our daily lives, we consciously or unconsciously make conclusions based on what we have observed, heard or felt. Sometimes, we make claims based on what we have experienced and further check them against our subsequent experiences – leading to the rejection, adjustment or confirmation of the claims. Similarly, Charmaz (2014) calls this process, in a grounded theory data analysis, abductive inference. It involves making conclusions about what you have initially observed in your data and matching the claims against new data with the aim of refining or rejecting the claims. As Charmaz (2014) puts it, "abductive inference entails considering all plausible theoretical explanations for surprising data, forming hypotheses for each possible explanation, and checking these hypotheses empirically by examining data to arrive at the most plausible explanation" (p. 200). In the same way, with the presumption-focused coding strategy, we look at the evidence in the data (i.e. empirical indicators) and make conclusions or claims out of which codes are developed. The codes are then compared with new empirical indicators so as to adjust and/or confirm them.

The more evidence you have in the data, the better the support you have for the codes created. There is the possibility that some of the codes (i.e. claims) may not have empirical indicators (i.e. evidence) to support them. In this case, you could collect more data for further assessment of the unconfirmed codes. This technique is similar to theoretical sampling in the grounded theory approach (Charmaz, 2014). It involves collecting data from sources (normally participants) which the researcher believes could help him/her address unanswered questions raised during the initial development of a theory. The goal is to determine whether the proposed theory could explain the new data (Adu, 2017a; Charmaz, 2014).

Since presumption-focused coding is all about generating claims and looking for specific evidence in the data to support them, researchers need to be flexible when developing presumption-focused codes – being willing to adjust or replace presumption-focused claims (codes) when needed. *Can you use presumption-focused coding alone?* Yes, especially when you have the research purpose and question implying that you should come up with claims based on the evidence. However, this strategy is better used when utilizing it with description-focused coding, interpretation-focused coding, or both, in a linear or non-linear format. In a linear process, you could start the coding process by generating descriptive labels, followed by developing codes to capture what the initial codes mean and then ending with crafting presumption-focused codes using interpretive codes as evidence. Following a non-linear pattern, you could use the coding strategies concurrently. For instance, you could be describing participants' behavior and at the same time figuring out what conclusions should be made based on the description-focused codes.

Characteristics of presumption-focused coding

- There is a high tendency for the researcher to have an influence on the development of the claims
- There is a possibility of using one empirical indicator to support more than one claim
- Codes created are more abstract in nature compared to the description-focused codes

When to use presumption-focused coding

- *When a study has a presumption-focused purpose:* Presumption-focused coding is appropriate for studies with the main purpose of making claims, judgment and recommendations based on the data.
- *When you have a presumption-focused research question:* Presumption-focused coding is normally used for a research question which has a goal of making a judgement, explaining a phenomenon, describing a process or drawing a conclusion. The question may start with *'What conclusions can be made…?'*, *'What may be the reason for…?'*, *'How can we conceptualize the process of…?'* and *'Was the* [state that you want to assess] *effective, accurate or adequate?'*
- *When using data to support a claim:* Presumption-focused coding is appropriate if you plan to use the data as evidence to make claims or draw conclusions.

Demonstration 3.3

The data we will be using for this demonstration is about the experience of domestic violence victims. The transcripts were not from real people but were created for the purpose of this demonstration. In all, five participants were involved – with the majority of them being: single, female, Caucasian, with children, and employed (see Tables 3.3 and 3.4). Let's assume I'm interested in addressing the following research question: *Why did domestic violence victims decide to initially stay in an abusive relationship/marriage?* Based on this question, the main goal of the qualitative analysis is to identify specific reasons for their initial decision to stay in an abusive relationship/marriage. My preliminary plan or idea is to go through the data and code the rationales participants presented. With this plan, I could use either the description-focused or interpretation-focused coding strategy to generate the reasons why domestic violence victims didn't initially leave. To make the coding process even easier, I could only focus on the structured interview question (i.e. *Why did you initially decide to stay?*) and code participants' responses to that question. However, if I implement my earlier plan of using the description-focused or interpretation-focused coding strategy, I will end up having themes with limited evidence from the data. In addition, without using presumption-focused coding, potentially rich evidence supporting why they stayed will be left unexamined.

Before using the presumption-based coding strategy, there are useful notations you should familiarize yourself with. They are: **'Pre'**, **'C'**, **'PreC'**, **'E'** and **'→'** (see Table 3.5). All of these tags are used to label empirical indicators. We use **'Pre'** to tag an empirical indicator that is an indication of a presumption or claim. This means that not all empirical indicators become evidence to claims. Some are triggers or catalysts to the development of claims while others are actual evidence which are used to

Table 3.3 First part of participants' demographics (domestic violence victims)

ID	Age	Marital status	Gender	Race/ethnicity	Educational level
A1	25	Married	Female	Caucasian	High school diploma
A2	56	Single	Female	Caucasian	Bachelor's degree
A3	35	Single	Male	Caucasian	Bachelor's degree
A4	18	Single	Female	African American	High school diploma
A5	42	Married	Female	African American	Doctorate

Table 3.4 Second part of participants' demographics (domestic violence victims)

ID	Duration of the relationship	When the abuse started	Number of children	Participant's employment status	Partner's employment status
A1	3 years	1st year	2	Unemployed	Employed
A2	6 months	2nd month	3	Employed	Employed
A3	2 years	1st year	None	Employed	Employed
A4	1 year	8th month	None	Unemployed	Unemployed
A5	10 years	9th year	4	Employed	Employed

Table 3.5 Prefix, letters and symbol used in presumption-focused coding

Prefix, letters and symbol	Meaning
Pre	Presumption-focused code
C	Confirmed
PreC	Presumption-focused code Confirmed
E	Evidence (or Evidence code)
→	Based on
PreC → E 1,2,...	Presumption-focused code based on Evidence 1, 2,...

confirm claims. Evidence is labeled as **'E'**. If a presumption is confirmed, **'C'** is added to the **'Pre'** to be **'PreC'**. Whenever supporting evidence is identified and coded, the empirical indicator that has been tagged **'Pre'** would change to **'PreC → E'**. This means that the presumption-focused code has been confirmed (**'PreC'**) based on ('→') supporting evidence (**'E'**).

With the research question in mind and taking into consideration participants' demographic information, I went through each transcript to identify potential evidence for the reason why participants initially stayed in their relationship/marriage. There are two main options you could choose from when generating potential evidence. One option is to go through the data and tag empirical indicators with the letter **'E'** if you think they could be supporting evidence for the presumption-focused code to be generated. You then review the indicators and assign presumption-focused codes to them.

The second option (which was what I used) involves using description-focused and interpretation-focused coding strategies to help develop codes for each of the potential evidence. In other words, after identifying each empirical indicator (i.e. potential evidence), I generated a description-focused or an interpretation-focused code. Then, in parentheses, I indicated the **'E'** with its assigned number (see Exhibits 3.11–3.15).

As I was coding the evidence, I kept on asking myself, *what claim (related to participants' reason for staying) can I make?* Examining Participant 'A1's' response to interview question 14, I identified two reasons why she initially stayed in the marriage: (1) *"I don't believe in divorce…"* and (2) *"…I love my husband"* (see Exhibit 3.11). These empirical indicators directly address the research question: *Why did domestic violence victims decide to initially stay in an abusive relationship/marriage?* I saw the two indicators as claim triggers – informing the generation of presumption-focused codes, namely: *'Belief against divorce'* and *'Love for partner'*. They represent the first and second reason why Participant A1 stayed.

I initially tagged both presumption-focused codes as **'Pre'** since they had not yet been confirmed. To confirm a presumption-focused code, you need to search for evidence coded to see whether any of the evidence supports the code. For instance, I used an evidence code, *'Seeking family counseling (E6)'* to support the presumption-focused code, *'Belief against divorce (Pre)'*; I strongly believed Participant 'A1' didn't want to divorce due to religious reasons. She tried to address her abusive marriage by going for family counseling. Applying this assertion, I revised the code tag for the presumption-focused code, *'Belief against divorce'* from **'Pre'** to **'PreC → E6'** – meaning the presumption-focused code has been confirmed by the evidence code, *'Seeking family counseling (E6)'* (see Exhibit 3.11).

As I continued to code empirical indicators, I concurrently sought evidence to support my initially developed and confirmed presumption-focused codes. As you may know, the more supporting evidence you discover for a presumption-focused code, the stronger the code (presumption/claim) becomes. For example, a presumption-focused code, *'Committed to the relationship (PreC → E9)'*, which was initially confirmed when coding Participant 'A2's' transcript (see Exhibit 3.12), had four additional pieces of evidence (E7, 12, 15 and 16) after completing coding the last transcript (see Exhibit 3.15). At the end, I had *'Believing abusive*

A1 (Domestic Violence Survivor)

1. **How old are you?** 25
2. **What is your marital status?** Married
3. **What is your highest educational level?** High school diploma
4. **What is your gender?** Female
5. **What is your race?** Caucasian
6. **How long were you in the relationship?** 3 years
7. **Were you employed when you were in the relationship?** No
8. **How many children do you have?** 2
9. **Was your partner employed at the time of the relationship?** Yes
10. **How was your relationship with your partner? Good, complicated or bad? Please explain.** The relationship started out very good, but my partner became very controlling of where I went, and who I spoke to. It then increased to verbal outbursts, and physical abuse.
11. **When did the abuse start?** It started off after about the 1ˢᵗ year of our marriage; when our first child arrived, and we had some stressors in our life with balancing a job and family responsibilities.
12. **What kinds of abuse did you sustain?** Verbal, and physical.
13. **How did you cope with the abuse?** I depended upon my family and close friends to help me get through it. I also reached out to our local pastor, who counselled us as a family, and became a father figure to my husband, who lacked this structure in his life.
14. **Why did you initially decide to stay?** I don't believe in divorce, and I love my husband.
15. **At what stage did you decide to leave?** I never left, and my husband continues to work on changing his behavior and his attitude towards us as a family.

PA
Displaying 'controlling' behavior (E1)

PA
Abusing verbally and physically (E2)

PA
Having a stressful life (E3)

PA
Difficulty 'balancing' job-family roles (E4)

PA
Abusing verbally and physically (E2)

PA
Seeking family and friends support (E5)

PA
Seeking family counseling (E6)

PA
Belief against divorce (PreC → E6)

PA
Love for partner (PreC→ E7)

PA
Working to address abusive behavior (E7)

PA
Believing abusive behavior would end (PreC → E6,7)

Exhibit 3.11. Participant 'A1' transcript with codes generated using presumption-focused coding

A2 (Domestic Violence Survivor)

1. **How old are you?** 56
2. **What is your marital status?** Single
3. **What is your highest educational level?** Bachelor's degree
4. **What is your gender?** Female
5. **What is your race?** Caucasian
6. **How long were you in the relationship?** 6 months
7. **Were you employed when you were in the relationship?** Yes
8. **How many children do you have?** 3
9. **Was your partner employed at the time of the relationship?** Yes
10. **How was your relationship with your partner?** *Good, complicated or bad? Please explain.* We were both widowers and found friendship in each other; we knew each other from work, and our relationship when it began was good. However, not too long after it began he wanted me only to be with him; and did not want me to speak with my family or children anymore. He wanted to isolate me from my normal routines, and I could only go to and from work to home. It was all about controlling my daily activity. I found the courage to leave him safely, and I am no longer with him.
11. **When did the abuse start?** About 2 months into the relationship
12. **What kinds of abuse did you sustain?** Verbal abuse, and control.
13. **How did you cope with the abuse?** I turned to my children, and my church friends.
14. **Why did you initially decide to stay?** He was my friend, and I thought I could trust him.
15. **At what stage did you decide to leave?** After I realized he was not adding anything but stress and fear to my life, I knew I had to leave in order to do what was best for me.

PA
Displaying 'controlling' behavior (E1)

PA
Having a sense of insecurity (E8)

PA
Displaying 'controlling' behavior (E1)

PA
Abusing verbally (E9)

PA
Seeking family and friends' support (E5)

PA
Committed to the relationship (PreC → E9)

PA
Having a sense of trust (E9)

Exhibit 3.12. Participant 'A2' transcript with codes generated using presumption-focused coding

A3 (Domestic Violence Survivor)

1. **How old are you?** 35
2. **What is your marital status?** Single
3. **What is your highest educational level?** Bachelors
4. **What is your gender?** Male
5. **What is your race?** Caucasian
6. **How long were you in the relationship?** 2 years
7. **Were you employed when you were in the relationship?** Yes
8. **How many children do you have?** None
9. **Was your partner employed at the time of the relationship?** Yes
10. **How was your relationship with your partner?** ***Good, complicated or bad? Please explain.*** It was very good, as it usually is in many relationships, but it started to take a turn for the worse. My girlfriend told me I could never be with anyone else, and she wanted me never to talk to any other females outside of my close family circle. She then became more than verbally abusive, and started to physically injure me. It actually turned out so bad, that I had to call the police in order to prevent the abuse from turning fatal.
11. **When did the abuse start?** It started after about 1 year.
12. **What kinds of abuse did you sustain?** Verbal, emotional, and physical.
13. **How did you cope with the abuse?** I would turn inwards, as I was too embarrassed to let others know that my girlfriend was abusing me. So I would just keep to myself, and try to deal with it alone.
14. **Why did you initially decide to stay?** I cared a lot about her, and I wanted to give her a chance.
15. **At what stage did you decide to leave?** When the abuse started to escalate, and there was a potential that both of us could get injured.

PA
Displaying 'controlling' behavior (E1)

PA
Having a sense of insecurity (E8)

PA
Abusing verbally and physically (E2)

PA
Abusing verbally and physically (E2)

PA
Ashamed of seeking outside help (E10)

PA
Addressing the abuse independently (E11)

PA
Believing abusive behavior would end (PreC → E6,7,10,11)

PA
Cared about the partner (E12)

PA
Committed to the relationship (PreC → E7,9,12)

PA
Working to address abusive behavior (E7)

Exhibit 3.13. Participant 'A3' transcript with codes generated using presumption-focused coding

A4 (Domestic Violence Survivor)

1. **How old are you?** 18
2. **What is your marital status?** Single
3. **What is your highest educational level?** High school diploma
4. **What is your gender?** Female
5. **What is your race?** African American
6. **How long were you in the relationship?** 1 year
7. **Were you employed when you were in the relationship?** No
8. **How many children do you have?** None
9. **Was your partner employed at the time of the relationship?** No
10. **How was your relationship with your partner? *Good, complicated or bad? Please explain.*** It started out difficult; but I thought it was because we were both young, and because it was our first relationship. However, it started to become stressful to be with my boyfriend. I did not feel happy, or joyful when I was with him, as he would point out all my supposed flaws, and try to isolate me from my friends and family.
11. **When did the abuse start?** It started after about 8 months into the relationship.
12. **What kinds of abuse did you sustain?** Verbal
13. **How did you cope with the abuse?** I turned to my friends, but was too afraid to tell my family for fear of what they would do to my boyfriend.
14. **Why did you initially decide to stay?** He was my friend, and I thought we could make it work.
15. **At what stage did you decide to leave?** I realized I had to leave, when I was no longer the happy and joyful person I was before knowing him. I knew that I never wanted to be in a relationship that caused me to be less than my true self.

PA
Making partner feel worthless (E13)

PA
Displaying 'controlling' behavior (E1)

PA
Abusing verbally (E9)

PA
Seeking friends support (E14)

PA
Trying to preserve the relationship (E15)

PA
Committed to the relationship (PreC → E7,9,12,15)

PA
Believing abusive behavior would end (PreC → E6,7,10,11)

Exhibit 3.14. Participant 'A4' transcript with codes generated using presumption-focused coding

A5 (Domestic Violence Survivor)

1. **How old are you?** 42
2. **What is your marital status?** Married
3. **What is your highest educational level?** PhD
4. **What is your gender?** Female
5. **What is your race?** African American
6. **How long were you in the relationship?** 10 years
7. **Were you employed when you were in the relationship?** Yes
8. **How many children do you have?** 4
9. **Was your partner employed at the time of the relationship?** Yes
10. **How was your relationship with your partner?** *Good, complicated or bad? Please explain.* Our relationship was good. However, after my husband suffered an injury, and he could no longer work or provide for the family, he became very resentful and angry. He than projected his stress on myself and our children, and told us he could not live with us anymore.
11. **When did the abuse start?** About 9 years into our marriage
12. **What kinds of abuse did you sustain?** Verbal and physical
13. **How did you cope with the abuse?** I turned to my pastor, and my church friends.
14. **Why did you initially decide to stay?** I stayed because I am committed to my husband and family, and we have 4 children. I did it for us.
15. **At what stage did you decide to leave?** I have never left; he has decided to move away from us: but if he is willing to work it through, our door is always open. However, he must make major changes in himself in order for us to live safely together.

PA
Abusing verbally and physically (E2)

PA
Seeking friends' support (E14)

PA
Committed to the relationship
(PreC →
E7,9,12,15,16)

PA
Avoiding separation/ divorce (E16)

PA
Avoiding separation/ divorce (E16)

Exhibit 3.15. Participant 'A5' transcript with codes generated using presumption-focused coding

behavior would end (PreC → E6,7,10,11)' and *'Committed to the rela-tionship (PreC → E7,9,12,15,16)'* as presumption-focused codes with the highest number of pieces of evidence. Here is a list of all of the codes with their respective evidence:

1. Belief against divorce **(PreC → E6)**
   a. *Seeking family counseling* **(E6)**
2. Love for partner **(PreC→ E7)**
   a. *Working to address abusive behavior* **(E7)**
3. Believing abusive behavior would end **(PreC → E6, 7, 10, 11)**
   a. *Seeking family counseling* **(E6)**
   b. *Working to address abusive behavior* **(E7)**
   c. *Ashamed of seeking outside help* **(E10)**
   d. *Addressing the abuse independently* **(E11)**
4. Committed to the relationship **(PreC → E7,9,12,15,16)**
   a. *Working to address abusive behavior* **(E7)**
   b. *Having a sense of trust* **(E9)**
   c. *Cared about the partner* **(E12)**
   d. *Trying to preserve the relationship* **(E15)**
   e. *Avoiding separation/divorce* **(E16)**

At this stage, I can present my findings by using the confirmed presumption-focused codes to address the research question. However, there are interesting discoveries which could be made if I continue to fur-ther examine the relationship among evidence and presumption-focused codes. It could lead to the development of an initial theory which could be further compared to new data to determine whether it could be confirmed, adjusted or rejected (Charmaz, 2014). Let me give you an example of a potential theory based on the presumption-focused code, *'Believing abusive behavior would end'* and its four pieces of evidence, *'Seeking family counseling (E6)'*, *'Working to address abusive behavior (E7)'*, *'Ashamed of seeking outside help (E10)'* and *'Addressing the abuse independently (E11)'*. I have two potential theories:

Theory 1

Some domestic violence victims decide to initially stay because they believe that the abuse will end one day. They feel it is their respon-sibility to help their partner deal with the abusive behavior. Because they are ashamed of seeking outside help, they isolate themselves from family and friends and try to address the abuse independently.

Theory 2

Some domestic violence victims decide to initially stay because they believe that the abuse will end one day. They feel it is their responsibility to help their partner deal with the abusive behavior. Due to this, they seek family counseling to address their partners' abusive behavior.

CONCLUSION

Qualitative coding is like reviewing artwork. You could start by describing the art so that your audience knows what it is. Your role is to relay to your audience the characteristics of the art in terms of its dimension, texture, color and resemblance without making an interpretation or inference. Similarly, if the aim of the qualitative analysis is to describe significant information found in the data, description-focused coding is an appropriate coding strategy to use. As an artwork reviewer, you could go beyond just describing the art by telling your audience what it means. Making meaning of art starts from learning about the person who created it – finding out who he/she was, his/her background and the source of his/her inspiration. In addition, you could look into what he/she wanted to communicate, who were his/her audience, what was his/her intent, and what was the political, economic or social situation at the time the art was created. It also involves preventing your background and biases from influencing your interpretation of the art. In the same way, the coding strategy appropriate for making meaning of the empirical indicators in data is interpretation-focused coding. The final task you could perform as an art critic is to make a logical conclusion or claim based on the characteristics and meaning of the art. Likewise, presumption-focused coding is used to draw conclusions from the data and look for evidence in the data to support the inference made.

I view these qualitative coding strategies as tools; they have strengths and weaknesses (see Table 3.6). When utilized appropriately, they will help generate codes, categories, themes and/or theories that reflect the data collected. If the aim of your coding process is to describe, interpret or infer, you could use description-focused, interpretation-focused or presumption-focused coding, respectively (see Table 3.7). In other words, within the DIP coding method toolbox are three coding strategies. Each of them could be independently applied (*i.e. single use*) to identify empirical indicators and assign codes to them. However, description-focused and interpretation-focused coding work well together (*i.e. multiple use*) if the coding aim is to interpret data. In a case where the coding objective is to infer from data, you could use description-focused and/or interpretative-focused coding with presumption-focused coding. These coding strategies are not only used for reviewing transcripts but are also appropriate for coding artifacts (which include pictures, artwork, documents, etc.), videos and audio.

Table 3.6 Strengths and weaknesses of the coding strategies

Coding strategy	Strengths	Weaknesses
Description-focused coding	• Easy to develop codes • Close connection between the codes and the empirical indicators • Less mental effort needed to generate codes • Less time needed to generate codes • Less influence of researcher's background and biases	• Difficult when coding existing data (such as archival data, artifacts or an annual report of a company) • Difficult to categorize codes and develop themes without engaging in some sort of interpretation of the empirical indicators • Limited in what to code because some portions of the data may need interpretation before creating codes
Interpretation-focused coding	• Easy to move from codes to categories and themes due to the codes' abstractive features • Could be used alongside description-focused coding • Helps in determining the underlying meaning of significant portions of the data	• Challenging to select an appropriate interpretation from potential meanings of an empirical indicator • Time-consuming due to generating meaning – this is not free from the researcher's background influence • More mental effort needed to generate codes
Presumption-focused coding	• Could be used alongside description-focused and interpretation-focused coding • Could facilitate the development of categories, themes and theories • Promotes creativity – aiding the researcher to come up with claims and use evidence in the data to support them	• Time-consuming since the researcher needs to identify the empirical indicators, and arrive at conclusions based on the indicators – not totally free from his/her background influence • More mental effort needed to generate codes • Presumption-focused codes can be refuted if contrary evidence is discovered

Table 3.7 Qualitative research methods and their respective purpose, data analysis goal and potential coding strategy

Research method	Main purpose of the method	Main goal of the data analysis	Potential coding strategy
Phenomenological approach	Examine participants' experience	Develop themes or concepts which represent participants' experience	Description-focused and interpretation-focused coding
Hermeneutic phenomenological approach	Examine and interpret documents to capture their underlying meaning (i.e. making sense of text)	Provide the meaning of the text in a condensed form	Interpretation-focused coding
Interpretative phenomenological analysis	Explore participants' thoughts about a phenomenon experienced	Assess participants' perspectives of their experience and interpret their views	Interpretation-focused coding
Transcendental phenomenological approach	Examine participants' experience and make sense of the experience from a bias-free perspective	In a bias-free state, develop themes which reflect participants' experience and determine the essence of the experience	Description-focused coding
Ethnography	Explore a phenomenon or an event as it happens in its natural setting	Develop themes to describe or generate a theory to explain a process, phenomenon or event which occurred in its natural environment	Description-focused and interpretation-focused coding
Narrative approach	Gather participants' stories with the aim of restating those narratives	Combine participants' stories and narrate them in a chronological order and/or specified themes	Description-focused coding
Case study	Understand a case or bring to light a unique case – collecting multiple kinds of data	Develop themes, models or theories to explain a case, describe a unique case or compare cases	Description-focused, interpretation-focused and/or presumption-focused coding
Grounded theory	Explain a process, behavior, event or phenomenon	Develop a statement, model or theory to explain a process, behavior, event or phenomenon	Interpretation-focused and presumption-focused coding

Qualitative data for practice:

To access the data used in this chapter for practice purposes, go to www.routledge.com/A-Step-by-Step-Guide-to-Qualitative-Data-Coding/Adu/p/book/9781138486874. The folder, *'Data for instruction and practice purposes'* contains the following:

- 'Domestic Violence Survivor' Data
- 'African American Physician' Data
- 'Mental Health Stigma' Data

NOTE

1 See Chapter 1 for detailed discussion of philosophical assumptions.

REFERENCES

Adu, P. (2013) Qualitative analysis coding and categorizing. [PowerPoint slides]. SlideShare. Retrieved from www.slideshare.net/kontorphilip/qualitative-analysis-coding-and-categorizing

Adu, P. (2017a). Using grounded theory approach: From start to finish. [PowerPoint slides]. SlideShare. Retrieved from www.slideshare.net/kontorphilip/using-grounded-theory-approach-from-start-to-finish

Adu, P. (2017b). Conducting qualitative analysis: What you need to know. [PowerPoint slides]. SlideShare. Retrieved from www.slideshare.net/kontorphilip/conducting-qualitative-analysis-what-you-need-to-know

Adu, P. (2018). What to do with your data: Qualitative research [PowerPoint slides]. SlideShare. Retrieved from www.slideshare.net/kontorphilip/what-to-do-with-your-data-qualitative-research

Auerbach, C. F., & Silverstein, L. B. (2003). *Qualitative data: An introduction to coding and analysis*. New York, NY: New York University Press.

Bazeley, P. (2013). *Qualitative data analysis: Practical strategies*. London, England: Sage.

Bentz, V. M., & Shapiro, J. J. (2001). *Mindful inquiry in social research*. Thousand Oaks, CA: Sage.

Charmaz, K. (2014). *Constructing grounded Theory*. London: Sage.

Creswell, J. W., & Poth, C. N. (2018). *Qualitative inquiry & research design: Choosing among five approaches*. Los Angeles, CA: Sage.

Hoffmann, J. E. (2008, February 07). Gold processing. Retrieved October 4, 2018, from www.britannica.com/technology/gold-processing

Moustakas, C. (1994). *Phenomenological research methods*. Thousand Oaks, CA: Sage.

Saldaña, J. (2016). *The coding manual for qualitative researchers*. Los Angeles, CA: Sage.

Strauss, A. L. (1989). *Qualitative analysis for social scientists*. Cambridge, England: Cambridge University Press.

Preparing data to code

OBJECTIVES

Readers will be able to:

1. Determine what kind of data could be qualitatively analyzed
2. Describe the steps needed to make data ready for analysis

WHAT KIND OF DATA CAN BE QUALITATIVELY ANALYZED?

Before conducting qualitative coding or analysis, a researcher needs to collect data. So what is qualitative data? It is anything collected using one or more data collection strategies (such as interviews, observations, focus groups, document/artifact collection and open-ended surveys), with the intention of analyzing it to address a research problem or research question(s), or to meet the purpose of a study. Qualitative data includes interview transcripts, documents, objects made or used by a person or a group of people, and audio, video or text produced by the researcher.

An interview is one of the widely used qualitative data collection strategies. It is a powerful data collection technique that helps us to capture what participants have experienced, their thoughts about a phenomenon, and the rationales behind their decisions and actions. With permission from participants, we can record our conversation with them during the interview process using an audio recording device. After compiling the audio files and saving them in a secure location, the next step is to transcribe the data.

TRANSCRIBING AUDIO FILES

Transcribing is the process of transforming audio or video, usually from interviews or focus groups, into text (Davidson, 2009). Depending on the time and resources available, you could hire a transcriptionist or use one of the available automatic transcription software programs to transcribe the audio files (see Adu, 2018a). However, there are huge benefits of engaging in "the traditional listen-and-type method" (MacLean, Meyer, & Estable, 2004, p. 91). By doing it yourself, you get a unique opportunity to review participants' responses to each question – discovering patterns and obtaining a picture of what the data portrays (Easton, McComish, & Greenberg, 2000; Patton, 2015). As Johnson (2011) indicates, "transcribing one's own interviews means that the researcher gets closer and more familiar with data interpretation and analysis" (p. 92). Available transcription software programs could facilitate the manual transcription of your audio files. Some of them are: Audacity (www.audacityteam.org/), Express Scribe Transcription (www.nch.com.au/scribe/) and oTranscribe (http://otranscribe.com/) (Adu, 2018a).

It can take about four hours to manually transcribe an interview which lasted for an hour, and the transcription could yield 15–25 pages if it is typed single-spaced (Bazeley, 2013; Patton, 2015). Even if you use a transcriptionist or automatic transcription software, it is recommended to review the transcripts to make sure they are a true reflection of the content of the audio files (Easton et al., 2000). At the end, you would have verbatim transcripts containing all the "conversational fillers" participants used during the interview (MacLean et al., 2004, p. 116).

Filler words, which are sometimes seen as a demonstration of disfluencies, can be a great way of understanding what participants have expressed (Bazeley, 2013; Laserna, Seih, & Pennerbaker, 2014; Patton, 2015; Roulston, 2014). According to Laserna et al. (2014), there are two main types of filler words: filler pauses (such as "um" and "uh") and discourse markers (such as "I mean, you know, like") (p. 328). Interviewees sometimes use a filler pause when they are thinking about what they want to say and preventing others (especially in a focus group) from cutting in as they look for words to express themselves (Laserna et al., 2014). Similarly, they use discourse makers such as 'you know' and 'I mean' to seek confirmation and provide clarification, respectively (Laserna et al., 2014).

USING EXISTING DATA FOR QUALITATIVE ANALYSIS DEMONSTRATIONS

Before going further with the data preparation process, here is some brief information about the data I will be using for demonstration purposes in the rest of the chapters. The data is from a research project conducted between 1997 and 2002. The main purpose of the case study was to examine the strategies that genetic modification (GM) specialists used to communicate their GM crop research to the general public (Cook & Robbins, 2005). A total of 29 interviews were conducted. Participants included GM scientists and staff from a public university in England and consultations which were not affiliated with the institution (Cook &

Robbins, 2005). In addition to the interviews, data from GM seminars, and committee reports and minutes were collected and analyzed. Throughout this book, I will be referring to this research project as *'GM crop case study'*. This study was conducted at a time when there were growing concerns about genetically modified (GM) foods among the British public (Moseley, 2002).

GM crops are produce whose genes have been altered by scientists to reflect desired characteristics in terms of their size, color, speed of growth, resistance to certain pests, taste, smell, and the like (Harlander, 2002). This technological innovation has led to high crop yield, wide varieties of fruits, vegetables and grains, reduction in food prices, and access to certain seasonal foods (Kurzgesagt, 2017). However, the public, including some non-governmental organizations, have raised concerns related to ethics, safety and fairness (see Krimsky, 2015; Moseley, 2002).

Taking a fresh look at the data that Cook and Robbins (2005) collected and similar to the purpose of the initial project, I want to explore the UK public's concerns about GM foods and the strategies GM scientists should use to present the GM crop research to the public. The following are the questions I want to address:

1. What were the factors contributing to public concerns about GM research and foods in the UK?
2. What were the challenges faced by GM scientists when communicating GM crop research to the public?
3. How should GM crop research be communicated to the public to address their concerns?

To address these questions and ensure that females are well represented, I selected all three female, and at random seven male, interview transcripts. Out of 17 GM scientists and seven university staff, I chose seven (41%) scientists' and three (43%) staff's transcripts, respectively (see Table 4.1). In total, I selected ten transcripts.

The transcripts consist of 167 pages in total with an average of 17 pages per interview transcribed. Each transcript contains (1) *participant ID*, (2) *label for the interviewer*, and (3) *label for the interviewee*. They are verbatim transcripts rich with: (4) *repetitions*, (5) *non-verbal behaviors of participants*, (6) *non-verbal behaviors of the interviewer*, (7) *conversational fillers* and (8) *pauses* (see Exhibit 4.1). As indicated earlier, these conversational elements play a huge role in better understanding not only what participants said but also what they meant.

USING QUALITATIVE ANALYSIS TOOLS

After transcribing the interview data, the next step is to decide whether to use manual qualitative analysis tools or qualitative data analysis (QDA)

Table 4.1 Demographics of participants (GM scientists and university staff)

Participant ID	Occupation	Gender	No. of pages (interview transcript)
S3	GM scientist	Male	31
S4	GM scientist	Male	17
S5	GM scientist	Male	20
S6	GM scientist	Male	20
S9	GM scientist	Female	14
S13	GM scientist	Female	11
S16	GM scientist	Male	14
NS1	Academic staff	Male	21
NS2	Student/staff	Female	7
NS5	Student/staff	Male	12

software to create codes, categories and themes. Conducting qualitative analysis manually involves using 'hands-on' coding tools (such as pen, pencil, paper, highlighter and index cards) and/or electronic coding tools (such as Microsoft Word and Excel) to select relevant information from the data, label them, sort the labels, and generate themes.

Using manual qualitative analysis tools

Using manual coding tools, you could print out all the transcripts (see Saldaña, 2016). You then read through each of them as you underline (with a pen or pencil) or highlight empirical indicators, and assign labels to the indicators by stating the codes on the margins of the printout. Alternatively, using index cards to record the codes generated could be a very worthwhile option. On the front of the card, you state the code and location in terms of where the indicator was found (using the participant's ID, transcript page and line numbers). On the back of the card, you describe the meaning including characteristics of the code generated. The next stage is to sort the cards based on the relationships between the codes, and based on the content of the clusters created, you come up with labels – leading to the development of themes. If index cards were not used, compile a list of codes on a piece of paper and start the sorting process.

Using Microsoft Word as an electronic coding tool, you select empirical indicators, and then click on the *'New Comment'* function under the *'Review'* tab to create a code (Adu, 2017; Saldaña, 2016). After developing codes, compile all of them and indicate their respective

Participant S13

A: OK . can I start by asking you of what in your opinion accounts for the . reaction to GM . products in Britain?

B: OK . I think it's . probably . a number of a number of things . one is . the . is perceived lack of knowledge and uncertainty . perceived uncertainty of . possible potential future outcomes that . it's not people are not . able to control so it is lack of control lack of knowledge . uncertainty about . potential . you know .

A: lack of knowledge of the technology itself ?or of the uncertainties? or

B: both . I think both yes . I don't know some some . some research we're . we're doing and we're only . pretesting the questionnaire what comes out is that . people . do not really know much they . people do not know much . about . food production technology . in general we've been asking questions about . enzymes and . you know the very basic . you know is . tomatoes have . DNA true or false and people . clearly . a number of people clearly do not know their whereabouts in in this sense so you know when you talk about biotechnology there is . perhaps partly . a bit of confusion because there are so many . ways of talking about . the issue and . biotechnology is different from genetic modification and that's different from . other . other terms . and so I think that that somehow adds to . to the confusion and . the lack of understanding and knowledge

A: what do you think would be a good strategy . to communicate . research concerning genetic modification?

B: that's a one million dollar question [both laugh] . I don't know I suppose .biased view because I'm doing some research on that . is . the the idea is . I don't know my impression is that perhaps . rather than focussing on on . on risk communication given that risks are not assessed . at the moment . and may take . years and years and years . to be able to do that . perhaps start thinking about possible benefits . of such products so . so that . if people say if- sorry if people see . trade-offs between accepting something that is new and to some extent . unknown . and . benefits there are quite tangible like perhaps . health benefits . if you know if . products are developed that can . can be either either . functional . type of foods or or can can give . you know . specific benefits then that may be an idea otherwise . I but I don't know I don't know what . what did you have in mind I'm not sure
that's the

1
Participant ID

2
Label for interviewer

3
Label for interviewee

7
Conversational filler

4
Repetition

8
Pause

7
Conversational filler

8
Pause

2
Label for the interviewer

3
Label for the interviewee

5
Non-verbal behavior of the participant

6
Non-verbal behavior of the interviewer

8
Pause

4
Repetition

7
Conversational filler

Exhibit 4.1. Participant 'S13' transcript excerpt showing elements of a verbatim transcript

frequency (which is how many times a code is assigned to empirical indicators). Group them to develop categories and themes. I have provided detailed information about this process in Chapters 7 and 8.

When to use manual qualitative analysis tools

- When you have a single kind of data such as interview transcripts
- When you have a small amount of data (preferably where all transcripts total 30 pages or less)
- When you are skilled in properly organizing and documenting data analysis steps
- When you have difficulty learning or using qualitative data analysis software (QDAS)

Using qualitative data analysis software (QDAS)

Imagine having a computer program that: accepts importing multiple kinds of data into a single workspace, facilitates manual transcription of video and audio files, helps in running a quick preliminary analysis to learn more about the data before the coding process starts, aids in connecting participants' demographic information to the data files imported, and enables assigning codes to relevant portions of the data and automatically providing code counts and cases (see Chapters 10, 11 and 12). Just think of a program that could aid in clustering codes into categories – leading to the development of themes and theories – allow for the organization and documentation of the coding process, assist in making comparisons of themes across data sources (or participants) and promote the visualization of findings. These are the main functions that most of the QDAS have. However, the "software will not do an analysis for you... Rather, its data management and querying capacity supports you to carry out your analysis by removing the limitations imposed by paper processing and human memory" (Bazeley & Jackson, 2014, p. 18).

There are numerous QDAS available. However, when looking for good software program, I recommend taking the following factors into consideration:

1. **Affordability:** There are a lot of well-developed software programs with useful interfaces available. However, they may be costly for a single user. The good news is that some of them have a student license/package/version that may be affordable to you. Therefore, I suggest you first review the cost when deciding on which one to choose. Alternatively, there are a number of QDAS that are free to use. However, make sure they meet your needs and are easy to use (Adu, 2018a). Another issue is there might be

hidden costs related to training and software upgrades, which you should keep in mind when making a decision.

2. **Compatibility:** When looking for an appropriate QDAS, don't only look into whether it is compatible with the operating system you have (i.e. Microsoft Windows or Mac OS) but also whether it functions optimally based on your system. You could find out the software performance by going through users' reviews. Another way is to determine whether there are instructional videos customized to your operating system. Lastly, having an online (web-based) version of the software could be a great option since you don't need to download it on your computer and it can be used anywhere irrespective of the type of operating system you may have. The most important thing is to have internet access. However, make sure you review the software developer's privacy agreement, especially the questions about who owns the data imported into their system, what protections it has, and what a third party can access and use.

3. **Functionality:** When choosing an appropriate QDAS, ensure that it performs at least the basic functions such as importing data, running word frequencies, developing codes, categories and themes, visualizing findings, and exporting outputs (Adu, 2018b). The questions I would ask when selecting a QDAS are: what does it do? Would I be able to import my data considering the kind of data I have? Before I start my coding process, can I quickly run an analysis to determine which kind of words were frequently used? Can I code the data and categorize the codes? And can I visualize and export the findings? Looking at the developer's description and demonstration videos would help in addressing the above questions.

4. **Usability:** Another factor you should take into consideration is whether the software is easy to learn and use. Think about specific tasks and goals you want to perform and achieve, respectively, with a QDAS (Adu, 2018a). You can then review the software manual and instructional videos to see whether the tool would help you to accomplish your data analysis objectives. Imagine having a qualitative software program with a familiar QDAS interface, icons and functions. You wouldn't need to spend a significant amount of time to learn how to use the functions and commands. In other words, look for the kind of QDAS which could promote spending more time intensively interacting with the data to generate codes, categories and themes, and less time learning about how to use the software. Also, using a trial version of a QDAS could help you to determine the usability.

5. **Availability:** When deciding on an appropriate QDAS, find out whether it has supporting resources such as a manual, instructional videos and a help service. I would reflect on the following

questions: Is there a manual (either incorporated into or separate from the software) that you could make a quick reference to when needed? Are there instructional videos that provide a step-by-step process of importing and analyzing data and visualizing and exporting findings? Is there a helpline or customer service available which you could easily access when needed? It would also be a plus if there is an online support group which you could join and ask questions related to the QDAS.

PAT Research (2018) has reviewed the top 16 widely used qualitative data analysis software programs (see: www.predictiveanalyticstoday. com/top-qualitative-data-analysis-software/#whatisqualitativedataanalys issoftware). It would be helpful to review them before deciding on which one to use. In addition, there are reviews on the top 21 free software programs that could be used to analyze qualitative data (see: https:// www.predictiveanalyticstoday.com/top-free-qualitative-data-analysis-software/). In this book, I will be demonstrating how to analyze qualitative data using the following QDAS: QDA Miner Lite (see Chapter 10), NVivo 12 (see Chapter 11), and Dedoose (see Chapter 12).

When to use QDAS

- ✓ When you have multiple kinds of data such as interview and focus group transcripts, documents, and field notes
- ✓ When you have a large amount of data (all transcripts total 30 pages or more)
- ✓ When you want to save time in organizing and documenting data analysis steps
- ✓ When you have little or no difficulty learning or using QDAS

Box 4.1 Data preparation steps

1. Compile audio files
2. Transcribe the audio files (i.e. producing verbatim transcriptions)
3. Remove any identifiable information
4. Assign IDs to your participants' data
5. Read through all of the transcripts
6. Decide on the qualitative analysis tools or software you want to use

---

CONCLUSION

Preparing your data is the first action that is needed before conducting data analysis. Making data (especially interview audio files) ready involves producing verbatim transcription. It is important to maintain data which are an exact reflection of what you and participants said, including conversational fillers and non-verbal communication. It helps in fully understanding the data and avoiding losing its richness. The decision to conduct manual coding or to use QDAS depends mainly on the amount and kinds of data to be analyzed, time available to analyze the data and familiarity with QDAS. With manual coding, all attention is directed towards the data analysis process, compared to using QDAS where you need to spend time to learn its functions before conducting the analysis. However, some of the advantages of using software are having the option to: quickly run the kind of words participants frequently used (i.e. word frequency), develop a visual representation of data and findings, and easily organize and categorize codes. Don't be too quick to start analyzing your data after selecting an appropriate QDAS. Spend time gaining the skills needed to efficiently and effectively use the software before starting the coding process.

REFERENCES

Adu, P. (2017). Conducting manual qualitative analysis using Word document [PowerPoint slides]. SlideShare. Retrieved from www.slideshare.net/kontorphilip/conducting-manual-qualitative-analysis-using-word-document

Adu, P. (2018a). What to do with your data: Qualitative research [PowerPoint slides]. SlideShare. Retrieved from www.slideshare.net/kontorphilip/what-to-do-with-your-data-qualitative-research

Adu, P. (2018b). Introduction to NVivo: Making good use of the qualitative software [PowerPoint slides]. SlideShare. Retrieved from www.slideshare.net/kontorphilip/introduction-to-nvivo-making-good-use-of-the-qualitative-software

Bazeley, P. (2013). *Qualitative data analysis: Practical strategies*. London, England: Sage.

Bazeley, P., & Jackson, K. (2014). *Qualitative data analysis with NVivo*. Los Angeles, CA: Sage.

Cook, G., & Robbins, P. T. (2005). *Presentation of genetically modified (GM) crop research to non-specialists, 1997–2002: A case study*. [data collection]. UK Data Service. SN: 5069, http://doi.org/10.5255/UKDA-SN-5069-1

Davidson, C. (2009). Transcription: Imperatives for qualitative research. *International Journal of Qualitative Methods, 8*(2), 35–52. doi:10.1177/160940690900800206

Easton, K. L., McComish, J. F., & Greenberg, R. (2000). Avoiding common pitfalls in qualitative data collection and transcription. *Qualitative Health Research, 10*(5), 703–707. doi:10.1177/104973200129118651

Harlander, S. K. (2002). Safety assessments and public concern for genetically modified food products: The American view. *Toxicologic Pathology, 30*(1), 132–134. doi:10.1080/01926230252824833

Johnson, B. E. (2011). The speed and accuracy of voice recognition software-assisted transcription versus the listen-and-type method: A research note. *Qualitative Research, 11*(1), 91–97. doi:10.1177/1468794110385966

Krimsky, S. (2015). An illusory consensus behind GMO health assessment. *Science, Technology, & Human Values, 40*(6), 883–914. doi:10.1177/0162243915598381

Kurzgesagt. (2017, March 30). Are GMOs good or bad? Genetic engineering & our food. Retrieved February 19, 2018, from www.youtube.com/watch?v=7TmcXYp8xu4

Laserna, C. M., Seih, Y., & Pennebaker, J. W. (2014). Um … who like says you know. *Journal of Language and Social Psychology, 33*(3), 328–338. doi:10.1177/0261927x14526993

MacLean, L. M., Meyer, M., & Estable, A. (2004). Improving accuracy of transcripts in qualitative research. *Qualitative Health Research, 14*(1), 113–123. doi:10.1177/1049732303259804

Moseley, B. E. (2002). Safety assessment and public concern for genetically modified food products: The European view. *Toxicologic Pathology, 30*(1), 129–131. doi:10.1080/01926230252824824

Patton, M. Q. (2015). *Qualitative research & evaluation methods: Integrating theory and practice.* Los Angeles, CA: Sage.

PAT Research. (2018, February 3). Top 16 qualitative data analysis software in 2018. Retrieved March 1, 2018, from www.predictiveanalyticstoday.com/top-qualitative-data-analysis-software/#whatisqualitativedataanalysissoftware

Roulston, K. (2014). Analysing interviews. In U. Flick (Ed.), *The SAGE handbook of qualitative data analysis* (pp. 297–312). London, England: Sage. doi: 10.4135/9781446282243

Saldaña, J. (2016). *The coding manual for qualitative researchers.* Los Angeles, CA: Sage.

Reflecting on, acknowledging and bracketing your perspectives and preconceptions

OBJECTIVES

Readers will be able to:

1. Discuss their perspectives and biases
2. Understand the concept of bracketing
3. Develop an appropriate bracketing strategy

KNOWING THE 'SELF'

When I was preparing to write this chapter, the word that continued to come into mind is 'self'. According to Zhao (2014), "the self is an individual's own person viewed from the standpoint of that individual, which may differ from what others perceive from their distinct standpoints" (p. 199). The 'self' includes the researcher's demographic characteristics, perspectives, preconceptions, lens and expectations (Berger, 2013). As you may know, in qualitative study, the researcher who is the 'self' is an instrument (Lincoln & Guba, 2003; Roulston & Shelton, 2015). Also, the 'self' has a close connection with what is being studied, the participants involved and data collected (Creswell & Poth, 2018). This implies that there is a possibility of the 'self' having an influence on the research process (including data analysis procedures and outcomes).

As qualitative researchers, it is important to know the 'self' by examining our views, expectations and preconceived ideas about the phenomenon of study, and the lens through which it is being studied. We also need to communicate our viewpoints and preconceptions to our audience (i.e. consumers of our research report) and demonstrate how we set them aside to prevent them from excessively affecting how we code the data, develop categories and themes, and report the findings.

During the data analysis stage, I see myself as a channel through which data is filtered, compressed and transformed – arriving at findings that are meaningful and credible. This channel, which is also known as the 'self', needs to be examined. Self-examination starts with asking myself the following questions: *Who am I? What do I know about this phenomenon of study? How am I connected to the phenomenon? What do I want to know in relation to the phenomenon? What are my views about the phenomenon? What lens (if any) am I using to examine the phenomenon? What do I want my audience to know about me?* I understand that some of the above questions may be challenging to address and you may not have answers to some. However, trying to address most of these questions could pave the way to knowing the 'self' (instrument or channel) as it relates to what you're studying. Moreover, knowing more about the 'self' opens doors of opportunity to share with your audience demographic characteristics (if necessary), perspectives, lens and predetermined ideas. Lastly, they tend to understand the findings and appreciate how the results are interpreted – positively influencing the credibility of the study (Creswell & Miller, 2000).

Knowing your perspectives

Our perspectives are continuously being shaped by what we experience and learn as we interact with the environment and people within it (Berger, 2013). To put it differently, who we are now (which is the 'self', including our perspectives) is partly a product of our past experience and knowledge, which in effect could impact the actions we take in a study. Let's assume a researcher plans to conduct a qualitative study on homelessness among veterans in his community. In all his adult life, he has been working with an organization as a volunteer to provide shelter, food, health service, counseling and job training to people without a place to stay. He became passionate about fighting against homelessness when he realized that a close relative had lost his home some time ago. In reflecting on his perspectives on the phenomenon of homelessness and the experience of people without a home, he could think about his personal interaction with them – looking into what he learned about the circumstances that led to them being homeless, and how they were surviving in the streets. After that he could then document his beliefs and views on homelessness and attitudes toward people without a home to stay in, especially among veterans. By engaging in this reflective activity, the researcher became conscious of his perspectives and used them strategically to aid in addressing the purpose of the study. He could either embrace his perspectives (using them as potential lenses) or set them aside (preventing their influence on the study).

What if you haven't directly or indirectly experienced the phenomenon of a study? You could discover your perspectives by assessing your prior knowledge – asking yourself, *what do I know about this phenomenon and based on what I know, what are my beliefs, views and attitudes in relation to the focus of my study?*

Knowing your preconceptions

Preconceptions are thoughts and conclusions we have about what we are studying. These preconceived ideas could adversely affect the research findings if not checked. During the qualitative coding process, these biases could prevent us from extensively interacting with the data and fully probing all potential evidence in the data. Consequently, having unexamined preconceptions leads to the temptation of cherry-picking portions of the data that are consistent with what we expect – leaving seemingly rich parts unexplored. In some situations, when our biases are overlooked, we risk developing codes which have no connection with the data analyzed – making our audience question the credibility of the findings. To address these adverse effects, we should be aware of our biases in relation to the phenomenon of study, disclose them to our audience and block them from having an effect on the analysis process.

Knowing your lens

To bring everything together, we all have unique experiences in life and these experiences inform our perspectives which include our beliefs, views and attitudes. These perspectives govern "what we see" and how we interpret it (Robinson, 2009, p. 302). Therefore, our lens is the perspective we knowingly or unknowingly choose and/or use to assess what we are experiencing (Robinson, 2009). Similarly, in qualitative coding, our "…lens [is meant] for filtering the information gathered from participants and making meaning of it…" (Berger, 2013, p. 217). So, what lens are you using to examine your data and select relevant information? There are many lenses you could select from (Robinson, 2009). I put them into three categories: experiential, conceptual and theoretical lens.

- **Experiential lens:** This involves using a perspective which is directly based on a phenomenon one is experiencing such as dealing with mental illness, grief, racism and discrimination, and success; or has experienced such as divorce, gun violence, unemployment, homelessness and poverty. Also, a researcher who is an activist (*such as one fighting for human rights, equal wage irrespective of gender and equal treatment irrespective of race*) or an advocate (*such as one protecting the rights of children and people with disabilities*) could use his/her role as an experiential lens to review and analyze qualitative data.
- **Conceptual lens:** This is a kind of lens which is based on a concept or group of concepts. It is normally created or adapted from

research literature or disciplines, and used in viewing data and searching for significant information in the data. For instance, the conceptual framework could be used as a conceptual lens to comb through the data (Jabareen, 2009).

- **Theoretical lens:** As the term implies, it encompasses theories and philosophical paradigms through which data is examined (Auerbach & Silverstein, 2003). For example, one can use Ainsworth's (1963) theory of attachment, Latané and Darley's (1970) bystander effect or Levinger's (1976) stage theory as a theoretical lens to explore how they apply to information collected from participants. The theoretical lens can also be referred to as a paradigm which is a set of beliefs held by a group of people in a field or research community, and used to inform how research inquiry should be conducted (Hanson, Creswell, Plano Clark, Petska, & Creswell, 2005). This type of theoretical lens guides the researcher's explorative eyes as he/she goes through the data, and influences how he/she makes sense of the empirical indicators found in the data. For instance, a researcher with a transformative paradigm as a lens could analyze data with the intention of improving the livelihood of the disadvantaged (Creswell & Poth, 2018; Mertens, 2003).

BRACKETING YOUR PERSPECTIVES AND PRECONCEPTIONS

Bracketing is simply preventing our perspectives and preconceptions from influencing the qualitative analysis process. As Tufford and Newman (2010) indicate, "bracketing is a method used by some researchers to mitigate the potential deleterious effects of unacknowledged preconceptions related to the research and thereby to increase the rigor of the project" (p. 81). Although bracketing is widely used within the qualitative research community, not all qualitative researchers, especially among the pioneers of the phenomenological approach, agree to the need to set aside views, opinions and knowledge we hold about what is being studied. Husserl (1962), who is a proponent of the phenomenological approach (specifically, the descriptive phenomenological method), argues that pure description of participants' experience is best attained when we engage in epoché. Epoché is the process of blocking our background, thoughts and preconceived ideas from influencing a qualitative research process, particularly during the data analysis stage (Moustakas, 1994; Patton, 2015).

Heidegger, who was once a student of Husserl and is the founder of the hermeneutic phenomenological approach, claims that practicing bracketing is a challenging undertaking which cannot be fully attained (Tufford & Newman, 2010). He suggests that when interpreting participants' experiences, rather than practicing an unattainable endeavor of epoché, why don't we embrace our unique characteristics we have as researchers and use them to help make sense of participants' stories and thoughts (Heidegger, 1962)? On the contrary, Smith, Flowers, and Larkin (2012) endorse bracketing for interpretative phenomenological analysis (IPA), which is similar to the hermeneutic phenomenological approach. Likewise, Charmaz (2014) and Moustakas (1994) recommend the use of epoché when conducting grounded theory and transcendental phenomenological analysis, respectively. So, why is it important to bracket our perspectives and preconceptions?

Importance of bracketing at the data analysis stage

- *Increases credibility of the findings:* Bracketing your pre-conceived ideas during the data analysis stage, in some cases, assures your audience that you have thoughtfully examined your "personal characteristics" including past experience and prior knowledge (Berger, 2013, p. 220). Besides, you have carefully selected those which have the potential of unduly influencing how you identify empirical indicators, assign codes and generate themes. These systematic actions make the audience believe what you found – contributing to the credibility of the findings (Tufford & Newman, 2010).
- **Promotes self-awareness:** Practicing bracketing is a profound moment for you to look inwardly – learning more about yourself as a qualitative researcher and your role in the analysis process (Smith, Flowers, & Larkin, 2012). It is also an opportunity for you to continuously check your decisions and actions to make sure you are working within the boundaries set for the selected qualitative coding strategy. Lastly, it intensifies the awareness of the influence of your perspectives and preconceived ideas on the data analysis process (Roulston, 2014).
- **Encourages giving balanced attention to all parts of the data:** Through bracketing, you are able to give all parts of the data equal scrutiny – preventing the risk of consciously or unconsciously leaving some areas of the data unexamined (Patton, 2015).
- **Intensifies engagement with the data:** Bracketing increases your level of engagement with the data (Sullivan, 2012). It also helps you not to take any aspect of the data for granted, exploring all possible meanings of each empirical indicator (Charmaz, 2014).

Steps in engaging in Epoché (bracketing) at the data analysis stage

The steps below are informed by Moustakas' (1994) suggested first steps of conducting data analysis under the transcendental phenomenological approach (see Adu, 2016). For demonstration purposes, I will be using the GM crop case study data (Cook & Robbins, 2005) to explain each epoché step (see Chapter 4).

1. **Create a peaceful space and time to engage in epoché:** How do I embark on a peaceful and meditative journey of epoché? I start this process by creating a serene atmosphere for myself – finding a peaceful place and time with no or minimal distractions. The place could be a coffee shop, library, office or the like.

2. **Review research purpose or questions:** To make sure I'm working within the research boundaries, I review the purpose of the study, which in this case is *to explore the process through which genetically modified (GM) crop research is communicated to the public*. I move a step further to go through all the questions I plan to address to remind myself of what is expected of me as a qualitative data analyst. The research questions are as follows: *What were the factors contributing to public concerns about GM research and foods in the UK? What were the challenges faced by GM scientists when communicating GM crop research to the public? And how should GM crop research be communicated to the public to address their concerns?*

3. **Brainstorm my perspectives and preconceived ideas about the phenomenon:** I list all my views, thoughts, beliefs and biases about GM foods and research. At this stage, I'm not concerned about whether the ideas are well-stated or not. I just list whatever comes into mind provided it is related to GM foods and research. *Please note that the thoughts below are my personal opinions and should only be used for teaching and learning purposes.*

   a. *My perspectives and preconceptions about GM foods and research*
      i. *Technological innovation (+/-)*
         1. *What specific problem does the GM invention intend to solve?*
         2. *Who are the beneficiaries?*
         3. *Who are the losers?*
         4. *What are unintended consequences?*
      ii. *Food safety (+): Less use of pesticide*
      iii. *Affordable food (+)*
      iv. *Availability of seasonal food at all times (+)*
      v. *No known GM-related food safety issues reported (+)*
      vi. *Uncertainty about the long-term effects of GM foods on our health (-)*
      vii. *Implications of GM research for farmers in developing countries (-/+)*
      viii. *Sense of dependence on GM companies (-)*

REFLECTING ON YOUR PERSPECTIVES

    ix. *The need for transparency of the motives of GM com-panies and funders of GM research*

    x. *I prefer all food to be labeled – indicating whether or not they are from genetically modified organisms (GMOs)*

    xi. *More research should be done on the long-term effects of consuming GM foods*

Commentary 5.1. *I indicated '+/-' for all mixed attitudes or feelings, and '+' and '-' for positive and negative attitudes, respectively. Brainstorming could include questions you are thinking about. As shown above, under 'technological innovation', I have four questions that I don't completely have answers to. I may have answers to them after I have completed analyzing the data. Some of the statements listed (such as 'no known GM-related food safety issues reported' and 'sense of dependence on GM companies') are beliefs that may not be valid in some cases. However, my role at this stage is to list my preconceptions and perspectives free from critical review of their accuracy. In this phase, do not worry about the quality of the information you generate.*

4. **State the sources of my perspectives and preconceptions:** As was stated earlier in this chapter, our past experience and knowledge contribute to our beliefs, biases, attitudes, feelings and thoughts. Under this step, I examine each brainstormed statement (or question) and determine factors related to my background that may have influenced it. The outcome of this activity would be helpful when explaining my perspectives and preconceptions to my audience. Sometimes, an audience will best understand your perceptions and biases if you introduce them to some background information. The questions I ask myself when engaging in this activity are: *what factors inform this perspective or preconception? And why do I hold this perspective or preconception?*

   a. ***My perspectives and preconceptions about GM foods and research and their respective sources***

     i. *Technological innovation (+/-) [Past knowledge: Literature reviewed and YouTube videos watched on GM foods and research]*

       1. *What specific problem does the invention intend to solve?*

       2. *Who are the beneficiaries?*

       3. *Who are the losers?*

       4. *What are unintended consequences?*

     ii. *Food safety (+): Less use of pesticide [Past knowledge: Literature reviewed and YouTube videos watched on GM foods and research]*

iii. *Affordable food (+) [Personal experience: Comparing foods labeled as non-GMO (non-genetically modified organism) with those not labeled as non-GMO]*

iv. *Availability of seasonal foods at all times (+) [Personal experience at the grocery store]*

v. *No known GM-related food safety issues reported (+) [Past experience: I haven't heard any food safety issues directly linked to GMO]*

vi. *Uncertainty about the long-term effects of GM foods on our health (-) [Prior knowledge and experience: Making me not completely certain about the GM foods' long-term impact on my health]*

vii. *Implications of GM research for farmers in the developing countries (-/+) [Demographic characteristics: I'm originally from Ghana, West Africa; my father had a palm oil farm when I was a child; recently, small-scale farmers' maize farms were destroyed by African armyworms in Ghana]*

viii. *Sense of dependence on GM companies (-) [Prior knowledge: Farmers who grow GM crops depend on GM companies to provide seeds every planting season; farmers could be in legal trouble if they preserve GM seeds for future planting (Genetic Literacy Project, n.d)]*

ix. *The need for transparency of the motives of GM companies and funders of GM research [Past experience and knowledge: The need for more disclosure of the funders of the GM research and their goals]*

x. *I prefer all foods to be labeled – indicating whether or not they are GM [Past experience and knowledge: This is my preference]*

xi. *More research should be done on the long-term effect of consuming GM foods [Past experience and knowledge: This is my recommendation]*

Commentary 5.2. *This is an intensively reflective activity, focusing on bringing to consciousness information I have learned and what I have experienced. I only focused on those experiences and knowledge that have either direct or indirect impact on my perceptions and preconceptions. Going through the outcome of the activity, you can see that I have mixed reactions about GM food and research. For instance, I know that there could be maize (corn) seeds which have been genetically modified to be pest resistant. However, I'm concerned about the unintended consequence such as farmers' dependence on GM companies for GM seed supply. Moreover, there is the possibility of driving non-GM crop farmers out of business due to the high price of their produce compared to*

GM foods. These assertions could be refuted but at this stage of the epoché process, my aim was to deliberate on what my views were and connect them to their respective contributing factors.

5. **State my expectations based on the research purpose or questions:** Our expectations shape the kind of information we look for and pay attention to when analyzing the data. However, if they are kept unchecked, we could run the risk of overlooking potentially rich parts of data – arriving at findings that are only in line with what we expect. The question I plan to address at this fifth stage is: *Considering my perspectives and preconceptions about GM foods and research, what do I expect to find after analyzing the data?* Here are my expectations based on the research questions:

   a. **What were the challenges faced by GM scientists when communicating GM crop research to the public?**
      i. *Reporting the GM research findings in such a way that they were less likely to ignite controversy*
      ii. *Concerns about the public misinterpretation of the GM research findings*
      iii. *Using the findings to address the public concerns about GM foods*
   b. **What were the factors contributing to public concerns about GM research and foods in the UK?**
      i. *Public concerns about GM foods are mostly driven by unverified information produced by non-GMO groups*
      ii. *Public fears about GM foods are most likely not based on GM research findings*
      iii. *The more GM scientists explain their findings, the less the public fears about GM foods*
   c. **How should GM food research be communicated to the public to address their concerns?**
      i. *Not sure*

Commentary 5.3. This is one of the challenging epoché steps to take since it involves coming up with answers to the research questions based on my past knowledge and experience, standpoints and preconceived ideas. As you can see, I had difficulty stating my expectations for the third research question. Engaging in this activity, you may end up having no, some or substantial expectations. If you have any expectations, the next step is to prevent them from overly influencing the data analysis process. This doesn't mean that when you find significant information in the data consistent with your expectations, you shouldn't include it as part of the findings. This activity helps you to be aware of your inclinations – preventing the tendency of ignoring the portions of data that are not consistent with your expectations.

6. **Creating a mental state free from my perspectives, preconceptions and expectations:** Moustakas (1994) calls this practice "reflective-meditation" (p. 89). This involves reviewing all my perspectives, preconceptions and expectations about GM foods and research (see steps 3–5) and thinking about their consequences for how I describe and interpret the interview transcripts. During this meditative process, I imagine having no perspectives, preconceptions and expectations about GM foods and research, and I am willing to consider all views, descriptions, meanings and interpretations (Charmaz, 2014). In this perspective, preconception and expectation-free state, I'm prepared to pay equal attention to all kinds of information including conversational fillers in the data (Moustakas, 1994). All information in the data is treated as potential empirical indicator until proven otherwise.

Commentary 5.4. This last stage is the core feature of epoché and according to Moustakas (1994), it should be repeated anytime you return to analyze the data. Epoché is a meditative practice that needs time to perfect. It is very challenging to reach a complete state of epoché (Moustakas, 1994). It takes continuous practice. Since this is a subjective experience, you may not know whether you have reached the highest level of epoché. However, you may know your level after assessing whether some of the perspectives, preconceptions and expectations came into consciousness when describing and/or interpreting the data. Another strategy of checking for any influence of your preconceived ideas on the coding process is to investigate alternative descriptions and interpretations of the significant information identified in the data.

DISCLOSING YOUR PERSPECTIVES, PRECONCEPTIONS, LENS AND EXPECTATIONS

As indicated earlier in this chapter, your perspectives, preconceptions, lens and expectations could influence the actions you take and decisions you make, whether conducting qualitative or quantitative study (Bentz & Shapiro, 2001; Guest, MacQueen, & Namey, 2012). You may ask, *should I share my "personal characteristics" with my audience?* (Berger, 2013, p. 220). Besides identifying your views and preconceived ideas about the focus of the study, it is important to let the audience know about them. Guest et al. (2012) report regarding researchers' biases that "if you do not report all of your biases, then your reporting itself is biased" (p. 98). Although deciding what to disclose is a subjective process, the benefit of reporting your biases outweighs the risk of not sharing. In other words, anytime we share our narrative, we move a step closer to making our interpretations and findings understandable and credible, respectively.

The unique aspect of the disclosure process is that you have control over your narrative. So, what factors should be considered when determining what to disclose? I recommend thinking about the following questions when deciding what to report:

- *Do you feel comfortable sharing your narrative?*
- *Does the narrative relate to the phenomenon of study?*
- *Will the information to-be-disclosed help readers or the audience to understand the findings and your interpretation of the results?*
- *Will the information positively contribute to the credibility of the findings?*

In summary, here are some examples of the information you could report:

- Demographic characteristics (*e.g. gender, profession, educational level and ethnicity etc.*)
- Past experience (*e.g. domestic violence, racial discrimination, substance abuse and health experiences*)
- Prior knowledge (*e.g. understanding of depression, how organisms are genetically modified and benefits of taking the influenza vaccine*)
- Perspectives, preconceptions and expectations
- Bracketing process
- Lens (if any)

Demonstration 5.1

My narrative

As a pragmatist, I embrace technological innovations which alleviate the problems we face and improve our lives. When thinking about my views about genetically modified organisms (GMOs), the questions that come to mind are: *What specific problem does the invention intend to solve? Who are the beneficiaries? Who are the losers? And what are the unintended consequences?* I believe that genetic modification (GM) innovations have a place in our modern world. I also believe that the development of GMOs has enormous benefits to mankind. They have the potential to address: destruction of crops by pests, frequent use of pesticides to contain the destruction, reductions in crop yields, decreases in revenue for farmers, high food prices, and food insecurity. For instance, "in Ghana [West Africa], armyworms... ravaged around 1.4 million hectares [or 3.5 million acres] of maize and cowpea plantations in six regions [out of ten in 2017]" – contributing to the rise of food prices

(Reliefweb, 2018, para. 3). This could have been solved by providing GM seeds that are armyworm-resistant to the farmers, preventing the devastating effects of the armyworm influx.

However, I know that supplying GM seeds could create a sense of dependence among farmers, especially in developing countries: every planting season, they are expected to buy the seeds from the producers of GM seeds. Additionally, they may be in legal trouble if they preserve the seeds for future planting or cultivate them on an undisclosed field (Genetic Literacy Project, n.d). Also, I think the lower prices of GM food products puts small-scale farmers who use non-GM seeds at a disadvantage – they are competing with 'affordable' GM foods produced by big corporations.

In terms of food safety, I'm concerned about the long-term health-related effects of consuming GM foods. Based on my past knowledge, I haven't heard of any food safety issues directly linked to GMOs. Nevertheless, I think that more studies should be done to determine the long-term effects of GM foods on our health. Also, I'm in favor of labeling all food to show whether or not they have been genetically modified, as required in EU countries.

Considering the focus of the study and the research questions I plan to address, I expect to find that GM scientists are mindful of the public concerns about GM foods and the potential misinterpretation of GM findings. They are also aware of the difficulty of making sure their press releases about GM research findings do not ignite controversy. I also foresee GM scientists accepting the need to do more to lessen public concerns.

To conduct a qualitative analysis free from the above views, thoughts, biases and expectations about GM scientists, research and foods, I engaged in epoché (Moustakas, 1994). Epoché is an introspective practice carried out to suspend my above narrative with the aim of analyzing the data with an open mind (Moustakas, 1994). I started this process by creating an intrusion-free space and reflecting on my thoughts about GM research and foods. I then listed all my views and biases connected to the phenomenon of study, and determined the potential sources: whether they were from personal experience, based on my previous knowledge or informed by my demographic characteristics. The essence of looking into the sources was to help me understand the rationale behind my opinions. In addition, I reviewed the research questions and listed my expected findings. The final stage of epoché was to think about my perspectives and biases listed, and try to mentally block them from coming into consciousness when working on the data. This final stage was repeated any time I came back to analyzing the data.

Commentary 5.5. *The above narrative is an example of how your perspectives, preconceptions, expectations and epoché process should be communicated. As you can see, there was no discussion* *about a specific lens since I didn't have a perspective through which I would be analyzing the data. If you have a lens, I recommend sharing it with your audience. I started my narrative by acknowledging my appreciation for the benefits of GMO innovations (see para. 1). Also, I briefly mentioned my philosophical paradigm which informed my assessment of GM innovations. Although pragmatism could be used as a lens, I was utilizing it to help me to better conceptualize my views about GM research and foods. I also shared the reservations I have about GM research and foods (see para. 2–3). It was challenging for me to articulate my mixed feelings about GM research and foods, but I think it would help my audience to know my stance. I then shared my expected findings and described my epoché process (see para. 4–5).*

Box 5.1 Epoché (bracketing) steps

1. Create a peaceful space and time to engage in epoché
2. Review research purpose or questions
3. Brainstorm perspectives and preconceived ideas about the phenomenon
4. State the sources of the perspectives and preconceptions listed
5. State expected results based on the research purpose or questions
6. Assume a mental stage free from the perspectives, preconceptions and expectations

---

CONCLUSION

Because we are a research instrument as qualitative researchers, it is possible that our demographic characteristics, perspectives, preconceptions, expectations and lens will influence how we analyze qualitative data and arrive at findings. Before we begin to analyze the data, it is important to conduct self-reflection with the aim of uncovering our "personal characteristics" related to the phenomenon of study (Berger, 2013, p. 220). Since there are huge benefits to be derived from making ourselves known to our audience, after identifying our views, biases, beliefs and lens, we should decide on which of them are relevant to share. There are four factors that should be considered when deciding what to disclose. They include: how comfortable we are sharing our thoughts, how relevant the yet-to-be-disclosed information is in helping our audience to know us and make sense of the findings, and whether sharing them will positively influence the credibility of the findings. Moreover, to promote transparency, we should also present our epoché experience. In a nutshell, there are unquestionable benefits of thinking about ourselves, setting aside our opinions, preconceived ideas and expected results, embracing our lens, and sharing relevant stories with our audience.

REFERENCES

Adu, P. (2016). Using NVivo to conduct transcendental phenomenological analysis [PowerPoint slides]. SlideShare. Retrieved from www.slideshare.net/kontorphilip/using-nvivo-to-conduct-transcendental-phenomenological-analysis

Ainsworth, M. D. S. (1963). The development of infant-mother interaction among the Ganda. In B. M. Foss (Ed.), *Determinants of infant behavior* (pp. 67–104). New York, NY: Wiley.

Auerbach, C. F., & Silverstein, L. B. (2003). *Qualitative data: An introduction to coding and analysis*. New York, NY: New York University Press.

Bentz, V. M., & Shapiro, J. J. (2001). *Mindful inquiry in social research*. Thousand Oaks, CA: Sage.

Berger, R. (2013). Now I see it, now I don't: Researcher's position and reflexivity in qualitative research. *Qualitative Research*, *15*(2), 219–234. doi:10.1177/1468794112468475

Charmaz, K. (2014). *Constructing grounded theory*. London: Sage.

Cook, G., & Robbins, P. T. (2005). *Presentation of genetically modified (GM) crop research to non-specialists, 1997–2002: A case study*. [data collection]. UK Data Service. SN: 5069, http://doi.org/10.5255/UKDA-SN-5069-1

Creswell, J. W., & Miller, D. L. (2000). Determining validity in qualitative inquiry. *Theory into Practice*, *39*(3), 124–130. doi:10.1207/s15430421tip3903_2

Creswell, J. W., & Poth, C. N. (2018). *Qualitative inquiry & research design: Choosing among five approaches*. Los Angeles, CA: Sage.

Genetic Literacy Project. (n.d). Does Monsanto sue farmers who save patented seeds or mistakenly grow GMOs? #GMOFAQ. Retrieved March 13, 2018, from https://gmo.geneticliteracyproject.org/FAQ/monsanto-sue-farmers-save-patented-seeds-mistakenly-grow-gmos/

Guest, G., MacQueen, K. M., & Namey, E. E. (2012). *Applied thematic analysis*. Los Angeles, CA: Sage.

Hanson, W. E., Creswell, J. W., Plano Clark, V. L., Petska, K. S., & Creswell, D. J. (2005). Mixed methods research designs in counseling psychology. *Journal of Counseling Psychology*, *2*(55), 224–235. doi:10.1037/0022-0167.52.2.224

Heidegger, M. (1962). *Being and time* (J. Macquarrie & E. Robinson, Trans.). Malden, MA: Blackwell.

Husserl, E. (1962). *Ideas: General introduction to pure phenomenology*. London, England: Allen & Unwin.

Jabareen, Y. (2009). Building a conceptual framework: Philosophy, definitions, and procedure. *International Journal of Qualitative Methods*, *8*(4), 49–62. doi:10.1177/160940690900800406

Latané, B., & Darley, J. M. (1970) *The unresponsive bystander: Why doesn't he help?* Englewood Cliffs, NJ: Prentice Hall.

Levinger, G. (1976) A social psychological perspective on marital dissolution. *Journal of Social Issues, 32*(1), 21–47.

Lincoln, Y. S., & Guba, E. G. (2003). Paradigmatic controversies, contradictions, and emerging confluences. In N. K. Denzin & Y. S. Lincoln (Eds.), *The landscape of qualitative research* (2nd ed., pp. 253–291). Thousand Oaks, CA: Sage.

Mertens, D. M. (2003). Mixed methods and the politics of human research: The transformative-emancipatory perspective. In A. Tashakkori & C. Teddlie (Eds.), *Handbook of mixed methods in social and behavioral research* (pp. 135–164). Thousand Oaks, CA: Sage.

Moustakas, C. (1994). *Phenomenological research methods*. Thousand Oaks, CA: Sage.

Patton, M. Q. (2015). *Qualitative research & evaluation methods: Integrating theory and practice*. Los Angeles, CA: Sage.

Reliefweb. (2018). West Africa: Armyworm infestation – Mar 2017. Retrieved March 18, 2018, from https://reliefweb.int/disaster/2017-000055-gha

Robinson, M. L. (2009). *Just conflict: Transformation through resolution: Maps for harnessing the transformative power of conflict to create mutually accountable relationships*. Rhinebeck, NY: Epigraph Books.

Roulston, K. (2014). Analysing interviews. In U. Flick (Ed.), *The SAGE handbook of qualitative data analysis* (pp. 297–312). London, England: Sage. doi: 10.4135/9781446282243

Roulston, K., & Shelton, S. A. (2015). Reconceptualizing bias in teaching qualitative research methods. *Qualitative Inquiry, 21*(4), 332–342. doi:10.1177/1077800414563803

Smith, J. A., Flowers, P., & Larkin, M. (2012). *Interpretative phenomenological analysis: theory, method and research*. London, England: Sage.

Sullivan, P. (2012). *Qualitative data analysis: Using a dialogical approach*. Los Angeles, CA: Sage.

Tufford, L., & Newman. P. (2010). Bracketing in qualitative research. *Qualitative Social Work, 11*(1), 80–96. doi: 10.1177/1473325010368316

Zhao, S. (2014). Self as an emic object: A re-reading of William James on self. *Theory & Psychology, 24*(2), 199–216. doi:10.1177/0959354314527181

6

Documenting personal reflections and the analytical process

OBJECTIVES

Readers will be able to:

1. Explain the art of writing a memo
2. Recognize the benefits of writing a memo
3. Document thoughts about the coding process

MEMO WRITING

Memo writing, which is also known as memoing or journaling, is the art of recording your thoughts, procedures and reactions before, during and after collecting and analyzing qualitative data (Birks, Chapman, & Francis, 2008; Charmaz, 2014; Strauss, 1989). As you intensively engage in data analysis – developing codes, categories and themes to represent the data – new ideas come to mind. Since the information may not stay in your consciousness for long, it is important to document them for future reference (Bazeley & Jackson, 2014; Becker & Richards, 1986). Memoing is a great opportunity for you to save information which could be revisited for further examination (Emerson, Fretz, & Shaw, 2011).

Memo writing encourages brainstorming ideas, practicing self-reflection and keeping check of your bracketed views and preconceived ideas. Moreover, it helps in leaving footprints of your thought process, decisions and actions – facilitating the chronological presentation of how codes were assigned, categories were created, and themes were developed. Memoing helps bring to light the road map of the data analysis process, making it more likely for your audience to believe and appreciate your findings, and contributing to the credibility of the study.

Memos generated when analyzing data are notes for yourself; they keep track of the steps taken and the rationale behind them (Charmaz,

2014). For instance, some of the "decisions and actions" that could be documented are: data analysis tool used, type of coding strategy chosen and reasons for selecting particular codes as dominant during the code categorization process (Charmaz, 2014, p. 168). Since they are notes to yourself, there is no specific rule on what to document, how they should be documented and what tool to use to create memos (Birks et al., 2008). Your notes could be in texts, outlines and/or visuals (Strauss, 1989). You could also decide on what, how much, and how to share the memos with your audience (Charmaz, 2015).

As you intensively interact with the data, you don't want to lose focus by attending to interesting but unrelated ideas that come into your consciousness. This is where memoing becomes a useful strategy – you can keep notes of the ideas and come back to them after completing the initial data analysis task (Emerson et al., 2011). Similarly, the memos could be a reservoir of reminders so that you attend to the task listed when needed.

As you know, qualitative analysis is an art and creative undertaking, and rich ideas could come anywhere and anytime. Just like artists' and musicians' experience, great ideas could come when coding the data, taking a break from coding, relaxing, bathing, driving and even sleeping. Due to this, you need to be ready to document them. Personally, I had a similar experience when working on this book. Whenever I thought of something which would be useful, I jotted it down on my notepad. I also used the 'Voice Memos' and the 'Notes' app on my mobile phone to document my thoughts.

Importance of memo writing

- **Promotes new discoveries:** When you glance at your documented ideas, they may look like disjointed and unrefined pieces of information (Bazeley & Jackson, 2014; Emerson et al., 2011). However, as you find time to extensively review every piece of the puzzle, rich discoveries related to underlying meanings, themes and theories are made.
- **Helps keep track of your thought process:** Ideas comes you're your consciousness and fade quickly if attention is not paid to them (Becker & Richards, 1986). Note taking helps in keeping those ideas and coming back to them when needed. It encourages building on initially documented thoughts – preventing a situation of not knowing what you were thinking about before taking a break from the data analysis activity. As Johnson and Christensen (2014) state, "because qualitative data analysis is an interpretative process, it is important that you keep track of your ideas... so that you do not have to rely on your memory later" (p. 589).

- **Aids in categorizing codes:** As you identify relevant information in the data and create appropriate labels or codes to represent them, thoughts about the potential relationships between codes run through your mind. Documenting them helps in determining the underlying meaning and relationships among a group of codes when working on categorizing the codes (Strauss, 1989).
- **Facilitates detailing an account of the coding process:** Imagine being asked to share specific steps you took during the data analysis phase. It would be challenging to recall the main actions taken if you don't have a documentation of the procedure from 'how empirical indicators were identified' to 'how themes and/or theories were developed' (Charmaz, 2014).

TYPES OF MEMOS

Memos can be grouped into three main types (see Chapter 7 for examples): initial, analytical and procedural memos (see Auerbach & Silverstein, 2003; Bazeley & Jackson, 2014; Birks et al., 2008; Charmaz, 2014; Emerson et al., 2011; Strauss, 1989).

- **Initial memos:** Memos that contain initial thoughts about the data as a whole, empirical indicators identified and codes created. They are normally created at the early stage of the data analysis process. Initial memos tend to have unfiltered, raw, mostly disconnected and yet-to-be-examined ideas (Birks et al., 2008; Charmaz, 2014; Emerson et al., 2011). They could be transformed into analytical memos after extensive examination of the initial reflections.
- **Analytical memos:** Memos produced as a result of examining the characteristics of codes and how they represent empirical indicators. They are also used to explore emerging themes. To put it differently, analytical memos house emerging ideas as you make comparisons between data, codes, themes and theories (Charmaz, 2014). Emerson et al. (2011) refer to these as "interpretive memos" because they capture the transformation of initially documented unpolished ideas into a coherent and meaningful form (p. 193).
- **Procedural memos:** As you go through the data analysis process, you make plans and take appropriate actions. Procedural memos contain your data analysis steps and processes. These memos are also called operational memos (Birks et al., 2008; Charmaz, 2014; Strauss & Corbin, 1998). As Birks et al. (2008) put it, "we used operational memos to map the steps that we took at each and every stage in conducting our research, including the rationale for decisions made and actions taken" (p. 72).

Box 6.1 Memoing steps

1. Decide on a tool you plan to use to create memos
2. As you read through your transcripts for the first time, document your thoughts
3. After the completion of the initial review of the data, find some time to review the *initial memo* – refining the ideas and generating new ideas
4. Continue to update the *analytical memo* as you start the coding process, generate codes and think about the features of the codes
5. Concurrently, create a *procedural memo* – documenting the actions you are taking and the reason why it is necessary to take them

CONCLUSION

It takes a considerable amount of time and mental effort to recall coding-related ideas and actions that were not documented compared to the time and effort needed to create memos. Memoing is not only for documenting thoughts but is also used as a tool to facilitate the development of codes, categories, themes and theories. When used appropriately, memoing could help contribute to the credibility of a study. Due to the huge benefits of memoing, especially at the data analysis stage, I suggest you document your thoughts, a critical review of your initial ideas and a step-by-step outline of the procedures. There isn't one strict way of creating your memo. You could audio record, visualize and/or document in written form your reflections. You could document your thoughts anywhere and anyhow you want. Develop a strategy that works for you (Birks et al., 2008). It may be challenging at the beginning if the art of memoing is new to you but when you become used to it, the experience will be rewarding.

REFERENCES

Auerbach, C. F., & Silverstein, L. B. (2003). *Qualitative data: An introduction to coding and analysis*. New York, NY: New York University Press.

Bazeley, P., & Jackson, K. (2014). *Qualitative data analysis with NVivo*. Los Angeles, CA: Sage.

Becker, H. S., & Richards, P. (1986). *Writing for social scientists: How to start and finish your thesis, book, or article*. Chicago, IL: The University of Chicago Press.

Birks, M., Chapman, Y., & Francis, K. (2008). Memoing in qualitative research Probing data and processes. *Journal of Research in Nursing, 13*(1), 68–75. doi:10.1177/ 1744987107081254

Charmaz, K. (2014). *Constructing grounded theory*. London, England: Sage.

Charmaz, K., (2015, February 4). A discussion with Prof Kathy Charmaz on grounded theory (Interview by G. R. Gibbs) [Video file]. Retrieved October 9, 2018, from www.youtube.com/watch?v=D5AHmHQS6WQ

Emerson, R. M., Fretz, R. I., & Shaw, L. L. (2011). *Writing ethnographic field notes* (2nd ed.). Chicago, IL: University of Chicago Press.

Johnson, R. B., & Christensen, L. (2014). *Educational research: Quantitative, qualitative, and mixed approaches*. Thousand Oaks, CA: Sage.

Strauss, A. L. (1989). *Qualitative analysis for social scientists*. Cambridge, England: Cambridge University Press.

Strauss, A.L., & Corbin, J. M. (1998) *Basics of qualitative research: Techniques and procedures for developing grounded theory* (2nd ed.). Thousand Oaks, CA: Sage.

7

Manually assigning codes to data

OBJECTIVES

Readers will be able to:

1. Assign labels to research question(s)
2. Determine appropriate coding strategies
3. Identify relevant information in the data
4. Create codes for the relevant information identified
5. Conduct manual coding using Microsoft Word

OVERVIEW

As described in Chapter 4, I will be using existing data on the communication of GM crop research to demonstrate how qualitative data should be coded (Cook & Robbins, 2005). The case study focused on data collected between 1997 and 2002 in the UK, at a time when there was growing concern among the public about GM crop research and foods (Moseley, 2002). The purpose of this qualitative coding is to explore UK public concerns about GM foods and the strategies GM scientists should use to present the GM crop research to the public. A total of ten interview transcripts will be used to demonstrate the qualitative coding process (see Table 7.1). The three research questions guiding this coding process are:

1. What were the factors contributing to public concerns about GM research and foods in the UK?
2. What were the challenges faced by GM scientists when communicating GM crop research to the public?
3. How should GM crop research be communicated to the public to address their concerns?

Also, I'll be using Microsoft Word to demonstrate how codes are generated. Microsoft Word is one of the qualitative analysis tools that could be used to conduct manual coding (Adu, 2017a). Manual coding

Table 7.1 Demographics of participants (GM scientists and university staff)

Participant ID	Occupation	Gender
S3	GM scientist	Male
S4	GM scientist	Male
S5	GM scientist	Male
S6	GM scientist	Male
S9	GM scientist	Female
S13	GM scientist	Female
S16	GM scientist	Male
NS1	Academic staff	Male
NS2	Student/staff	Female
NS5	Student/staff	Male

is generally viewed as a cost-effective way of analyzing qualitative data. However, a significant amount of time is needed to code qualitative data without the use of any qualitative analysis software – especially when working with a huge amount of data (Saldaña, 2016).

DECIDING ON AN APPROPRIATE CODING STRATEGY

Comprehensively, there are four main factors to be considered when determining an appropriate coding strategy: function of the research approach, kind of research purpose, characteristics of the research question(s) and nature of the data (see Table 7.2). Looking at the research approach function, if you plan to use the selected research method to describe a phenomenon of study, then you are more likely to use description-focused coding. Similarly, if the purpose of the study and research questions are descriptively focused, you could use this coding strategy – especially if you do not plan to interpret empirical indicators (i.e. significant information identified in the data) in order to create codes.

However, you could choose interpretation-focused coding if it is consistent with the nature of the research approach, purpose and questions (see Table 7.2). Sometimes, interpretation-focused coding may not be sufficient to aid in addressing a research question. A research question with the focus of making a judgement, claim or conclusion based on the evidence found in the data requires presumption-focused coding. You're more likely to use this coding strategy if you have questions such as: *What conclusions could be made based on participants' experience of mental health stigma?* And *what may be the reasons for the high level of childhood obesity in the U.S.?*

Table 7.2 Factors to be considered when choosing an appropriate coding strategy

Contributing factors of the coding strategy choice	Description-focused coding	Interpretation-focused coding	Presumption-focused coding
Main function of research approach	• Case study • Ethnography • Narrative approach • Phenomenological approach • Transcendental phenomenological approach	• Case study • Ethnography • Grounded theory • Hermeneutic phenomenological approach • Interpretative phenomenological analysis • Phenomenological approach	• Case study • Grounded theory
Kind of research purpose	To identify or describe specific behaviors, settings, phenomena, experiences or events.	To explore, explain or understand specific behaviors, settings, phenomena, experiences or events.	To make a judgment, recommendations, rationales and/or draw conclusions based on the evidence in the data.
Features of research question	This coding strategy is normally used for research questions that start with 'what', 'where', 'when', or 'who'.	This coding strategy is normally used for research questions that start with 'what' or 'how'.	This coding strategy is normally used for research questions which have the goal of making a judgment, explaining a phenomenon, describing a process or making a conclusion.
Nature of qualitative data	Having data with explicit empirical indicators: Working with data in which the information you plan to code is easy to find without engaging in a critical and intensive review	Having data with implicit empirical indicators: Working with data in which the information you plan to code is difficult to find without engaging in a critical and intensive review	Not only having data with implicit empirical indicators but also having a goal of using the data as evidence to make claims or draw conclusions

Note: This table is based on the information presented in Chapter 3.

Demonstration 7.1

To determine appropriate coding strategies for my analysis, I will examine the functions of the case study approach, the research purpose which is to explore UK public concerns about GM foods and the strategies GM scientists should use to present the GM crop research to the public, the three research questions, and the characteristics of participants' responses (see Table 7.3). As shown in Table 7.2, the case study method is compatible with any of the three coding strategies. With respect to the GM crop research and foods study (Cook & Robbins, 2005), the research approach plays a role in helping me: to understand the public concerns about GM foods from the perspective of GM scientists and university staff, and to develop strategies for communicating GM crop research. With these functions of the case study approach, interpretation-focused coding is suitable for the analysis.

Correspondingly, the operative word *'explore'* used in the purpose statement implies that my motive is actively seeking understanding about the GM foods' concerns and GM crop research communication strategies – making the coding tool more of interpretation-focused coding. My final decision on determining the appropriate coding strategy is hugely based on the assessment of the research questions and the content of the data. As I review the data to search for potential empirical indicators, the question I keep on asking myself is *'what information am I looking for to help me address my research questions?'*

With respect to the first research question (*What were the factors contributing to public concerns about GM research and foods in the UK?*), I will be looking for specific behaviors and situations that have either a direct or indirect link to public concerns about GM foods. Similarly, for question two (*What were the challenges faced by GM scientists when communicating GM crop research to the public?*), I will be searching for behaviors and situations that hindered GM scientists' communication of GM-related information. Question three (*How should GM crop research be communicated to the public to address their concerns?*) is quite different from the first two questions. Most of the time, if a question starts with 'how', the information you will be looking for are processes and/or actions. With this research question, I'll be coming up with the strategies GM scientists could use to communicate GM crop research. Using mostly gerunds (verbs plus 'ing') when creating codes for the last research question will be the best way of developing consistent codes that capture processes and actions related to GM communication strategies (Charmaz, 2014).

When examining participants' responses to the interview questions, I realized that most of the potential relevant information (i.e. empirical indicators) needs to be extensively assessed to draw meanings from it (see Exhibits 7.1–7.3). In other words, the meanings of the potential empirical indicators are implicit – requiring my interpretation in order

Table 7.3 Coding strategy decision made based on the research method, purpose, question, and data to be analyzed

Contributing factors of the coding strategy choice	Description-focused coding	Interpretation-focused coding	Presumption-focused coding
Case study functions: • To help understand public concerns about GM foods • To produce strategies for communicating GM crop research		✓	
Purpose: • To explore UK public concerns about GM foods and the strategies GM scientists should use to present the GM crop research to the public		✓	
Research questions:		✓	
1. What were the factors contributing to public concerns about GM research and foods in the UK?		✓	
2. What were the challenges faced by GM scientists when communicating GM crop research to the public?		✓	
3. How should GM crop research be communicated to the public to address their concerns?		✓	
Nature of the data Considering the nature of the data, a critical and intensive review of the data is required to generate answers to address the research questions		✓	

to address the research questions. This confirms the need to use the interpretation-focused coding strategy.

Commentary 7.1. As you can see, deciding on an appropriate coding strategy mainly depended on the characteristics of the research questions and data content. Critically scrutinizing the research questions helped me to know what I would be looking

Participant S9

A: can I start by asking you . what in your opinion accounts for the
response to genetic modification in this country?

B: you mean what people find important what?

A: mhmh what kind of reason has caused . this controversy here in the
UK with genetic modification?

B: mhmh . mainly I believe it's the her . media . and the first
because the first reaction was not bad . from what I know . OK from
Syngenta's . seminars about the tomato paste . on the on the shelves
. it was not bad the first reaction but . after a while I don't know
for why for which reason . the media started to campaign against . GM
products so . in general I think the media has a very . high impact
on public opinion

Potential empirical indicator:
Addressing research question 1

A: and so . would you would you say that without the media
intervening there would have been . no big mess about it?

B: no it's not the truth either you know I believe that people are
afraid of new things . you can see that all through . the time you
know at first they were afraid of the car they thought that it was
something bad well . it turned out to be something bad but anyway .
they were they are afraid of new things . they are reluctant to try
something completely new . different from what they know . so I
believe that this combination media and this . fear of human beings .
it's you know . it creates this . this reaction

Potential empirical indicator:
Addressing research question 1

Exhibit 7.1. Participant 'S9' transcript excerpt showing potential empirical indicators for research question 1

for in the data. My goal was to find out whether the information I will be seeking was clearly displayed in the data (i.e. explicit) or hidden in the data (i.e. implicit), which needs further examination to bring to light. I realized that most of the potential empirical indicators were implicit in nature – hence the need to use the interpretation-focused coding strategy. At this stage of the coding process, it is not about choosing a right or wrong coding strategy. However, it is about choosing the one which will best help you to identify empirical indicators and adequately address the research questions.

Participant S6

A: so you think once people . have achieved this . kind of basic knowledge then they would be . less . in opposition to genetic modification?

Potential empirical indicator: Addressing research question 2

B: I don't see automatically there'd be less in opposition but it would be . easier to have informed debate which is is the important thing . and the second thing would be it would be . harder for the people to use . or the particularly things like the tabloid press to simple scare . tactics . I mean it's very very easy . to make claims . which are completely unsubstantiated . if people are in ignorance . so you can say . this food is Frankenstein . food and all the rest of it you need no knowledge to answer them . a scientists you feel you could have evidence you've got to give people irrationally they say is there . any risk associated with this . and you can't put your hand on your heart as a scientist and say there is no risk . you have to say well our experiments have not shown anything that we need to be worried about and . and of course . the public are quite rightly concerned about those kind of statements whereas if they're more familiar . with what's happening and things they would . perhaps understand those statements more and also look at the horror . type of story and say well OK but that hasn't got any basis . so it would tend to . at least bring the . the two things a bit closer together and perhaps on a on a basis on which you could discuss rat- . rather than just this blanket well it's so horrible it's gonna . wipe out the world and therefore we can't talk about it

A: do you do you feel that at the moment it's . this lack of knowledge in the public that . pushes you as scientists to have to say there is no risk . a position that you say is not . what you would . say?

B: you you do feel that there's a certain amount of pressure . from people wanting you to say this

A: from the public?

Potential empirical indicator: Addressing research question 2

B: yes . yes . yes and people who . want you to say that to the public . as well . and as a scientist if yo- you know you really . can't . do that easily . you can only say there is no evidence for or . you know we have not found any . and that's it's it's a different . thing and it's not because . it feels I think to the public as though therefore your hiding something or your trying to make a clever statement which fools them into whereas in fact that's what science is . it's you know you try and base everything on factual . statements although I still agree there's a lot of . subjectivity in . in in . in science despite what's said about it because of interpretation but . yes

Exhibit 7.2. Participant 'S6' transcript excerpt showing potential empirical indicators for research question 2

Participant S4

A: ehm what do you see as the best strategy to . communicate .
research about . GM food or . products?

B: it's a difficult one that one isn't it really . I think . to be
honest . we need . more in depth . coverage . and less . headline .
coverage . I think we need more . documentaries and less news items
for instance . because when people see the comp- it's it's the
complexity . and the knowledge base which needs to be . improved not
the opinions . and whereas . documentary and feature writers tend to
provide information . to allow you to to come to a . a decision at
the end I think . headline writers . it tends to be far more .
superficial . and opinion is . far more in the forefront [xxx] . in
order to communicate it effectively I think . some people . would say
that it's a softly softly approach I wouldn't say that I would say .
that it's it . it's far more . seeking to provide information . so
that people become . more able to . be rational in the . areas that
they are worried about . and . and become more relaxed in the areas
that are really frankly . nothing to worry about

Potential empirical indicator:
Addressing research question 3

A: and can you see a difference in strategy that you would apply . if
you were talking to one audience of lay- . of non-specialists or?

B: yes . yes . simply because their knowledge bases are different .
so . if you are . talking to an ehrm an an audience which does not
have . a wide knowledge base in the area . whether or not they have
strong opinions it's it's it's irrelevant really . the st- the
strategy that I always have is to provide the facts . I do not .
really have strong opinions . a priori myself . I base . what I .
consider to have the higher risk and the lower risk on the basis of .
the results that come back and the and on the literature . so when I
talk to a lay audience what I start off with is the basis of the
technology and then I . outlying what the major areas are perceived
as . and I give a . a detailed either a detailed case study . or I'll
give . in broad terms . how we go about . trying to quantify those
risks . for a . an audience which is . fairly well . tuned into GM .
and GM technology . again it depends on what the audience is . for
instance if I talked to an audience which . is . very much informed
on . how the technology works . I'll probably concentrate on the
areas which I feel they will be weaker . on . which will be . perhaps
on the areas of agriculture and . ecology .. on the other hand if I
am talking to . a . room full of ecologists . I'll probably spend
more time talking about . technology . how gene interactions . work
and how . the transformation technology works . and what our .
capabilities are .. and then . bring in the ecology so

Potential empirical indicator:
Addressing research question 3

Exhibit 7.3. Participant 'S4' transcript excerpt showing potential empirical
indicators for research question 3

ASSIGNING LABELS TO THE RESEARCH QUESTIONS

The next step is to create anchor codes for your research questions. Anchor codes are labels which are generated to represent the questions you want to address in your study (Adu, 2013). So, why do you need to develop an anchor code for each of your research questions? This is mainly for a code organizational purpose. By developing anchor codes, you are able to easily organize codes under their respective research questions. Also, it facilitates the grouping of the codes into categories and themes – thereby saving data analysis time and eliminating the stress of figuring out which code belongs to which question.

Demonstration 7.2

Based on the content of the research questions, I created anchor codes. Below are the research questions and their anchor codes (in parentheses):

1. What were the factors contributing to public concerns about GM research and foods in the UK? *(GM concerns factors)*
2. What were the challenges faced by GM scientists when communicating GM crop research to the public? *(GM communication challenges)*
3. How should GM crop research be communicated to the public to address their concerns? *(GM communication strategies)*

Commentary 7.2. The anchor codes created don't have to be perfect. The most important thing is to construct them in such a way that they remind you of the research questions they are representing. I suggest you make each research question label not too long. It would be ideal if you could have a label which is not more than five words' long.

CREATING CODES USING THE INTERPRETATION-FOCUSED CODING STRATEGY

As discussed previously, interpretation-focused coding will be used to code the GM crop research project data (Cook & Robbins, 2005). Under this coding strategy, there are five main steps leading to the development and description of an appropriate code. They are:

1. Identifying a potential *empirical indicator* with the research question in mind → *(e)*
2. Determining the *meaning* of the indicator → *(m)*
3. Providing an *answer* to the research question based on the interpretation of the indicator → *(a)*
4. Creating a *code* based on the answer to the question → *(c)*
5. Developing a *description* of what the code represents → *(D)*

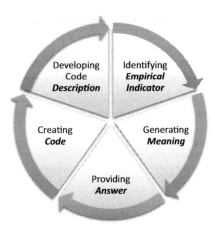

Figure 7.1. Five steps of code generation using the interpretation-focused coding strategy

When using interpretation-focused coding, think of the acronym **'emacD'** (which stands for the **empirical indicator** identified, **meaning** of the indicator generated, **answer** to the research question provided, **code** created, and **description** of the code developed; see Figure 7.1). Going through these steps would help you to develop codes that best represent the empirical indicators selected, capture the underlying meanings of the indicators and address your research questions.

Demonstration 7.3

There are four main documents I use for manual coding: transcripts, initial memo, analytical memo and codebook. I conduct the main coding (such as selecting empirical indicators and assigning codes) in the transcript documents using the **'New Comment'** function under the **'Review'** tab on the Word document toolbar. The initial memo is used to write my reactions to some of the codes generated. Concurrently, I construct my initial memo and analytical memo – documenting my personal reflections about the codes and the process through which the codes are developed, respectively. I then create a codebook – compiling a list of codes and their respective definitions and exemplary empirical indicators (Decuir-Gunby, Marshall, & McCulloch, 2010).

STEP 7.1. SETTING UP INITIAL MEMO, ANALYTICAL MEMO AND CODEBOOK

1. After opening a blank Word document, state the type of document (whether it is an initial memo, analytical memo or codebook) as a header and provide a brief description underneath it

2. State the research questions and their labels (i.e. anchor codes) in parentheses
3. Create a table that corresponds to the characteristics of the type of document (see Exhibits 7.4–7.6)
   a. *The initial memo should have the following columns (see Exhibit 7.4):*
      i. **Anchor code column:** This contains labels of the research questions that are connected to empirical indicators.
      ii. **Empirical indicator column:** This contains the relevant information selected from the data.
      iii. **Code column:** This has the codes generated.
      iv. **Reflections column:** This contains thoughts about the empirical indicator and/or the code representing the indicator.
   b. *The analytical memo should have the following columns (see Exhibit 7.5):*
      i. **Anchor code column:** This contains labels of the research questions that are connected to empirical indicators.
      ii. **Empirical indicator column:** This contains the relevant information selected from the data.
      iii. **Empirical indicator meaning column:** This contains your interpretation or understanding of the significant excerpts identified.
      iv. **Research question answer column:** This is where you provide your answer to the research question based on your interpretation of the empirical indicator.
      v. **Code column:** This contains the label generated out of an extensive examination of the empirical indicators and your answers to the research questions. To ensure consistency and clarity of the codes developed, each code shouldn't be more than five words' long.
      vi. **Code description column:** In this column, you address the question, *what kind of relevant information in the data will the code be representing?*
   c. *The codebook should have the following columns (see Exhibit 7.6):*
      i. **Anchor code column:** This contains labels of the research questions that are connected to empirical indicators.
      ii. **Empirical indicator source column:** This is the source or location of the relevant information selected. In this column, you could indicate the participant ID and the line numbers of the empirical indicators in the transcript documents (example: NS1, lines 39–40).

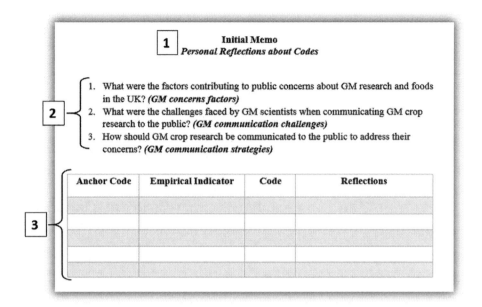

Exhibit 7.4. Initial memo

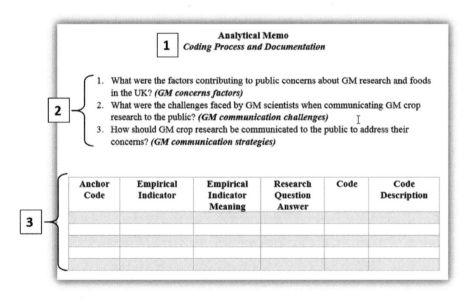

Exhibit 7.5. Analytical memo

    iii. Code column: This contains labels given to the empirical indicators.

    iv. Code description column: The essence of having code descriptions in a codebook is to guide you to decide which specific empirical indicator belongs to which code. It is also helpful when you have more than one coder. Using agreed

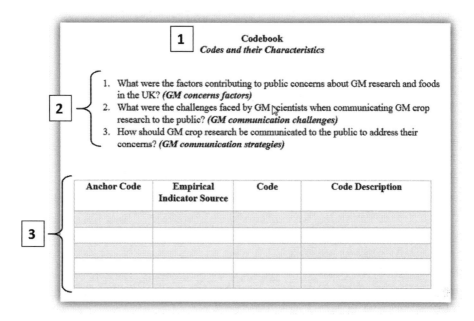

Exhibit 7.6. Codebook

code definitions promotes the likelihood of coders arriving at similar outcomes in terms of relevant texts selected in the data and the codes assigned to them (MacPhail, Khoza, Abler, & Ranganathan, 2015).

STEP 7.2. GOING THROUGH THE TRANSCRIPTS AND SELECTING EMPIRICAL INDICATORS (SEE EXHIBIT 7.7)

1. Open the transcript
   a. To display line numbers on the transcript, go to the *'Layout'* tab, click on *'Line Numbers'* and select *'Continuous'*
2. With the research questions in mind, actively read through the texts – looking for empirical indicators
3. After locating an empirical indicator, copy it *(ready to be pasted into the analytical memo)*

STEP 7.3. MAKING MEANING OF THE SELECTED EMPIRICAL INDICATOR AND CREATING A CODE (SEE EXHIBIT 7.8)

1. In the analytical memo, paste the selected excerpt into the *'Empirical Indicator'* column, and in parentheses state the source of the text
2. Indicate the research question linked to the empirical indicator by stating the anchor code of the question (with the research question number in parentheses) in the *'Anchor code'* column

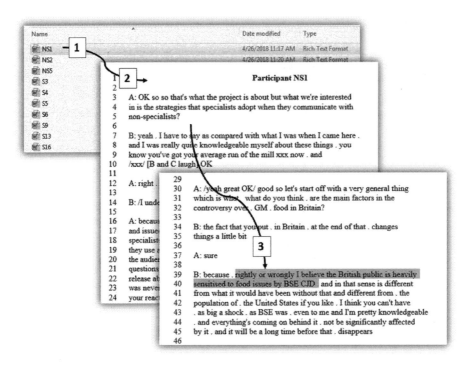

Exhibit 7.7. Selecting empirical indicators

3. Based on the content of the empirical indicator, state what it means
4. Based on the interpretation of the empirical indicator, provide the answer to the research question
5. Create a code from the answer – making sure that:
   a. It represents the empirical indicator
   b. It captures the interpretation of the empirical indicator
   c. It addresses the research question
   d. It is not more than five words in length
6. Describe what the code represents – addressing the question, *what kind of empirical indicators or its interpretations should be represented by the code?*

Commentary 7.3. The table in the analytical memo is a perfect work area to engage in an intensive "interaction with" the empirical indicators selected (Charmaz, 2014, p. 252). The objective of this activity is to produce a simple but condensed phrase called a code which best represents the significant excerpts captured. Since I'm using interpretation-focused coding, my role is to: make sense of the text captured, adjust my interpretation of the empirical indicator to address the research question without distorting its meaning, build a code which is informed by the answer to the

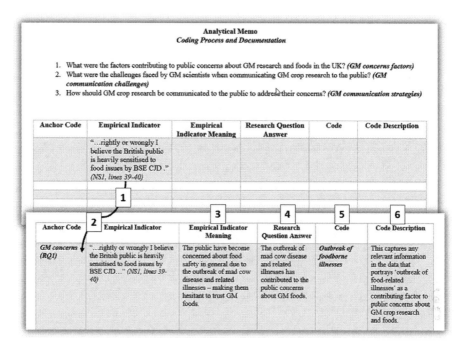

Exhibit 7.8. Creating a code in the analytical memo

research question, and describe what the code exemplifies. There is flexibility in this process. I can always go back to make adjustments to the information documented under each column of the analytical memo table.

I want to emphasize that not all empirical indicators are examined in the analytical memo. Also, not all codes were created in the analytical memo. As you develop codes in the memo, you may reach a stage where you could generate codes without following all the steps needed to create them. You could just look at an empirical indicator, think about the potential interpretation and answer to the research question without documenting them in the analytical memo, and generate an appropriate code and its description. That was exactly what I did when coding the data. In effect, I created 14 codes in the memo (see Appendix A, Table A.1), which is just a fraction of the codes I'll be generating. The essence of having this type of memo is to help create new codes but you don't have to create all the codes in it.

STEP 7.4. ASSIGNING CODES GENERATED TO THE EMPIRICAL INDICATOR ON THE TRANSCRIPT (SEE EXHIBITS 7.9–7.12)

1. In the transcript document, select the empirical indicator
2. Go to the toolbar and click on the **'Review'** tab

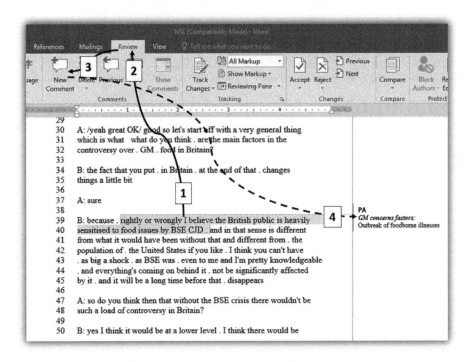

Exhibit 7.9. Excerpt from Participant 'NS1' transcript showing how an empirical indicator is selected and coded

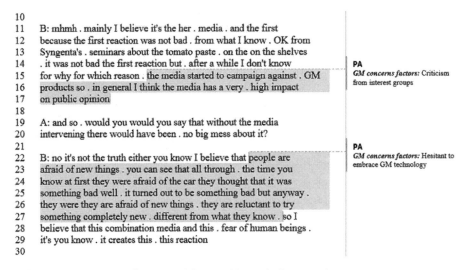

Exhibit 7.10. Excerpt from Participant 'S9' coded transcript

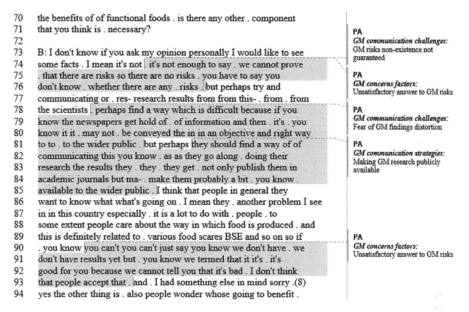

Exhibit 7.11. Excerpt from Participant 'S13' coded transcript

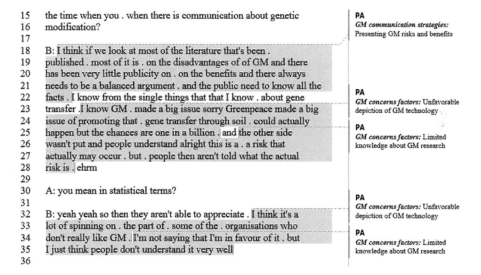

Exhibit 7.12. Excerpt from Participant 'NS5' coded transcript

3. Under the **'Review'** tab, click on **'New Comment'**
4. In the comment box, type the anchor code of the research question connected to the empirical indicator, type a colon (:), then a space and state the code which represents the indicator (example: '**GM concerns factors:** Outbreak of foodborne illnesses')

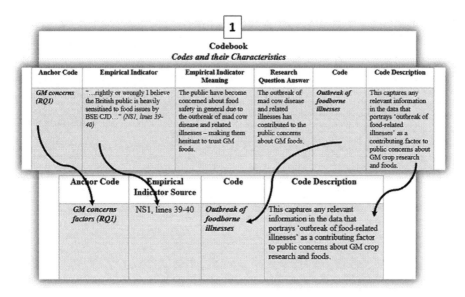

Exhibit 7.13. Copying information from the analytical memo to the codebook

STEP 7.5. CREATING A CODEBOOK (SEE EXHIBITS 7.13–7.14)

1. Copy information about the anchor code, empirical indicator source, code and code description from the analytical memo to the codebook
2. With respect to adding the codes and their characteristics that didn't appear in the analytical memo, state the location of the empirical indicator in the **'Empirical Indicator Source'** column of the codebook table
3. Copy the label of the research question from the transcript and paste it into the **'Anchor Code'** column
4. Copy the assigned code from the transcript and paste it into the **'Code'** column
5. Describe what the code represents in the **'Code Description'** column

Commentary 7.4. *I view a codebook as a reservoir of all the codes generated, including their anchor codes, sources of exemplary empirical indicators and code descriptions. Some of the codes and their characteristics in the codebook are taken from the analytical memo while others are copied from the transcripts, as indicated above. At the end of the coding process, you may have more codes in the codebook compared to those in the analytical memo.*

STEP 7.6. CREATING AN INITIAL MEMO (SEE EXHIBITS 7.15–7.17)

1. In the initial memo, document thoughts about the empirical indicators and/or codes generated

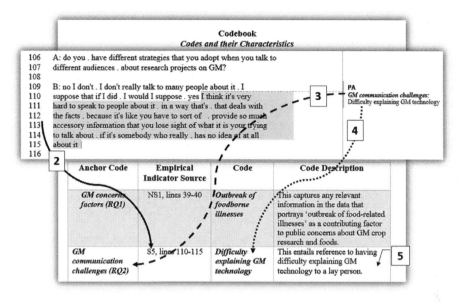

Codebook
Codes and their Characteristics

		Anchor Code	Empirical Indicator Source	Code	Code Description
106	A: do you . have different strategies that you adopt when you talk to				
107	different audiences . about research projects on GM?				
108					
109	B: no I don't . I don't really talk to many people about it . I				**PA**
110	suppose that if I did . I would I suppose . yes I think it's very			**3**	*GM communication challenges:* Difficulty explaining GM technology
111	hard to speak to people about it . in a way that's . that deals with				
112	the facts . because it's like you have to sort of . provide so much				
113	accessory information that you lose sight of what it is you trying			**4**	
114	to talk about . if it's somebody who really . has no idea of at all				
115	about it				
116	**2**				
		Anchor Code	**Empirical Indicator Source**	**Code**	**Code Description**
		GM concerns factors (RQ1)	NS1, lines 39-40	*Outbreak of foodborne illnesses*	This captures any relevant information in the data that portrays 'outbreak of food-related illnesses' as a contributing factor to public concerns about GM crop research and foods.
		GM communication challenges (RQ2)	S5, lines 110-115	*Difficulty explaining GM technology*	This entails reference to having difficulty explaining GM technology to a lay person. **5**

Exhibit 7.14. Copying information from the transcript to the codebook

Initial Memo
Personal Reflections about Codes

1. What were the factors contributing to public concerns about GM research and foods in the UK? *(GM concerns factors)*
2. What were the challenges faced by GM scientists when communicating GM crop research to the public? *(GM communication challenges)*
3. How should GM crop research be communicated to the public to address their concerns? *(GM communication strategies)*

Anchor Code	Empirical Indicator	Code	Reflections
GM communication strategies (RQ3)	"I think . you need to . communicate what the main aims of doing it are . because a lot of the time people don't really know . why it was done in the first place . so the sort of background to the research and the use of GM foods..." *(NS2, lines 38-41)*	*Presenting GM research rationale*	I think the public are potential consumers of GM products and they have the right to know the rationale behind GM research and the process through which GM foods are produced. But how much information about GM should be provided to satisfy the public quest for answers since GM scientists and companies don't want to provide information that may help their competitors?

Exhibit 7.15. Creating an initial memo

Anchor Code	Empirical Indicator	Code	Reflections	
GM concerns factors (RQ1)	"...the way the media portrayed . GM foods as being . sort of . Frankenstein foods or whatever . the way it was put across in the media ..." (NS2, lines 13-15)	Unfavorable depiction of GM technology	This may have some connection with one of the codes under the 'GM communication challenges (RQ2)' research question.	Potential relationship
GM communication strategies (RQ3)	"I think . you need to . communicate what the main aims of doing it are . because a lot of the time people don't really know . why it was done in the first place . so the sort of background to the research and the use of GM foods..." (NS2, lines 38-41)	Presenting GM research rationale	I think the public are potential consumers of GM products and they have the right to know the rationale behind GM research and the process through which GM foods are produced. But how much information about GM should be provided to satisfy the public quest for answers since GM scientists and companies don't want to provide information that will help their competitors?	Rhetorical question
GM concerns factors (RQ1)	"...it's very nature it's like . very technical and it's not about . being . subjective it's about being objective so" (NS2, lines 67-69)	Objective-driven nature of scientific research	Due to the objective nature of science, GM scientists can't just assure the public that there is no risk associated with GM research and foods when there is currently no evidence to support or refute this assertion.	Opinion
Other	"...I think it would be good if the Government could pay for some research . and some independent research as well" (NS2, lines 82-84)	Government funding for GM research	I was thinking that if the government sponsors GM research, wouldn't GM scientists be pressured to produce favorable results especially on issues about GM risks?	Unanswered question

Exhibit 7.16. First excerpt of an initial memo table

Anchor Code	Empirical Indicator	Code	Reflections	
GM communication strategies (RQ3)	"...more or to concentrate on the both the . the good part of it and the side effects of it . but it's like they have been highlighting more on the . the good part of . GM . than the bad part of it" (S16, lines 47-50)	Emphasizing GM's positive side	This code may come under the 'communicating GM innovation benefits' code. Emphasizing the positive side makes sense since they are not certain about the potential side effects of GM. As the same time, they need to be open to the public – having a conversation about the people's concerns.	Possible relationship
GM concerns factors (RQ1)	"...even when you . genetically modified genes it's when you're cha- changing the genes so people think if you're changing genes . then it will have some side effects probably in the human body when you eat it ." (S16, lines 55-58)	Belief in GM product side effects	I coded this empirical indicator as 'Belief in GM product side effects' although I used this code to label an indicator previously. This is because, in this case, the 'side effects' were being discussed in a different context under a different interview question.	Reason why this empirical evidence was coded
GM communication challenges (RQ2)	"...those side effects I am not I'm . not very sure of what exactly side effects it had it's always speculating but I think there should be some side effects" (S16, lines 59-61)	Not sure about GM risks	This supports the assertion that GM scientists are not in the position to emphatically assure the general public about GM safety because (1) it takes time to know the effects and (2) not much research has been done on the risk.	Making sense of the empirical indicator

Exhibit 7.17. Second excerpt of an initial memo table with comments

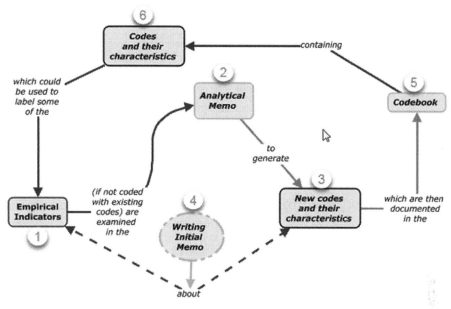

Figure 7.2. Manual qualitative coding process

Note: Repeat Steps 7.2–7.6 until all the transcripts are coded

Commentary 7.5. As you can see from the comments made in the initial memo tables (see Exhibits 7.16–7.17), initial thoughts could be about potential relationships between codes, rhetorical or unanswered questions, or views about an empirical indicator coded. Sometimes you may want to document your understanding about an empirical indicator or the rationale behind your decision to code specific information in the data. All these reflections would be helpful when categorizing codes, developing themes, determining relationships among the themes and even presenting your findings.

In sum, the coding process starts with selecting an empirical indicator and examining it in the analytical memo to help generate a code to represent the indicator. You then transfer the code and its characteristics to the codebook (see Figure 7.2). As I stated earlier, not all new codes are created in the analytical memo but all of the new codes are documented in the codebook. During the coding process, you can document your thoughts in the initial memo. Also, whenever an empirical indicator is identified, you first need to find out whether any of the existing codes can be used to label it.

COMPILING CODES AND TALLYING CODE FREQUENCIES

The next step of the coding process is to copy all the codes from the transcripts and paste them into a separate sheet called the *'Code*

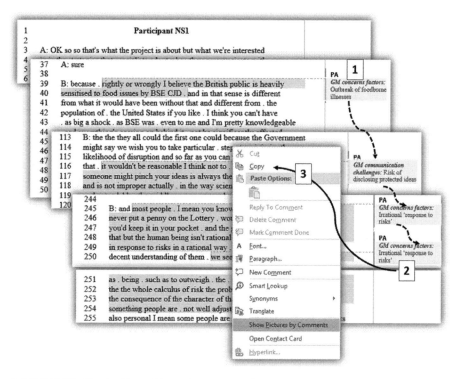

Exhibit 7.18. Illustration of how to copy codes

Compilation Sheet'. In the sheet, you compute code frequency, which is "the number of times" a particular code is assigned to empirical indicators (Guest, MacQueen, & Namey, 2012, p. 128). In addition, it is very important for you to tally the number of cases or participants connected to a specific code. So at the end, you would have the number of counts (i.e. frequency) and number of cases for each code.

Demonstration 7.4

Below are the final steps of the coding process. The **'Code Compilation Sheet'** is the main document used in computing the counts and cases for each code.

STEP 7.7. COPYING CODES AND PASTING THEM INTO THE **'CODE COMPILATION SHEET'** *(SEE EXHIBITS 7.18–7.19)*

1. On the transcript, select the first code, press and hold the **'Shift'** key on the keyboard and then press and hold the **'Down'** ('↓') key until the last code is selected
2. Right-click any of the selected codes
3. Click on **'Copy'** in the menu options

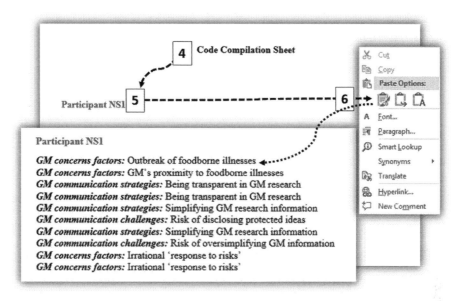

Exhibit 7.19. Illustration of how to paste codes

Note: If you have a Mac computer, disregard the last two actions (i.e. Actions 2 and 3). Press and hold the **'Command'** key and then press the **'C'** key to copy.

4. Open a blank document and name it **'Code Compilation Sheet'**
5. State the case (participant ID)
6. Right-click on the document and under **'Paste Options'**, click on the first option (which is **'Keep Source Formatting (K)'**)

Note: For Mac computer users, press and hold the **'Command'** key and then press the **'V'** key to paste

STEP 7.8. TALLY THE CODES UNDER EACH CASE
(SEE EXHIBITS 7.20–7.21)

1. Select all the codes under the case
2. Go to the **'Home'** tab
3. Under the **'Home'** tab click on the **'Sort'** ($\frac{A}{Z}\downarrow$) command to open the **'Sort Text'** dialog box
4. Click on **'OK'** to alphabetically arrange the codes
5. Tally the codes, and in parentheses state the number of counts for each code

Note: Follow Steps 7.7 and 7.8 to alphabetically arrange the codes and tally them under each case

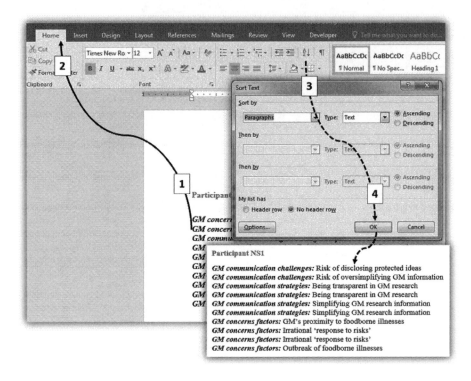

Exhibit 7.20. Alphabetically assigning the codes under a case

Code Compilation Sheet

Participant NS1

GM communication challenges: Risk of disclosing protected ideas *(1 count)*
GM communication challenges: Risk of oversimplifying GM information *(1 count)*
GM communication strategies: Being transparent in GM research *(2 counts)*
GM communication strategies: Simplifying GM research information *(2 counts)*
GM concerns factors: GM's proximity to foodborne illnesses *(1 count)*
GM concerns factors: Irrational 'response to risks' *(2 counts)*
GM concerns factors: Outbreak of foodborne illnesses *(1 count)*

Exhibit 7.21. Tallying the codes under a case

STEP 7.9. BRING ALL THE CODES TOGETHER AND COMPUTE THE OVERALL COUNTS AND NUMBER OF CASES ASSIGNED TO EACH CODE (SEE EXHIBIT 7.22)

1. Bring all the codes together on a separate page on the *'Code Compilation Sheet'*
2. Select all the codes
3. Go to the *'Home'* tab

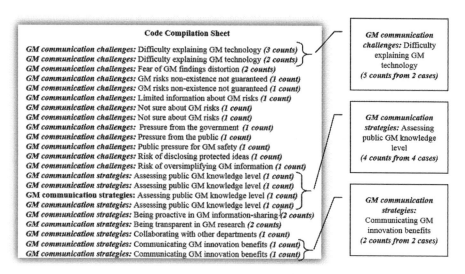

Exhibit 7.22. How overall counts and cases are computed

4. Under the **'Home'** tab click on the **'Sort'** ($\frac{A}{Z}\downarrow$) command to open the **'Sort Text'** dialog box
5. Click on **'OK'** to alphabetically arrange the codes
6. Tally the overall counts for each code and the number of cases connected to it (see Exhibit 7.22)
7. Create a table for the codes under each research question (see Tables 7.4–7.7)

Commentary 7.6. In the end, I created 22, 10, and 23 codes under *'GM concerns factors (RQ1)'*, *'GM communication challenges (RQ2)'*, and *'GM communication strategies (RQ3)'*, respectively. In addition, I coded some portions of the data which I thought were relevant but which didn't belong to any of the three research questions. Consequently, I generated five codes under the umbrella of *'Other issues'*. I'm now ready to move to the next stage of the data analysis process, which comprise categorizing codes and developing themes. The counts and number of cases for each code will play a huge role in the next phase. The number of times empirical indicators are linked to a particular code (i.e. code frequency) is as important as the number of participants connected to the code (i.e. code case). Manual coding is generally time-consuming compared to utilizing qualitative data analysis software (QDAS). Moreover, when compiling and tallying the codes manually, there is always the possibility of making computation errors. Lastly, when coding manually, there is a challenge of keeping track of all the coding materials such as the transcripts, analytical memo, initial memo and codebook.

Table 7.4 Codes and their respective counts and cases under *'GM concerns factors (RQ1)'*

Code (GM concerns factors)	Count/ frequency	Number of cases
Belief in GM product side effects	5	2
Conflicting views about GM safety	1	1
Criticism from interest groups	4	3
Disinterested in learning about GM	1	1
Extensively unexamined GM side effects	1	1
GM scientists' ineffective communication	1	1
GM's proximity to foodborne illnesses	3	3
Hesitant to embrace GM technology	1	1
Hesitant to explain GM research	3	2
Inadequate promotion of GM benefits	1	1
Irrational 'response to risks'	2	1
Lack of effective government communication	2	2
Limited knowledge about GM research	10	6
'Mistrust of commercial companies'	3	2
Mistrust of scientists	4	2
Mistrust of the government	2	2
Multiple meanings of GM concepts	2	1
Objective-driven nature of scientific research	1	1
Outbreak of foodborne illnesses	3	3
Uncertain about GM research	1	1
Unfavorable depiction of GM technology	7	3
Unsatisfactory answer to GM risks	3	2

Table 7.5 Codes and their respective counts and cases under *'GM communication challenges (RQ2)'*

Code (GM communication challenges)	Count/ frequency	Number of cases
Difficulty explaining GM technology	3	3
Fear of GM findings distortion	2	1
GM risks non-existence not guaranteed	2	2
Limited information about GM risks	1	1
Not sure about GM risks	2	2
'Pressure from the government'	1	1
Pressure from the public	1	1
Public pressure for GM safety	1	1
Risk of disclosing protected ideas	1	1
Risk of oversimplifying GM information	1	1

Table 7.6 Codes and their respective counts and cases under *'GM communication strategies (RQ3)'*

Code (GM communication strategies)	Count/ frequency	Number of cases
Assessing public GM knowledge level	4	4
Being proactive in GM information-sharing	2	1
Being transparent in GM research	2	1
Collaborating with other departments	1	1
Communicating GM innovation benefits	2	2
Creating awareness of GM risks	1	1
Creating press releases	1	1
Debating with pressure groups	1	1
Discussing specific GM case	3	3
Educating the public about GM	3	2
Emphasizing crossbreeding/GM similarities	2	2
Emphasizing GM's positive side	2	1
Giving the public some time	3	3
Having conversations about GM risks	2	2
Having public debate about GM	1	1
Listening to the public concerns	1	1
Making GM research publicly available	1	1
Making in-depth GM presentations	4	3
Organizing seminars for the public	1	1
Presenting GM research rationale	2	2
Presenting GM risks and benefits	3	1
Simplifying GM research information	2	2
Tailoring GM information	2	1

Table 7.7 Codes and their respective counts and cases under *'Other issues'*

Code (Other issues)	Count/ frequency	Number of cases
Difficulty in labeling products	1	1
Finding out GM research sponsor	1	1
Government funding for GM research	2	2
More research on GM risks	2	2
Single definition of GM concepts	2	2

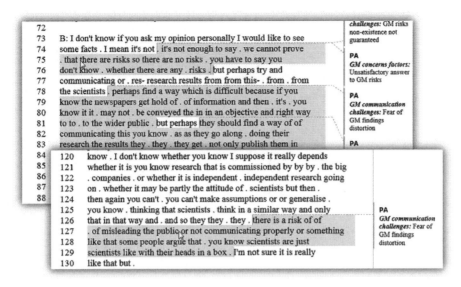

Exhibit 7.23. Excerpt from Participant 'S13' coded transcript

Q&A ABOUT QUALITATIVE CODING

Q1. Can an empirical indicator (a relevant excerpt) be coded more than one time?

A. *Yes, you can code an empirical indicator again if it addresses more than one research question.*

Q2. Let's say I code an empirical indicator as *'difficulty in understanding GM research'* and in the same transcript I find another indicator which can be coded as *'difficulty in understanding GM research'*, should I give the same code to it?

A. *Yes, you can do that provided the indicator is presented in a different context or in response to a different interview question. For instance, when reviewing Participant S13's transcript, I coded two empirical indicators as* 'Fear of GM findings distortion' *under different interview questions and in different contexts (see* Exhibit 7.23*). In a qualitative analysis, the importance of a code is partly based on the number of times it is assigned to empirical indicators in the data.*

Q3. If a portion of the data is important but doesn't fall under any of the research questions, should I code it?

A. *You could code it if you think it will be helpful for further examination in the future and/or the audience will be interested in the findings that are unrelated to your research questions. If you decide to code it, you could put it under a separate anchor code called* 'Other issues' *(see* Exhibit 7.24*).*

Q4. How do I maintain consistency among the codes I generate in terms of the structure?

A. *Having a consistent code structure as shown in* Table 7.6 *begins with deciding on an appropriate coding strategy, finding information*

351 so . I think in that sense it's a positive . you know there is there
352 are opportunities . but I don't think that . it's good that industry
353 . I mean it is a very danger in industry . dictating . what goes on
354 in universities because . everybody in University is funded by   **PA**
355 industry it's . you know I think a bit of industry funding's fine .   *Other issues:* Government
356 there has to be . money that comes from . non-industry sources   funding for GM research
357
358 A: the Government or
359
360 B: yes I suppose . so that . I mean the Research Council money I
361 think is . even though they are closer to industry than they used to
362 be . it doesn't . seem yet to have got so bad that . that one is
363 dictated to . although I think research is a bit more focused than it
364 used to . you have to sort of talk in the grant proposals about . you
365 know what are the . what are the industry applications for doing this
366

Exhibit 7.24. Excerpt from Participant 'S5' coded transcript

55
56 B: I think the Government want   . I think the Government want to hear
57 that there are no risks with this . I think part of the . initiative
58 for . starting in the first place was because because of Governments
59 and because of political reasons . and once you've given backing to
60 something politically it's to you need to hear that . it's safe for the   **PA**
61 people who've . elected you to represent them if you see what I mean .   *GM communication*
62 so . I think there is pressure from the Government on scientists . to   *challenges:* Pressure
63 make sure that they can make it safe and that they can . say that it's   from the government
64 safe . and I think also the public want to hear that as well . but I   **PA**
65 don't think that's necessarily a good thing that there's just this this   *GM communication*
66 pre-pressure especially from the Government because . you don't you   *challenges:* Public
67 can't really . put that kind of pressure on science . because . by it's   pressure for GM
68 very nature it's like . very technical and it's not about . being .   safety
69 subjective it's about being objective so   **PA**
70   *GM concerns factors:*
71 A: what do you think of the links between . business and University in   Objective-driven
                                                                               nature of scientific
                                                                               research

Exhibit 7.25. Excerpt from Participant 'NS2' coded transcript

*in the data which would help in addressing the research question(s),
and addressing the question based on the empirical indicator captured.
You then reduce the answer to a word or usually a phrase (which is
no longer than five words in length) – describing a behavior (such
as a thought, feeling or action), process, situation, setting and the
like. All these steps are contributing to the data reduction process –
transforming specific and practical information to general and abstract
concepts (Saldaña, 2016). Alternatively, you could develop consistent
codes by converting each research question to a "focus prompt" (Kane
& Trochim, 2007, p. 10). In qualitative coding, a focus prompt is a
phrase which is used to construct structurally consistent codes (Adu,
2017b; Kane & Trochim, 2007). For example, for the research question,*
**What were the factors contributing to public concerns about
GM research and foods in the UK?** *I can state its focus prompt as:*
**'The factor(s) contributing to the public GM research and food
concerns was (were)…'.** *Using this technique, I can create codes such*

as: **'Mistrust of scientists', 'Multiple meanings of GM concepts', 'Unfavorable depiction of GM technology'** *and* **'Unsatisfactory answer to GM risks'** *(see Table 7.4). Note that I didn't use the focus prompt technique for my coding process but this is an alternative strategy you could consider.*

Q5. When should I stop using the analytical memo at the coding stage?
A. *The main purpose of the analytical memo at the coding stage is to facilitate the development of codes. In other words, it shouldn't be seen as a way of completing a code development protocol or 'ritual' but should be viewed as one of the numerous techniques of generating codes. The time to stop using the memo for coding generation purposes differs from person to person. For me, I stopped using the analytical memo tool when coding my second transcript and had created 14 codes (see Appendix A, Table A.1). After developing the 14th code, I realized I could effortlessly create new codes without completing the table in the memo. So, you can cease using the analytical memo tool when you feel that you can create codes without following the five code generation steps discussed in this chapter.*

Q6. Can participants' own words be used to code when utilizing the interpretation-focused coding strategy?
A. *Yes, if they best represent the interpretation of the empirical indicators selected (see Exhibit 7.25).*

Q7. Can I adjust an existing code after realizing it doesn't fully represent the empirical indicators?
A. *Yes, you always need to be flexible in the coding process. Be open to examining new and alternative interpretations of the empirical indicators and if it requires an adjustment of the code initially developed, you could do it.*

Q8. Is it possible to have an empirical indicator addressing more than one research question?
A. *Yes, it is possible. For example, the empirical indicator below was coded as* **'GM risks non-existence not guaranteed'** *and* **'Unsatisfactory answer to GM risks'** *under* **'GM communication challenges (RQ2)'** *and* **'GM concerns factors (RQ1)',** *respectively.*

> "...it's not enough to say. we cannot prove. that there are risks so there are no risks. you have to say you don't know. whether there are any. risks."
>
> *(S13, lines 74–76)*

Q9. At the coding stage, should I be concerned about determining potential relationships between empirical indicators or codes?
A. *Your main focus in the coding stage is to identify significant text in the data and assign codes to them. At this stage, any idea including potential*

connections among empirical indicators or codes can be documented in the initial memo. You could review the memo after completing the initial coding process.

Q10. How many codes should I develop?
A. The number of codes doesn't matter. The most important thing is to select relevant information and assign codes which best represent them and address the research question(s).

Q11. Should every code created have a description?
A. Yes, you should have descriptions for all codes in terms of what they stand for.

Q12. Where are all the code descriptions stored?
A. All codes are stored in the codebook.

Q13. What is the use of code description in the coding stage?
A. As you transform specific information into abstract concepts, there is the likelihood that the meaning of the concepts (codes) becomes broad and ambiguous. Having a description for each code helps draw boundaries in terms of what they represent – reducing the level of ambiguity of what they mean (Guest et al., 2012). Take a few minutes to reflect on the following questions: What do you think the code **'Unfavorable depiction of GM technology'** *means or represents? Does your answer to this question come close to the description, "this code represents the media and interest groups' negative prediction of GM products or distortion of GM research findings"? You see how different your understanding of the code could be if there was no description? A code description could also be used as a criterion for deciding whether or not to assign a code to an empirical indicator. It also helps at the code categorization stage.*

Box 7.1 Qualitative coding steps

1. Decide on an appropriate coding strategy
2. Assign labels to the research questions
3. Create codes using the selected coding strategy
4. Compile codes and tally code frequencies

CONCLUSION

The two main factors that should not be overlooked when deciding on an appropriate coding strategy are the nature of the research question(s) and the data you plan to analyze. Irrespective of the coding strategy selected, you need to generate codes that best reflect the empirical indicators selected and address the research question(s) or purpose of the study. Memos play a prominent role in code development, especially in the analytical memo. An initial memo helps keep track of your thoughts about codes and empirical indicators; an analytical memo also expedites the smooth creation of codes. You may ask, where should I store all the codes created? A codebook is useful – documenting all codes and their respective characteristics. After coding all the transcripts, the next step is compiling and computing all the frequencies and cases assigned to each code in preparation for the code categorization stage.

REFERENCES

Adu, P. (2013). Qualitative analysis coding and categorizing [PowerPoint slides]. SlideShare. Retrieved from www.slideshare.net/kontorphilip/qualitative-analysis-coding-and-categorizing

Adu, P. (2017a). Conducting manual qualitative analysis using Word document [PowerPoint slides]. SlideShare. Retrieved from www.slideshare.net/kontorphilip/conducting-manual-qualitative-analysis-using-word-document

Adu, P. (2017b). Conducting qualitative analysis: What you need to know [PowerPoint slides]. SlideShare. Retrieved from www.slideshare.net/kontorphilip/conducting-qualitative-analysis-what-you-need-to-know

Charmaz, K. (2014). *Constructing grounded theory*. London: Sage.

Cook, G., & Robbins, P. T. (2005). *Presentation of genetically modified (GM) crop research to non-specialists, 1997–2002: A case study*. [data collection]. UK Data Service. SN: 5069, http://doi.org/10.5255/UKDA-SN-5069-1

Decuir-Gunby, J. T., Marshall, P. L., & McCulloch, A. W. (2010). Developing and using a codebook for the analysis of interview data: An example from a professional development research project. *Field Methods*, *23*(2), 136–155. doi:10.1177/1525822x10388468

Guest, G., MacQueen, K. M., & Namey, E. E. (2012). *Applied thematic analysis*. Los Angeles, CA: Sage.

Kane, M., & Trochim, W. M. K. (2007). *Concept mapping for planning and evaluation* (Applied Social Research Methods Series: Vol. 50; Series Eds.: L. Bickman & D. J. Rog). Thousand Oaks, CA: Sage.

MacPhail, C., Khoza, N., Abler, L., & Ranganathan, M. (2015). Process guidelines for establishing Intercoder Reliability in qualitative studies. *Qualitative Research*, *16*(2), 198–212. doi:10.1177/1468794115577012

Moseley, B. E. (2002). Safety assessment and public concern for genetically modified food products: The European view. *Toxicologic Pathology*, *30*(1), 129–131. doi:10.1080/01926230252824824

Saldaña, J. (2016). *The coding manual for qualitative researchers*. Los Angeles, CA: Sage.

8

Developing categories and themes

OBJECTIVES

Readers will be able to:

1. Distinguish between the presumption-focused coding strategy and the sorting strategy
2. Distinguish between the individual-based and the group-based sorting strategy
3. Use the presumption-focused coding strategy and the sorting strategy to develop categories and themes

TRANSFORMING CODES INTO CATEGORIES AND THEMES

Out of a sequentially systematic process of coding, I generated codes under each research question (see Chapter 7). The next step is to create categories and themes based on the codes. Categorizing involves assessing the characteristics of each code, reviewing commonalities among them and grouping them based on their shared characteristics (Charmaz, 2014; Creswell & Poth, 2018; Dey, 1993; Saldaña, 2016). This process is also called clustering or sorting – since it entails grouping codes into clusters based on what they have in common. So, clusters of codes are called categories. Consequently, themes normally emerge as the result of the further examination of categories – reducing them to concepts which represent sets of codes and empirical indicators that address the research question(s).

In simple terms, a code comes before a category and a category precedes a theme (Saldaña, 2016). Moreover, the level of abstraction of concepts generated increases as you move from codes to categories and then to themes. In some cases, the distinction between a code, category and theme becomes blurry, in that after qualitatively analyzing data you can end up with a small number of codes. In this case, a researcher could call these codes themes. Moreover, after generating codes, a qualitative analyst could select a dominant code (i.e. a code with the highest frequency and connected to the most participants) and label it as a theme. He/she could even call the categories created themes if no further analysis is needed. You could also have sub-categories and sub-themes, if you plan to demonstrate the unique characteristics of categories or themes under them when addressing the research question(s).

CODE TRANSFORMATION OR CATEGORIZATION STRATEGIES

There are numerous strategies used in transforming codes into categories and themes (see Charmaz, 2014; Creswell & Poth, 2018; Dey, 1993; Guest, MacQueen, & Namey, 2012; Richards, 2015; Saldaña, 2016; Smith, Flowers, & Larkin, 2012). Two that I will be discussing in this book are the presumption-focused coding strategy and the sorting strategy. Presumption-focused coding was discussed in Chapter 3 as one of the coding strategies. The unique aspect of this coding strategy is that it could also be used to build categories and themes. Alternatively, the sorting strategy is a widely used code categorization technique (see Adu, 2017).

Presumption-focused coding strategy

The presumption-focused coding strategy involves making conclusions based on the evidence provided. In this case, the evidence comprises the codes generated. The strategy begins with reviewing the codes under a research question, making claims or assertions typically in phrases, and looking for evidence (codes) to confirm, reject or revise the claims. At the end, claims supported by evidence are labeled as categories or themes. As described in Chapter 3, *'Pre'*, *'E'* and *'→'* are used to represent *'Presumption-focused code'*, *'Evidence'* and *'Based on'*, respectively. In this context of code transformation, if a claim (i.e. presumption-focused code) is confirmed by evidence, the notation would be *'Pre→E'*. In addition, numbering the *'Pre'* and *'E'* helps in keeping track of the claims created and evidence assigned to them. For example, the seventh piece of evidence (code) assigned to the third claim would be notated as *'Pre3→E7'*. Also, you indicate *'R'* before the sign *'→'* if a claim has been revised. I want to emphasize that the notations for the presumption-focus coding strategy in the categorization stage are slightly different from the signs used in the initial coding stage (see Chapter 3).

Demonstration 8.1

To demonstrate how the presumption-focused coding strategy is used to develop themes, I will be utilizing all 22 codes under the first research question: *What are the factors contributing to public concerns about GM research and foods in the UK?* (see Table 7.4).

STEP 8.1. SETTING UP THE LIST OF CODES AND REVIEWING THEM

1. Transfer the list of codes under the research question to the analytical memo
2. Number the codes by clicking on the **'Numbering'** command in the **'Home'** tab
3. Review the codes and their descriptions *(to learn more about codes and to think about possible claims that could be made)*

STEP 8.2. DEVELOPING CLAIMS AND CONNECTING THEM TO EVIDENCE (SEE EXHIBIT 8.1)

1. In the analytical memo, select the code (which is to be connected to a claim)
2. Go to the toolbar and click on the **'Review'** tab
3. Under the **'Review'** tab, click on **'New Comment'**
4. In the comment box, type the claim, and in parentheses state its notation
5. Go through the codes to look for evidence to support the claim
6. When additional evidence is identified, assign the claim to it and indicate the notation

Note: Repeat the actions (under Step 8.2) until all codes are examined as potential evidence for the claims *(Exhibit 8.2)*

Commentary 8.1. After reviewing the description of the code, **'Belief in GM product side effects'** and the empirical indicators it represents, I came up with a claim that the UK public believe that GM innovations and products have side effects on the environment and their health. Based on this claim, I developed a presumption-focused code, **'Existence of GM side effects'** and notated it as **'Pre1→E1'**, meaning it is the first claim supported by the first piece of evidence (see Exhibit 8.1). As I reviewed additional potential evidence, I revised the label of the claim from **'Existence of GM side effects'** to **'Perceived existence of GM risks'**. Additional pieces of evidence which prompted the revision of the claim were **'Hesitant to embrace GM technology'** and **'Irrational "response to risks"'** – making it necessary to create their notations as **'Pre1R→E8'** and **'Pre1R→E11'** (see Exhibit 8.2). One of the unique characteristics of the presumption-focused coding strategy is that a piece of evidence (a code) can be used to support more than one claim. For instance, **'E11'** (**'Irrational**

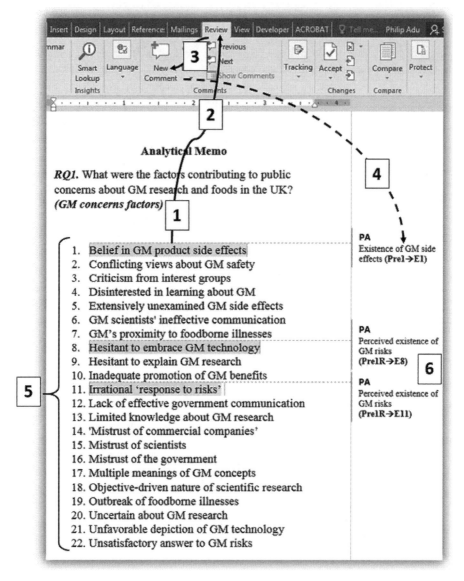

Exhibit 8.1. Analytical memo depicting how claims are created and supported

"response to risks"') was used to support **'Pre1R'** (**'Perceived existence of GM risks'**) and **'Pre7'** (**'Misunderstanding of GM risks'**).

STEP 8.3. COMPILING AND ARRANGING THE CLAIMS (SEE EXHIBIT 8.3)

1. In the analytical memo, select the claim (i.e. **'Existence of GM side effects (Pre1→E1)'**) in the first **'Comment box'**, press

and hold the *'Shift'* key and then press and hold the *'Down'* (*'↓'*) key until the claim (i.e. *'Misunderstanding of GM risks' (Pre7→E22)'*) in the last *'Comment box'* is selected
2. Right-click any of the selected claims
3. Click on *'Copy'*

Note: If you have a Mac computer, disregard the last two steps. Press and hold the **'Command'** key and then press the **'C'** key to copy.

4. Right-click on the document and under *'Paste Options'*, select the first option *('Keep Source Formatting (K)')*

Note: For Mac computer users, press and hold the **'Command'** key and then press the **'V'** key to paste
5. Select all of the claims *(presumption-focused codes)*
6. Go to the *'Home'* tab
7. Under the *'Home'* tab, click on the *'Sort'* (*'$\overset{A}{Z}\downarrow$'*) command to open the *'Sort Text'* dialog box
8. Click on *'OK'* to alphabetically arrange the claims *(presumption-focused codes)*

- ***Here is the outcome of Action 8 under Step 8.3:***
  Existence of GM side effects **(Pre1→E1)**
  GM risks uncertainties **(Pre8→E18)**
  GM risks uncertainties **(Pre8→E20)**
  GM risks uncertainties **(Pre8→E5)**
  GM scientists' ineffective communication **(Pre3→E6)**
  Lack of effective communication **(Pre3R→10)**
  Lack of effective communication **(Pre3R→E12)**
  Lack of effective communication **(Pre3R→E17)**
  Lack of effective communication **(Pre3R→E9)**
  Limited knowledge about GM research **(Pre6→E13)**
  Limited knowledge about GM research **(Pre6→E4)**
  Mistrust towards GM stakeholders **(Pre5→E14)**
  Mistrust towards GM stakeholders **(Pre5→E15)**
  Mistrust towards GM stakeholders **(Pre5→E16)**
  Misunderstanding of GM risks **(Pre7→E11)**
  Misunderstanding of GM risks **(Pre7→E19)**
  Misunderstanding of GM risks **(Pre7→E22)**
  Misunderstanding of GM risks **(Pre7→E7)**
  Mixed messaging about GM safety **(Pre2→E2)**
  Perceived existence of GM risks **(Pre1R→E11)**
  Perceived existence of GM risks **(Pre1R→E8)**
  Unfavorable depiction of GM technology **(Pre4→E21)**
  Unfavorable depiction of GM technology **(Pre4→E3)**

RQ1. What were the factors contributing to public concerns about GM research and foods in the UK? (**GM concerns factors**)

	PA	Existence of GM side effects (**Pre1→E1**)
1. Belief in GM product side effects	**PA**	Mixed messaging about GM safety (**Pre2→E2**)
2. Conflicting views about GM safety	**PA**	Unfavorable depiction of GM technology (**Pre4→E3**)
3. Criticism from interest groups	**PA**	Limited knowledge about GM research (**Pre6→E4**)
4. Disinterested in learning about GM	**PA**	GM risks uncertainties (**Pre8→E5**)
5. Extensively unexamined GM side effects	**PA**	GM scientists' ineffective communication (**Pre3→E6**)
6. GM scientists' ineffective communication	**PA**	Misunderstanding of GM risks (**Pre7→E7**)
7. GM's proximity to foodborne illnesses	**PA**	Perceived existence of GM risks (**Pre1R→E8**)
8. Hesitant to embrace GM technology	**PA**	Lack of effective communication (**Pre3R→E9**)
9. Hesitant to explain GM research	**PA**	Lack of effective communication (**Pre3R→10**)
10. Inadequate promotion of GM benefits	**PA**	Perceived existence of GM risks (**Pre1R→E11**)
11. Irrational 'response to risks'	**PA**	Misunderstanding of GM risks (**Pre7→E11**)
12. Lack of effective government communication	**PA**	Lack of effective communication (**Pre3R→E12**)
13. Limited knowledge about GM research	**PA**	Limited knowledge about GM research (**Pre6→E13**)
14. Mistrust of commercial companies'	**PA**	Mistrust towards GM stakeholders (**Pre5→E14**)
15. Mistrust of scientists	**PA**	Mistrust towards GM stakeholders (**Pre5→E15**)
16. Mistrust of the government	**PA**	Mistrust towards GM stakeholders (**Pre5→E16**)
17. Multiple meanings of GM concepts	**PA**	Lack of effective communication (**Pre3R→E17**)
18. Objective-driven nature of scientific research	**PA**	GM risks uncertainties (**Pre8→E18**)
19. Outbreak of foodborne illnesses	**PA**	Misunderstanding of GM risks (**Pre7→E19**)
20. Uncertain about GM research	**PA**	GM risks uncertainties (**Pre8→E20**)
21. Unfavorable depiction of GM technology	**PA**	Unfavorable depiction of GM technology (**Pre4→E21**)
22. Unsatisfactory answer to GM risks	**PA**	Misunderstanding of GM risks (**Pre7→E22**)

Exhibit 8.2. Analytical memo showing claims and their respective evidence

STEP 8.4. GROUPING AND COMPARING CLAIMS TO DETERMINE THEMES AND SUB-THEMES (SEE EXHIBITS 8.4–8.5)

1. Group the claims and state their respective evidence (see Exhibit 8.4)
2. Compare the relationship among claims to determine themes and sub-themes (see Exhibit 8.5)

Commentary 8.2. I was able to transform 22 codes under the anchor code '**GM concerns factors (RQ1)**' into eight supported claims. I further examined the claims – looking at the relationship among them to determine the themes and sub-themes. At this stage, it is important to always document your thought process

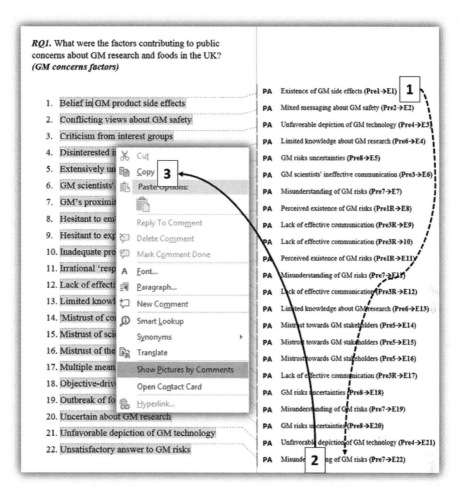

Exhibit 8.3. Analytical memo showing how claims (presumption-focused codes) are copied

since it will be helpful when connecting themes and sub-themes to describe or explain a phenomenon.

Individual-based sorting strategy

Sorting is the process of grouping codes in a way that would help address a research question or meet the purpose of a study. Applying a sorting strategy involves examining what the codes represent, comparing them to each other and categorizing them based on shared similarities. There are two main ways of using the sorting strategy: it could be used individually or in a group setting. With the individual use, after assessing the features of each code, you put them into clusters and with the research question(s) in mind, you label each cluster based on the characteristics of the codes within it (see Figure 8.1).

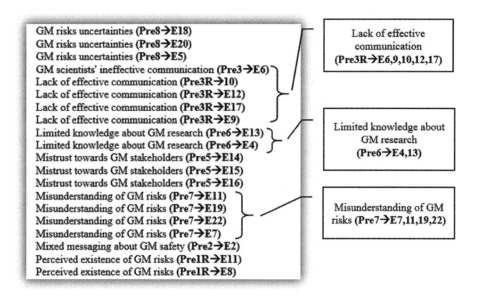

Exhibit 8.4. Analytical memo showing how claims (presumption-focused codes) are grouped

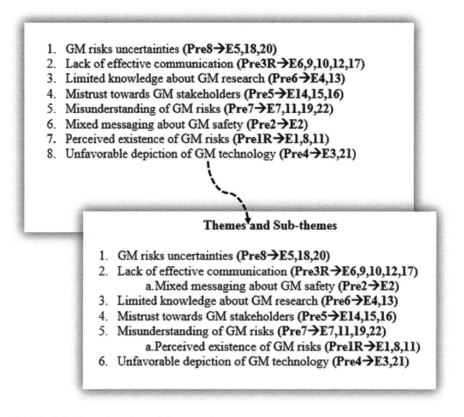

Exhibit 8.5. Transforming claims to themes

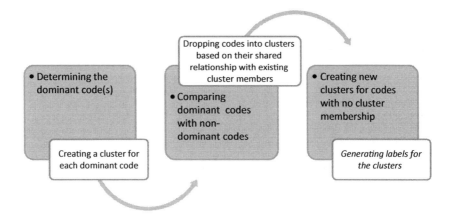

Figure 8.1. The process of clustering codes using the individual-based sorting strategy

Demonstration 8.2

In this demonstration, I use the individual-based sorting strategy to develop themes for the third research question: *'How should GM crop research be communicated to the public to address their concerns?'*

STEP 8.1. DETERMINING THE DOMINANT CODE(S)
(SEE EXHIBIT 8.6)

1. Transfer the list of codes with their frequency and number of cases under the research question to the analytical memo
2. Select the dominant code (which is the code with the highest frequency and cases)

STEP 8.2. PUTTING THE DOMINANT CODE(S) INTO INDIVIDUAL CLUSTERS (SEE EXHIBIT 8.7)

1. Create a cluster table – labeling the columns as clusters and numbering them
2. Transfer the dominant code to the cluster 1 column and indicate the number of counts in parentheses

STEP 8.3. COMPARING THE REMAINING CODES TO THE DOMINANT CODE(S)

1. Review the characteristics of each code by looking at their descriptions and some of the empirical indicators connected to them

Analytical Memo

RQ3. How should GM crop research be communicated to the public to address their concerns? *(GM communication strategies)*

Code	Counts/ Frequency	Number of Cases
Assessing public GM knowledge level	*4*	*4*
Being proactive in GM information-sharing	2	1
Being transparent in GM research	2	1
Collaborating with other departments	1	1
Communicating GM innovation benefits	2	2
Creating awareness of GM risks	1	1
Creating press releases	1	1
Debating with pressure groups	1	1
Discussing specific GM case	3	3
Educating the public about GM	3	2
Emphasizing crossbreeding/GM similarities	2	2
Emphasizing GM's positive side	2	1
Giving the public some time	3	3
Having conversations about GM risks	2	2
Having public debate about GM	1	1
Listening to the public concerns	1	1
Making GM research publicly available	1	1
Making in-depth GM presentations	4	3
Organizing seminars for the public	1	1
Presenting GM research rationale	2	2
Presenting GM risks and benefits	3	1
Simplifying GM research information	2	2
Tailoring GM information	2	1

Dominant code

Exhibit 8.6. Displaying the dominant code under 'GM communication strategies (RQ3)'

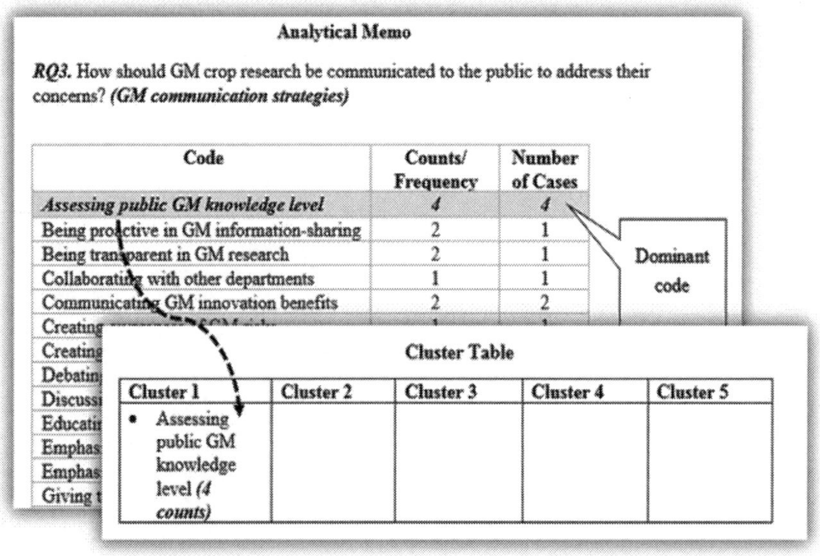

Exhibit 8.7. Displaying the transfer of the dominant code to the 'Cluster 1' column

2. Compare them to the dominant code to determine their shared relationships
3. Drop the codes into the cluster with the dominant code, if they have things in common

STEP 8.4. CREATING NEW CLUSTERS FOR CODES WITH NO CLUSTER MEMBERSHIP (SEE TABLES 8.1–8.2)

1. Create a new cluster for any code that is not related to any member of the existing cluster(s)
2. After completing the initial clustering of codes, review the members within each cluster to make sure each code is in an appropriate cluster

STEP 8.5. GENERATING LABELS FOR THE CLUSTERS

1. With the research question in mind and considering the features of the codes under each cluster, create labels for the groupings (see Table 8.3)
2. For each label, state the total number of counts (code frequency) in parentheses
   Outcome of Action 2 under Step 8.5
   Cluster 1: Assessing public views about GM *(5 counts)*
   Cluster 2: Sharing GM risks and benefits *(14 counts)*
   Cluster 3: Giving the public some time *(3 counts)*
   Cluster 4: Making GM research publicly available *(3 counts)*
   Cluster 5: Proactively engaging with the public *(12 counts)*
   Cluster 6: Simplifying GM research information *(9 counts)*
3. Describe what the categories/themes represent in a similar way to how codes were defined

Commentary 8.3. Sometimes, determining the dominant code becomes challenging since there could be more than one top code. If you encounter this situation, you could put them in separate clusters (i.e. one cluster for each dominant code). In terms of the number of clusters to create in the cluster table, in the initial stage, you could construct cluster columns as needed. However, in order for you to extensively explore the relationships among codes, it would be useful for the total number of clusters to be less than half the total number of codes. One of the main differences between the presumption-focused coding strategy and the individual-based sorting strategy is that with the former, a code (as evidence) can be used to support more than one claim while with the latter, a code can only be in one cluster.

As you can see from Tables 8.1–8.2, there is flexibility in assigning codes to clusters. After completing the initial clustering of codes, I reviewed the codes under each cluster and reassigned cluster membership when necessary. Below are the thoughts behind creating cluster membership:

Cluster 1: I realized that adding *'Listening to the public concerns'* as a member of cluster 1 throws more light on what *'Assessing public GM knowledge level'* would involve as part of the GM communication strategies. To confirm a potential connection between the above codes, I reviewed some of the empirical indicators. One of the indicators that supports the supplementary relationship between the two codes is:

I think there are a lot of reasons why. people. have genuine concerns about it it's just a question of. being able to. hear those in a sensible way rather than. just being reactionary about it.

(NS2, lines 28–31)

Cluster 2: I dropped all the codes related to GM content (that need to be communicated to the public) into the second cluster. I saw that there was a complementary relationship among the cluster members. In other words, they need each other to be whole. For example, *'Being transparent in GM research'* could involve *'Presenting GM research rationale'* and *'Presenting GM risks and benefits'*. Also, *'Having conversations about GM risks'* may imply *'Being transparent in GM research'*. So, I perceived the members of this cluster as pieces of the GM communication strategy of openly *'Sharing GM risks and benefits'* (see Table 8.3).

Cluster 3: This has one standalone member which better addresses the research question by not linking it with other codes. It supports the assertion that communication is not only about listening and exchanging ideas but giving each party time to digest what was received.

Cluster 4: I was thinking that the code, *'Creating press releases'* is supplementing what *'Making GM research publicly available'* may comprise. I also thought that the above codes are preceded by GM scientists *'Collaborating with other departments'* in their institution.

Cluster 5: Initially, I created this cluster to store all specific GM information-sharing activities. However, as I assigned more codes to the cluster, I became aware of the shared relationship among the codes – implying the need to actively engage with the public in understanding GM research. Ultimately, the last cluster

Table 8.1 Initial version of the cluster table

Cluster 1	Cluster 2	Cluster 3	Cluster 4	Cluster 5	Cluster 6
• Assessing public GM knowledge level **(4 counts)** • Listening to the public concerns **(1 count)**	• Being transparent i n GM research **(2 counts)** • Creating awareness of GM risks **(1 count)** • Communicating GM innovation benefits **(2 counts)** • Emphasizing GM's positive side **(2 counts)** • Having conversations about GM risks **(2 counts)** • Presenting GM research rationale **(2 counts)** • Presenting GM risks and benefits **(3 counts)**	• Giving the public some time **(3 counts)**	• Creating press releases **(1 count)** • Making GM research publicly available **(1 count)** • Being proactive in GM information-sharing **(2 counts)** • Collaborating with other departments **(1 count)**	• Debating with pressure groups **(1 count)** • Discussing specific GM case **(3 counts)** • Educating the public about GM **(3 counts)** • Having public debate about GM **(1 count)** • Making in-depth GM presentations **(4 counts)** • Organizing seminars for the public **(1 count)**	• Simplifying GM research information **(2 counts)** • Tailoring GM information **(2 counts)** • Emphasizing crossbreeding/GM similarities **(2 counts)**

Table 8.2 Revised version of the cluster table

Cluster 1	Cluster 2	Cluster 3	Cluster 4	Cluster 5	Cluster 6
• Assessing public GM knowledge level (*4 counts*) • Listening to the public concerns (*1 count*)	• Being transparent in GM research (*2 counts*) • Creating awareness of GM risks (*1 count*) • Communicating GM innovation benefits (*2 counts*) • Emphasizing GM's positive side (*2 counts*) • Having conversations about GM risks (*2 counts*) • Presenting GM research rationale (*2 counts*) • Presenting GM risks and benefits (*3 counts*)	• Giving the public some time (*3 counts*)	• Creating press releases (*1 count*) • Making GM research publicly available (*1 count*) • Collaborating with other departments (*1 count*)	• Debating with pressure groups (*1 count*) • Discussing specific GM case (*3 counts*) • Having public debate about GM (*1 count*) • Making in-depth GM presentations (*4 counts*) • Organizing seminars for the public (*1 count*) • Being proactive in GM information-sharing (*2 counts*)	• Simplifying GM research information (*2 counts*) • Tailoring GM information (*2 counts*) • Emphasizing crossbreeding/GM similarities (*2 counts*) • Educating the public about GM (*3 counts*)

Table 8.3 Final version of the cluster table with cluster labels

Cluster 1 (Assessing public views about GM)	Cluster 2 (Sharing GM risks and benefits)	Cluster 3 (Giving the public some time)	Cluster 4 (Making GM research publicly available)	Cluster 5 (Proactively engaging with the public)	Cluster 6 (Simplifying GM research information)
• Assessing public GM knowledge level *(4 counts)* • Listening to the public concerns *(1 count)*	• Being transparent in GM research *(2 counts)* • Creating awareness of GM risks *(1 count)* • Communicating GM innovation benefits *(2 counts)* • Emphasizing GM's positive side *(2 counts)* • Having conversations about GM risks *(2 counts)* • Presenting GM research rationale *(2 counts)* • Presenting GM risks and benefits *(3 counts)*	• Giving the public some time *(3 counts)*	• Creating press releases *(1 count)* • Making GM research publicly available *(1 count)* • Collaborating with other departments *(1 count)*	• Debating with pressure groups *(1 count)* • Discussing specific GM case *(3 counts)* • Having public debate about GM *(1 count)* • Making in-depth GM presentations *(4 counts)* • Organizing seminars for the public *(1 count)* • Being proactive in GM information-sharing *(2 counts)*	• Simplifying GM research information *(2 counts)* • Tailoring GM information *(2 counts)* • Emphasizing crossbreeding/ GM similarities *(2 counts)* • Educating the public about GM *(3 counts)*

member, *'Being proactive in GM information-sharing'*, sums up the connection between the codes.

Cluster 6: This cluster contains codes that tell me what *'Educating the public about GM'* means. Based on the empirical indicators coded, it is about: *'Simplifying GM research information'*, *'Tailoring GM information'*, and *'Emphasizing crossbreeding/GM similarities'*.

With respect to labeling clusters, you can use the name of a cluster member as a cluster label as I did for cluster 6. When composing labels for the clusters, I made sure they represented the features of the cluster members and at the same time address the research question. At the end of the sorting process, I had developed six clusters which could be called categories. Since I don't plan to further categorize these clusters, I can call them themes. It is possible to develop sub-categories or sub-themes under a cluster or group of clusters. You can create sub-categories/sub-themes out of a further categorization of codes under a cluster. Another option is to examine the clusters created to see whether any of them could be brought under one of the clusters. An optional step is to document the meaning of the clusters and what they represent. This would be helpful when you move to the stage where you want to determine the connections among them.

Group-based sorting strategy

The group-based sorting strategy entails involving a group of people to assist in categorizing the codes generated. The group could be project stakeholders, research participants, experts in a field or co-analysts of your qualitative data. This strategy is adopted from the concept mapping approach, which involves engaging "…participants to generate, sort and rate statements, conducting statistical analyses such as Multidimensional Scaling and Hierarchical Cluster Analysis, and developing a visual representation that reflects the sorted and rated statements" (Adu, 2015, slide 4).

> The creation of concept mapping was influenced by the constructivist perspective of learning (Bedi & Alexander, 2009). The constructivist is of the view that our knowledge about the world or our interpretation of the things around us is shaped by our culture, past experience and prior knowledge (Plotnick, 1997). This means that we may have diverse interpretations of the same situation: concept mapping is used to integrate these diverse meanings into a meaningful visual representation.
>
> (Adu, 2011, pp. 34–35)

According to Kane and Trochim (2007), to sort the sorting statements (which are based on the codes generated), you need at least ten participants. The sorting process starts with transforming the codes created into research question-informed statements, determining where the sorting activity will take place, and recruiting participants who qualify to sort the statements (Adu, 2011; Johnsen, Biegel, & Shafran, 2000; Kane & Trochim, 2007). It ends with having a cluster map on a Scatter Plot – displaying clusters and their respective members (Kane & Trochim, 2007). In essence, you are systematically utilizing quantitative and qualitative techniques to develop clusters of codes which best represent how participants sorted the data.

Demonstration 8.3

Imagine working with ten qualitative analysts to develop themes based on the 22 codes under research question 1 *(what were the factors contributing to public concerns about GM research and foods in the UK?)*. How would you involve them to create clusters? The following are the 22 codes that will be used for this demonstration:

1. Belief in GM product side effects
2. Conflicting views about GM safety
3. Criticism from interest groups
4. Disinterested in learning about GM
5. Extensively unexamined GM side effects
6. GM scientists' ineffective communication
7. GM's proximity to foodborne illnesses
8. Hesitant to embrace GM technology
9. Hesitant to explain GM research
10. Inadequate promotion of GM benefits
11. Irrational 'response to risks'
12. Lack of effective government communication
13. Limited knowledge about GM research
14. 'Mistrust of commercial companies'
15. Mistrust of scientists
16. Mistrust of the government
17. Multiple meanings of GM concepts
18. Objective-driven nature of scientific research
19. Outbreak of foodborne illnesses
20. Uncertain about GM research
21. Unfavorable depiction of GM technology
22. Unsatisfactory answer to GM risks

STEP 8.1. TRANSFORMING CODES INTO STATEMENTS

1. Develop a focus prompt for the research question
    *   A focus prompt, in this context, is a constructed phrase (based on the research question) that is used to introduce the codes (Adu, 2015; Kane & Trochim, 2007). In this case, the focus prompt would be: *'One of the factors contributing to public concerns about GM research and foods in the UK was…'*
2. Use the focus prompt to develop a sorting statement for each of the 22 codes
    *   Examples of sorting statements are:
        i.   *One of the factors contributing to public concerns about GM research and foods in the UK was* **'Belief in GM product side effects'**
        ii. *One of the factors contributing to public concerns about GM research and foods in the UK was* **'Conflicting views about GM safety'**
        iii. *One of the factors contributing to public concerns about GM research and foods in the UK was* **'Criticism from interest groups'**
    *   To make sure all the ten analysts know what the codes represent, you should provide them with the **'codebook'** for review before the sorting activity.
3. Provide a tag for each of the statements
    *   The first statement would be 's1' and the last statement would 's22' since you have 22 statements/codes.

STEP 8.2. SETTING UP A LOCATION OR AN ONLINE PLATFORM IN WHICH THE SORTING OF THE STATEMENTS WILL TAKE PLACE

1. Determine where the sorting activity will take place
    *   If it is a physical location, you could write each statement/code on an index card – ready to be given to each analyst for sorting purposes.
    *   If you plan to do it online, you could set up the statement for sorting on an online survey platform (see Adu, 2011, 2015). Alternatively, you could use a concept mapping software for this activity (see Concept Systems, 2018; Kane & Trochim, 2007).

STEP 8.3. FACILITATING THE SORTING ACTIVITY

1. As a facilitator of the sorting activity, review the sorting statements with the analysts and address any questions they may have
2. Instruct them to sort the statements (considering the yet-to-be-addressed research questions)

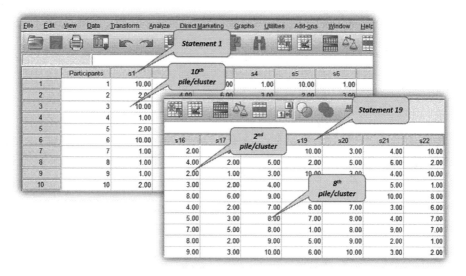

Exhibit 8.8. SPSS data of participants' responses to sorting statements

- One rule is that every statement can be sorted into one cluster (Kane & Trochim, 2007).
- Asking them to group the statements into clusters which are not more than half of the total statements would be great.

STEP 8.4. COMPILING THE SORTING (SORTED) DATA AND TRANSFERRING THEM TO STATISTICAL PACKAGE FOR THE SOCIAL SCIENCES (SPSS) SOFTWARE (VERSION 23.0; IBM CORP, 2015) (SEE EXHIBIT 8.8)

1. Bring together the sorting data
2. Transfer the data to SPSS for analyses
   - SPSS is a statistical analysis tool used to conduct descriptive and inferential statistical tests.
   - As shown in Exhibit 8.8, 'Participant 3' put the first sorting statement (s1) into the 10th pile/cluster and the 16th statement (s16) into the 2nd pile.
   Note that the data in SPSS were not from real participants. They were created for the purpose of demonstrating how to conduct 'Multidimensional Scaling' and 'Hierarchical Cluster Analysis'.

STEP 8.5. RUNNING MULTIDIMENSIONAL SCALING TO CREATE XY COORDINATES FOR EACH STATEMENT (SEE EXHIBITS 8.9–8.11)

1. To run Multidimensional Scaling, click on the **'Analyze'** tab on the SPSS toolbar
2. In the dropdown menu, go to **'Scale'**

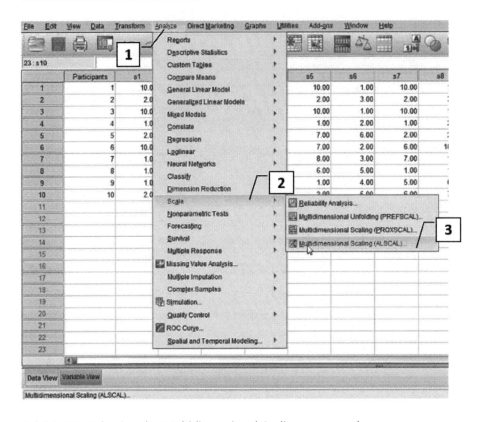

Exhibit 8.9. Selecting the Multidimensional Scaling command

3. Click on *'Multidimensional Scaling (ALSCAL)'*
4. In the *'Multidimensional Scaling'* dialog box, move all the sorting statements (i.e. s1–s22) to the box under *'Variables'*
5. In the dialog box, check *'Create distances from data'*
6. Click on *'Measure'* to make sure *'Euclidean distance'* is selected
7. Click on *'OK'* to run the analysis and create XY coordinates for the sorting statements
   • Transforming the sorting data into two-dimensional coordinates helps in determining the distance among sorting statements (see Exhibit 8.11). The closer the distance among statements, the more likely they are to be put in one cluster.

Commentary 8.4. Exhibit 8.11 shows XY coordinates representing the sorted data. You may ask, how best do the two-dimensional coordinates reflect the data? Stress index and R square values are used to determine the degree of connection between the coordinates generated and the sorting data collected (Adu, 2011). The stress test is used to assess the degree to which the two-dimensional coordinates generated best represent the sorted

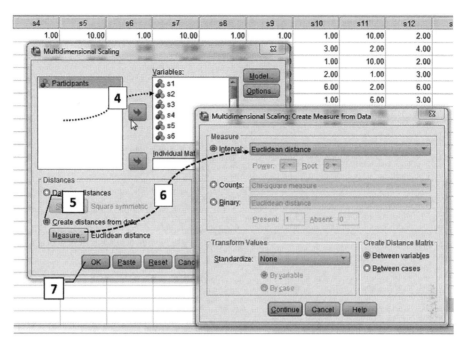

Exhibit 8.10. Selecting sorting statements for the analysis

data (Kane & Trochim, 2007). As shown in Exhibit 8.11, the stress value was .15, which is within the range of a good stress index. According to Kane and Trochim (2007), the stress values of most of the concept mapping projects "range between about 0.205 and 0.365" (p. 98). The lower the stress value the better the XY indices represent the data (Dipeolu et al., 2016; Salvador-Piedrafita et al., 2017). Similarly, the R square value (.89) was very good – showing that the two-dimensional solution explains 89% of the variability of the sorting data. All of these indicators support the assertion that the XY coordinates accurately reflect the sorted data – paving the way to the running of the Hierarchical Cluster Analysis (see Figure 8.2).

STEP 8.6. TRANSFERRING THE XY COORDINATES FROM THE SPSS OUTPUT PAGE TO THE SPSS 'DATA VIEW' (SEE EXHIBITS 8.12–8.15)

1. Copy the two-dimensional table (with XY coordinates) from the SPSS output and paste it into a Word document
2. In the document, select the table and click on the *'Insert'* tab
3. Click on the *'Table'* ribbon
4. In the dropdown menu, click on *'Convert Text to Table'*
5. In the *'Convert Text to Table'* dialog box, click on *'OK'*

```
                     For  matrix
      Stress  =   .15210       RSQ =  .88855



              Configuration derived in 2 dimensions



                      Stimulus Coordinates

                          Dimension

    Stimulus   Stimulus      1          2
    Number       Name


       1         s1        2.1834      .8489
       2         s2        -.3709     1.1740
       3         s3         .1986      .1986
       4         s4        -.5899      .3158
       5         s5        1.7059     -.7386
       6         s6        -.9138      .2897
       7         s7        1.6532     -.1607
       8         s8        -.6872     1.4423
       9         s9       -1.2305      .3370
      10         s10       -.8099      .9012
      11         s11       1.9571      .4516
      12         s12       -.6084      .1466
      13         s13       -.1545      .4942
      14         s14       -.6811    -1.2465
      15         s15      -1.3560     -.1758
      16         s16      -1.1800     -.3096
      17         s17        .5223      .5092
      18         s18      -1.1826    -1.2315
      19         s19       1.6389     -.1302
      20         s20      -1.1750    -1.2332
      21         s21       -.5098     -.9958
      22         s22       1.5900     -.8872
```

Exhibit 8.11. SPSS output showing stress, R square value and XY coordinates

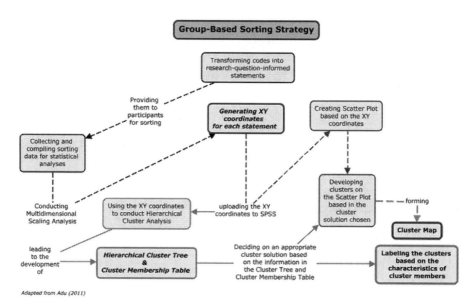

Figure 8.2. The process of clustering codes using the group-based sorting strategy

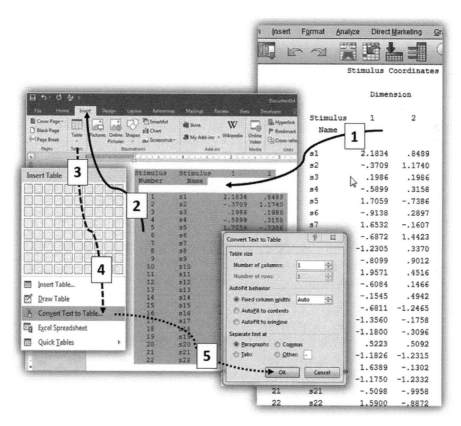

Exhibit 8.12. Preparing the two-dimensional table for Hierarchical Cluster Analysis

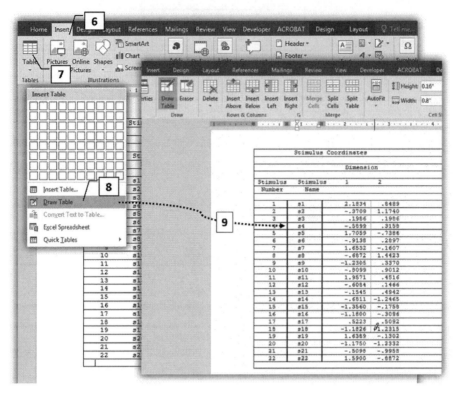

Exhibit 8.13. Drawing lines in-between the columns of the table with XY coordinates

6. Click on the **'Insert'** tab
7. Click on the **'Table'** ribbon
8. In the dropdown menu, click on **'Draw Table'**
9. Draw lines in-between the columns, starting from the row with the first statement (*s1*)
10. Copy the second to third columns
11. Open a new SPSS window and in the **'Data View'**, paste the table
12. Click on the **'Variable View'** tab
13. Under the **'Name'** column, name the data (such as '*Statement*', '*Dimension1*' and '*Dimension2*')

STEP 8.7. RUNNING HIERARCHICAL CLUSTER ANALYSIS TO DETERMINE THE NUMBER OF CLUSTERS AND CLUSTER MEMBERS (SEE EXHIBITS 8.16–8.19)

1. To run Hierarchical Cluster Analysis, click on the **'Analyze'** tab on the SPSS toolbar
2. In the dropdown menu, go to **'Classify'** and click on **'Hierarchical Cluster'**

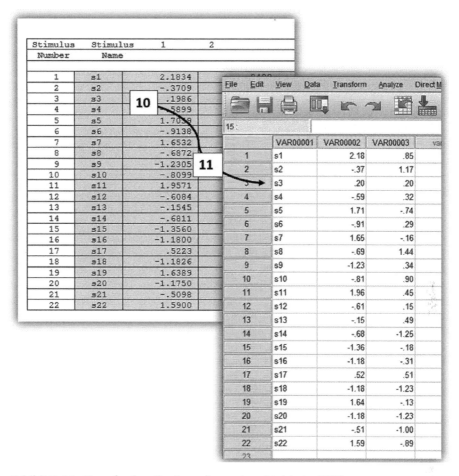

Exhibit 8.14. Transferring the two-dimensional table to SPSS

3. In the **'Hierarchical Cluster Analysis'** dialog box, move **'Dimension1'** and **'Dimension2'** to the box under **'Variables'**
4. Click on **'Statistics'** to open the **'Hierarchical Cluster Analysis: Statistics'** dialog box
5. In the dialog box, check **'Range of solutions'** and state '2' as the **'Minimum number of clusters'** and '10' as the **'Maximum number of clusters'**
   - I indicated the minimum clusters as '2' because it is the smallest number of clusters I expect participants to create. Also, I stated '10' as the maximum cluster because participants were informed to create no more than ten clusters.
6. Click on **'Continue'** to close the dialog box
7. In the **'Hierarchical Cluster Analysis'** dialog box, click on **'Plots'** to open the **'Hierarchical Cluster Analysis: Plots'** dialog box and check **'Dendrogram'**

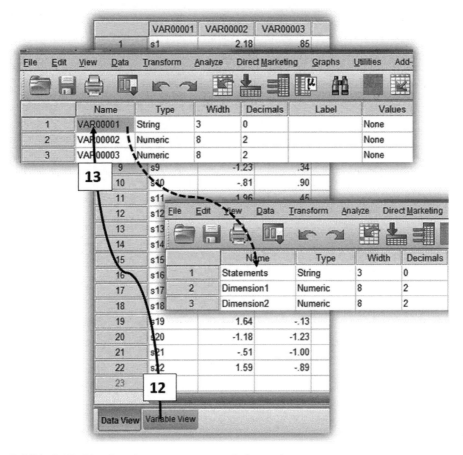

Exhibit 8.15. Naming the statements and dimensions

- Dendrogram is also called Cluster Tree (Adu, 2011; Kane & Trochim, 2007).
8. In the dialog box, check *'None'* under *'Icicle'*
9. Click on *'Continue'* to close the dialog box
10. In the *'Hierarchical Cluster Analysis'* dialog box, click on *'Method'* to open the *'Hierarchical Cluster Analysis: Method'* dialog box and select *'Ward's method'* as the *'Cluster Method'*
11. Click on *'Continue'* to close the dialog box
12. Click on *'OK'* in the *'Hierarchical Cluster Analysis'* dialog box to run the analysis
    - The SPSS output will display:
      Cluster Membership Table: This shows the sorting statement cluster membership across the cluster solutions suggested in the columns (see Table 8.4)
      Dendrogram/Cluster Tree: This visualizes the potential numbers of clusters and their respective cluster members (see Exhibit 8.19)

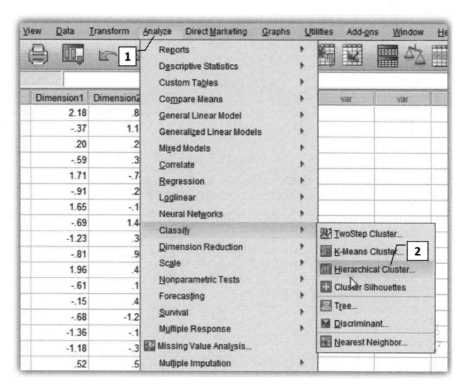

Exhibit 8.16. Selecting the Hierarchical Cluster Analysis command

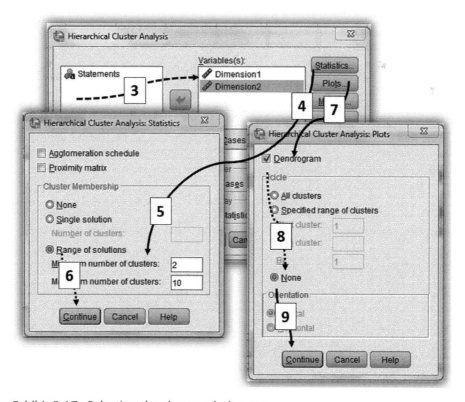

Exhibit 8.17. Selecting the cluster solution range

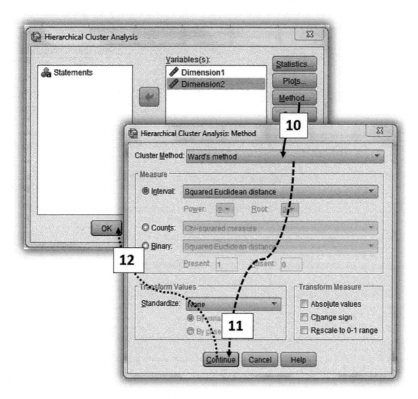

Exhibit 8.18. Selecting Ward's cluster method

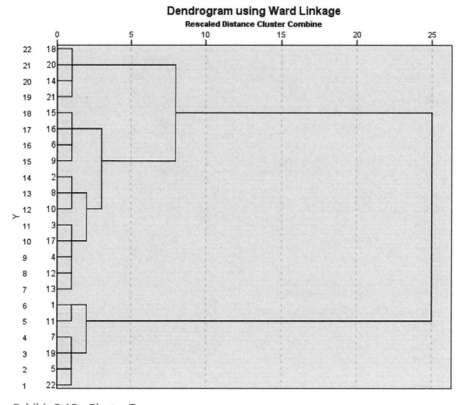

Exhibit 8.19. Cluster Tree

Table 8.4 Cluster membership table

Statement	10 clusters	9 clusters	8 clusters	7 clusters	6 clusters	5 clusters	4 clusters	3 clusters	2 clusters
s1	1	1	1	1	1	1	1	1	1
s2	2	2	2	2	2	2	2	2	2
s3	3	3	3	3	3	2	2	2	2
s4	4	4	4	4	3	2	2	2	2
s5	5	5	5	5	4	3	1	1	1
s6	6	6	6	6	5	4	3	2	2
s7	7	7	7	5	4	3	1	1	1
s8	2	2	2	2	2	2	2	2	2
s9	6	6	6	6	5	4	3	2	2
s10	2	2	2	2	2	2	2	2	2
s11	1	1	1	1	1	1	1	1	1
s12	4	4	4	4	3	2	2	2	2
s13	4	4	4	4	3	2	2	2	2
s14	8	8	8	7	6	5	4	3	2
s15	9	6	6	6	5	4	3	2	2
s16	9	6	6	6	5	4	3	2	2
s17	3	3	3	3	3	2	2	2	2
s18	10	9	8	7	6	5	4	3	2
s19	7	7	7	5	4	3	1	1	1
s20	10	9	8	7	6	5	4	3	2
s21	8	8	8	7	6	5	4	3	2
s22	5	5	5	5	4	3	1	1	1

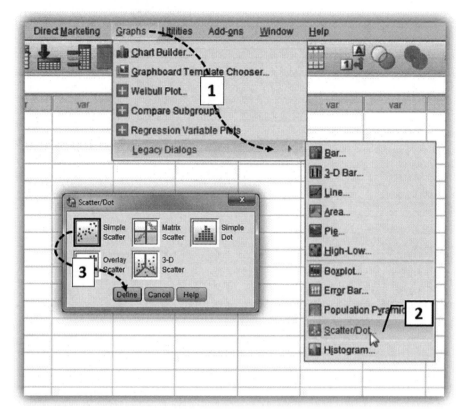

Exhibit 8.20. Selecting the 'Graphs' command to create a Scatter Plot

STEP 8.8. USING THE XY COORDINATES TO CREATE A SCATTER PLOT (SEE EXHIBITS 8.20–8.23)

1. On the toolbar, click on the **'Graphs'** tab and go to **'Legacy Dialogs'**
2. Click on the **'Scatter/Dot'** option to open the **'Scatter/Dot'** dialog box
3. In the dialog box, select **'Simple Scatter'** and click on **'Define'** to open the **'Simple Scatter'** dialog box
4. In the dialog box, move **'Dimension1'**, **'Dimension2'** and **'Statements'** to **'Y Axis'**, **'X Axis'** and **'Label Cases by'**, respectively
5. Click on **'OK'**
6. Go to the SPSS output and double-click on the Scatter Plot
7. On the Scatter Plot duplicate, right-click on one of the data points
8. Select **'Show Data Labels'** to display sorting statements connected to the data points
9. Close the Scatter Plot duplicate

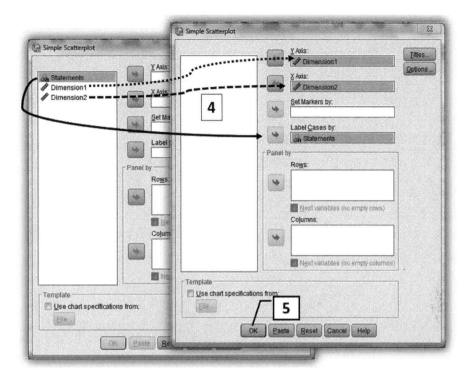

Exhibit 8.21. Path to creating a Scatter Plot

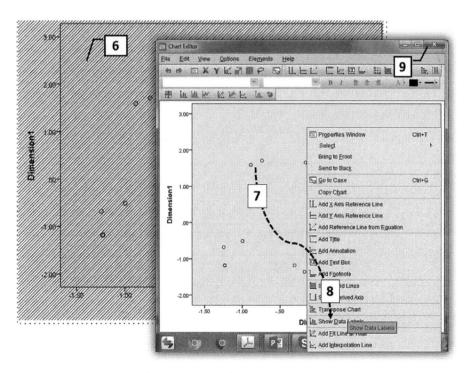

Exhibit 8.22. Labeling data points on the Scatter Plot

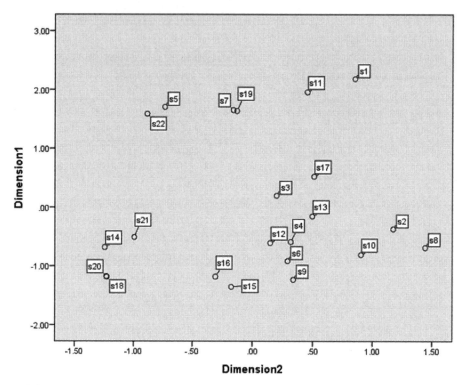

Exhibit 8.23. Scatter Plot with labeled data points

STEP 8.9. CREATING CLUSTERS ON THE SCATTER PLOT WITH THE HELP OF THE CLUSTER MEMBERSHIP TABLE AND CLUSTER TREE (SEE EXHIBITS 8.24–8.27)

1. Decide on the cluster solution by examining the Cluster Membership Table, Cluster Tree and Scatter Plot
   - All three SPSS outputs help to determine the cluster solution which best reflects the way participants grouped the statements. In deciding, you could first look at the Cluster Tree. As shown in Exhibit 8.24, you could choose from one of the three cluster solutions. Let's say you chose the six-cluster solution; the next step is to map the six clusters on the Scatter Plot. Here are the cluster members for the six-cluster solution:
     Cluster 1
     - 'Mistrust of commercial companies' (s14)
     - Objective-driven nature of scientific research (s18)
     - Uncertain about GM research (s20)
     - Unfavorable depiction of GM technology (s21)
     Cluster 2
     - GM scientists' ineffective communication (s6)
     - Hesitant to explain GM research (s9)

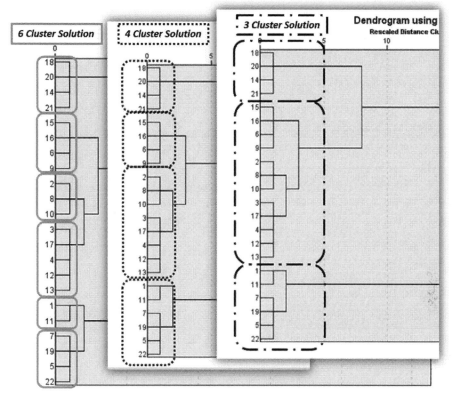

Exhibit 8.24. Cluster Tree with potential cluster solutions

- Mistrust of scientists (s15)
- Mistrust of the government (s16)

Cluster 3

- Conflicting views about GM safety (s2)
- Hesitant to embrace GM technology (s8)
- Inadequate promotion of GM benefits (s10)

Cluster 4

- Criticism from interest groups (s3)
- Disinterested in learning about GM (s4)
- Lack of effective government communication (s12)
- Limited knowledge about GM research (s13)
- Multiple meanings of GM concepts (s17)

Cluster 5

- Belief in GM product side effects (s1)
- Irrational 'response to risks' (s11)

Cluster 6

- Extensively unexamined GM side effects (s5)
- GM's proximity to foodborne illnesses (s7)
- Outbreak of foodborne illnesses (s19)

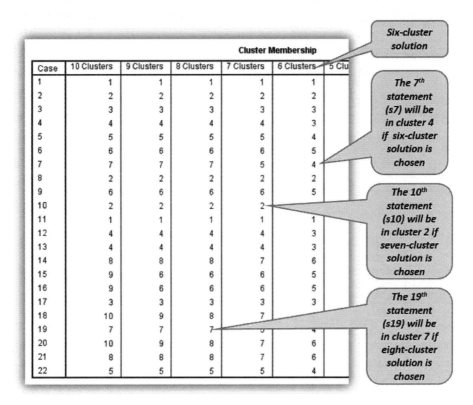

Case	10 Clusters	9 Clusters	8 Clusters	7 Clusters	6 Clusters	5 Clu...
1	1	1	1	1	1	
2	2	2	2	2	2	
3	3	3	3	3	3	
4	4	4	4	4	3	
5	5	5	5	5	4	
6	6	6	6	6	5	
7	7	7	7	5	4	
8	2	2	2	2	2	
9	6	6	6	6	5	
10	2	2	2	2		
11	1	1	1	1	1	
12	4	4	4	4	3	
13	4	4	4	4	3	
14	8	8	8	7	6	
15	9	6	6	6	5	
16	9	6	6	6	5	
17	3	3	3	3	3	
18	10	9	8	7		
19	7	7	7		4	
20	10	9	8	7	6	
21	8	8	8	7	6	
22	5	5	5	5	4	

Cluster Membership

Six-cluster solution

The 7th statement (s7) will be in cluster 4 if six-cluster solution is chosen

The 10th statement (s10) will be in cluster 2 if seven-cluster solution is chosen

The 19th statement (s19) will be in cluster 7 if eight-cluster solution is chosen

Exhibit 8.25. Interpreting the Cluster Membership table

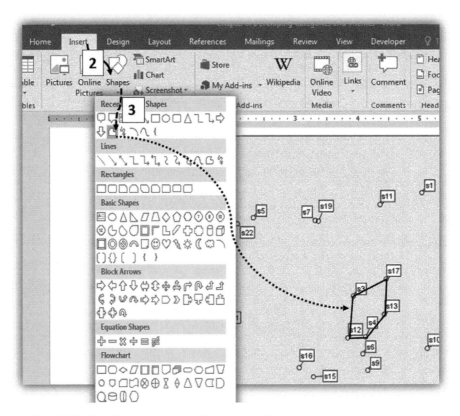

Exhibit 8.26. Creating clusters on the Scatter Plot

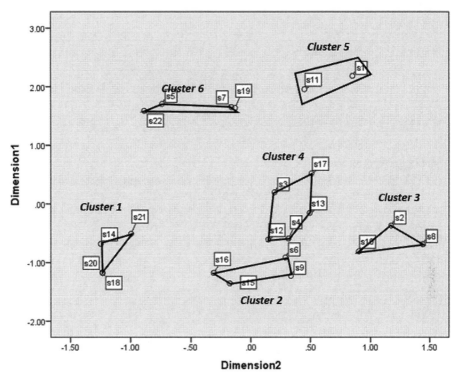

Exhibit 8.27. Cluster Map

- Unsatisfactory answer to GM risks (s22)
2. Based on the solution chosen, map the clusters on the Scatter Plot (which is pasted into a Word document) by going to the **'Insert'** tab and clicking on **'Shapes'** (see Exhibit 8.26)
3. Click on the **'Freeform'** option to start the mapping of the clusters on the Scatter Plot (see Exhibit 8.26)

STEP 8.10. LABELING EACH CLUSTER

1. Examine the characteristics of each statement (code) under each cluster
2. For each cluster, come up with a label that best represents the cluster members
   - An optional step that you could take is to involve some of the participants (if not all) in the cluster labeling process – by asking them to suggest potential labels for the clusters created.
3. Describe what the categories/themes (clusters) represent, in a similar way to how codes were defined

Commentary 8.5. I view incorporating a group-based coding strategy into the qualitative analysis process as adding a quantitative approach to your study. It involves qualitatively creating codes from interview data, transforming the codes into statements for participants to sort and quantitatively analyzing the sorting statements to generate potential cluster solutions (see Figure 8.2). This falls under a sequential mixed methods design (Hanson, Creswell, Plano Clark, Petska, & Creswell, 2005).

CONCLUSION

Qualitative analysis encompasses breaking down data, selecting and labeling significant segments of data, and grouping codes to form categories and themes (Dey, 1993). Two of the strategies you could use in grouping codes are the presumption-focused coding strategy and the sorting strategy. While presumption-focused coding is about making claims and using codes (which is viewed as evidence) to support them, the sorting strategy involves clustering codes that share common characteristics. For novice qualitative analysts, I suggest familiarizing yourself with the sorting strategy and using it before trying out the presumption-focused coding strategy. However, if you intend to develop a theory at the end of the qualitative analysis, then presumption-focused coding would be the better strategy. With the sorting strategy, you can cluster the codes yourself (using the individual-based sorting strategy) or involve at least ten people to conduct the categorization (using the group-based sorting strategy). The latter is time-consuming compared to the former since it entails transforming the codes into clear and succinct statements, purposely selecting participants, briefly training them about sorting and what each statement represents, collecting sorted statements, and conducting statistical analyses to help produce the suitable cluster solution. Irrespective of the strategy used, the categories or themes generated should address or be close to addressing the research question(s). In some cases, you could best address the research question by moving from categorizing the codes to connecting the categories (see Chapter 9).

REFERENCES

Adu, P. (2015). Using concept mapping as a research approach: Collecting, analyzing, and visualizing data [PowerPoint slides]. SlideShare. Retrieved from www.slideshare.net/kontorphilip/using-concept-mapping-as-a-research-approach-collecting-analyzing-and-visualizing-data

Adu, P. (2017). Using sorting strategy in qualitative analysis [PowerPoint slides]. SlideShare. Retrieved from www.slideshare.net/kontorphilip/using-sorting-strategy-in-qualitative-analysis

Adu, P. K. (2011). *Conceptualizing doctoral advising from professors' and doctoral students' perspectives using concept mapping.* (Order No. 3531922, West Virginia University). *ProQuest Dissertations and Theses*, 210. Retrieved from http://search.proquest.com/docview/1221263677?accountid=34120. (1221263677).

Charmaz, K. (2014). *Constructing grounded theory.* London, England: Sage.

Concept Systems. (2018). How it works. Retrieved May 22, 2018, from www.conceptsystems.com/gw/software

Creswell, J. W., & Poth, C. N. (2018). *Qualitative inquiry & research design: Choosing among five approaches.* Los Angeles, CA: Sage.

Dey, I. (1993). *Qualitative data analysis: A user-friendly guide for social scientists.* London, England: Routledge.

Dipeolu, A., Cook-Cottone, C., Lee, G. K., Donnelly, J. P., Janikowski, T. P., Reynolds, A. L., & Boling, T. (2016). A concept map of campers' perceptions of camp experience. *The Family Journal*, *24*(2), 182–189. doi:10.1177/1066480716628566

Guest, G., MacQueen, K. M., & Namey, E. E. (2012). *Applied thematic analysis.* Los Angeles, CA: Sage.

Hanson, W. E., Creswell, J. W., Plano Clark, V. L., Petska, K. S., & Creswell, D. J. (2005). Mixed methods research designs in counseling psychology. *Journal of Counseling Psychology*, *2*(55), 224–235. doi:10.1037/0022-0167.52.2.224

IBM Corp. (2015). *IBM SPSS Statistics for Windows.* Version 23.0 [Computer software] Armonk, NY.

Johnsen, J. A., Biegel, D. E., & Shafran, R. (2000). Concept mapping in mental health: Uses and adaptations. *Evaluation and Program Planning*, *23*(1), 67–75. doi:10.1016/s0149-7189(99)00038-5

Kane, M., & Trochim, W. M. K. (2007). *Concept mapping for planning and evaluation* (Applied Social Research Methods Series: Vol. 50; Series Eds.: L. Bickman & D. J. Rog). Thousand Oaks, CA: Sage.

Richards, L. (2015). *Handling qualitative data: A practical guide.* Los Angeles, CA: Sage.

Saldaña, J. (2016). *The coding manual for qualitative researchers.* Los Angeles, CA: Sage.

Salvador-Piedrafita, M., Malmusi, D., Mehdipanah, R., Rodríguez-Sanz, M., Espelt, A., Pérez, C., Solf, E., del Rincón, M. A., & Borrell, C. (2017). Evaluating the impact of structure policies on health inequalities – Care giving and quality of life: Views on the effects of the Spanish dependency law on caregivers' quality of life using concept mapping. *International Journal of Health Services*, *47*(2), 233–257. doi: 10.1177/0020731416685494

Smith, J. A., Flowers, P., & Larkin, M. (2012). *Interpretative phenomenological analysis: Theory, method and research.* London, England: Sage.

9

Connecting themes, and developing tables and diagrams

OBJECTIVES

Readers will be able to:

1. Examine the relationships among themes
2. Connect themes and confirm the connections
3. Develop tables and diagrams to represent findings

WHEN TO EXAMINE THE RELATIONSHIPS AMONG CATEGORIES/THEMES

In the previous chapters, I demonstrated that the qualitative coding process involves breaking apart data to fish for significant information called empirical indicators, and developing codes out of them (see Figure 9.1). The codes are then brought together to form categories and/or themes, which are further examined to determine the connections among them (Dey, 1993). You may ask, *after generating themes, is it important to determine the relationship among them?* It depends on whether you could address the research question(s) without looking into the connections among the themes. If each category/theme could be independently used to address the research question, then you don't have to go further to explore links among them. However, if a theme needs to be connected to other themes to adequately address the research question, then an examination of the associations is required. For instance, almost all of the themes, *'Assessing public views about GM'*, *'Sharing GM risks and benefits'*, *'Giving the public some time'*, *'Making GM research publicly available'*, *'Proactively engaging with the public'*, and *'Simplifying GM research information'* cannot independently and adequately address the research question: *How should GM crop research be communicated to the public to address their concerns?* I view each of them as an aspect of how GM crop research should be shared with the public; hence there is a need to assess how the themes are related to each other.

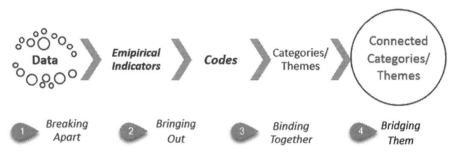

Figure 9.1. Simplifying the data analysis process

HOW RELATIONSHIPS AMONG CATEGORIES/THEMES ARE BUILT

As you methodically move from developing categories and themes to creating relationships, there is a temptation to allow your past knowledge and preconceived ideas to dictate which category/theme should be linked. To avert this pitfall, I suggest you continue to practice epoché whenever you are about to interact with the data and categories/themes (concepts) generated (see Chapter 5). In addition, any potential relationship among concepts discovered should be compared with the data for confirmation. Charmaz (2014) refers to this technique as "constant comparative methods" (p. 131) – which involves (in this case) comparing one category/theme with another in terms of their meaning, what they represent, and the empirical indicators and codes they are connected to (Freeman, 2017; Strauss, 1989). As Dey (1993) states, "this way of analysing dynamics infers connections from the regular association of categories in the data" (p. 178).

After establishing that there are connections among the concepts you are examining, the next step is to determine the kind of relationships that exist. In his book, *Qualitative Data Analysis: A User-Friendly Guide for Social Scientists*, Dey (1993) discusses in detail the different types of relationship that may be found among categories/themes (see pp. 177–200). Most of the relationship types he reviews are concurrent, chronological, overlapping, embedded, explanatory and causal relationships. Below are brief definitions of the relationship types (Dey, 1993):

- **Concurrent relationship:** Two concepts, events, behaviors or processes have a concurrent relationship if they exist, happen, change or impact at the same time.
- **Chronological relationship:** Two concepts, events, behaviors or processes have a chronological relationship if one concept precedes or follows the other.
- **Overlapping relationship:** Two concepts have an overlapping relationship if they have aspect(s) of their characteristics in common in

terms of explaining a phenomenon, influencing another concept(s), or representing a concept, process, behavior or an event.

- **Embedded relationship:** Two concepts have an embedded relationship if the entire characteristics of one concept are completely shared with a portion of another concept's features in terms of explaining a phenomenon, influencing another concept(s), or representing a process, behavior or an event.
- **Explanatory relationship:** Two concepts have an explanatory relationship if one concept plays the role of clarifying, elaborating or exemplifying another.
- **Causal relationship:** Two concepts have a causal relationship if the existence of or changes in a concept leads (or contributes) to the emergence or adjustment of another.

At this stage, constant documentation of your thought process in the analytical memo is highly recommended. In the memo, you are able to transform initially documented ideas of links among concepts – building and refining them as you continuously compare their characteristics. In effect, you create a narrative (description/statement) that reflects data-driven relationships of concepts and addresses the research question, explains a phenomenon, and describes a process, a behavior or an event.

Demonstration 9.1

To demonstrate how relationships among themes are built, I will be utilizing all the six themes developed under the third research question: *How should GM crop research be communicated to the public to address their concerns?* (see Table 9.1).

STEP 9.1. REVIEWING CHARACTERISTICS OF THE THEMES
INCLUDING THEIR DESCRIPTIONS, CODES, COUNTS (FREQUENCY)
AND EMPIRICAL INDICATORS

1. To easily explore the theme connections and patterns, create a table which contains the relevant characteristics of each theme (see Table 9.1)
2. Review one theme at a time and compare it with the rest of the themes
3. In the analytical memo, document the potential relationships that emerge
   Outcome of Action 3 under Step 9.1
   - *'Assessing public views about GM'* is followed by *'Simplifying GM research information'*
   - *'Assessing public views about GM'* could inform the GM scientists' decision of *'Giving the public some time'*

- *'Making GM research publicly available'* and *'Proactively engaging with the public'* could concurrently be done after *'Assessing public views about GM'*
- *'Sharing GM risks and benefits'* is part of *'Making GM research publicly available'* and *'Proactively engaging with the public'*
- *'Simplifying GM research information'* and *'Sharing GM risks and benefits'* have a shared idea of simplifying and balancing the GM information being communicated

STEP 9.2. COMPARING THE PROPOSED RELATIONSHIP WITH EMPIRICAL INDICATORS

1. Review the empirical indicators to assess how they reflect the proposed connection among the themes
2. Confirm or reject the proposed relationship based on the interpretation of the empirical indicators

   Outcome of Action 2 under Step 9.2
   - *'Assessing public views about GM'* is followed by *'Simplifying GM research information'* (Supported – see: S13, lines 58–64; NS1, lines 210–217 in Table 9.1)
   - *'Assessing public views about GM'* could inform GM scientists' decision of *'Giving the public some time'* (Not supported)
   - *'Making GM research publicly available'* and *'Proactively engaging with the public'* could concurrently be done after *'Assessing public views about GM'* (Supported – see: S13, lines 58–64; S13, lines 81–84; S6, lines 127–131 in Table 9.1)
   - *'Sharing GM risks and benefits'* is part of *'Making GM research publicly available'* and *'Proactively engaging with the public'* (Supported – see: NS5, lines 18–22; S13, lines 81–84; S6, lines 127–131 in Table 9.1)
   - *'Simplifying GM research information'* and *'Sharing GM risks and benefits'* have a shared idea of simplifying and balancing the GM information being communicated (Supported – see: NS1, lines 210–217; NS5, lines 18–22 in Table 9.1)

Commentary 9.1. When examining the potential relationship between *'Assessing public views about GM'* and *'Giving the public some time'*, I thought GM scientists may give the public time to familiarize themselves with GM innovations if the outcome of the assessment of public views suggests this. However, the empirical indicators I have don't support this assertion. As I indicated earlier, at this stage of determining connections, you may be tempted to allow your preconceived ideas to influence the process – trying to

Table 9.1 Themes under 'Communication strategies (RQ3)' and their descriptions, codes, frequencies and example empirical indicators

Theme	Description	Code	Frequency	Example empirical indicator
1. Assessing public views about GM	As part of the GM communication strategies, GM scientists need to assess the public knowledge and views about genetically modified crops and research. Assessing the public concerns about GM also involves taking time to listen to them.	• Assessing public GM knowledge level • Listening to the public concerns	5	"…in that sense we don't I mean because we want their views we're not. providing a lot of information. except for the very basic. you know. what they call biotechnology and. you know that genetic modification can be used to do. one of two things just just to. sort of introduce. the topic to them but. we don't want to give too much information because we want to see. how much they know and what kind of. attitudes they have…" (S13, lines 58–64)

| 2. **Sharing GM risks and benefits** | In terms of making GM research known to the public, GM scientists should be transparent – sharing not only the benefits of GM innovations but the rationale behind their studies and risks involved. | • Being transparent in GM research
• Creating awareness of GM risks
• Communicating GM innovation benefits
• Emphasizing GM's positive side
• Having conversations about GM risks
• Presenting GM research rationale
• Presenting GM risks and benefits | 14 | "I think if we look at most of the literature that's been. published . most of it is. on the disadvantages of of GM and there has been very little publicity on. on the benefits and there always needs to be a balanced argument. and the public need to know all the facts…." *(NS5, lines 18–22)* |
| 3. **Giving the public some time** | This theme is about giving the public time to digest the GM information presented to them, which is another communication strategy. Also, because the public is uncertain about the risks associated with GM foods, they need time to observe the implications that result from the GM innovation. | • Giving the public some time | 3 | "…I think after a while people would begin to accept them. and I think a lot of the initial fears and stuff have already died down." *(NS2, lines 96–97)* |

(continued)

Table 9.1 (Cont.)

Theme	Description	Code	Frequency	Example empirical indicator
4. Making GM research publicly available	Collaborating with an appropriate department in their institution, GM scientists could make information about GM research publicly available and easily consumable.	• Creating press releases • Making GM research publicly available • Collaborating with other departments	3	"...they should find a way of communicating this you know. as as they go along. doing their research the results they. they . they get. not only publish them in academic journals but ma-. make them probably a bit. you know. available to the wider public..." (S13, lines 81–84)
5. Proactively engaging with the public	GM scientists should actively engage the public, including in terest groups, in discussing, debating and having an honest conversation about specific issues related to GM innovations.	• Debating with pressure groups • Discussing specific GM case • Having public debate about GM • Making in-depth GM presentations • Organizing seminars for the public • Being proactive in GM information-sharing	12	"...there should be much more public debate and much more information. for public so that. when decisions are made. they may or not be. absolutely what people want but they can see why they're made. and I think the same's true with GM." (S6, lines 127–131)

| 6. Simplifying GM research information | As part of educating the public, GM scientists should present GM research information in a simplified form so that the public can understand it. | • Simplifying GM research information
• Tailoring GM information
• Emphasizing crossbreeding/ GM similarities
• Educating the public about GM | 9 | "...if we assume to begin with that an article in a scientific journal captures. 100% of what the scientist was doing wanted to say. that itself actually is not always the case. but if we make that assumption when that work gets translated into an article in my weekend newspaper. there will have been made. inevitably . simplifications . roundings up roundings down. fillings out all kinds. of things will have happened to the. pristine information to make it fit the. public format..." (NS1, lines 210–217) |

establish relationships where there aren't any, considering the data you have. If you want to further explore potential relationships that are not supported by the data, you could collect more data – using the grounded theory technique called theoretical sampling (see Charmaz, 2014).

STEP 9.3. DETERMINING THE TYPE OF RELATIONSHIP THAT EXISTS AMONG THE THEMES BEING REVIEWED

1. After confirming that a relationship exists among specific themes, the next step is to determine whether they have concurrent, chronological, overlapping, embedded, explanatory or causal relationships

   Outcome of Action 1 under Step 9.3
   - **'Assessing public views about GM'** is followed by **'Simplifying GM research information'** *(Chronological relationship)*
   - **'Making GM research publicly available'** and **'Proactively engaging with the public'** could concurrently be done after **'Assessing public views about GM'** *(Concurrent with chronological relationship)*
   - **'Sharing GM risks and benefits'** is part of **'Making GM research publicly available'** and **'Proactively engaging with the public'** *(Embedded relationship)*
   - **'Simplifying GM research information'** and **'Sharing GM risks and benefits'** have a shared idea of simplifying and balancing the GM information being communicated *(Overlapping relationship)*

STEP 9.4. WRITING STATEMENTS THAT DEPICT THE RELATIONSHIPS DISCOVERED

1. With the research question (or the phenomenon of study) in mind, write a statement or group of statements that portrays the relationships established

   Outcome of Action 1 under Step 9.4
   - *In terms of how GM scientists should communicate the GM crop research to the public, the first and most important step is to assess the public views about GM crops, research and innovations. The outcome of this assessment would help them to prepare simplified GM information tailored to address the public concerns about GM technology. As GM scientists make available the information, they should proactively engage with the public in discussion and debate. The information they*

share shouldn't only be simplified but balanced – creating an atmosphere of honest conversation about GM risks and benefits. Another unique communication strategy suggested was the need to give the public time to reflect on, experience and observe the implications of GM innovations. By so doing, the fears and misunderstanding about GM crops and research would subside.

Commentary 9.2. Constructing a good statement about an established relationship among themes takes time. I suggest you continue to refine the initial statement until it best fits the connections identified, and addresses the research question or explains a phenomenon of study. If you intend to develop a theory, you could further conduct a constant comparison and collect more data if necessary to help refine and confirm the proposed theory (see Adu, 2017; Charmaz, 2014).

USING TABLES AND DIAGRAMS

Since our origin as humans, signs and symbols have been an integral part of our daily lives – playing an integral role in constructing, discovering and sharing knowledge. We use visual representations to symbolize our thoughts, feelings, verbal and non-verbal communications, and things around us. In the context of analyzing qualitative data, tables and diagrams can play a huge role in exploring the links among themes before writing a statement to reflect the connections established. For instance, I use Table 9.1 (containing the main characteristics of the themes) when working on the potential relationships that exist among themes under research question 3.

Tables and diagrams are also used to enhance the presentation of the findings – helping to simplify the narration of results. Constructing tables and diagrams is also a way of bringing to light a creative way of communicating our findings (especially the connections among themes). Moreover, words may not be sufficient in expressing how themes are linked. Visualizing the results could complement what we want to convey to our audience. It is a way of condensing seemingly lengthy assertions about themes – making it easy for readers to make a quick review of the findings if needed.

Although visualizing findings has numerous benefits, if not properly done, it could cause miscommunication and confusion among our audience. Presenting tables and diagrams without any narrative to describe what they are could lead to misunderstanding, leaving the audience to interpret them in multiple ways. Visual representations should be less complicated in design, and easy to explain and understand.

Tables can be used to display participants' demographic information (see Tables 3.1, 3.2, 3.3 and 7.1). We can also use them to create a matrix showing shared relationship between cases (participants) and themes (Dey, 1993). Lastly, we can develop a table to show themes and their respective characteristics. Saldaña (2016) refers to this kind of table as a summary table (see Tables 9.1, 13.4). Besides these examples, you could create any table that you think would help to complement and promote a better understanding of the findings. Similarly, diagrams can be a powerful visual representation of how often specific words were used (i.e. word frequency) in participants' responses to interview questions (see Figure 9.3), and charts of categories/themes frequencies (see Figure 9.2) and illustrations of relationships among categories/themes (concepts) (see Exhibits 9.1– 9.6) can be used.

Dey (1993) extensively discusses how to create maps to adequately represent connections among categories/themes (concepts). In summary, aligning two concepts as shown in Exhibit 9.1 implies there is a concurrent relationship between concept A and B. You could design a similar map if more than two categories/themes occur at the same time. Also, if concepts A, B and C occur in a sequential manner, you could use chronological relationship related maps as shown in Exhibit 9.2. In demonstrating an overlapping relationship, you could create overlapping circles – depicting shared features among concepts with each circle representing a concept (see Exhibit 9.3). Further, there are a variety of ways you could show an embedded connection among concepts. For

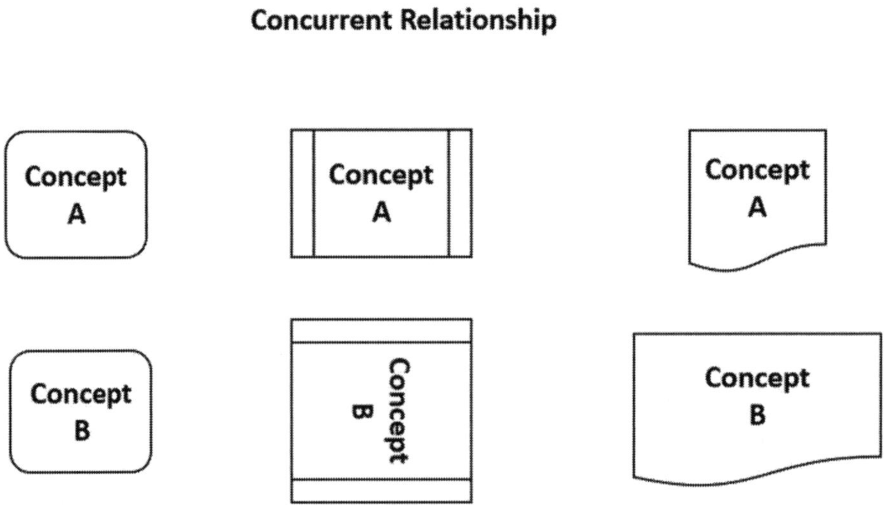

Concurrent Relationship

Exhibit 9.1. Diagram showing concurrent relationship between concepts

Chronological Relationship

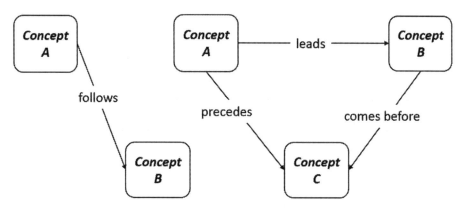

Exhibit 9.2. Diagram showing chronological relationship between concepts

Overlapping Relationship

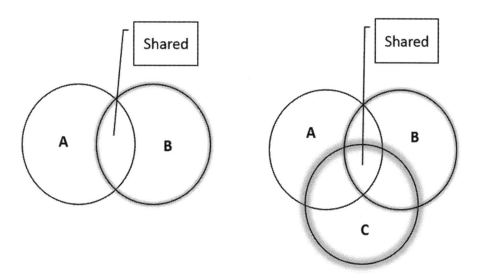

Exhibit 9.3. Diagram showing overlapping relationship between concepts

instance, when illustrating that concept B is nested in concept A, you could create one large circle to represent concept A and draw another circle (i.e. concept B) within concept A (see Exhibit 9.4). Another option is to create rectangles/squares or rounded rectangles/squares and use

Embedded Relationship

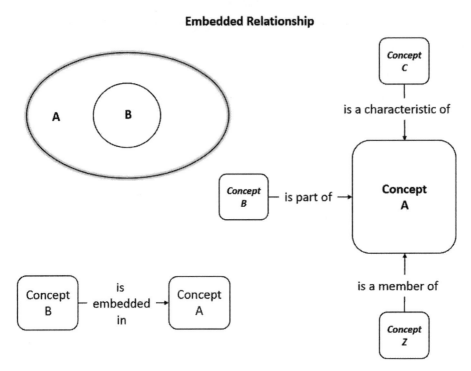

Exhibit 9.4. Diagram showing embedded relationship between concepts

Explanatory Relationship

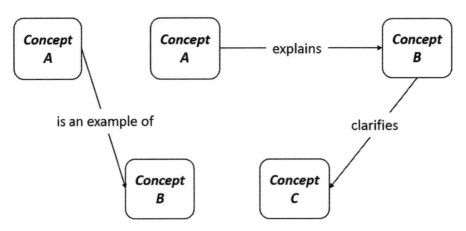

Exhibit 9.5. Diagram showing explanatory relationship between concepts

arrows with labels to portray the embedded relationships as shown in Exhibit 9.4. In the same way, rounded rectangles/squares and labeled arrows could be used to demonstrate explanatory and causal relationships among concepts (see Exhibits 9.5–9.6). To learn more, I recommend

Causal Relationship

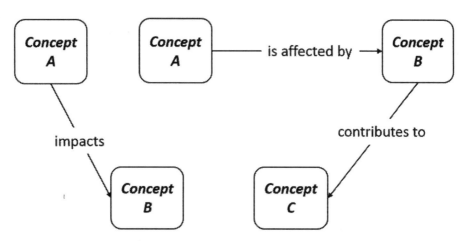

Exhibit 9.6. Diagram showing causal relationship between concepts

reviewing Day's (1993) book, *Qualitative Data Analysis: A User-Friendly Guide for Social Scientists* (see Chapter 13).

TOOLS FOR DESIGNING TABLES AND DIAGRAMS

There are a good number of tools available to create tables, maps and charts. Using the 2016 version of Microsoft Word, you could create tables, shapes, art and maps by going to the **'Insert'** tab and clicking on '**Table'**, **'Shapes'** and **'SmartArt'** and create charts by clicking on **'Chart'**. In addition, Microsoft Word could be utilized to create word clouds which display the kinds of words participants frequently use. This is done by going to the **'Developer'** tab and clicking on **'Add-ins'** and searching for **'Pro Word Cloud'** (Version 1.0.0.3; Orpheus Technology Ltd, 2014). Another software program capable of developing maps is **'CmapTools'** (Version 6.03; IHMC, 2018a). It is free software which is used to create connections among concepts, including codes and categories. It is also a helpful tool when engaging in brainstorming ideas and visualizing models and theories (IHMC, 2018b). Lastly, some qualitative data analysis software programs are capable of generating tables and diagrams (see Chapters 10–12).

Demonstration 9.2

In this demonstration, I use the **'Chart'** command under the **'Insert'** tab (in a Word document) to create a bar chart displaying the themes and their frequencies for research question 3. To review the six themes with their frequencies, see Table 9.1.

STEP 9.1. SETTING UP A TABLE FOR THE DEVELOPMENT OF THE CHART (SEE EXHIBIT 9.7)

1. In the Word document, click on the **'Insert'** tab
2. Click on the **'Chart'** ribbon
   - ✓ In the **'Insert Chart'** dialog box, make sure **'Column'** and **'Clustered Column'** are selected
3. In the **'Insert Chart'** dialog box, click on **'OK'**

STEP 9.2. ENTERING THE THEMES AND THEIR FREQUENCIES IN THE TABLE (SEE EXHIBITS 9.8–9.9; FIGURE 9.2)

1. In the **'Chart in Microsoft Word'** table, delete the last two columns by selecting the two columns and right-clicking on them
2. In the right-click menu, click on **'Delete'** and then **'Table Column'**
3. Since there are six themes, press and hold the intersection of the column line (*which is between the first and second column*) and

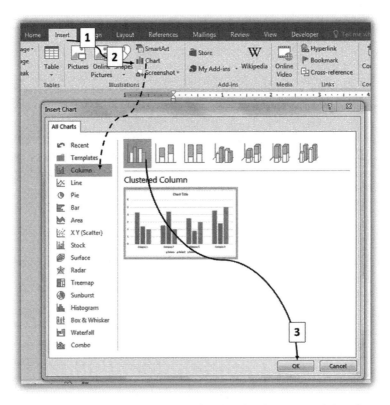

Exhibit 9.7. Steps for setting up a table for the development of the chart

the border line under the last entry, and move it down to the seventh row

4. Enter the themes and their frequencies
5. Close the table after completing entering the themes and their counts
    ✓ You could double-click on the chart to make the necessary adjustments.

Demonstration 9.3

Word Cloud is a visual display of the number of times participants used certain words in their response to the interview questions. The size of a word in Word Cloud is based on how often it is used compared to other words in segments of the data you are examining. Therefore, "the most frequent word or phrase from a text appears larger than the others" (Saldaña, 2016, p. 222). Assuming you want to create a Word Cloud (in Microsoft Word) based on all the empirical indicators for research question 3 (*GM communication strategies*) using **'Pro Word Cloud'**

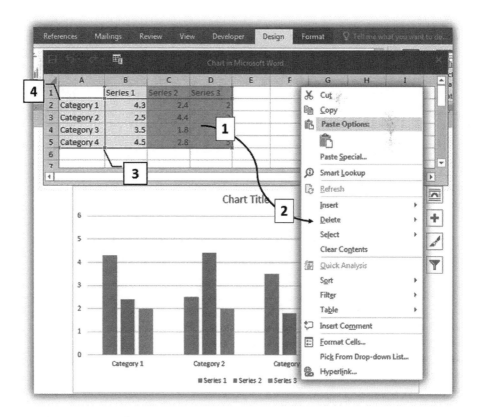

Exhibit 9.8. Steps for customizing the table and entering the themes and frequencies

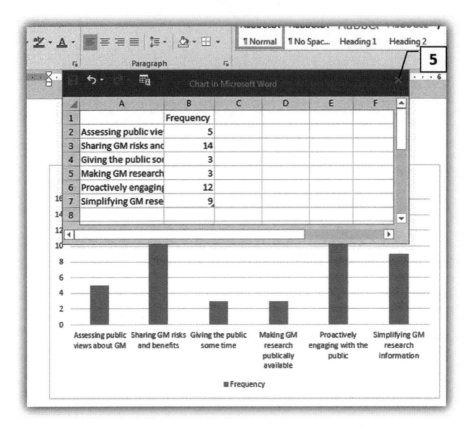

Exhibit 9.9. Completed table and its chart

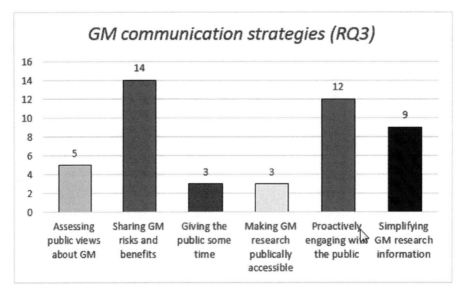

Figure 9.2. Chart showing themes and frequencies under 'GM communication strategies (RQ3)'

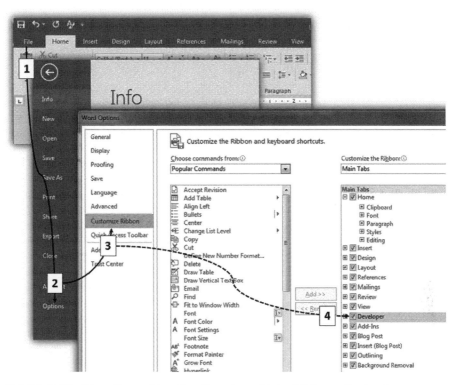

Exhibit 9.10. Steps for making the 'Developer' tab visible on the toolbar

(Version 1.0.0.3; Orpheus Technology Ltd, 2014), here is an example of the steps to follow:

*STEP 9.1. MAKING THE **'DEVELOPER'** TAB VISIBLE ON THE TOOLBAR (SEE EXHIBIT 9.10)*

1. In the Word document, click on the **'File'** tab
2. Click on **'Options'** to open the **'Word Options'** dialog box
3. In the dialog box, click on **'Customize Ribbon'**
4. Under **'Main Tabs'**, check **'Developer'** and click on **'OK'** to close the **'Word Options'** dialog box

*STEP 9.2. SEARCHING FOR THE WORD CLOUD APP FROM THE **'OFFICE STORE'** (SEE EXHIBIT 9.11)*

1. In the Word document, click on the **'Developer'** tab
2. Click on **'Add-ins'** to open the **'Office Add-ins'** dialog box
3. Click on **'Office Store'** to open the search box
4. Search for **'Pro Word Cloud'** in the search box
5. When the **'Pro Word Cloud'** app is found, click on **'Add'** to launch the app on the right-hand side of the Word document

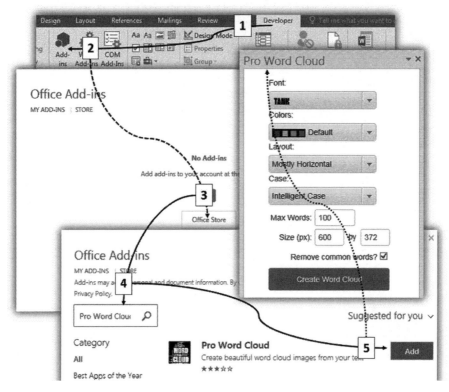

Exhibit 9.11. Steps for launching the 'Pro Word Cloud' app

STEP 9.3. CREATING THE WORD CLOUD USING *'PRO WORD CLOUD'* (SEE EXHIBIT 9.12; FIGURE 9.3)

1. In the *'Pro Word Cloud'* window/platform, make your preferred adjustments to the *'Font'*, *'Colors'*, *'Layout'* and *'Case'*
2. Select the text of interest (*in this case, all the empirical indicators under the third research question are selected*)
3. In the *'Pro Word Cloud'* window, click on *'Create Word Cloud'* to generate the Word Cloud
   ✓ To copy the Word Cloud, you right-click on it and click on *'Copy'* in the menu options. You then paste it into the Word document.

Commentary 9.3. The main purpose of creating Word Clouds is to add meaning to the themes and/or connection among them. If you realize that they are not playing their auxiliary roles, you don't have to share them with your audience. It would be great if you could ensure a diagram makes sense to you before presenting it to your readers. As shown in Figure 9.3, participants used four main words when talking about communication strategies needed to address

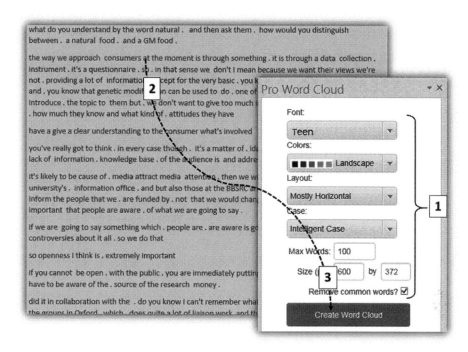

Exhibit 9.12. Steps for creating a Word Cloud using the 'Pro Word Cloud' app

Figure 9.3. Word Cloud based on the empirical indicators under *'GM communication strategies (RQ3)'*

public concerns about GM crops and research: *'GM'*, *'know'*, *'think'* and *'people'*. To have a better understanding of the Word Cloud, it is important to look into how these dominant words were used in the empirical indicators. You could also explore the context in which some of the less dominant words were utilized. Lastly, you could create and examine Word Clouds under each theme.

Demonstration 9.4

In this demonstration, I use **'CmapTools'** (Version 6.03; IHMC, 2018a) to create a map representing the narrative of the relationship among the confirmed communication strategy themes (see Demonstration 9.1). The outcomes of Steps 9.3 and 9.4 under Demonstration 9.1 would be helpful in creating the map. The diagrams showing relationship types would also be a good reference when developing concept maps (see Exhibits 9.1–9.6).

*STEP 9.1. SETTING UP A WORK AREA FOR **'CMAPTOOLS'**
(SEE EXHIBIT 9.13)*

1. Open the **'CmapTools'** software, click on the **'File'** tab and in the menu options, click on **'New Cmap'** to open a blank work area
2. In the toolbar of the work area, click on the **'Window'** tab and in the menu options, click on **'Show Style Palette'** to open the **'Styles'** toolbox

STEP 9.2. CREATING SHAPES FOR THE THEMES AND CONNECTING THEM TO REFLECT THE RELATIONSHIPS DISCOVERED (SEE EXHIBITS 9.14–9.17)

1. Double-click on the work area to create a shape for each theme
2. Based on the relationship established (see Steps 9.3 and 9.4 under Demonstration 9.1), connect the themes by clicking on the theme of interest to show the arrow icon
3. Click and hold the arrow icon and drag to connect it to another theme
   ✓ The shapes can be moved to any preferred location in the work area.
4. Label the arrow reflecting the established relationship

STEP 9.3. MAKING ADJUSTMENTS TO THE INITIAL CONCEPT MAP FOR ESTHETIC AND SIMPLICITY PURPOSES (SEE EXHIBIT 9.17)

1. Using the **'Style'** toolbox, adjust the initial concept to make it simple, esthetic and reflective of the assertion about the connection among the themes (see Step 9.4 in Demonstration 9.1)

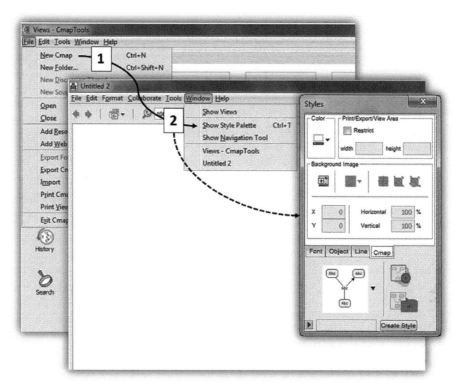

Exhibit 9.13. Steps for setting up a work area for the development of a map

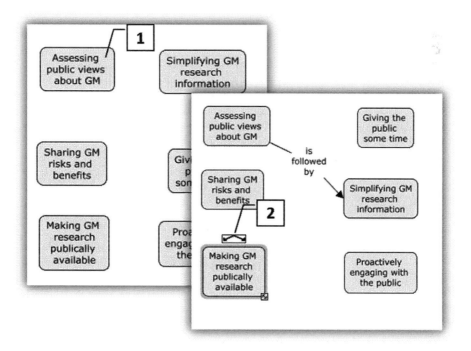

Exhibit 9.14. Steps for creating shapes for the themes

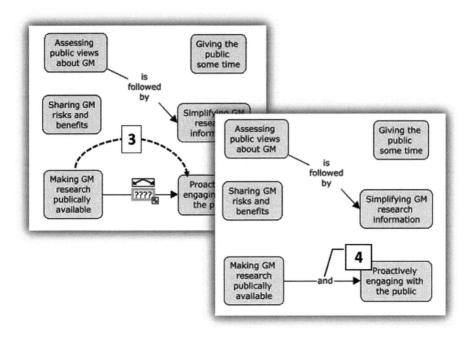

Exhibit 9.15. Steps for connecting the themes

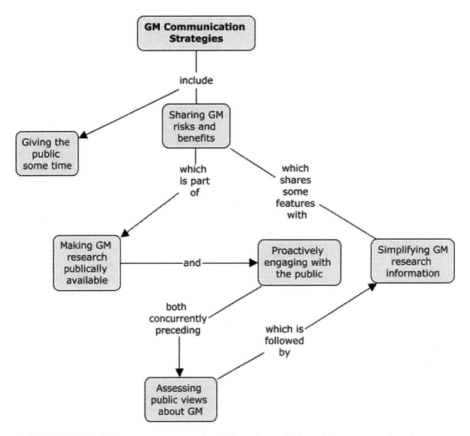

Exhibit 9.16. Initial concept map depicting the relationship among the themes

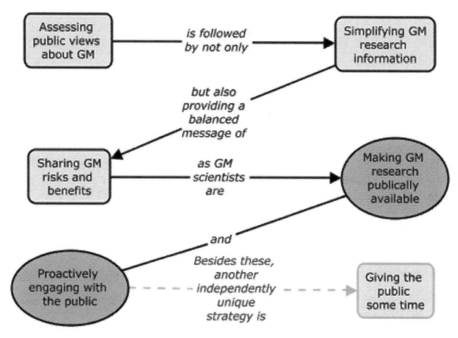

Exhibit 9.17. Concept map depicting the relationship among the themes

STEP 9.4. SAVING AND EXPORTING THE CONCEPT MAP

1. To save the map, go to the **'File'** tab and click on **'Save Cmap As'** and name the map
2. To export the map, go to the **'File'** tab, move to the option **'Export Cmap As'** and select either **'Image File'** or **'PDF (Portable Document Format)'**

Box 9.1 Theme synthetization and visualization steps

1. Engage in epoché
2. Explore potential relationship among themes
3. Compare potential relationships with empirical indicators for confirmation
4. Create a description of the confirmed relationships
5. Choose appropriate tools to visualize the established associations among themes
6. Design a simple table and/or diagram that represents findings including established associations among themes

---

CONCLUSION

Begin thinking about exploring the connection among categories/
themes if your research question is process or explanatory-based.
What do I mean by having a process or explanatory-based question?
A process-based research question normally starts with 'how' while
an explanatory question opens with 'why'. Also, if the individual cat-
egories/themes generated cannot independently address the research
question, then you could examine potential relationships. Before
assessing potential links, you should engage in epoché to prevent any
preconceived ideas and past experiences from informing the theme relationship building process. During the exploration, you review potential
connections among categories/themes and find out whether the data
support those relationships. After the confirmation of a relationship, you
create a description of the established relationship. The next step is to
select appropriate tools to visualize the established associations among
themes. At the end you should have simple tables and/or diagrams that
are rich with information which accurately mimic the description of the
established relationships among themes and the findings as a whole.

REFERENCES

Adu, P. (2017). Using grounded theory approach: From start to finish [PowerPoint
slides]. SlideShare. Retrieved from www.slideshare.net/kontorphilip/
using-grounded-theory-approach-from-start-to-finish

Charmaz, K. (2014). *Constructing grounded theory*. London, England: Sage.

Dey, I. (1993). *Qualitative data analysis: A user-friendly guide for social scientists*.
London, England: Routledge.

Freeman, M. (2017). *Modes of thinking for qualitative data analysis*. New York,
NY: Routledge.

IHMC. (2018a). CmapTools. Version 6.03 [Computer software]. Retrieved from
https://cmap.ihmc.us/products/

IHMC. (2018b). CmapTools. Retrieved from https://cmap.ihmc.us/cmaptools/

Orpheus Technology Ltd. (2014). *Pro Word Cloud*. Version 1.0.0.3 [Computer
software]. Oxford, UK.

Saldaña, J. (2016). *The coding manual for qualitative researchers*. Los Angeles,
CA: Sage.

Strauss, A. L. (1989). *Qualitative analysis for social scientists*. Cambridge,
England: Cambridge University Press.

10

Using QDA Miner Lite to analyze qualitative data

OBJECTIVES

Readers will be able to:

1. Recognize the features and functions of QDA Miner Lite
2. Prepare qualitative data for analysis
3. Code qualitative data using QDA Miner Lite
4. Build already generated categories/themes in QDA Miner Lite
5. Use QDA Miner Lite tools to visualize findings

QDA MINER LITE OVERVIEW

QDA Miner Lite (Version 2.0.5; Provalis Research, 2018a) is a free qualitative analysis software program with basic user-friendly functions. You could utilize it to: import data; create demographic variables and assign demographic attributes to participants; develop and organize codes under their research questions; visualize codes, categories and themes with their respective frequencies, empirical indicators and sources; and download findings (Adu, 2018; Provalis Research, 2018b). Qualitative data analysis can be grouped into five main stages: preparing qualitative data, exploring data, coding empirical indicators, developing categories/themes, and generating tables and diagrams (see Figure 10.1). I will be using QDA Miner Lite (with a Windows 10 operating system) to show how qualitative analysis is conducted in the five stages. You can download this free software by going to: https://provalisresearch.com/products/qualitative-data-analysis-software/freeware/.

PREPARING QUALITATIVE DATA

At this stage, it is assumed that all of the data preparation steps discussed in Chapter 4 have been followed (see Box 4.1) and the interview

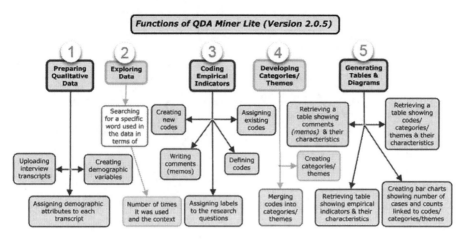

Figure 10.1. Functions of QDA Miner Lite

transcripts are ready to be imported into QDA Miner Lite (Version 2.0.5; Provalis Research, 2018a). For the purpose of this demonstration, I will be using the ten interview transcripts from the case study, *Presentation of Genetically Modified (GM) Crop Research to Non-Specialists* by Cook and Robbins (2005) (see Chapter 4). The aim of this analysis is to examine UK public concerns about GM foods and the strategies GM scientists should use to present the GM crop research to the public. The research questions are as follows:

1. What were the factors contributing to public concerns about GM research and foods in the UK?
2. What were the challenges faced by GM scientists when communicating GM crop research to the public?
3. How should GM crop research be communicated to the public to address their convcerns?

Importing the interview transcripts

The first main feature in the QDA Miner Lite software you're likely to use is the **'Project'** tab. With this command, you can import your interview transcripts. The software recognizes each file of the transcript as a case. I view a case as a container that contains all information about a participant or a group of participants. Therefore, a case should include the participant's demographic information and responses to the interview questions. Similarly, if you were to analyze data from focus groups, each of the groups could have one case which contains all of the information collected from participants in that group.

Demonstration 10.1

The following are the actions I take to import the ten interview transcript files; one for each participant. The documents are in a Rich Text Format (.rtf) and the file names correspond to IDs given to participants.

STEP 10.1. OPENING THE QDA MINER LITE SOFTWARE (SEE EXHIBIT 10.1)

1. Open the QDA Miner Lite software on your computer and click on **'Use Free Edition'**
2. Click on **'Create a new project'**
3. Click on **'Create a project from a list of documents/images'**

STEP 10.2. LOCATING AND SELECTING THE INTERVIEW TRANSCRIPTS (SEE EXHIBIT 10.2)

1. In the **'Import Documents and Images'** window, look for the interview transcripts
   a. To select all files, click on the first document, press and hold the **'Shift'** key on the keyboard, and click on the last document
2. Click on **'Add'** to move the files into the import transit space

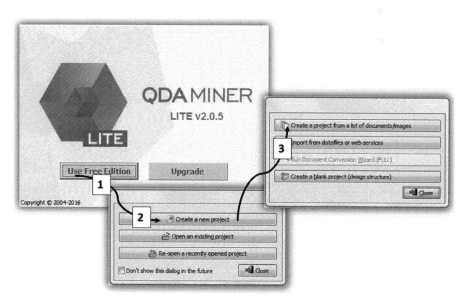

Exhibit 10.1. The first three steps for importing the transcripts

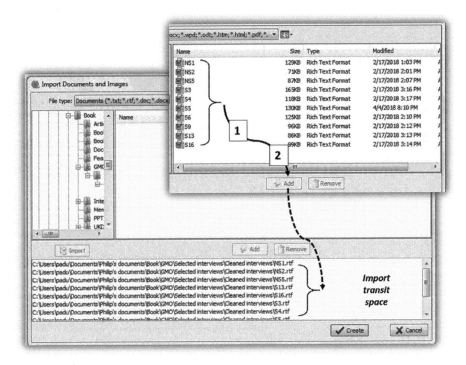

Exhibit 10.2. Steps on locating and selecting the transcripts

STEP 10.3. SAVING THE DATA ANALYSIS PROJECT AND IMPORTING THE FILES (SEE EXHIBIT 10.3)

1. In the **'Import Documents and Images'** window, click on **'Create'**
2. Click on **'OK'** in the **'Importation Options'** dialog box
3. In the **'Save As'** window, type the name of the project (in this case, 'GM Crop Research and Foods Project')
4. Click on **'Save'** to import the files

Overview of the QDA Miner lite software interface (see Exhibit 10.4)

1. **Toolbar:** This contains all the tools necessary to conduct the analysis. It displays the following tabs:
   - **Project:** With the **'Project'** tab, you can save and open the data analysis project. Also, using the **'Export'** function under the tab, you can export the interview files – especially if you have made adjustments to them in the software and want to save them on your computer. Lastly, you can use the **'Notes'** function under the **'Project'** tab to document your reflections about the project, and to record reminders. It can also be used

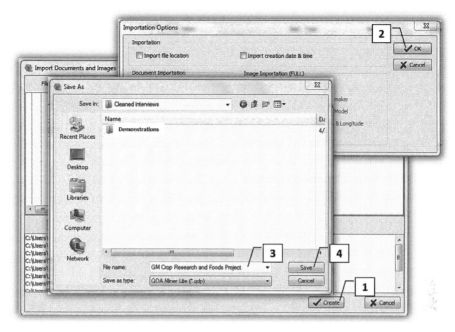

Exhibit 10.3. Steps on saving the data analysis project and finalizing the importing of files

to create analytical and procedural memos (Birks, Chapman, & Francis, 2008; Charmaz, 2014; Emerson, Fretz, & Shaw, 2011; Strauss & Corbin, 1998).

- **Cases:** Think about cases as containers that store participants' information, including their transcripts. Since each participant has one case, having ten participants will provide ten cases. With the **'Cases'** tab, you can add a new case (i.e. participant's transcript) to existing cases using the **'Append'** function. Similarly, if you want to create a case within the software, the **'Add'** function is appropriate. Lastly, if you plan to group cases based on demographic attributes, you could explore the **'Grouping/Descriptor'** function.

- **Variables:** Variables are "characteristics that can take on more than one value, such as age, achievement, or ethnicity" (Slavin, 2007, p. 9). In other words, any feature that varies across the files imported, cases created or participants involved in the study can be labeled as a variable. So, the **'Variables'** tab helps in creating variables such as type of document imported and gender of participants. Using the **'Add'** function, you would be able to create new variables and assign their respective attributes such as male, female and other for a gender variable. You also have an option to delete a variable using the

'Delete' function or to change a variable name by using the *'Properties'* function.

- **Codes:** The *'Codes'* tab is meant to create codes to represent empirical indicators using the *'Add'* function. Besides this, functions such as *'Delete'*, *'Edit'*, and 'Merge into' can be very useful tools when reviewing and merging your codes. Also, you have an option to print the codes created by clicking on the *'Print Codebook'* function.

- **Document:** This tab is useful if you want to edit or format a document. Two functions under the *'Document'* tab that could facilitate the coding process are *'Coded text'* and *'Text View'*. If you want to make a distinction in terms of text display between the text coded and text that is not coded, you could use the *'Coded text'* function. If you want to display line numbers in your document, you could click on *'View Line Numbers'* under the *'Text View'* option.

- **Retrieve:** The *'Retrieve'* tab helps in searching for a specific word from participants' transcripts (utilizing the *'Text Retrieval'* function). Imagine that after completing the coding process you want a summary table containing a list of codes with their assigned research questions and their sources: the *'Coding Retrieval'* function would be an appropriate option for you. Similarly, *'List Comments'* helps create a table containing all memos written (or comments made) about the empirical indicators selected and codes developed.

- **Analyze:** With this free version of the software, there is one available function under the *'Analyze'* tab, namely *'Coding Frequency'*. Using this function, you can create a table of codes, their descriptions and counts/frequencies, and number of cases (participants) connected to the codes.

- **Help:** The *'Help'* tab is a useful tool for addressing questions you have about the software. Moreover, if you prefer to make visible only the functions that work for the QDA Miner Lite version of the software, you could check *'Hide Full Function Menu Items'*.

2. **Cases window:** This window displays all the cases imported. To view the content of each case (file) in the workspace **[6]**, click on the case of interest. Additionally, the *'Cases'* window serves as a small work area to add, edit, delete and group cases. It is similar to the functions of the *'Cases'* tab. To view the *'Add Cases'*, *'Append'*, *'Delete Cases'*, *'Filter Cases'* and *'Case Descriptor'* functions, right-click on the work area in the *'Cases'* window.

3. **Variables window:** This window displays all the variables created linked to the cases. To view variable attributes/values for each case (file/participant) in the *'Variables'* window work area, click

on the case of interest in the *'Cases'* window work area **[2]**. Additionally, the *'Variables'* window functions as a work area to add, delete and edit variables – similar to the functions of the *'Variables'* tab. To view the *'Add Variables'*, *'Delete Variables'* and *'Edit Properties'* functions, right-click on the work area in the *'Variables'* window.

4. **Codes window:** This window shows all the codes created under their respective research questions. Also, the *'Codes'* window serves as a work area to add, edit, delete and group codes. It is similar to the functions of the *'Codes'* tab. To view the *'Add Code'*, *'Edit Code'*, *'Delete Code'*, *'Search & Replace'* and *'Merge Code'* functions, right-click in the work area in the *'Codes'* window.

5. **Document toolbar (ribbon):** Similar to what you find in the Microsoft Word interface, the functions shown on the toolbar are used to make edits to the transcripts imported.

6. **Workspace:** This an area where files are displayed mainly for coding purposes. In this workspace, you are able to review text, identify empirical indicators and assign codes to them.

7. **Coding icons:** Besides using the *'Codes'* tab and *'Codes'* window to create, edit and delete codes, you could alternatively use the coding icons to conduct these three main coding functions.

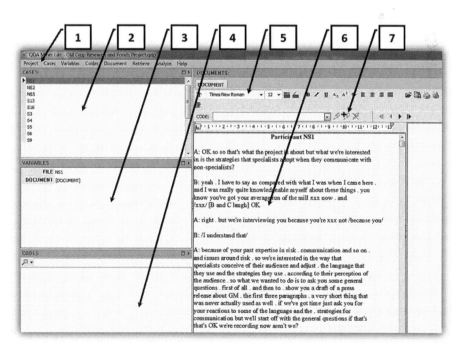

Exhibit 10.4. QDA Miner Lite interface displaying the main functions

Creating demographic variables and attributes

After importing all of the interview transcripts into the software, the next step is to input demographic information collected, and assign attributes or values to participants' files in the **'Cases'** window. As discussed in Chapter 5, my background, past knowledge and preconceived ideas can influence how I view and interpret data. In the same way, there is a possibility that participants' views (data) collected were shaped by their past experiences and demographic features. Therefore, in order for me to better understand and successfully interpret their responses, I need to take into consideration their demographic information. With respect to the data I'm analyzing, there are two main demographic variables: gender and occupation.

Demonstration 10.2

Before creating the variables in the '**Variables**' window, you have to know the type of variable in terms of their level of measurement. For categorical and ordinal variables, you are expected to state the names of the groups and labels of the ranks, respectively, in the **'Value editor'** window (see Exhibits 10.5–10.6). If the level of measurement of a variable is numerical, you are expected to indicate whether the values given to participants are integers (whole numbers) or floating points (decimal numbers).

STEP 10.1. CREATING THE GENDER VARIABLE (SEE EXHIBIT 10.5)

1. Right-click on the **'Variables'** window work area and then click on **'Add Variables'**
2. In the **'Variable Definition'** dialog box:
   ✓ State the **'Variable name'** (i.e. GENDER)
   ✓ Provide the **'Description'** (i.e. Participants' gender)
   ✓ Indicate the **'Data type'** (i.e. Nominal/Ordinal)
3. Under **'Values'** click on **'Edit'** to open the **'Value editor'** window
4. In the **'Value editor'** window, state the categories for the gender variable (which are: Male and Female)
   ✓ **Note:** Each category should be on a separate line. So, I typed **'Male'** and pressed **'Enter'** on the keyboard and typed **'Female'**
5. In the **'Value editor'** window, click on **'OK'** to save and close the window
6. In the **'Variable Definition'** dialog box, click on **'Add'**

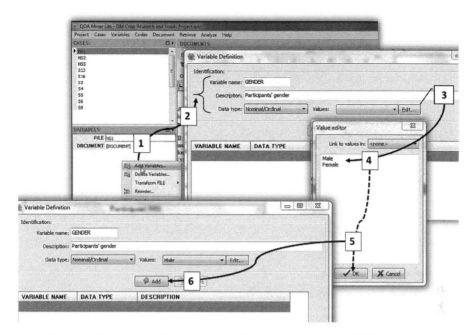

Exhibit 10.5. QDA Miner Lite interface displaying how the GENDER variable is created

STEP 10.2. CREATING THE OCCUPATION VARIABLE
(SEE EXHIBIT 10.6)

1. In the **'Variable Definition'** dialog box:
   a. State the **'Variable name'** (i.e. OCCUPATION)
   b. Provide the **'Description'** (i.e. Participants' occupation)
   c. Indicate the **'Data type'** (i.e. Nominal/Ordinal)
2. Under **'Values'** click on **'Edit'** to open the **'Value editor'** window
3. In the **'Value editor'** window, state the categories for the occupation variable (Academic staff, Student/staff and GM Scientist)
4. In the **'Value editor'** window, click on **'OK'** to save and close the window
5. In the **'Variable Definition'** dialog box, click on **'Add'**
6. Click on **'Create'**

STEP 10.3. ASSIGNING PARTICIPANTS TO THEIR RESPECTIVE
CATEGORIES UNDER GENDER AND OCCUPATION VARIABLES
(SEE EXHIBIT 10.7)

1. In the **'Cases'** window, click on one of the cases
2. In the **'Variables'** window, click in front of the **'GENDER'** variable to open the drop-down menu and select the appropriate category

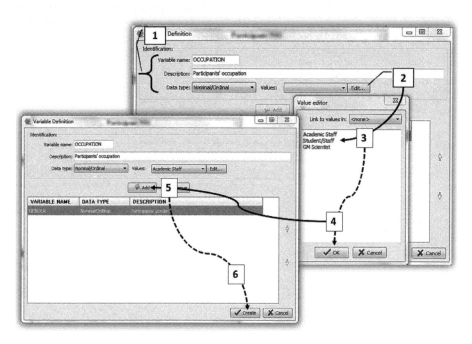

Exhibit 10.6. QDA Miner Lite interface displaying how the OCCUPATION variable is created

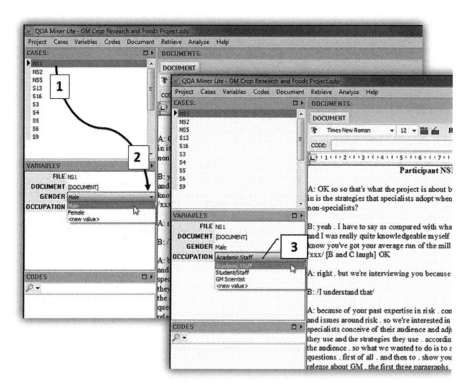

Exhibit 10.7. QDA Miner Lite interface displaying how demographic attributes are assigned to participants

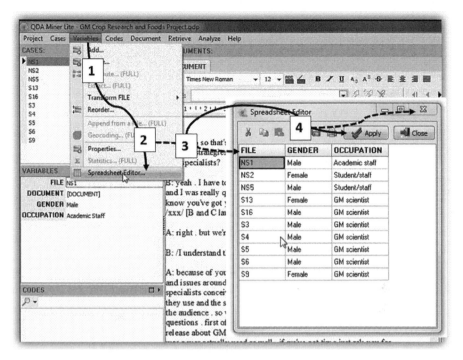

Exhibit 10.8. QDA Miner Lite interface displaying a spreadsheet with participants' demographics

3. Click in front of the **'OCCUPATION'** variable to open the drop-down menu and select the appropriate category
   Note: Repeat Actions 1–3 until all the cases have been assigned to their respective demographic attributes

STEP 10.4. REVIEWING AND REVISING THE DEMOGRAPHIC SPREADSHEET (SEE EXHIBIT 10.8)

1. To review and revise (if needed), click on the **'Variables'** tab
2. In the drop-down menu, click on **'Spreadsheet Editor'** to open a **'Spreadsheet Editor'** window
3. Review the spreadsheet to make sure all the entries are correct and make appropriate revisions if needed
4. Click on **'Apply'** and close the **'Spreadsheet Editor'** window

EXPLORING DATA

As part of knowing your data at the initial stage of the data analysis, you could explore it to learn more about the number of times and the context in which a particular word was used. The **'Retrieve'** tab is the appropriate command to help conduct a word search query. However,

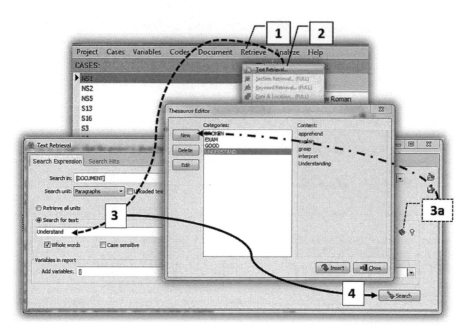

Exhibit 10.9. QDA Miner Lite interface displaying the text retrieval process

searching for a specific word in the data is not a requirement for the development of codes, categories or themes.

Demonstration 10.3

Let's assume I'm interested in knowing how participants used the word *'understand'* and the number of times they used it. Here are the actions under Step 10.1:

STEP 10.1. RETRIEVING THE INFORMATION ASSOCIATED WITH THE WORD 'UNDERSTAND' (SEE EXHIBITS 10.9–10.10)

1. Go to the *'Retrieve'* tab
2. In the drop-down menu, click on *'Text Retrieval'* to open the *'Text Retrieval'* dialog box
3. Type the word of interest (in this case *'Understand'*) in the text area under the checked '*Search for text*' option and make sure the *'Whole words'* option is checked
   a. Alternatively, if you also want to retrieve words related to the word of interest, you could click on the book icon, and click on *'New'* in the *'Thesaurus Editor'* window to state the word of interest, and associated words under *'Categories'* and *'Content'*, respectively. You then click on *'Insert'*.
4. In the *'Text Retrieval'* dialog box, click on *'Search'* to retrieve the word of interest and its context

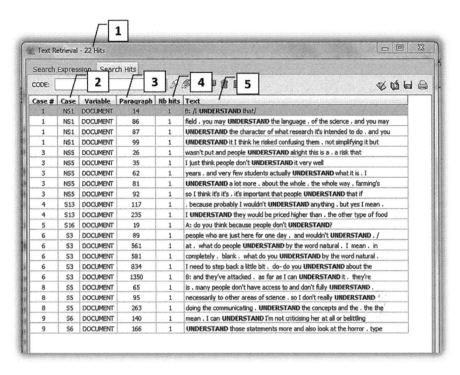

Exhibit 10.10. QDA Miner Lite interface displaying the text retrieval outcome

Commentary 10.1. Exhibit 10.10 shows the outcome of the retrieval of the words used before and after the word of interest (i.e. **'Understand'**). Below are the main features of the **'Text Retrieval'** table:

1. As shown on the topmost left-hand side of the table, the word **'Understand'** was used 22 times.

2. The second column of the table shows the specific case or source of the word **'Understand'**. For instance, in the first row, you can see "/I UNDERSTAND that/" is from case 'NS1'.

3. The **'Paragraph'** column shows the location of the text retrieved in terms of which paragraph. For example, in the third row, it shows that the text is from the 87th paragraph of the NS1 document.

4. The column, **'Nb hits'** indicates the number of times **'Understand'** was referenced with a paragraph.

5. The **'Text'** column displays the paragraph that contains the word **'Understand'**. To find out the location of a paragraph within a document, you click on the paragraph in question under the **'Text'** column and close the '**Text Retrieval**' table. You will see it in the workspace of the software main interface.

CODING EMPIRICAL INDICATORS

The next step is to open each case and conduct the coding process using the *'Codes'* command. Applying this command, you go through the data – identifying empirical indicators and assigning codes to them. You create new codes if the existing codes cannot represent the indicators identified. The software has been built in such a way that you are expected to create each code under a category. In this case, your research questions would be the categories. This supports the need to have labels (called anchor codes) for the research questions before you start the coding process. In effect, your goal is to create codes under their respective research questions. Whenever a new code is created, you should define it in terms of what it represents. You also have an option to write and attach memos to codes and their empirical indicators using the *'Comment'* command.

Demonstration 10.4

As discussed in Chapter 7, before starting the coding process, you should have anchor codes representing the research questions. Here are the research questions and their anchor codes:

1. What were the factors contributing to public concerns about GM research and foods in the UK? *(GM concerns factors)*
2. What were the challenges faced by GM scientists when communicating GM crop research to the public? *(GM communication challenges)*
3. How should GM crop research be communicated to the public to address their concerns? *(GM communication strategies)*

You should also have decided on the specific coding strategy you will be using. After critical analysis of the research approach, nature of the research question and data collected, I chose interpretation-focused coding as the appropriate coding strategy (see Chapter 7 for more information). The following are the steps to follow for coding interview transcripts using the interpretation-focused coding strategy.

STEP 10.1. ASSIGNING AN EMPIRICAL INDICATOR TO A NEW CODE UNDER A NEW CATEGORY (SEE EXHIBIT 10.11)

1. Click on the case/participant/transcript to be analyzed
2. Go through the transcript and select the empirical indicator identified

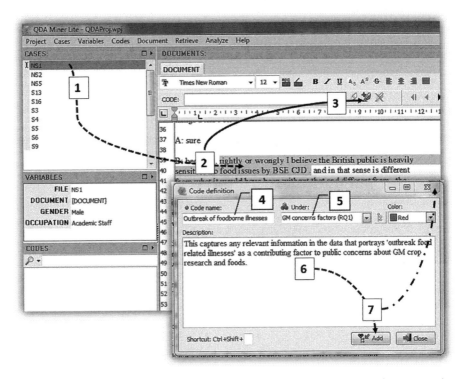

Exhibit 10.11. QDA Miner Lite interface displaying the generation of a new code

3. Click on the **'Add'** code icon on the document toolbar to open the **'Code definition'** window
4. In the **'Code definition'** window, type the code name
5. In the text area for **'Under'**, create a new category by typing the anchor code connected to the code created
   ✓ For easy recognition of what research question the anchor code is representing, you could add **'(RQ1)'**, **'(RQ2)'** or **'(RQ3)'** depending on the research question number. For instance, the anchor code **'GM concerns factors'** is a label for research question 1. So I would type **'GM concerns factors (RQ1)'**.
6. In the **'Description'** text area, provide what the code represents
7. Click on **'Add'** and then close the **'Code definition'** window
   ✓ To view all the coded segments in the transcripts, you can click on the **'Document'** tab, go to **'Coded text'** and click on **'Highlight'**.

Commentary 10.2. As discussed in Chapter 7, a new code is generated whenever the existing codes are not capable of representing the significant text (empirical indicator) identified.

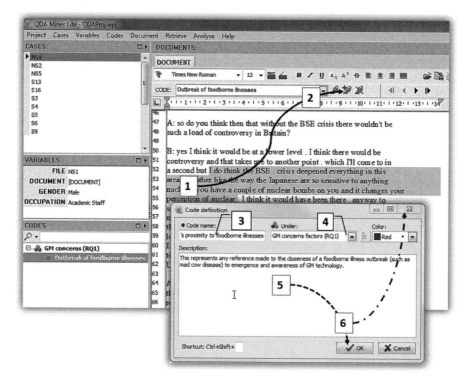

Exhibit 10.12. QDA Miner Lite interface displaying the process of linking a new code to an existing category

I recommend you make sure the code generated best represents the text selected and helps address the research question. Moreover, the code should not be more than five words' long. It is highly recommended to provide a description of every new code created. There are numerous benefits of describing the codes. Some of the benefits are: reducing ambiguity in terms of what the codes mean, helping to easily determine the codes to be assigned to empirical indicators, and facilitating the process of category and theme development, even during the presentation of findings.

STEP 10.2. ASSIGNING AN EMPIRICAL INDICATOR TO A NEW CODE UNDER AN EXISTING CATEGORY (SEE EXHIBIT 10.12)

1. Select the empirical indicator identified
2. Click on the **'Add'** code icon on the document toolbar
3. In the **'Code definition'** window, type the code name
4. In the text area for **'Under'**, click on the drop-down icon to select the category (i.e. the anchor code) associated with the code created

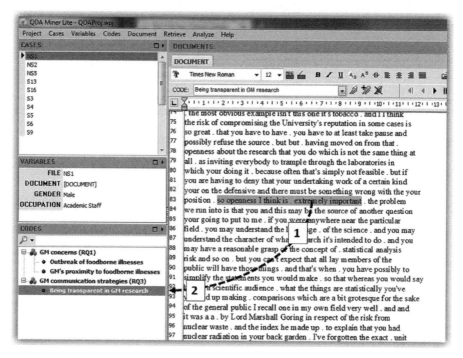

Exhibit 10.13. QDA Miner Lite interface displaying how an empirical indicator is linked to an existing code

5. In the **'Description'** text area, input what the code represents
6. Click on **'OK'** and then close the **'Code definition'** window

Commentary 10.3. At this stage, the ultimate goal is to create codes to reflect your interpretation of the empirical indicators selected and put them under their respective anchor codes. If the anchor code you are looking for has not been listed in the **'Under'** text box in the **'Code definition'** window, you just type the appropriate anchor code in the text box. You may encounter a situation where the codes created have no connection with the anchor codes you have. What you could do is to create a category called **'Other issues'** in the **'Under'** text box and link the codes to it.

STEP 10.3. ASSIGNING AN EMPIRICAL INDICATOR TO AN EXISTING CODE (SEE EXHIBIT 10.13)

1. Select the empirical indicator identified
2. Look for the appropriate existing code in the **'Codes'** window and double-click on it

STEP 10.4. CREATING INITIAL MEMOS (MAKING COMMENTS ABOUT CODES AND EMPIRICAL INDICATORS) (SEE EXHIBIT 10.14)

1. Right-click on the code of interest located at the right-hand side of the workspace and click on **'Comment'**
2. In the **'Comment'** window, write your reflection about the code and/or its associated empirical indicator
3. When finished, close the **'Comment'** window

Commentary 10.4. It is not required to comment on every code or empirical indicator. However, I highly recommend that you always document any thoughts about the codes and empirical indicators. These initial memos would be very helpful at the code categorization stage (see Chapters 6 and 8). To access a list of comments made, go to the **'Retrieve'** tab and click on **'List Comments'** (see Table B.1, Appendix B). I want to emphasize that all the steps about coding (provided above) should be followed for all of the transcripts. At the end of the coding process, I generated 22, 10, 23, and 5 codes under *'GM concerns factors (RQ1)'*, *'GM communication challenges (RQ2)'*, *'GM communication strategies (RQ3)'* and *'Other issues'*, respectively (see Tables 10.1–10.4). I produced these tables by going to the **'Analyze'** tab and clicking on the **'Coding Frequency'** command.

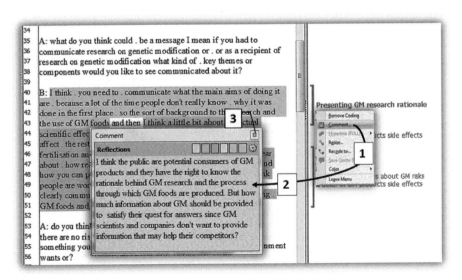

Exhibit 10.14. QDA Miner Lite interface displaying how a comment (memo) is created

Table 10.1 Codes and their respective description, count and cases under
'GM concerns factors (RQ1)'

Code	Description	Count	Cases
1. **Outbreak of foodborne illnesses**	This captures any relevant information in the data that portrays 'outbreak of food-related illnesses' as a contributing factor to public concerns about GM crop research and foods.	3	3
2. **GM's proximity to foodborne illnesses**	This represents any reference made to the closeness of a foodborne illness outbreak (such as mad cow disease) to the emergence and awareness of GM technology.	3	3
3. **Irrational 'response to risks'**	This code covers all relevant information that makes reference to issues related to unreasonable decisions and reactions of the public about potential GM risks.	2	1
4. **Limited knowledge about GM research**	This represents significant information in the data that explains how limited the public understanding of GM research and foods is.	10	6
5. **Uncertain about GM research**	This covers relevant portions of the data that depict the public sense of uncertainty about the GM research and products.	1	1
6. **Unsatisfactory answer to GM risks**	This covers any information in the data that makes reference to the fact that the public is not satisfied with the risks and uncertainty-related answers they received from GM scientists.	3	2
7. **Belief in GM product side effects**	This code covers information on the public belief in the adverse effects of consuming GM products.	5	2
8. **Extensively unexamined GM side effects**	This code represents parts of the data which imply that not many studies have been conducted on GM side effects.	2	1
9. **Unfavorable depiction of GM technology**	This code represents the media and interest groups' negative depiction of GM products or distortion of GM research findings.	7	3
10. **Objective-driven nature of scientific research**	This captures any reference made to the objective nature of conducting science.	1	1

(continued)

Table 10.1 (Cont.)

Code	Description	Count	Cases
11. Multiple meanings of GM concepts	This captures explanations of the concept of 'natural' and how the meaning differs between scientists and the public.	2	1
12. Conflicting views about GM safety	While the government is assuring the public about how safe GM products are, GM scientists are unsure about GM safety.	1	1
13. 'Mistrust of commercial companies'	This covers all references to the public mistrust of GM companies.	3	2
14. Mistrust of the government	This code covers all issues related to the public mistrust of the government in relation to assuring them of GM safety.	2	2
15. Hesitant to explain GM research	This covers empirical indicators that portray GM scientists' hesitance in explaining the GM research process to the public.	3	2
16. Criticism from interest groups	This captures any references to criticism of interest groups about GM research and foods.	4	3
17. Lack of effective government communication	This covers the lack of communication on the part of the government.	2	2
18. Inadequate promotion of GM benefits	This code depicts participants' expression of the poor promotion of GM benefits.	1	1
19. Mistrust of scientists	This covers all references to the public mistrust of scientists.	4	2
20. Disinterested in learning about GM	This focuses on representing the public as not being interested in learning about GM.	1	1
21. GM scientists' ineffective communication	This represents empirical indicators that imply that the GM scientists have poor communication – in terms of helping the public to understand GM.	1	1
22. Hesitant to embrace GM technology	This covers the public unwillingness to accept something new.	1	1

Note: 'Count' represents the number of times a code is assigned to empirical indicators found in the data. 'Cases' represents the number of cases/participants/transcript documents connected to a particular code.

Table 10.2 Codes and their respective description, count and cases under *'GM communication challenges (RQ2)'*

Code	Description	Count	Cases
1. Risk of disclosing protected ideas	This captures information about the dilemma of being open to the public and putting GM scientists' protected ideas at risk of being used by their competitors.	1	1
2. Risk of oversimplifying GM information	This code is about the challenge of presenting easy-to-understand GM crop research information, and at the same time making sure the information is not oversimplified and/or misleading.	1	1
3. Limited information about GM risks	This code focuses on GM scientists' inability to adequately address the public concerns about GM-related risks due to the limited research done.	1	1
4. GM risks non-existence not guaranteed	This code covers the communication challenges related to GM scientists' difficulty in satisfying the public interest in the assurance of there being no GM innovation-related risks.	2	2
5. Fear of GM findings distortion	This code represents relevant portions of the data that portray GM scientists' concern about the misrepresentation of GM crop research findings.	2	1
6. Not sure about GM risks	This is about empirical indicators that show expression of GM scientists not being sure about GM risks.	3	3
7. 'Pressure from the government'	This includes statements in the data that indicate government pressure on GM scientists to say that GM research and products are safe.	1	1
8. Public pressure for GM safety	This is about GM scientists being pressured by the public to declare that GM products are safe.	1	1
9. Difficulty explaining GM technology	This entails reference to having difficulty explaining GM technology to a lay person.	5	2
10. Pressure from the public	This represents relevant information that makes reference to public pressure on GM scientists regarding the issue of declaring that GM has no risk.	1	1

Note: 'Count' represents the number of times a code is assigned to empirical indicators found in the data. 'Cases' represents the number of cases/participants/transcript documents connected to a particular code.

Table 10.3 Codes and their respective description, count and cases under 'GM communication strategies (RQ3)'

Code	Description	Count	Cases
1. Being transparent in GM research	This represents all participants' responses that cover the need to be open when communicating GM research – including willingly sharing information on who funded the research.	2	1
2. Simplifying GM research information	This represents portions of the data that depict the need to present GM research and food information in a simplified format so that the public can understand it.	3	2
3. Communicating GM innovation benefits	This code captures ideas in the data which imply the need to put a greater emphasis on the benefits of GM research and foods than the potential risks when making a presentation.	2	2
4. Assessing public GM knowledge level	Any participants' expression related to the need to assess the public knowledge level and perceptions about GM innovations will be put under this code.	4	4
5. Making GM research publicly available	This code focuses on the need for GM scientists to make GM research available for public consumption.	1	1
6. Emphasizing GM's positive side	This focuses on the need to promote the benefits of GM more than its negative side.	2	1
7. Organizing seminars for the public	This is about the need to organize seminars for the public.	2	2
8. Giving the public some time	This code represents all information that indicates the need to give the public some time to understand issues related to GM.	4	4
9. Educating the public about GM	This covers the need to teach the public about GM innovations and products rather than just telling them what GM is about.	3	2
10. Listening to the public concerns	This code represents the need for GM scientists to meet the public and listen to what they are concerned about.	1	1

Table 10.3 (Cont.)

Code	Description	Count	Cases
11. Presenting GM research rationale	This is about the need to present the reason why GM research should be conducted. In addition, it represents information about why GM foods are needed.	2	2
12. Having conversations about GM risks	This code captures significant information that shows that GM scientists should have a conversation with the public about GM risks: what they are, the extent of the risks, how likely it is that they will occur, and a way to prevent them from happening.	2	2
13. Creating press releases	This focuses on reference to creating press releases as one of the communication strategies.	1	1
14. Making in-depth GM presentations	This focuses on the need to be more detailed when presenting GM information rather than just giving brief information.	4	3
15. Discussing specific GM case	This focuses on communication strategies related to discussing in detail a specific case study on GM, including risks. It also includes discussing both GM benefits and risks.	3	3
16. Tailoring GM information	This is about adjusting the GM information being presented based on the audience's GM knowledge level.	2	1
17. Emphasizing crossbreeding/ GM similarities	This covers the need to discuss the similarities between traditional crossbreeding practices and GM technology.	2	2
18. Being proactive in GM information-sharing	This is about the need to anticipate the public reactions to GM research and to devise ways of responding to them (including informing them about the source of research funding).	2	1
19. Creating awareness of GM risks	This is about the fact that the public should be aware of any potential risks related to GM crop research and products.	1	1

(continued)

Table 10.3 (Cont.)

Code	Description	Count	Cases
20. Presenting GM risks and benefits	This focuses on the need to present a balanced argument when communicating with the public about GM technology.	3	1
21. Debating with pressure groups	This covers the need to engage in a debate with pressure groups.	1	1
22. Having public debate about GM	This covers the need to have public debate about GM – discussing GM risks and benefits.	1	1
23. Collaborating with other departments	This covers parts of the data that suggest the need to work with university departments specializing in helping with the presentation of GM content to the public.	1	1

Note: 'Count' represents the number of times a code is assigned to empirical indicators found in the data. 'Cases' represents the number of cases/participants/transcript documents connected to a particular code.

Table 10.4 Codes and their respective description, count and cases under 'Other issues'

Code	Description	Count	Cases
1. Finding out GM research sponsor	This code is for any remarks by participants that recommend the need to look for the source of funding when reviewing a GM research article.	1	1
2. Government funding for GM research	This is part of the recommendations. It calls for the government to sponsor independent research on GM.	2	2
3. More research on GM risks	This focuses on the need for more research on potential side effects of GM.	2	2
4. Single definition of GM concepts	This captures the need to have a single definition of natural crops, health and safety.	2	1
5. Difficulty in labeling products	This represents the difficulty of differentiating GM products from non-GM products (especially processed foods) by labeling.	1	1

Note: 'Count' represents the number of times a code is assigned to empirical indicators found in the data. 'Cases' represents the number of cases/participants/transcript documents connected to a particular code.

DEVELOPING CATEGORIES/THEMES

When it comes to developing categories and themes facilitated by a QDAS program, there are two questions you should think about: Does the software have the ability to help generate categories/themes? And does it have the capability to support the transformation of the codes into already-generated categories/themes? The first question is referring to the **process** aspect of category/theme development while the second is about the **product** aspect of category/theme development.

In terms of the process aspect, QDA Miner Lite (Version 2.0.5; Provalis Research, 2018a) could be used to conduct the sorting of codes generated. Since the **'Notes'** window (which can be opened by going to the **'Project'** tab and then clicking on the **'Notes'** option) has functions similar to a Microsoft Word document, you could use the individual-based sorting strategy for the category/theme generation process (see Chapter 8). However, it is challenging to solely utilize the **'Notes'** window to categorize codes and develop themes with the presumption-focused coding strategy (see Table 10.5). This is because the **'Notes'** window does not have the function to label the codes as is available in a Microsoft Word document using **'New Comment'** under the **'Review'** tab (See Chapter 8, Demonstration 8.1).

Alternatively, I recommend you work on developing categories and themes in a Microsoft Word document using the presumption-focused coding strategy or the individual-based sorting strategy. After developing your categories/themes, you then move on to the product aspect of category/theme development. This is where you use the **'Codes'** command in the QDA Miner Lite software to create categories/themes and merge codes into them.

Demonstration 10.5

Let's imagine I have developed my themes for the first and third research questions (with Microsoft Word) (see Chapter 8, Demonstrations 8.1–8.2) and want to integrate them into the codes generated in the QDA Miner Lite software. I start the process by having a list of themes and their associated codes for each of the research questions (see below). The themes under *'GM concerns factors (RQ1)'* and *'GM communication strategies (RQ3)'* were outcomes of the utilization of the presumption-focused coding strategy and the individual-based sorting strategy, respectively. I also need to create a copy of the project by clicking on the **'Project'** tab, going to **'Save as'** in the menu options, and typing a preferred project name. The essence of having a duplicate is to keep the initial codes for future reference. For example, the project with all the codes created was named *'GM Crop Research and Foods Project'* and the one I will be working on is labeled *'GM Crop Research and Foods Project_Phase2'*.

Table 10.5 Analytical tools for generating categories/themes

Categorization strategy	Analytical tools		
	Microsoft Word	SPSS	QDA Miner Lite
Presumption-focused coding strategy	**'New Comment'** function under the **'Review'** tab		
Individual-based sorting strategy	**'Tables'** function under the **'Insert'** tab		**'Table'** function within the **'Notes'** window of the **'Notes'** option under the **'Project'** tab
Group-based sorting strategy	**'Tables'** and **'Shapes'** functions under the **'Insert'** tab	**'Multidimensional Scaling'** function of the **'Scale'** option under the **'Analysis'** tab **'Hierarchical Cluster'** function of the **'Classify'** option under the **'Analysis'** tab	

List of themes and their respective codes for
'GM concerns factors (RQ1)'

1. GM risks uncertainties
   i. Extensively unexamined GM side effects
   ii. Objective-driven nature of scientific research
   iii. Uncertain about GM research
2. Lack of effective communication
   i. GM scientists' ineffective communication
   ii. Hesitant to explain GM research
   iii. Inadequate promotion of GM benefits
   iv. Lack of effective government communication
   v. Multiple meanings of GM concepts
   vi. Mixed messaging about GM safety
      a. Conflicting views about GM safety
3. Limited knowledge about GM research
   i. Disinterested in learning about GM
   ii. Limited knowledge about GM research

4. Mistrust towards GM stakeholders
   i. 'Mistrust of commercial companies'
   ii. Mistrust of scientists
   iii. Mistrust of the government
5. Misunderstanding of GM risks
   i. GM's proximity to foodborne illnesses
   ii. Irrational 'response to risks'
   iii. Outbreak of foodborne illnesses
   iv. Unsatisfactory answer to GM risks
   v. Perceived existence of GM risks
      a. Belief in GM product side effects
      b. Hesitant to embrace GM technology
      c. Irrational 'response to risks'
6. Unfavorable depiction of GM technology
   i. Criticism from interest groups
   ii. Unfavorable depiction of GM technology

List of themes and their respective codes for
'GM communication strategies (RQ3)'

1. Assessing public views about GM
   i. Assessing public GM knowledge level
   ii. Listening to the public concerns
2. Sharing GM risks and benefits
   i. Being transparent in GM research
   ii. Creating awareness of GM risks
   iii. Communicating GM innovation benefits
   iv. Emphasizing GM's positive side
   v. Having conversations about GM risks
   vi. Presenting GM research rationale
   vii. Presenting GM risks and benefits
3. Giving the public some time
   i. Giving the public some time
4. Making GM research publicly available
   i. Creating press releases
   ii. Making GM research publicly available
   iii. Collaborating with other departments
5. Proactively engaging with the public
   i. Debating with pressure groups
   ii. Discussing specific GM case
   iii. Having public debate about GM
   iv. Making in-depth GM presentations
   v. Organizing seminars for the public
   vi. Being proactive in GM information-sharing

6. Simplifying GM research information
   i. Simplifying GM research information
   ii. Tailoring GM information
   iii. Emphasizing crossbreeding/GM similarities
   iv. Educating the public about GM

STEP 10.1. CREATING THEMES UNDER THE ANCHOR CODE (SEE EXHIBIT 10.15)

1. In the **'Codes'** window, right-click on the anchor code and select **'Add Code'**
2. In the **'Code definition'** window, type the name of the theme and state **'T'** in parentheses to show that it is a theme
3. In the **'Description'** text area, input what the theme represents
4. Click on **'Add'** and then close the **'Code definition'** window

STEP 10.2. CREATING DUPLICATES OF CODES BELONGING TO MORE THAN ONE THEME (SEE EXHIBITS 10.16–10.17)

✓ If you use the presumption-focused coding strategy for the development of categories/themes, there is a possibility that

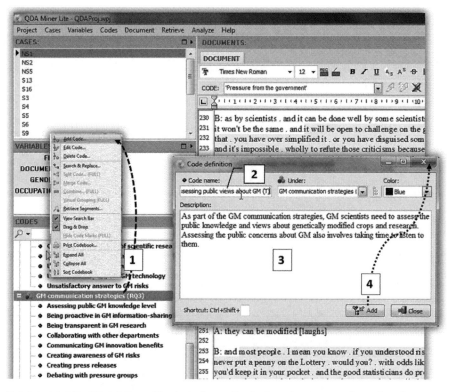

Exhibit 10.15. QDA Miner Lite interface displaying the generation of a theme

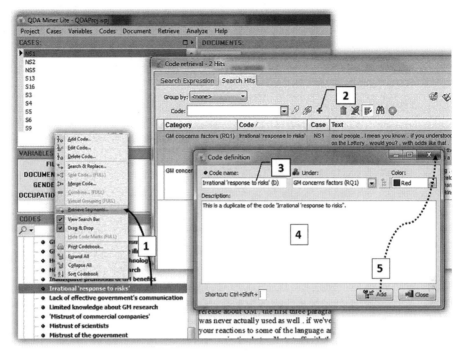

Exhibit 10.16. QDA Miner Lite interface displaying the generation of a duplicate code

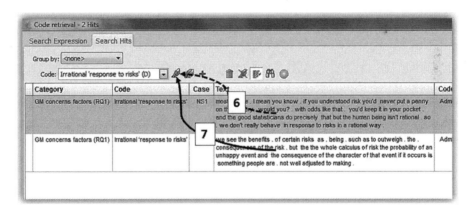

Exhibit 10.17. QDA Miner Lite interface displaying how empirical indicators are coded to the duplicate code

some codes would support more than one category/theme. By creating duplicates of the codes, you would be able to put the same code under multiple categories/themes.

1. In the **'Codes'** window, right-click on the code and select **'Retrieve Segments'**
2. In the **'Code retrieval'** window, click on the **'Define new code'** (**'+'**) icon to create a duplicate code

3. In the **'Code definition'** window, type the name of the code to be duplicated and state **'D'** in parentheses to show that it is a duplicate

4. Provide a description showing that the code created is a duplicate

5. Click on **'Add'** and then close the **'Code definition'** window

6. In the **'Code retrieval'** window, click on the first row to select the text (i.e. empirical indicator) connected to the original code and click on the **'Code'** icon

   ✓ The essence of taking this action is to code all the empirical indicators for the original code to the duplicate code.

7. Follow *'Action 6'* to code subsequent empirical indicators to the duplicate code

STEP 10.3. MERGING CODES INTO CATEGORIES/THEMES
(SEE EXHIBIT 10.18)

1. In the **'Codes'** window, right-click on the code and select **'Merge Code'**

2. In the **'Merge Code'** dialog box, select the corresponding theme

3. Click on **'OK'**

   Note: Repeat these actions until all the codes are merged into their respective categories/themes

Commentary 10.5. One limitation of using QDA Miner Lite (Version 2.0.5; Provalis Research, 2018a) for the product of category/theme development is that it does not allow you to put a code, sub-category or sub-theme under the categories/themes. The only option at this stage is to merge them into the categories/themes. As shown in Exhibit 10.19, all the codes (for the anchor codes, *'GM concerns factors (RQ1)'* and *'GM communication strategies (RQ3)'*) have been merged into their corresponding themes.

GENERATING TABLES AND DIAGRAMS

At the end of the analysis, you could retrieve all the outcomes that would help in presenting the results. The **'Retrieve'** and **'Analyze'** functions are used to extract visual representations of the findings such as tables and charts. Tables containing empirical indicators, memos and categories/themes would be useful information for the presentation of findings. Also, bar charts showing categories/themes and their respective number of cases and counts (frequencies) could serve as complementary information when writing the results. However, you won't be able to create maps to represent the confirmed relationships among categories/

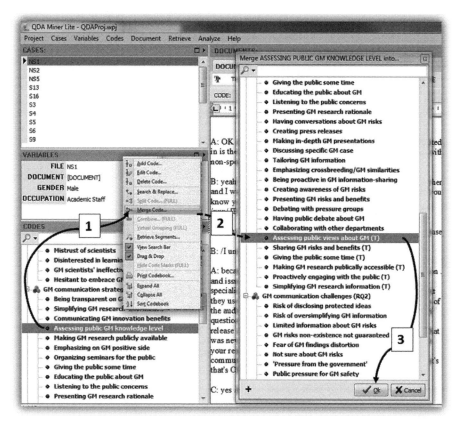

Exhibit 10.18. QDA Miner Lite interface displaying how codes are merged into themes

themes in the software (see Chapter 9 for a review of available tools for creating maps).

Demonstration 10.6

In this demonstration, I show you how to use the *'Analyze'* function to create and export tables and charts with themes and their associated counts and number of cases.

STEP 10.1. CREATING TABLES CONTAINING THEMES AND THEIR ASSOCIATED COUNTS AND NUMBER OF CASES (SEE EXHIBIT 10.20)

1. Go to the *'Analyze'* tab and in the drop-down menu click on *'Coding Frequency'* to open the *'Coding Frequency'* dialog box
2. In the dialog box, check *'Selected'* and click on the icon next to the drop-down menu

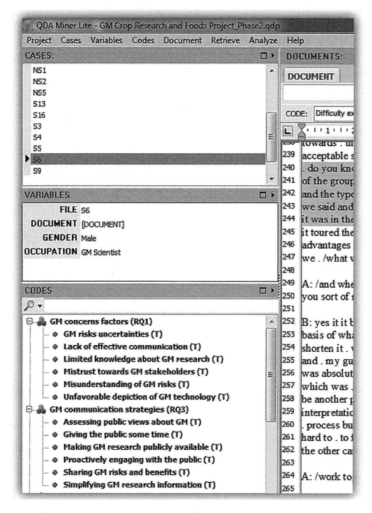

Exhibit 10.19. QDA Miner Lite interface displaying the outcome of the merging process

3. In the **'Code selection'** menu options, check the themes of interest and click on **'OK'**
4. Click on **'Search'**
5. In the **'Coding Frequency'** dialog box, click on the **'Table'** tab to display the table
   ✓ To export the table, click on the **'Save'** icon in the dialog box (see Tables 10.6–10.7)

Commentary 10.6. Tables 10.6 and 10.7 are clean versions of the tables exported from the software. These tables could be displayed when presenting the findings. You can present them with or without the description of the themes, as shown in the tables.

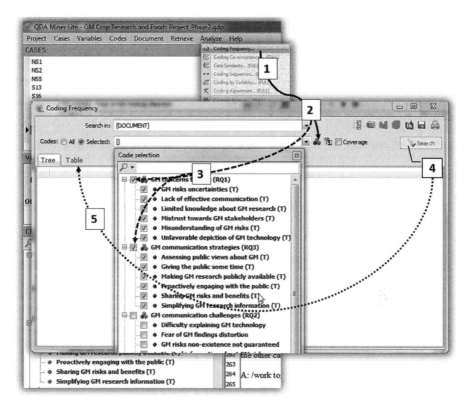

Exhibit 10.20. QDA Miner Lite interface displaying how to create a table with themes and their counts and cases

Table 10.6 Themes for the *'GM concerns factors (RQ1)'* with their count and cases

Theme	Count	Cases	% Cases
GM risks uncertainties	4	3	30.0%
Lack of effective communication	10	4	40.0%
Limited knowledge about GM research	11	6	60.0%
Mistrust towards GM stakeholders	9	3	30.0%
Misunderstanding of GM risks	19	8	80.0%
Unfavorable depiction of GM technology	11	5	50.0%

Table 10.7 Themes for the *'GM communication strategies (RQ3)'* with their description, count and cases

Theme	Description	Count	Cases	% Cases
Assessing public views about GM	As part of the GM communication strategies, GM scientists need to assess the public knowledge and views about genetically modified crops and research. Assessing the public concerns about GM also involves taking time to listen to them.	5	5	50.0%
Giving the public some time	Giving the public time to digest the GM information presented to them is another communication strategy. Also, because the public is uncertain about the risks associated with GM foods, they need time to observe the implications that result from the GM innovation.	4	4	40.0%
Making GM research publicly available	Collaborating with an appropriate department in their institution, GM scientists could make information about GM research publicly available.	3	3	30.0%
Proactively engaging with the public	GM scientists should actively engage the public, including interest groups in discussing, debating and having an honest conversation about specific issues related to GM innovations.	13	5	50.0%
Sharing GM risks and benefits	In terms of making GM research known to the public, GM scientists should be transparent – sharing not only the benefits of GM innovations but the rationale behind their studies and risks involved.	14	7	70.0%
Simplifying GM research information	As part of educating the public, GM scientists should present GM research information in a simplified form so that the public can understand it.	10	4	40.0%

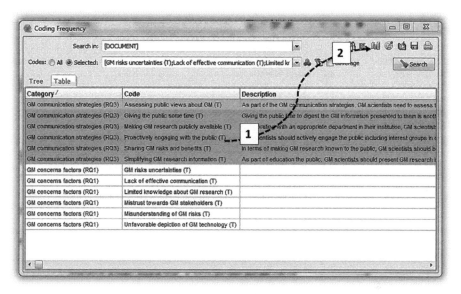

Exhibit 10.21. QDA Miner Lite interface displaying how to create a chart with themes and their counts and cases

STEP 10.2. CREATING CHARTS SHOWING THE THEME WITH COUNT AND NUMBER OF CASES (SEE EXHIBIT 10.21)

1. In the **'Coding Frequency'** dialog box, select the first row of the table, press and hold the **'Shift'** key and click on the last row containing the themes of interest
2. Click on the **'Chart'** icon to generate a chart (see Figures 10.2–10.5)

Box 10.1 Qualitative analysis steps using QDA Miner Lite

1. Prepare interview transcripts
2. Explore the data
3. Code empirical indicators
4. Create categories/themes
5. Generate tables and charts

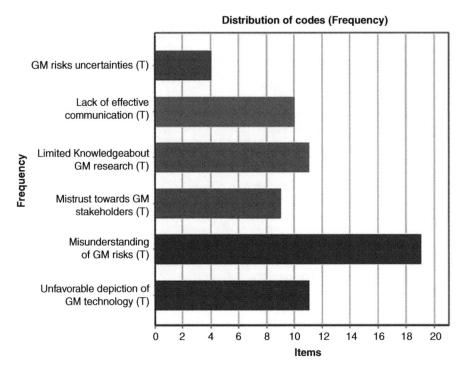

Figure 10.2. Bar chart showing the themes and frequency under *'GM concerns factors (RQ1)'*

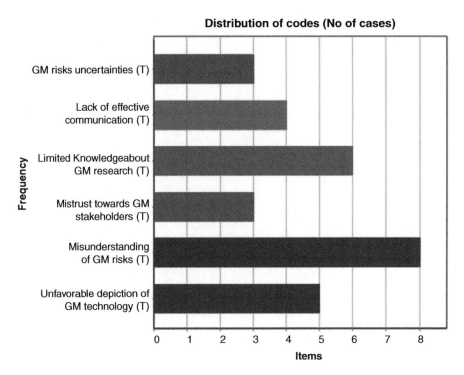

Figure 10.3. Bar chart showing the themes and number of cases under *'GM concerns factors (RQ1)'*

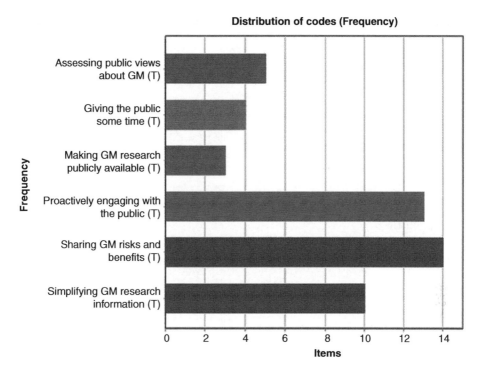

Figure 10.4. Bar chart showing the themes and frequency under *'GM communication strategies (RQ3)'*

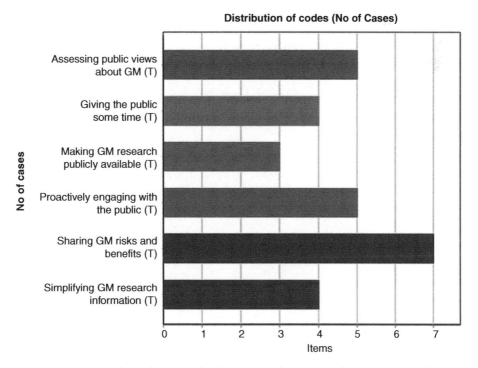

Figure 10.5. Bar chart showing the themes and number of cases under *'GM communication strategies (RQ3)'*

CONCLUSION

QDA Miner Lite (Version 2.0.5; Provalis Research, 2018a) is a QDAS program capable of importing data, creating variables, assigning associated attributes to cases (participants), and developing codes and transforming them into categories/themes. In terms of visualizing the results, the software helps to create tables and charts. It has unique basic functions of qualitative analysis and is free to use. The labels for the commands are self-explanatory and easy to use. This makes it particularly suitable for people who are new to QDAS and also for those who just want to use the software to conduct simple qualitative analyses.

REFERENCES

Adu, P. (2018). Familiarizing yourself with QDA Miner Lite: A free qualitative data analysis software [PowerPoint slides]. SlideShare. Retrieved from www.slideshare.net/kontorphilip/familiarizing-yourself-with-qda-miner-lite-a-free-qualitative-data-analysis-software

Birks, M., Chapman, Y., & Francis, K. (2008). Memoing in qualitative research: Probing data and processes. *Journal of Research in Nursing, 13*(1), 68–75. doi:10.1177/ 1744987107081254

Charmaz, K. (2014). *Constructing grounded theory*. London, England: Sage.

Cook, G., & Robbins, P. T. (2005). *Presentation of genetically modified (GM) crop research to non-specialists, 1997–2002: A case study*. [data collection]. UK Data Service. SN: 5069, http://doi.org/10.5255/UKDA-SN-5069-1

Emerson, R. M., Fretz, R. I., & Shaw, L. L. (2011). *Writing ethnographic field notes* (2nd ed.). Chicago, IL: University of Chicago Press.

Provalis Research. (2018a). QDA Miner Lite. Version 2.0.5 [Computer software]. Retrieved from https://provalisresearch.com/products/qualitative-data-analysis-software/freeware/

Provalis Research. (2018b). QDA Miner Lite – free qualitative data analysis software. Retrieved April 7, 2018, from https://provalisresearch.com/products/qualitative-data-analysis-software/freeware/

Slavin, R. E. (2007). *Educational research: In an age of accountability*. Boston, MA: Pearson Education, Inc.

Strauss, A. L., & Corbin, J. M. (1998). *Basics of qualitative research: Techniques and procedures for developing grounded theory* (2nd ed.). Thousand Oaks, CA: Sage.

11

Using NVivo 12 to analyze qualitative data

OBJECTIVES

Readers will be able to:

1. Recognize the features and functions of NVivo
2. Prepare qualitative data for analysis
3. Code qualitative data using NVivo
4. Generate categories/themes in NVivo
5. Visualize findings with the software

NVIVO 12 SOFTWARE OVERVIEW

NVivo 12 (Version 12.1.249; QSR International Pty Ltd, 2018) is a qualitative data analysis software (QDAS) program which facilitates the analysis of qualitative data in terms of coding relevant text, categorizing codes generated, and visualizing results (Adu, 2015, 2018; Bazeley & Jackson, 2014). It can be used to analyze audio, videos, text and illustrations. With the help of NVivo, you can manually transcribe your imported audio and videos. Additionally, another unique function of NVivo is the ability to submit your audio and videos for them to be automatically transcribed for a fee (NVivo Transcription, 2018). To submit, you click on the **'Create'** tab and then click on the **'NVivo Transcription'** command.

This user-friendly data analysis tool has an esthetic interface – making it easier to use commands under the **'Home'**, **'Import'**, **'Create'**, **'Explore'** and **'Share'** tabs. The option of hovering the cursor over the commands for a quick review of their functions saves time compared to going to **'Help'** under the **'File'** tab to learn about the tools.

NVivo 12 (Version 12.1.249; QSR International Pty Ltd, 2018) has numerous data analytical tools which make it possible to independently conduct qualitative data analyses from start to finish. With the **'Import'** tab, you are able to import data into the software. Each data file imported comprises participants' interview responses (provided that interviews were conducted). You then use the *'Cases'* command to create containers called cases to house participants' information including their transcripts. In terms of connecting participants' demographics to their transcripts, you can first create a Microsoft Excel spreadsheet with participants' information, and import and connect the information to their respective cases using the *'Classification Sheet'* under the *'Import'* tab. Alternatively, you could create attributes (i.e. demographic variables) in NVivo utilizing the *'Case Classification'* command under the *'Create'* tab.

There is another type of container that is created using the *'Node'* function (under the *'Create'* tab). It is called a node. Although node and code mean the same and can be used interchangeably, there is a slight difference between them. Whereas a node is a reservoir of empirical indicators, a code is the label given to the reservoir. Using NVivo terms, a code is referred to as a node, sub-category or sub-theme as a child node, and category or theme as a parent node (Adu, 2015). During the coding process, whenever you identify an empirical indicator, you use the *'Node'* function to create a node – giving the node a label and dropping the indicator into it. Concurrently, you could document your reflections during coding by employing the *'Memo'* command.

After completing generating codes, the next step is to develop categories/themes. Unique commands within a memo such as the *'Table'* and *'Insert'* functions help to apply the presumption-focused coding and individual-based sorting strategies to create categories/themes out of the initial codes. You then finalize the qualitative analysis process by creating nodes for the categories/themes built in the memo and dropping the initial nodes into them.

At the end of the analysis, you don't have to retrieve all outcomes but instead focus on exporting those that are relevant, to help address the research questions and those which would facilitate the presentation of the findings. By going to the *'Share'* tab, you could retrieve and export a codebook with the help of the *'New Report'* or *'Expert Codebook'* command. You could also create and export a matrix which displays the empirical indicators shared between cases and themes by clicking on the *'Framework Matrix'* command under the *'Create'* tab. Similarly, *'Matrix Coding'* and *'Crosstab'* under the *'Explore'* tab are very valuable tools in creating matrices depicting the number of empirical indicators shared between cases and themes and also between attributes and themes. Lastly, if you plan to map out cases or themes and their associations, the *'Project Map'* command is an appropriate tool.

NVivo 12 has a variety of versions to meet your qualitative analysis needs in terms of whether you are a student or not, the type of computer you have, and the type of analysis you plan to do (such as actively developing codes and assigning them to relevant text identified, auto coding sentiments, or determining the connections among cases using

'Sociogram Tools'). In this chapter, I use NVivo 12 Pro (for Window operating systems) for all the demonstrations. To review the versions, go to: www.qsrinternational.com/nvivo/nvivo-products.

My plan is to use NVivo 12 (Version 12.1.249; QSR International Pty Ltd, 2018) to analyze interview transcripts – generating themes to help address my research questions. With this purpose in mind, I have divided the qualitative data analysis process into six stages: preparing qualitative data, exploring data, coding empirical indicators, developing categories/themes, visualizing outcomes and exporting outcomes (see Figure 11.1). All analyses demonstrated in this chapter are run on a Windows 10 operating system.

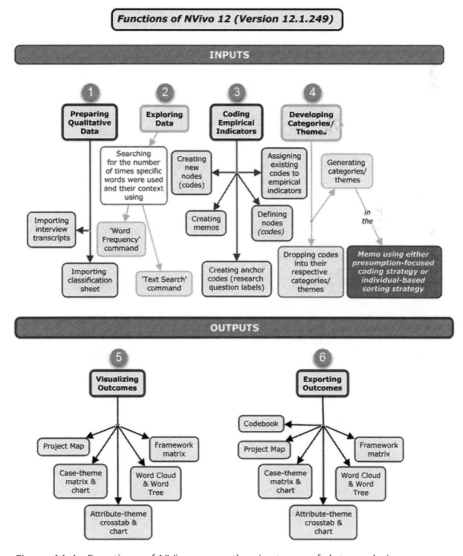

Figure 11.1. Functions of NVivo across the six stages of data analysis

PREPARING QUALITATIVE DATA

Qualitative data preparation involves making the data ready for importing into the NVivo 12 (Version 12.1.249; QSR International Pty Ltd, 2018) software. This involves all the steps discussed in Chapter 4 and also making sure all the interview transcript files have been labeled accordingly – preferably using the IDs you have generated for participants. With respect to participants' demographic information, I find it easy to create this on an Excel spreadsheet and import it into NVivo. I would emphasize that there should be consistency among participant IDs given, file labels created, and participant IDs stated in the spreadsheet. By so doing, you will be able to link participants' transcripts to their respective demographics when importing the demographic information into NVivo.

Before I delve into demonstrating the data preparation steps, let me introduce you to some of the terms used in NVivo. Classification represents what you want to assign values to (see Table 11.1). I'll come back to the concept of 'values' but think of classification as a "unit of analysis" – and thus a case to be examined (Baxter & Jack, 2008, p. 545). So, in NVivo, if you want to assess participants, the name of the classification could be **'Person'** (or **'Participant'**) while if you plan to analyze organizations, the classification could be **'Organization'**. Let's assume you collected data through focus groups and intend to analyze group

Table 11.1 NVivo terms and their meanings

NVivo terms	Meaning
Classification/case classification	Unit of analysis (Example: participant/person, organization or group)
Classification sheet	Excel spreadsheet with participants' demographic information
Attribute	Demographic variable (Example: gender, age, educational level or occupation)
Attribute type 1. Integer and decimal 2. Text and Boolean	Type of variable (in terms of the level of measure) 1. Continuous variable (ordinal, interval and ratio) 2. Categorical variable (nominal)
Attribute value	Assigned group/value/score (Example: male, female, 35 years or 20 points)
Cases	Containers created for files, participants, groups or organization
Node/code	Container which houses empirical indicators
Child node	Node created under another node
Parent node	Node that has child node(s)

characteristics such as average age and number of participants in each group; the name of the classification could be **'Group'**. In a nutshell, classification is a label given to cases you want to assign attribute values to (Bazeley & Jackson, 2014).

So what is an attribute? In NVivo, attribute represents a demographic variable such as gender, age, educational level or occupation. Each attribute is described by its type and values. Think about an attribute type as the level of measurement of a variable – whether it is a continuous variable (example: age) or categorical variable (example: gender) (Slavin, 2007). Attribute values are characteristics assigned to a case or group of cases. For instance, if a participant is a female, the classification, attribute name, attribute type and attribute value would be **'Person'**, **'Gender'**, **'Categorical variable'** and **'Female'**, respectively. Another example is, if she is 25 years old, the classification, attribute name, attribute type and attribute value would be **'Person'**, **'Age'**, **'Continuous variable'** and **'25 years'**, respectively.

Demonstration 11.1

I use ten interview transcripts for all of the demonstrations in this chapter (see Chapter 4). These transcripts are from a case study in the UK conducted between 1997 and 2002 (Cook & Robbins, 2005). The purpose of the research project was to assess strategies used by GM specialists to communicate GM crop research to the public (Cook & Robbins, 2005). Similarly, the aim of this analysis is to explore UK public concerns about GM foods and the strategies GM scientists should use to present the GM crop research to the public. The following are the steps you would take to prepare interview transcripts before importing them into the software.

STEP 11.1. USING PARTICIPANT IDS TO LABEL THE TRANSCRIPT FILES (SEE EXHIBIT 11.1)

1. After deciding on an ID for each participant, state it at the top of the transcript document
2. Use the ID as the name for the document when saving it and then close it
   Note: Repeat these actions for all the interview transcripts

STEP 11.2. PUTTING PARTICIPANTS' DEMOGRAPHIC INFORMATION INTO AN EXCEL SPREADSHEET (SEE EXHIBIT 11.2)

1. Open a blank Excel spreadsheet
2. Enter participant IDs with their demographic information

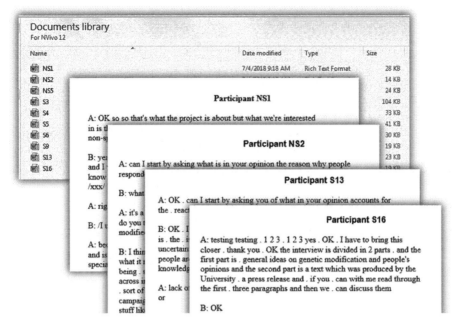

Exhibit 11.1. Display of the interview transcript files

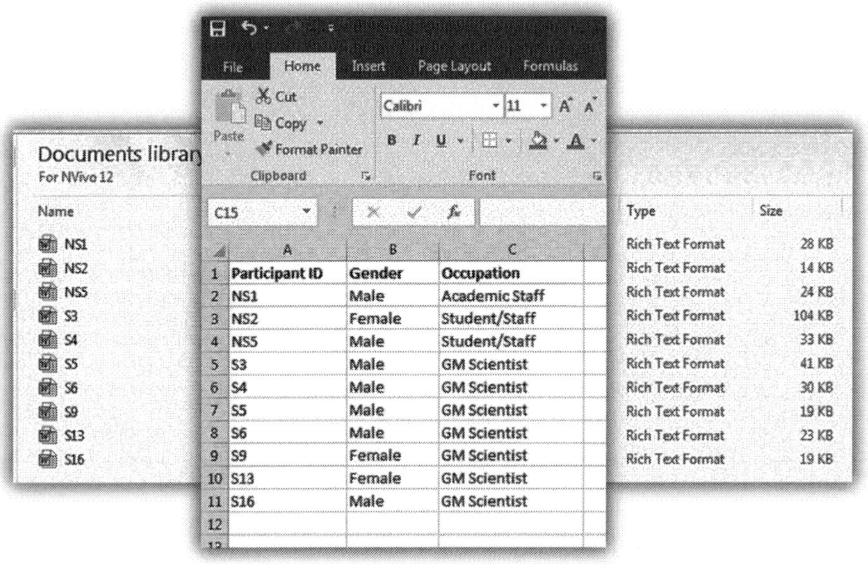

Exhibit 11.2. Display of the interview transcript files and Excel spreadsheet with demographic information

    ✓ Each row contains a participant's demographic information while each column holds values for a demographic attribute/variable.

3. After you finish entering all of the demographic information for each participant, save and close the file

STEP 11.3. OPENING NVIVO 12 SOFTWARE (SEE EXHIBIT 11.3)

1. Open the NVivo 12 software, and to start a new project, click on **'Blank Project'**
2. In the **'New Project'** window, state the title of the project and provide a brief description of the project in the **'Description'** textbox
3. Click on **'Browse'** to determine where to save the project and check **'Write user actions to project event log'** to automatically document steps taken when analyzing the data
4. Click on **'OK'**

STEP 11.4. IMPORTING TRANSCRIPT FILES (SEE EXHIBITS 11.4–11.5)

1. Click on the **'Import'** tab and click on the **'Files'** ribbon to open the **'Import Files'** window
2. In the **'Import Files'** window, locate and select the interview transcript files

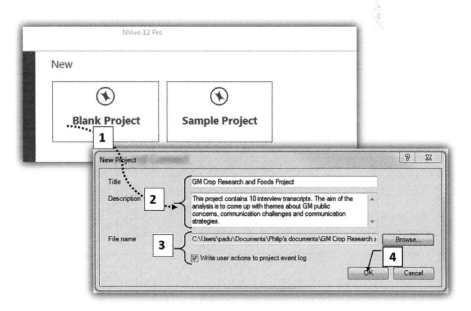

Exhibit 11.3. Opening NVivo 12 and creating a new project

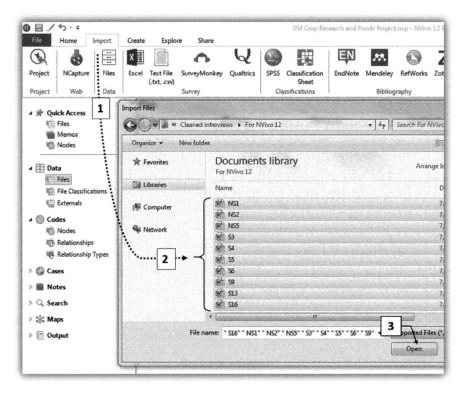

Exhibit 11.4. Locating and importing transcript files

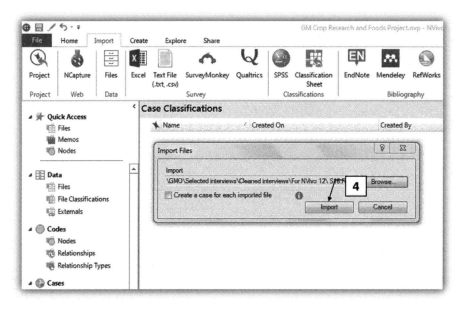

Exhibit 11.5. Importing transcript files

✓ To select all files, click on the first file, press and hold the **'Shift'** key on the keyboard, and click on the last file
3. Click on **'Open'** to display the **'Import Files'** dialog box
4. In the dialog box, click on **'Import'** to import all the transcript files

STEP 11.5. CREATING CASES FOR PARTICIPANTS' TRANSCRIPT FILES (SEE EXHIBITS 11.6–11.7)

1. In the Navigation View, click on **'Files'** to display the transcript files in the List View
2. Select all the transcript files and right-click on them to display menu options
   ✓ To select all files, click on the first file, press and hold the **'Shift'** key on the keyboard, and click on the last file
3. Go to **'Create As'** and select **'Create As Cases'** to open the **'Select Location'** dialog box
4. In the dialog box, click on **'OK'** after making sure that **'Cases'** is selected
5. In the Navigation View, click on **'Cases'** to view the cases created

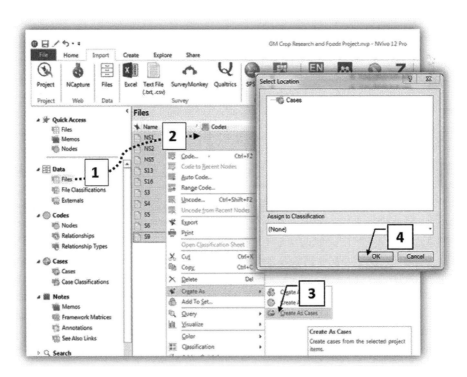

Exhibit 11.6. Creating cases for each transcript file

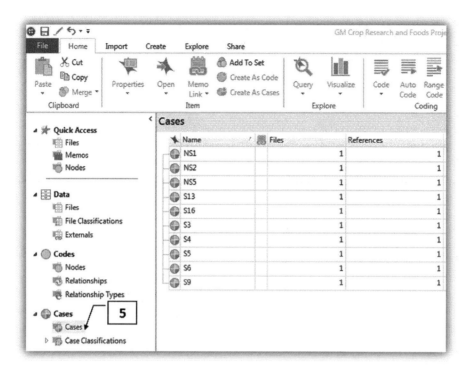

Exhibit 11.7. Display of cases created

STEP 11.6. IMPORTING THE EXCEL FILE (CONTAINING PARTICIPANTS' DEMOGRAPHIC INFORMATION) AS A CLASSIFICATION SHEET (SEE EXHIBITS 11.8–11.10)

1. Click on the *'Import'* tab and then click on the *'Classification Sheet'* ribbon to open the *'Import Classification Sheets Wizard – Step 1 of 4'* window
2. Click on *'Browse'* to locate and select the Excel spreadsheet, and click on *'Next'* to open the *'Import Classification Sheets Wizard – Step 2 of 4'* window
3. In the window, select *'Case Classification'* as the *'Classification type'* and click on *'Next'*
4. In the *'Import Classification Sheets Wizard – Step 3 of 4'* window, check *'As names'*
5. After making sure *'Cases'* is selected under the heading *'Location for these cases in this project'*, click on *'Next'* to open the *'Import Classification Sheets Wizard – Step 4 of 4'* window
6. Click on *'Finish'* to display the imported demographic information

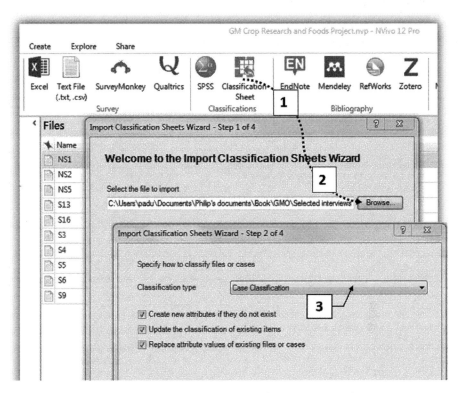

Exhibit 11.8. Locating and selecting the Excel file containing demographic information

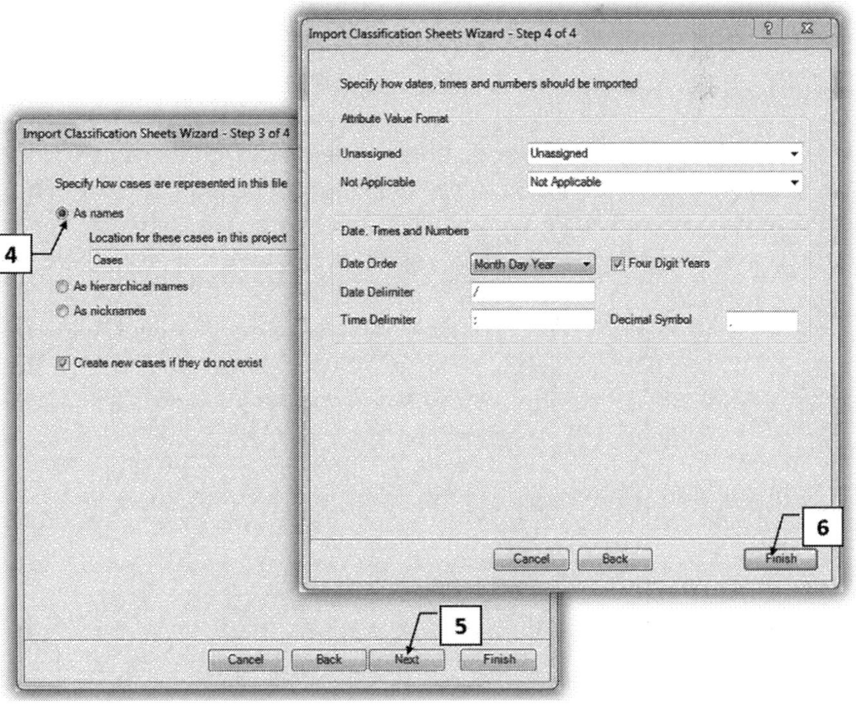

Exhibit 11.9. Indicating the location of the cases

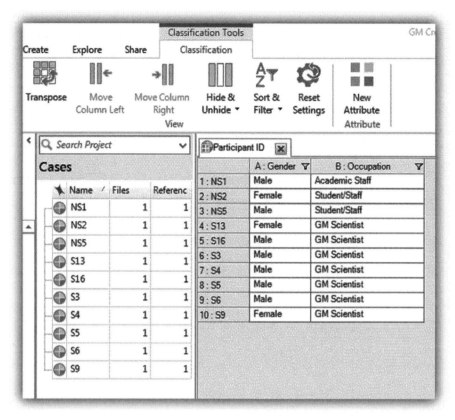

Exhibit 11.10. Display of the imported demographics

EXPLORING DATA

The more you learn about your qualitative data, the better the quality of the analysis. Getting to know the data starts with actively reviewing all the transcripts (see Chapter 4). NVivo software could also be an effective tool to further explore data which are yet to be analyzed. You could conduct a quick analysis to identify the kind of words participants frequently used and how some of them were utilized. The **'Word Frequency'** and **'Text Search'** commands are useful tools to help develop a good understanding of your data. In addition, the outcomes of these queries could inform the kind of codes you use in labeling the empirical indicators identified. However, I would emphasize that running a word frequency or text search is not a substitute for extensive qualitative coding.

Demonstration 11.2

The purpose of this demonstration is to show how to use the **'Word Frequency'** command to develop a Word Cloud and list of words with their counts. A word count is the number of times participants used a particular word. Also, I will illustrate how to search for a specific word employing the *'Text Search'* command, thereby creating a visual representation called a Word Tree.

STEP 11.1. RUNNING A WORD FREQUENCY SEARCH (SEE EXHIBITS 11.11–11.13)

1. Click on the *'Explore'* tab and then click on the *'Word Frequency'* ribbon
2. In the *'Word Frequency Criteria'* dialog box, click on *'Selected Items'* to open the *'Select Project Items'* window
3. In the window, click on *'Files'* (to display all the transcript files) and select each of them
4. Click on *'OK'* to close the window
5. In the *'Word Frequency Criteria'* dialog box, click on *'Run Query'*
6. If the word frequency table is not displayed, click on *'Summary'* on the sidebar to show it
7. On the sidebar, click on *'Word Cloud'* to create a Word Cloud

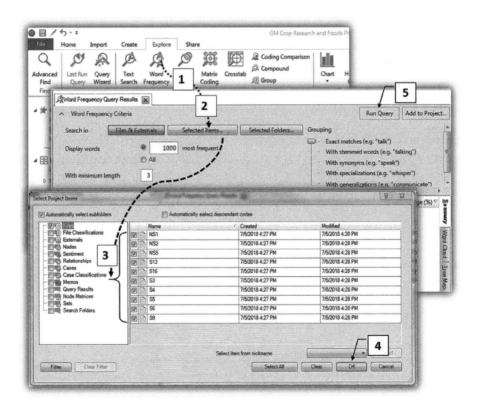

Exhibit 11.11. Running a word frequency search

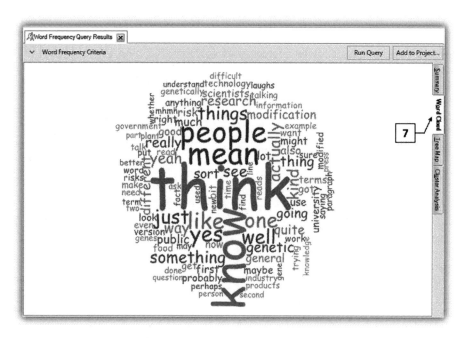

Word	Length	Count ▽	Weighted Percentage (%)
think	5	895	3.10
know	4	639	2.21
mean	4	411	1.42
people	6	398	1.38
like	4	288	1.00
yes	3	266	0.92
one	3	264	0.91
just	4	238	0.82
well	4	235	0.81
things	6	206	0.71
something	9	183	0.63
actually	8	182	0.63
kind	4	179	0.62
see	3	170	0.59
way	3	167	0.58
yeah	4	167	0.58
thing	5	154	0.53
really	6	151	0.52
genetic	7	150	0.52
research	8	140	0.49

Exhibit 11.12. Excerpt of a word frequency table

Exhibit 11.13. Display of a Word Cloud

Commentary 11.1. In the **'Word Frequency Criteria'** dialog box, I maintained the default settings for the options under **'Grouping'**, **'Display words'** and **'With minimum length'**. With the **'Grouping'** options, you could run a frequency search on an exact word (such as *'think'*) or groups of words associated with a specific word (such as *'think'* with *'thinking'*, *'reflecting'* and *'meditating'*). You could also indicate the number of the most frequent words you want to display and the minimum number of letters for the words under **'Display words'** and **'With minimum length'**, respectively. As shown in Exhibit 11.12, the word with the most counts (i.e. the most used word by participants) was **'think'** with a frequency of 895 times – accounting for 3.1% of the top 1000 words participants used. To locate the sources of the word **'think'**, you could double-click on it.

Similarly, the Word Cloud displayed in Exhibit 11.13 mirrors the information in the word frequency table. With this visual representation, the font size of a word depicts how often it was utilized (Saldaña, 2016). For instance, the font of the word **'research'** is smaller than **'think'** because the former was mentioned 140 times compared to 895 times for the latter. In case you decide to remove a word (such as **'yeah'**) from the Word Cloud, you can right-click on the word, select **'Add to Stop Words List'** on the menu options and click on **'OK'** in the **'Add Stop Words'** window. To completely remove the word, you then click on **'Run Query'** in the **'Word Frequency Criteria'** dialog box. Note that the word frequency outcomes may not perfectly reflect the frequency of participants' word usage since the interviewer's words forming the interview questions were also included. There is a way of excluding the interview questions from the transcripts before running the word frequency query (which involves using the **'Auto Code'** command – see Bazeley & Jackson, 2014) but this is beyond the scope of this chapter.

STEP 11.2. RUNNING A TEXT SEARCH (SEE EXHIBIT 11.14)

1. Click on the **'Explore'** tab and then click on the **'Text Search'** ribbon
2. In the **'Text Search Criteria'** dialog box, click on **'Selected Items'** to open the **'Select Project Items'** window
3. In the window, click on **'Files'** (to display all the transcript files) and select each of the files
4. Click on **'OK'** to close the window
5. In the **'Text Search Criteria'** dialog box, click on **'Run Query'**
   ✓ On the sidebar, click on **'Word Tree'** to display a Word Tree (see Figure 11.2)

Commentary 11.2. Similar to the **'Word Frequency Criteria'** dialog box, I made no change to the default settings (in the **'Word Search Criteria'** dialog box) for the options under **'Spread to'** and **'Find'**. When running the query, you could make adjustments to

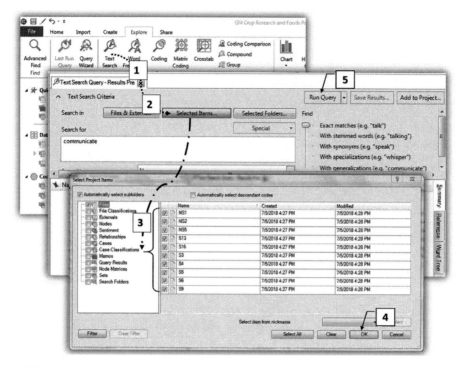

Exhibit 11.14. Running a text search

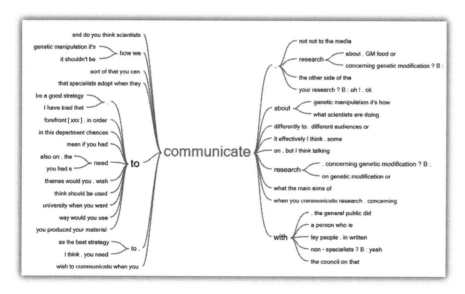

Figure 11.2. A Word Tree displaying the context in which 'communicate' was used

the options and see what you would get. The more you explore, the better you understand your data. Likewise, after running the Text Search query, you could further examine the Word Tree by double-clicking on the phrases or sentences. By so doing, you could review how the word of interest was used contextually and the sources of the information.

CODING EMPIRICAL INDICATORS

At this stage, with the research questions in mind, you go through each transcript – coding relevant segments under their respective research questions. In the same way with the NVivo 12 (Version 12.1.249; QSR International Pty Ltd, 2018) software, when an empirical indicator is identified, you create a node (which can be viewed as a container) (Adu, 2015, 2016; Bazeley & Jackson, 2014). Based on the coding strategy chosen, you label the node. Before creating a new node, see whether any of the existing nodes can house the empirical indicator selected. Additionally, you have an option to document your reflections by creating memos and connecting them to nodes.

Before starting the process of coding empirical indicators, you need to determine the appropriate coding strategy you plan to use. After examining the research approach, purpose of the study, research questions and data, I chose interpretation-focused coding as the suitable coding strategy to analyze the ten interview transcripts (see Chapter 7). I also assigned labels (called anchor codes) to the research questions. As I indicated in Chapter 7, the essence of generating anchor codes is to help organize the codes/nodes under each of the research questions. Here are the research questions and their anchor codes:

1. What were the factors contributing to public concerns about GM research and foods in the UK? **(GM concerns factors)**
2. What were the challenges faced by GM scientists when communicating GM crop research to the public? **(GM communication challenges)**
3. How should GM crop research be communicated to the public to address their concerns? **(GM communication strategies)**

Demonstration 11.3

Below are steps and actions you would follow if you plan to create: anchor codes, nodes for empirical indicators, and memos.

STEP 11.1. CREATING ANCHOR CODES (I.E. NODES FOR THE RESEARCH QUESTIONS) (SEE EXHIBIT 11.15)

1. In the Navigation View, click on **'Nodes'** to display the List View (which is the work area for generating nodes)
2. Right-click on the work area and select **'New Node'**
3. In the **'New Node'** window, type the node name, which is the anchor code
4. In the **'Description'** textbox, input what the anchor code represents
5. Check **'Aggregate coding from children'** and click on **'OK'** to close the **'New Node'** window
   - ✓ Checking **'Aggregate coding from children'** implies that the number of empirical indicators (i.e. references) for each node under the anchor code will be automatically summed to be the references (total frequencies or counts) for that anchor code.

   Note: The above actions are repeated for all the research questions

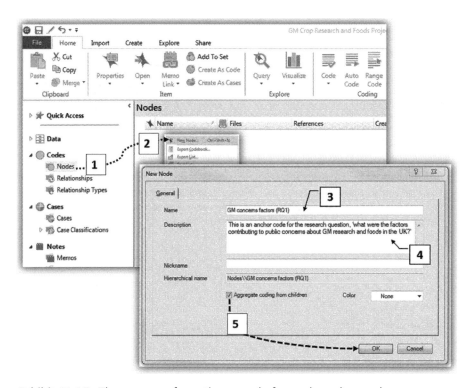

Exhibit 11.15. The process of creating a node for each anchor code

STEP 11.2. IDENTIFYING EMPIRICAL INDICATORS AND DROPPING THEM INTO NEW NODES (SEE EXHIBITS 11.16–11.17)

1. In the Navigation View, click on **'Files'** under **'Data'** to display all the transcript files in the List View
2. Open the transcript file to be reviewed by double-clicking on it to display it in the workspace (Detail View)
3. In the Navigation View, click on **'Nodes'** under **'Codes'** to display all the anchor codes in the List View
4. In the workspace (Detail View), go through the transcript and when an empirical indicator is identified, select and drag it to the List View – leading to the opening of a **'New Node'** window
5. In the window, type the node/code name
6. In the **'Description'** textbox, provide what the node/code represents
7. Click on **'Select'** to open the **'Select Location'** window
8. In the window, select the anchor code the new node belongs to (or should be put under)
9. Click on **'OK'** in the **'Select Location'** window to close it

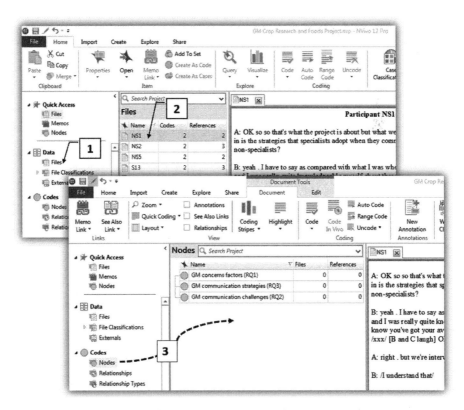

Exhibit 11.16. Setting up for the development of nodes

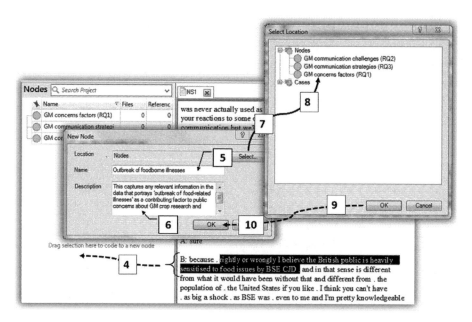

Exhibit 11.17. Actions taken to create a node

10. Click on **'OK'** in the **'New Node'** window to close it
   - ✓ To find areas in the transcript you have coded, **'Coding Stripes'** and **'Highlight'** under the **'Document'** tab are useful tools to use
   - ✓ To review all the empirical indicators connected to a node, double-click the node

STEP 11.3. SELECTING EMPIRICAL INDICATORS AND DROPPING THEM INTO EXISTING NODES (EXHIBIT 11.18)

1. If an existing node can be used to code an empirical indicator identified, select the indicator in the workspace (Detail View)
2. Drag and drop it into the existing node

STEP 11.4. CREATING MEMOS (EXHIBITS 11.19–11.20)

1. Right-click on the node which the memo will be linked to
2. Go to **'Memo Link'** and select **'Link to New Memo'** to open the **'New Memo'** description window
3. In the window, type the name of the memo
4. In the **'Description'** textbox, input what the memo is about
5. Click on **'OK'** to close the window and open a blank memo
6. On the toolbar under **'Memo Tools'**, click on **'Edit'**
7. Click on the **'Insert'** ribbon and then click on **'Insert Data/Time'**
8. In the memo, document reflections about empirical indicator (s) and/or the associated node and close it when done

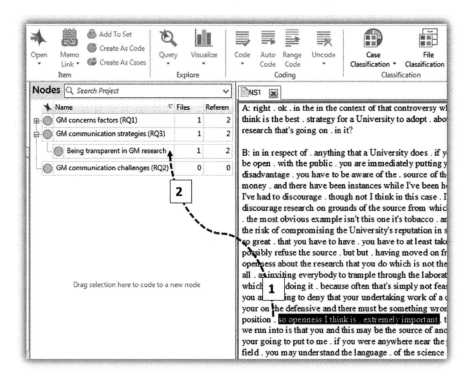

Exhibit 11.18. Dropping an empirical indicator into an existing node

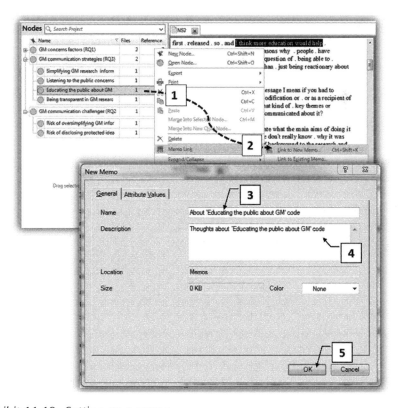

Exhibit 11.19. Setting up a memo

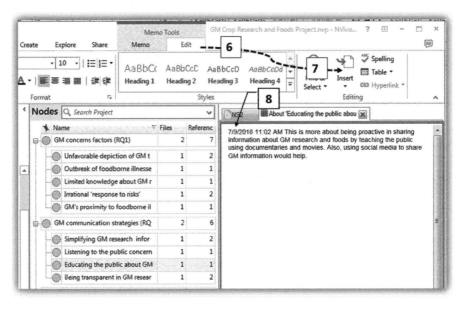

Exhibit 11.20. Writing a memo

Commentary 11.3. Note that the above steps are not strictly sequential. When coding, you have the flexibility of going back and forth in terms of creating new nodes, dropping empirical indicators into existing nodes and creating memos. You have the option to make changes to the name and the description of an existing node by right-clicking on the node and selecting *'Node Properties'* in the menu options. With regards to making adjustments or adding more information to an existing memo, you could click on *'Notes'* in the Navigation View and then *'Memos'* to display the memos created in the List View. To open the memo, you double-click on it.

In terms of how to develop appropriate labels for the nodes, there are a couple of steps you need to take. Chapter 7 has all the information and illustrations about creating codes. I recommend you first review that chapter before learning how to create codes with NVivo.

As shown in Exhibits 11.21–11.24 (the outcome of the initial coding process), the first column contains all the nodes created under each of the research questions. The second column indicates the nodes that have a memo connected to them. To see the content of the memos, go to the Navigation View and click on *'Memos'* under *'Notes'*. The column with the heading *'Files'* has the number of transcript files (cases) linked to a particular node. For example: the node *'Limited knowledge about GM research'* under the anchor code *'GM concerns factors (RQ1)'* represents empirical indicators from six out of ten files (cases) (see Exhibit 11.21).

The **'References'** column contains the number of the times empirical indicators were dropped into a particular node. It can also be referred to as counts or frequencies. In all, 22 nodes (with 61 counts), 10 nodes (with 18 counts), 23 nodes (with 48 counts) and 5 nodes (with 8 counts) were created under **'GM concerns factors (RQ1)'**, **'GM communication challenges (RQ2)'**, **'GM communication strategies (RQ3)'** and **'Other issues'**, respectively (see Exhibits 11.21–11.24). The next stage of the analysis process is to generate categories and themes out of the nodes developed.

DEVELOPING CATEGORIES/THEMES

Developing categories/themes using NVivo 12 (Version 12.1.249; QSR International Pty Ltd, 2018) software involves two main steps: building categories/themes and dropping nodes/codes into the categories/themes generated. With respect to building categories/themes, you could use one of the three categorization strategies, namely: presumption-focused

Name	Files	Reference ▽
Nodes		
GM concerns factors (RQ1)	10	61
Limited knowledge about GM research	6	10
Unfavorable depiction of GM technology	3	7
Belief in GM product side effects	2	5
Criticism from interest groups	3	4
'Mistrust of commercial companies'	2	4
Mistrust of scientists	2	4
Outbreak of foodborne illnesses	3	3
GM's proximity to foodborne illnesses	3	3
Unsatisfactory answer to GM risks	2	3
Hesitant to explain GM research	2	3
Irrational 'response to risks'	1	2
Lack of effective government communication	2	2
Multiple meanings of GM concepts	1	2
Objective-driven nature of scientific research	1	1
Inadequate promotion of GM benefits	1	1
Uncertain about GM research	1	1
Extensively unexamined GM side effects	1	1
Conflicting views about GM safety	1	1
Mistrust of the government	1	1
Disinterested in learning about GM	1	1
GM scientists' ineffective communication	1	1
Hesitant to embrace GM technology	1	1

Exhibit 11.21. Codes and their respective cases (files) and counts (frequencies) under *'GM concerns factors (RQ1)'*

Nodes

Name	Files	Reference ▽
⊟ ◯ GM communication challenges (RQ2)	8	18
◯ Difficulty explaining GM technology	2	5
◯ Not sure about GM risks	3	3
◯ GM risks non-existence not guaranteed	2	2
◯ Fear GM findings distortion	1	2
◯ Risk of disclosing protected ideas	1	1
◯ Risk of oversimplifying GM information	1	1
◯ 'Pressure from the government'	1	1
◯ Public pressure for GM safety	1	1
◯ Limited information about GM risks	1	1
◯ Pressure from the public	1	1

Exhibit 11.22. Codes and their respective cases (files) and counts (frequencies) under 'GM communication challenges (RQ2)'

Nodes

Name	Files	Reference ▽
⊟ ◯ GM communication strategies (RQ3)	9	48
◯ Making in-depth GM presentations	3	4
◯ Assessing public GM knowledge level	4	4
◯ Simplifying GM research information	2	3
◯ Educating the public about GM	2	3
◯ Giving the public some time	3	3
◯ Presenting GM risks and benefits	1	3
◯ Discussing specific GM case	3	3
◯ Being transparent in GM research	1	2
◯ Presenting GM research rationale	2	2
◯ Having conversations about GM risks	2	2
◯ Communicating GM innovation benefits	2	2
◯ Emphasizing GM's positive side	1	2
◯ Organizing seminars for the public	2	2
◯ Tailoring GM information	1	2
◯ Emphasizing crossbreeding-GM similarities	2	2
◯ Being proactive in GM information-sharing	1	2
◯ Listening to the public concerns	1	1
◯ Debating with pressure groups	1	1
◯ Making GM research publicly available	1	1
◯ Creating press releases	1	1
◯ Creating awareness of GM risks	1	1
◯ Having public debate about GM	1	1
◯ Collaborating with other departments	1	1

Exhibit 11.23. Codes and their respective cases (files) and counts (frequencies) under 'GM communication strategies (RQ3)'

Nodes		
↖ Name	📊 Files	References ▽
⊟ ◯ Other issues	4	8
◯ Government funding for GM research 📊	2	2
◯ More research on GM risks	2	2
◯ Single definition of GM concepts	1	2
◯ Finding out GM research sponsor	1	1
◯ Difficulty in labeling products	1	1

Exhibit 11.24. Codes and their respective cases (files) and counts (frequencies) under *'Other issues'*

coding, individual-based sorting and group-based sorting (see Chapter 8). Similar to Microsoft Word, the memo document in NVivo can play a huge role in generating categories/themes with the utilization of either the presumption-focused coding strategy or the individual-based sorting strategy (see Table 11.2). Microsoft Word, in comparison to the memo document in NVivo, is able to fully complement SPSS when implementing the group-based sorting strategy to develop categories/themes, while NVivo cannot at this time. After achieving the end goal of building categories/themes with one of the categorization strategies, the next stage is to create a node for each of the categories/themes and drop initial nodes/codes into them.

Demonstration 11.4

The demonstrations are on how to work on the memo document (in NVivo) to build categories/themes employing the presumption-focused coding strategy and the individual-based sorting strategy. These demonstrations end with the process of creating nodes for the categories/themes and dropping existing nodes/codes into them.

STEP 11.1A. BUILDING CATEGORIES/THEMES USING THE PRESUMPTION-FOCUSED CODING STRATEGY (SEE EXHIBITS 11.25–11.29)

1. In the Navigation View, click on **'Nodes'** under **'Codes'** to display the nodes in the List View
2. Under the **'Create'** tab, click on the **'Memo'** ribbon to set up the memo document
3. In the **'New Memo'** window, type the name of the memo (in this case, **'Analytical Memo_themes for GM concern factors'**)

Table 11.2 Analytical tools for generating categories/themes

Categorization strategy	Analytical tools		
	Microsoft Word	SPSS	NVivo
Presumption-focused coding strategy	**'New Comment'** function under the **'Review'** tab		**'Memo'** function under the **'Create'** tab
Individual-based sorting strategy	**'Tables'** function under the **'Insert'** tab		**'Memo'** function under the **'Create'** tab
Group-based sorting strategy	**'Tables'** and **'Shapes'** functions under the **'Insert'** tab	**'Multidimensional Scaling'** function of the **'Scale'** option under the **'Analysis'** tab **'Hierarchical Cluster'** function of the **'Classify'** option under the **'Analysis'** tab	

4. In the **'Description'** textbox, input what the memo is
5. Click on **'OK'** to open a blank memo
6. Input the heading as **'Analytical Memo'** and then input the research question for the categories/themes to be developed
7. Under the **'Edit'** tab, click on the **'Table'** ribbon and select **'Insert Text Table'**
8. In the **'Insert Text Table'** dialog box, indicate the number of columns and rows
9. Click on **'OK'** to display the table
10. Above the table, state the notations associated with the presumption-focused coding strategy (see Chapter 8 for more information about the notations)
    a. To insert the notation for **'Based on'**, click on the **'Insert'** ribbon
    b. Select the **'Insert Symbol'** to open the **'Insert Symbol'** window
    c. In the window, double-click on the forward arrow ('→') symbol to display it in parentheses after **'Based on'** and close the window
       ✓ To find the forward arrow symbol in the **'Insert Symbol'** window, select **'Wingdings 3'** and **'Private Use Area'** for the **'Font'** type and **'Subset'**, respectively

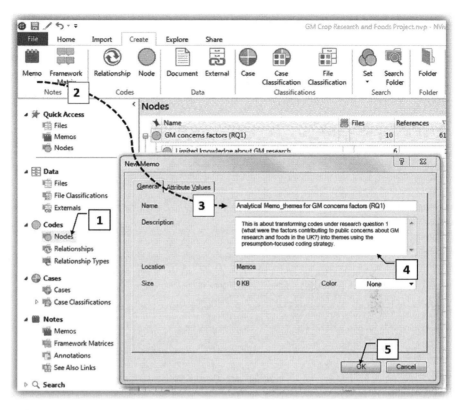

Exhibit 11.25. Setting up a memo document to generate themes under *'GM concerns factors (RQ1)'*

     d. After inserting the forward arrow symbol, check under the **'Edit'** tab to make sure the right font type is displayed (preferably **'Times New Roman'**)

11. In the table, provide a heading for each column: **'Code(Evidence)'** and **'Claim with Evidence'** for column 1 and column 2, respectively
    ✓ With the presumption-focused coding strategy, nodes/codes are seen as evidence. The goal is to develop claims and look for evidence (which are the codes) to support them (see Chapter 8).

12. Copy each node from the List View and paste it in the **'Code (Evidence)'** column
    ✓ After transferring all the nodes to the table, number them. The essence of numbering the nodes is to help with the development of notations.

13. After reviewing all nodes, including their descriptions, generate claims and link them to their respective evidence

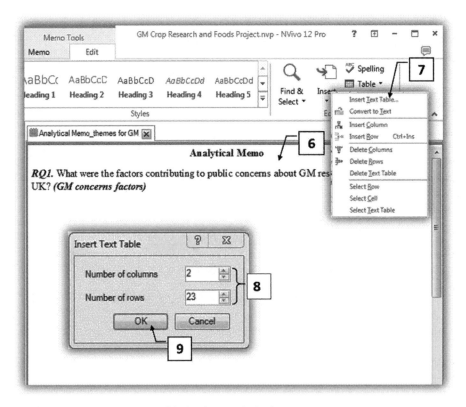

Exhibit 11.26. Creating a table in the analytical memo

✓ This is done by typing the claim in the cell corresponding to its evidence, and in parentheses stating its notation. For instance, the first claim supported by the first evidence would be written as *(Pre1→E1)*.

14. Go through the nodes to look for additional evidence to support the claim

✓ There is flexibility in this process. You could make adjustments to the original claim when needed. If a change is made to the claim due to an introduction of new evidence, *'R'* should be included in the notation. For example, I revised the first claim when the eighth piece of evidence was added to the existing evidence (see Exhibit 11.28). In this case, the notation would be *(Pre1R→E8)*. Also, you could use one piece of evidence to support more than one claim. For instance, the eleventh piece of evidence, *'Irrational "response to risks"'* was used to support two claims, namely: *'Perceived existence of GM risks'* and *'Misunderstanding of GM risks'* (see Table 11.3).

Note: Actions 13 and 14 are followed until all nodes are examined as potential evidence for the claims (see Table 11.3)

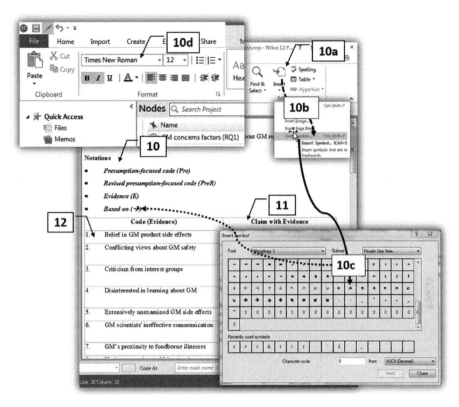

Exhibit 11.27. Transferring nodes to the table

15. Compile a list of claims and their respective evidence
16. State each claim (theme), and in parentheses indicate a notation that represents all the supporting evidence
17. Compare initial themes to determine whether there are sub-themes

STEP 11.1B. CREATING NODES UNDER AN ANCHOR CODE FOR THE THEMES AND SUB-THEMES DEVELOPED (SEE EXHIBIT 11.30)

1. Copy the theme/sub-theme developed
2. Right-click on the anchor code and select **'New Node'** to open the **'New Node'** window
3. In the window, paste the theme/sub-theme in the textbox for the node **'Name'** and state **'Pre'** with the assigned claim number in parentheses to distinguish it from the initial nodes
   ✓ You could provide a description for the theme/sub-theme if you want to.
4. Check **'Aggregate coding from children'**
5. Click on **'OK'** to create a node for the theme/sub-theme
   Note: The above actions are repeated for all the themes and sub-themes.

Code (Evidence)	Claim with Evidence 13
1. Belief in GM product side effects	Existence of GM side effects *(Pre1 →E1)*
2. Conflicting views about GM safety	
3. Criticism from interest groups	
4. Disinterested in learning about GM	
5. Extensively unexamined GM side effects	
6. GM scientists' ineffective communication	
7. GM's proximity to foodborne illnesses	
8. Hesitant to embrace GM technology	Perceived existence of GM risks 14 *(Pre1R →E8)*
9. Hesitant to explain GM research	
10. Inadequate promotion of GM benefits	
11. Irrational 'response to risks'	Perceived existence of GM risks *(Pre1R →E11)*
12. Lack of effective government communication	

Exhibit 11.28. Connecting claims to nodes (evidence)

STEP 11.1C. DROPPING THE NODES/CODES INTO THEIR RESPECTIVE THEMES AND SUB-THEMES (SEE EXHIBITS 11.31–11.32)

1. Use the table with the codes and associated claims as a reference
2. Select a node in the List View, and drag and drop it into the theme it belongs to
   ✓ If a code supports more than one claim, make a duplicate of it by right-clicking on it, selecting **'Copy'** and right-clicking on the node (claim/theme) you plan to drop it into and selecting **'Paste'**.

Note: The above actions are repeated until all the codes are dropped into their themes/sub-themes

STEP 11.2A. BUILDING CATEGORIES/THEMES USING THE INDIVIDUAL-BASED SORTING STRATEGY (SEE EXHIBITS 11.33–11.37)

1. In the Navigation View, click on **'Nodes'** under **'Codes'** to display the nodes in the List View
2. Under the **'Create'** tab, click on the **'Memo'** ribbon to set up the memo document

Table 11.3 List of codes and their respective claims

Code (evidence)	Claim with evidence
1. Belief in GM product side effects	Existence of GM side effects *(Pre1→E1)*
2. Conflicting views about GM safety	Mixed messaging about GM safety **(Pre2→E2)**
3. Criticism from interest groups	Unfavorable depiction of GM technology **(Pre4→E3)**
4. Disinterested in learning about GM	Limited knowledge about GM research **(Pre6→E4)**
5. Extensively unexamined GM side effects	GM risks uncertainties **(Pre8→E5)**
6. GM scientists' ineffective communication	GM scientists' ineffective communication **(Pre3→E6)**
7. GM's proximity to foodborne illnesses	Misunderstanding of GM risks **(Pre7→E7)**
8. Hesitant to embrace GM technology	Perceived existence of GM risks *(Pre1R→E8)*
9. Hesitant to explain GM research	Lack of effective communication **(Pre3R→E9)**
10. Inadequate promotion of GM benefits	Lack of effective communication **(Pre3R→E10)**
11. Irrational 'response to risks'	Perceived existence of GM risks **(Pre1R→E11)** Misunderstanding of GM risks **(Pre7→E11)**
12. Lack of effective government communication	Lack of effective communication **(Pre3R→E12)**
13. Limited knowledge about GM research	Limited knowledge about GM research **(Pre6→E13)**
14. 'Mistrust of commercial companies'	Mistrust towards GM stakeholders **(Pre5→E14)**
15. Mistrust of scientists	Mistrust towards GM stakeholders **(Pre5→E15)**
16. Mistrust of the government	Mistrust towards GM stakeholders **(Pre5→E16)**
17. Multiple meanings of GM concepts	Lack of effective communication **(Pre3R→E17)**
18. Objective-driven nature of scientific research	GM risks uncertainties **(Pre8→E18)**
19. Outbreak of foodborne illnesses	Misunderstanding of GM risks **(Pre7→E19)**
20. Uncertain about GM research	GM risks uncertainties **(Pre8→E20)**
21. Unfavorable depiction of GM technology	Unfavorable depiction of GM technology **(Pre4→E21)**
22. Unsatisfactory answer to GM risks	Misunderstanding of GM risks **(Pre7→E22)**

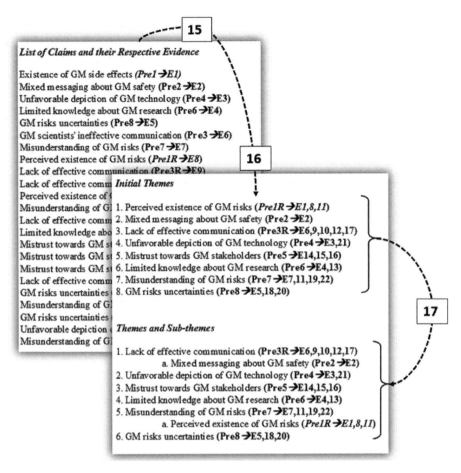

15

List of Claims and their Respective Evidence

Existence of GM side effects *(Pre1 →E1)*
Mixed messaging about GM safety **(Pre2 →E2)**
Unfavorable depiction of GM technology **(Pre4 →E3)**
Limited knowledge about GM research **(Pre6 →E4)**
GM risks uncertainties **(Pre8 →E5)**
GM scientists' ineffective communication **(Pre3 →E6)**
Misunderstanding of GM risks **(Pre7 →E7)**
Perceived existence of GM risks **(Pre1R →E8)**
Lack of effective communication **(Pre3R →E9)**
Lack of effective comm
Perceived existence of
Misunderstanding of G
Lack of effective comm
Limited knowledge abo
Mistrust towards GM s
Mistrust towards GM s
Mistrust towards GM s
Lack of effective comm
GM risks uncertainties
Misunderstanding of G
GM risks uncertainties
Unfavorable depiction
Misunderstanding of G

16

Initial Themes

1. Perceived existence of GM risks **(Pre1R →E1,8,11)**
2. Mixed messaging about GM safety **(Pre2 →E2)**
3. Lack of effective communication **(Pre3R →E6,9,10,12,17)**
4. Unfavorable depiction of GM technology **(Pre4 →E3,21)**
5. Mistrust towards GM stakeholders **(Pre5 →E14,15,16)**
6. Limited knowledge about GM research **(Pre6 →E4,13)**
7. Misunderstanding of GM risks **(Pre7 →E7,11,19,22)**
8. GM risks uncertainties **(Pre8 →E5,18,20)**

17

Themes and Sub-themes

1. Lack of effective communication **(Pre3R →E6,9,10,12,17)**
      a. Mixed messaging about GM safety **(Pre2 →E2)**
2. Unfavorable depiction of GM technology **(Pre4 →E3,21)**
3. Mistrust towards GM stakeholders **(Pre5 →E14,15,16)**
4. Limited knowledge about GM research **(Pre6 →E4,13)**
5. Misunderstanding of GM risks **(Pre7 →E7,11,19,22)**
      a. Perceived existence of GM risks **(Pre1R →E1,8,11)**
6. GM risks uncertainties **(Pre8 →E5,18,20)**

Exhibit 11.29. Transitioning from a list of claims to themes and sub-themes

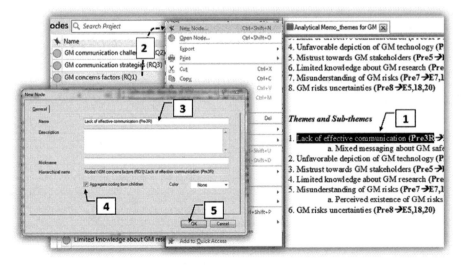

Exhibit 11.30. Creating a node under the anchor code for a theme

3. In the **'New Memo'** window, type the name of the memo (in this case, **'Analytical Memo_themes for the GM communication strategies (RQ3)'**)
4. In the **'Description'** textbox, input what the memo is
5. Click on **'OK'** to open a blank memo
6. Input the heading as **'Analytical Memo'** and then input the research question for the categories/themes to be developed
7. Under the **'Edit'** tab, click on the **'Table'** ribbon and select **'Insert Text Table'**
8. In the **'Insert Text Table'** dialog box, indicate the number of columns and rows
9. Click on **'OK'** to display the table
10. For each column header, state **'Cluster'** and number it
   ✓ At this point, the number of cluster columns you create doesn't matter. You could decide to work on between two cluster columns and any number not more than half of the total nodes/codes created under your research question. During the sorting process, be ready to create more columns when needed (see Chapter 8).

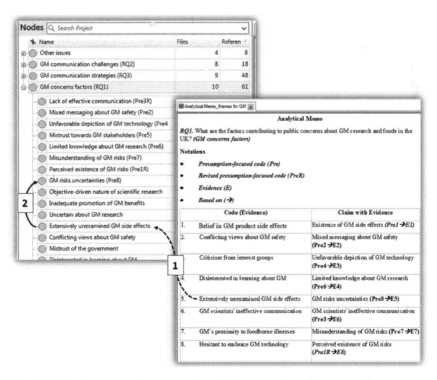

Exhibit 11.31. Dropping the codes into their respective themes and sub-themes

253

Nodes

Name	Files	References ▽
⊟ ◯ GM concerns factors (RQ1)	10	63
⊟ ◯ Misunderstanding of GM risks	8	19
⊞ ◯ Perceived existence of GM risks (Pre1R)	4	8
◯ GM's proximity to foodborne illnesses	3	3
◯ Outbreak of foodborne illnesses	3	3
◯ Unsatisfactory answer to GM risks	2	3
◯ Irrational 'response to risks'	1	2
⊟ ◯ Unfavorable depiction of GM technology	5	11
◯ Unfavorable depiction of GM technology 🖿	3	7
◯ Criticism from interest groups 🖿	3	4
⊟ ◯ Limited knowledge about GM research (Pre6)	6	11
◯ Limited knowledge about GM research	6	10
◯ Disinterested in learning about GM 🖿	1	1
⊟ ◯ Lack of effective communication	4	10
◯ Hesitant to explain GM research 🖿	2	3
◯ Lack of effective government communication	2	2
◯ Multiple meanings of GM concepts 🖿	1	2
◯ Inadequate promotion of GM benefits	1	1
◯ GM scientists' ineffective communication	1	1
⊞ ◯ Mixed messaging about GM safety (Pre2)	1	1
⊟ ◯ Mistrust towards GM stakeholders (Pre5)	3	9
◯ Mistrust of scientists	2	4
◯ 'Mistrust of commercial companies'	2	4
◯ Mistrust of the government	1	1
⊟ ◯ GM risks uncertainties (Pre8)	3	3
◯ Uncertain about GM research	1	1
◯ Extensively unexamined GM side effects 🖿	1	1
◯ Objective-driven nature of scientific research 🖿	1	1

Exhibit 11.32. Themes and sub-themes and their codes for *'GM concerns factors (RQ1)'*

11. Transfer the dominant code by copying it from the List View and pasting it into **'Cluster 1'** column
  ✓ The code with the highest frequency (**'References'**) and highest number of cases (**'Files'**) would be considered a dominant code. In case you encounter a situation where there is more than one dominant code, you could put them in separate columns.

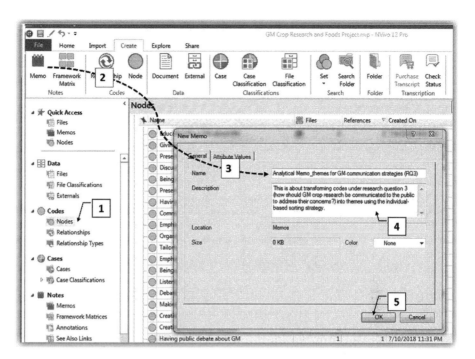

Exhibit 11.33. Setting up a memo document to generate themes under *'GM communication strategies (RQ3)'*

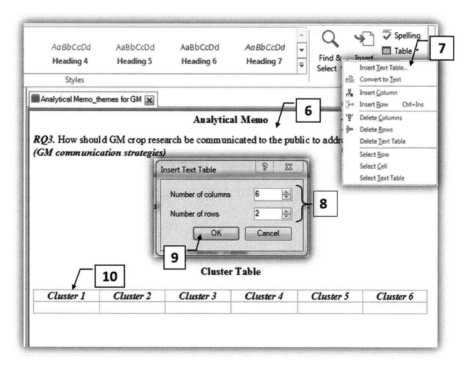

Exhibit 11.34. Creating a cluster table in the analytical memo

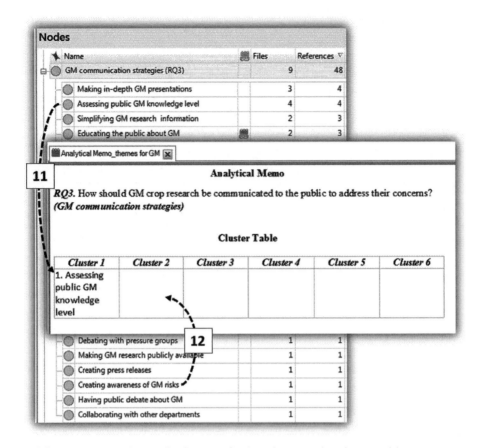

Exhibit 11.35. Sorting codes by transferring them to the cluster table

12. Review the rest of the codes to determine if they are related to the dominant code and if a code has no connection with the dominant code, put it under a new cluster column
   ✓ The rule is whenever a code has no relationship with the dominant code or any code in another existing cluster, you put such a code into a new cluster column.
13. Review the codes in the clusters and label each of them
   ✓ See Chapter 8 for more information on generating labels for clusters

STEP 11.2B. CREATING NODES UNDER AN ANCHOR CODE FOR THE THEMES DEVELOPED (SEE EXHIBIT 11.38)

1. Copy the theme (cluster label) developed
2. Right-click on the anchor code and select **'New Node'** to open the **'New Node'** window

Analytical Memo_themes for GM [x]

Analytical Memo

RQ3. How should GM crop research be communicated to the public to address their concerns? ***(GM communication strategies)***

Cluster Table

Cluster 1	Cluster 2	Cluster 3	Cluster 4	Cluster 5	Cluster 6
1. Assessing public GM knowledge level	**1.** Being transparent in GM research	**1.** Giving the public some time	**1.** Creating press releases	**1.** Debating with pressure groups	**1.** Simplifying GM research information
2. Listening to the public concerns	**2.** Creating awareness of GM risks		**2.** Making GM research publicly available	**2.** Discussing specific GM case	**2.** Tailoring GM information
	3. Communicating GM innovation benefits		**3.** Collaborating with other departments	**3.** Having public debate about GM	**3.** Emphasizing crossbreeding/ GM similarities
	4. Emphasizing GM's public side			**4.** Making in-depth GM presentations	**4.** Educating the public about GM
	5. Having conversations about GM risks			**5.** Organizing seminars for the public	
	6. Presenting GM research rationale			**6.** Being proactive in GM information-sharing	
	7. Presenting GM risks and benefits				

Exhibit 11.36. Sorted codes under six clusters

3. In the window, paste the theme in the textbox for the node **'Name'** and state **'T'** (which stands for 'theme') in parentheses to distinguish it from the initial nodes

4. In the **'Description'** textbox, input what the theme represents
   ✓ Providing a description is optional but recommended

5. Check **'Aggregate coding from children'**

6. Click on **'OK'** to create a node for the theme

Note: The above actions are repeated for all the themes

STEP 11.2C. DROPPING THE CODES INTO THEIR RESPECTIVE THEMES (SEE EXHIBITS 11.39–11.40)

1. Use the cluster table with cluster labels as a reference

Cluster Table with Cluster Label

Cluster 1 (Assessing public views about GM)	**Cluster 2** (Sharing GM risks and benefits)	**Cluster 3** (Giving the public some time)	**Cluster 4** (Making GM research publicly available)	**Cluster 5** (Proactively engaging with the public)	**Cluster 6** (Simplifying GM research information)
1. Assessing public GM knowledge level 2. Listening to the public concerns	1. Being transparent in GM research 2. Creating awareness of GM risks 3. Communicating GM innovation benefits 4. Emphasizing GM's positive side 5. Having conversations about GM risks 6. Presenting GM research rationale 7. Presenting GM risks and benefits	1. Giving the public some time	1. Creating press releases 2. Making GM research publicly available 3. Collaborating with other departments	1. Debating with pressure groups 2. Discussing specific GM case 3. Having public debate about GM 4. Making in-depth GM presentations 5. Organizing seminars for the public 6. Being proactive in GM information-sharing	1. Simplifying GM research information 2. Tailoring GM information 3. Emphasizing crossbreeding/GM similarities 4. Educating the public about GM

13

Exhibit 11.37. Labeled clusters

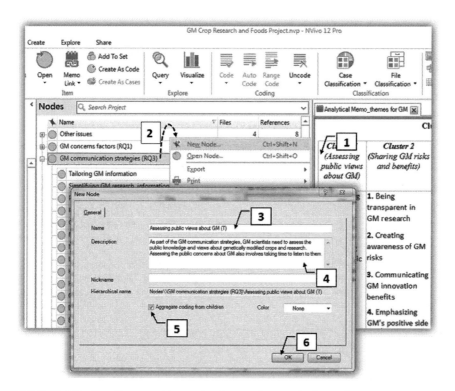

Exhibit 11.38. Creating a node under the anchor code for a theme

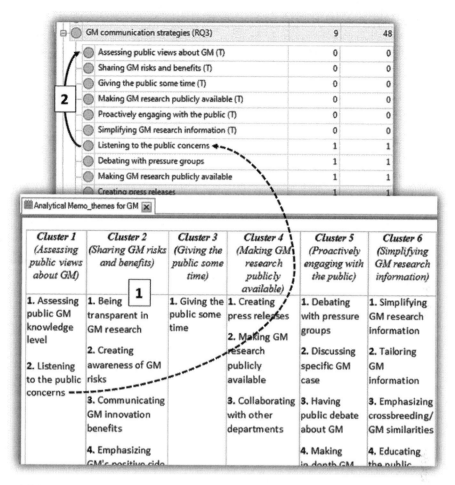

Exhibit 11.39. Dropping nodes/codes into their themes

2. Select a node in the List View, and drag and drop it into the theme it belongs to

Note: The above actions are repeated until all the codes are dropped into their themes

VISUALIZING OUTCOMES

In terms of visualizing qualitative data analysis outcomes, NVivo 12 (Version 12.1.249; QSR International Pty Ltd, 2018) software has numerous tools to create meaningful illustrations to help make sense of the findings and communicate them to your audience. You can use the **'Framework Matrix'** tool to create a table that shows the empirical indicators shared between cases (participants/files) and codes/themes. Similarly, another visualization tool, **'Matrix Coding'**, produces a table with shared relationships between cases and codes/themes. However, with this function, instead of displaying the empirical indicators in the cells of the table, it shows the number of empirical indicators (which could be called references, frequencies or counts). Further, imagine you want to create a table that shows the number of empirical indicators linked to both participants' attributes and themes: **'Crosstab'** would be useful here.

Word Cloud and Word Tree are products of running **'Word Frequency'** and **'Text Search'**, respectively. These visual representations can play a huge role when presenting your findings. They are based on the empirical indicators coded under an anchor code or a theme. They give your audience a new perspective about the results and assist them in understanding the kind of words (in the empirical indicators) participants frequently used and the context in which they utilized the words. Similarly, as you explore Word Clouds and Word Trees you can gain new insights into the themes and the results as a whole.

Lastly, another exploratory tool that I personally like is **'Project Map'**. I work with it to examine the demographic characteristics of participants who are linked to a specific theme or a group of themes. With this tool, I'm able to pull up all features of a theme including its child and parent nodes, and cases and files connected to it. Building this web of information helps in better comprehending my results and opens a new door to interesting patterns and discoveries which could be shared with my audience.

Demonstration 11.5

The following are demonstrations on how to create a framework matrix, case-theme matrix with chart, attribute-theme crosstab with chart, Word Cloud, Word Tree and Project Map.

STEP 11.1. CREATING A FRAMEWORK MATRIX (SEE EXHIBITS 11.41–11.43)

1. Click on the **'Create'** tab and click on **'Framework Matrix'** to open the **'New Framework Matrix'** window
2. In the window, name the matrix (example: **'Framework matrix for GM communication strategies (RQ3)'**)
3. Click on the **'Rows'** tab
4. Under **'Selected cases'**, click on **'Select'** to check cases of interest and click on **'OK'**
5. Under **'Select attributes to sort the rows by'**, click on **'Select'** to check participants' attributes of interest and click on **'OK'**
   ✓ This action is optional. You can create a framework matrix without including participants' demographics.

6. Click on the **'Columns'** tab
7. Under **'Selected theme codes'**, click on **'Select'** to check themes of interest and click on **'OK'**
8. In the **'New Framework Matrix'** window, click on **'OK'** to create the matrix
9. Under the **'Framework Matrix Tools'** tab, click on **'Auto Summarize'** to populate the matrix cells with the shared empirical indicators

STEP 11.2. CREATING A CASE-THEME MATRIX AND CHART (SEE EXHIBIT 11.44)

1. Click on the **'Explore'** tab and select **'Matrix Coding'** to open the **'Matrix Criteria'** dialog box
2. In the dialog box and under **'Rows'**, click on **'+'** to select cases of interest and click on **'OK'**
3. Under **'Columns'**, click on **'+'** to select themes of interest and click on **'OK'**
4. Click on **'Run Query'** to display the matrix
   ✓ To review the empirical indicators shared between a case and a theme, double-click on the cell of interest
   ✓ On the sidebar, click on **'Chart'** to display the chart (see Figure 11.3)

STEP 11.3. CREATING AN ATTRIBUTE–THEME CROSSTAB AND CHART (SEE EXHIBIT 11.45)

1. Click on the **'Explore'** tab and select **'Crosstab'** to open the **'Crosstab Criteria'** dialog box
2. In the dialog box and under **'Codes'**, click on **'+'** to select cases of interest and click on **'OK'**
3. Make sure the right type of **'Classification'** is selected and select the attribute(s) of interest
4. Click on **'Run Query'** to display the table
   ✓ To review the empirical indicators shared between specific attribute(s) and a theme, double-click on the cell of interest
   ✓ On the sidebar, click on **'Chart'** to display the chart (see Figure 11.4)

STEP 11.4. CREATING A WORD CLOUD AND WORD TREE (SEE EXHIBIT 11.46)

1. Click on the **'Explore'** tab and then click on the **'Word Frequency'** ribbon

Nodes

Name	Files	Referenc ▽
⊟ ◯ GM communication strategies (RQ3)	9	48
⊟ ◯ Proactively engaging with the public (T)	6	15
◯ Making in-depth GM presentations	3	4
◯ Discussing specific GM case	3	3
◯ Being proactive in GM information-sharing	1	2
◯ Having conversations about GM risks	2	2
◯ Organizing seminars for the public	2	2
◯ Debating with pressure groups	1	1
◯ Having public debate about GM	1	1
⊞ ◯ Sharing GM risks and benefits (T)	6	12
⊞ ◯ Simplifying GM research information (T)	4	10
⊟ ◯ Assessing public views about GM (T)	5	5
◯ Assessing public GM knowledge level	4	4
◯ Listening to the public concerns	1	1
⊞ ◯ Giving the public some time (T)	3	3
⊞ ◯ Making GM research publicly available (T)	3	3

Exhibit 11.40. Excerpt of the themes and their codes for *'GM communication strategies (RQ3)'*

2. In the *'Word Frequency Criteria'* dialog box, click on *'Selected Items'* to open the *'Select Project Items'* window
3. In the window, click on *'Nodes'* and select the themes of interest
    ✓ In this case, I checked all the themes under the 'GM concerns factors (RQ1)' anchor code.
4. Click on *'OK'* to close the window
5. In the *'Word Frequency Criteria'* dialog box, click on *'Run Query'*
    ✓ On the sidebar, click on *'Word Cloud'* to see the Word Cloud (see Figure 11.5)
    ✓ To create a Word Tree based on a word shown in the Word Cloud, right-click on the word of interest (which is *'Communication'*) and select *'Run Text Search Query for communication'* (see Figure 11.6)

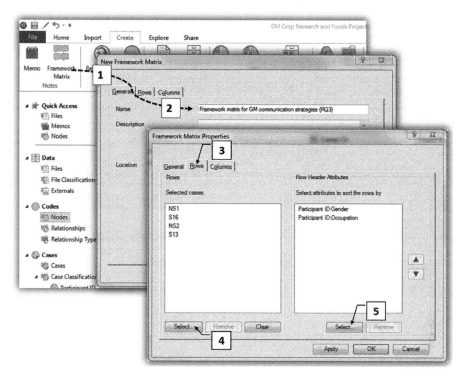

Exhibit 11.41. Setting up framework matrix properties related to cases and attributes of interest

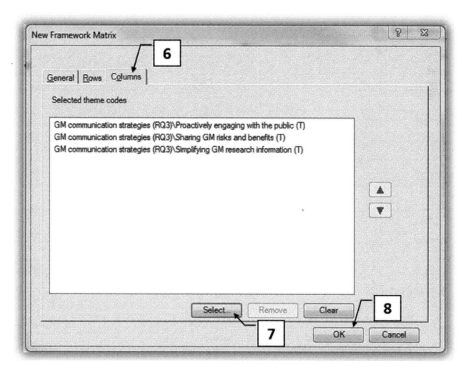

Exhibit 11.42. Setting up framework matrix properties related to themes of interest

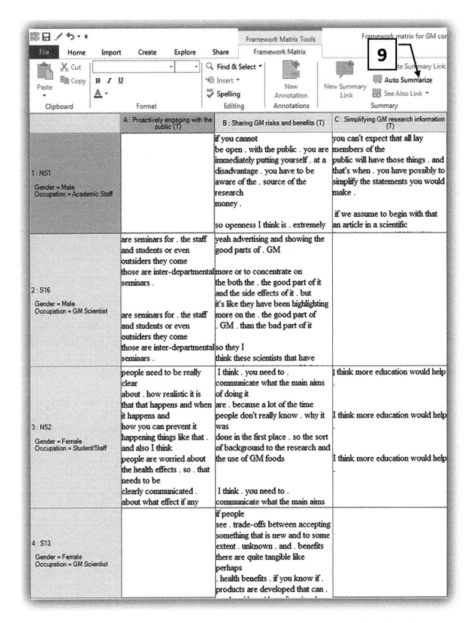

Exhibit 11.43. Populating the framework matrix cells with empirical indicators

STEP 11.5. CREATING PROJECT MAP (SEE EXHIBITS 11.47–11.49; FIGURE 11.7)

1. Click on the **'Explore'** tab and click on the **'Project Map'** to open the **'New Project Map'** window
2. In the window, name the Project Map
3. Click on **'OK'**

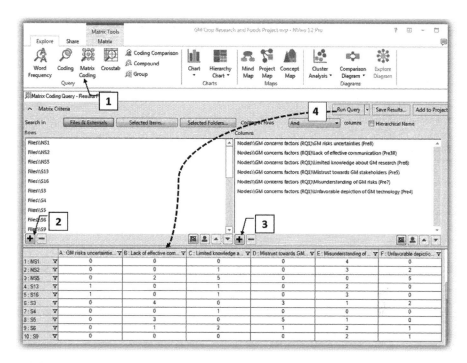

Exhibit 11.44. Creating a case–theme matrix

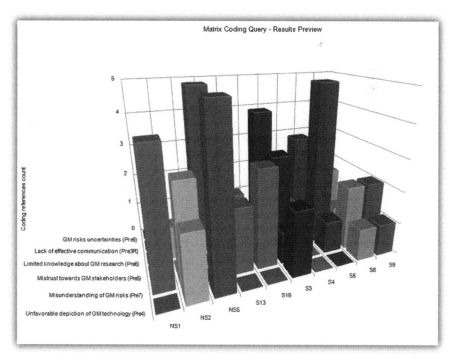

Figure 11.3. Bar chart (in 3D) showing shared counts between cases and themes

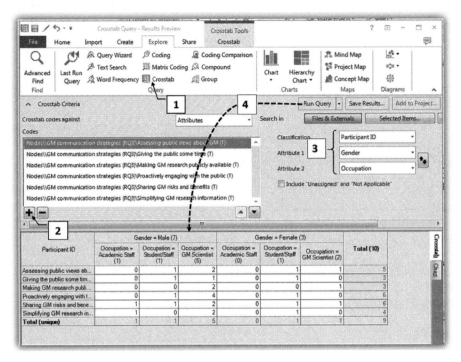

Participant ID	Gender = Male (7)			Gender = Female (3)			Total (10)
	Occupation = Academic Staff (1)	Occupation = Student/Staff (1)	Occupation = GM Scientist (5)	Occupation = Academic Staff (0)	Occupation = Student/Staff (1)	Occupation = GM Scientist (2)	
Assessing public views ab...	0	1	2	0	1	1	5
Giving the public some tim...	0	1	1	0	1	0	3
Making GM research publi...	0	0	2	0	0	1	3
Proactively engaging with f...	0	1	4	0	1	0	6
Sharing GM risks and bene...	1	1	2	0	1	1	6
Simplifying GM research in...	1	0	2	0	1	0	4
Total (unique)	1	1	5	0	1	1	9

Exhibit 11.45. Creating an attribute–theme crosstab

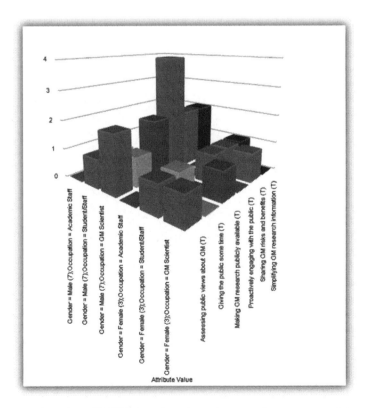

Figure 11.4. Bar chart (in 3D) showing shared counts between participants' attributes and themes

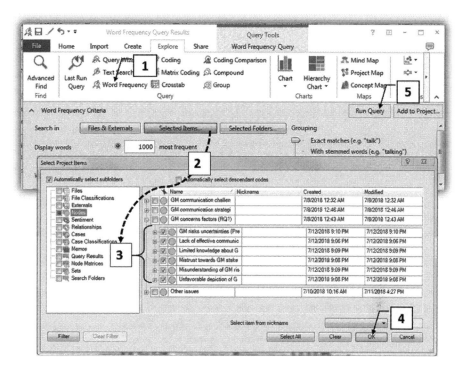

Exhibit 11.46. Running 'Word Frequency' search based on empirical indicators under *'GM concerns factors (RQ1)'*

4. In the Navigation View, click on **'Nodes'** under **'Codes'** to display the nodes in the List View, and select the theme of interest and drag it to the Project Map workspace

5. Right-click on the theme and select **'Show Association Items'** to show all the items linked to the theme

6. In the list of associated items, go to **'Cases'** and under it double-click on the cases connected to the theme to move them to the Project Map workspace

7. For each case, right-click on it and select **'Show Association Items'** to show all the items linked to the case, and in the list of associated items, double-click on the attribute values (example: **'Female'** and **'Student/Staff'**) to move the participant's demographics to the Project Map workspace

EXPORTING OUTCOMES

When planning to export qualitative analysis outcomes, think about retrieving those that will aid you in communicating your findings to your audience. Some of the important information you could export are

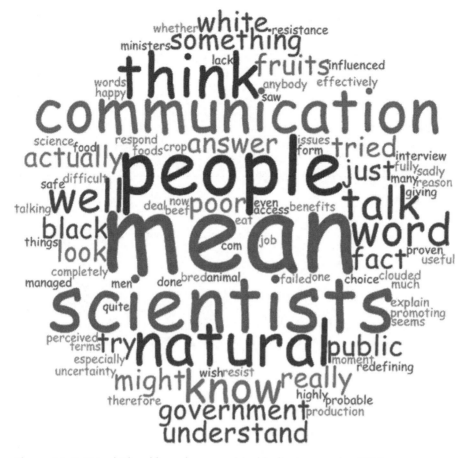

Figure 11.5. Word Cloud based on empirical indicators under *'GM concerns factors (RQ1)'*

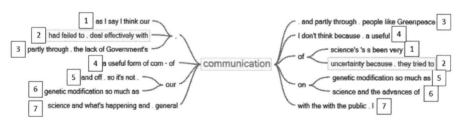

Figure 11.6. Word Tree of 'communication' based on empirical indicators under *'GM concerns factors (RQ1)'*

participants' demographics, codebook, and supplementary illustrations such as matrices, charts and maps featuring links among themes, cases, counts and attributes, and Word Clouds and Word Trees visualizing participants' word usage.

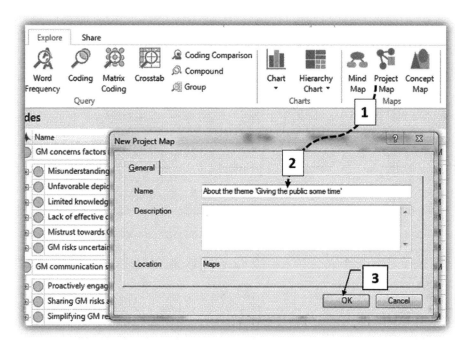

Exhibit 11.47. Setting up the development of a Project Map

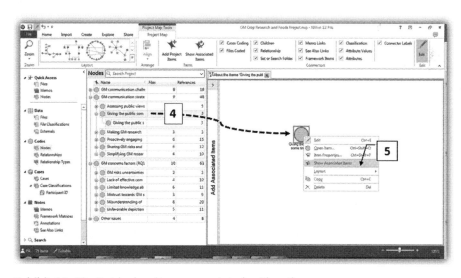

Exhibit 11.48. Retrieving items associated with a theme

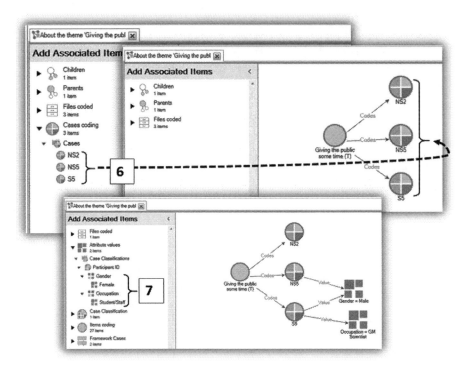

Exhibit 11.49. Connecting cases to the themes and values to the cases

Demonstration 11.6

The following are demonstrations on exporting data analysis outcomes.

STEP 11.1. RETRIEVING AND EXPORTING DEMOGRAPHIC INFORMATION (SEE EXHIBIT 11.50)

1. In the Navigation View, double-click on the unit of analysis (i.e. 'Participant ID') under **'Case Classification'** to open the demographic table in the Detail View
2. To export, right-click on the table and select **'Export Classification Sheet'** from the menu options
   ✓ Since the classification sheet is similar to the Excel file (with participants' demographic information) initially imported, you don't have to export it if no adjustment was made to it.

STEP 11.2. RETRIEVING AND EXPORTING A CODEBOOK (SEE EXHIBITS 11.51–11.55)

1. In the **'Share'** tab, click on the **'New Report'** ribbon and select the **'New Report via Wizard'** to open the **'Report Wizard'**

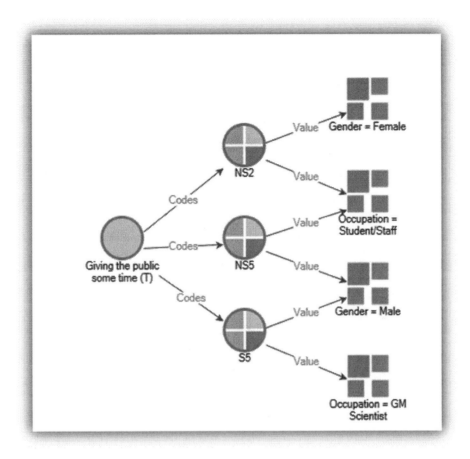

Figure 11.7. Project Map showing the theme 'Giving the public some time' and associated cases with their demographic features

2. In the **'Report Wizard 1 of 8'** under the question, **'How would you like to build your report?'**, make sure **'From a view'** is checked and select **'Code'**
3. Click on **'Next'** to open **'Report Wizard 2 of 8'**
4. Under **'Code'** in the **'Available fields'** select **'Parent Name'**, **'Name'**, **'Description'**, **'Hierarchical Name'**, **'Number Of Files Coded'**, and **'Number Of Coding References'**
   ✓ Taking into consideration the data I analyzed, here are what the selected items stand for:
   i. **'Parent Name':** This refers to the name of an anchor code (which is a label given to a research question).
   ii. **'Name':** This includes the code, sub-theme or theme created. In other words, the codebook would have a list of all the codes, sub-themes and themes developed.
   iii. **'Description':** This is about the definition of a code, sub-theme or theme in terms of what it represents.

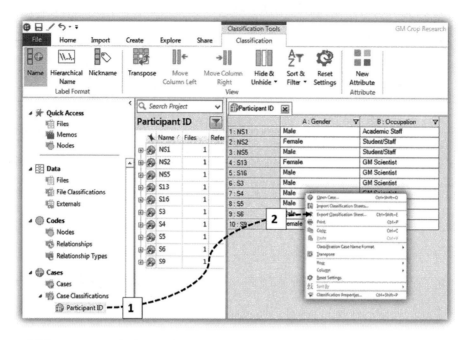

Exhibit 11.50. Retrieving and exporting participants' demographic information

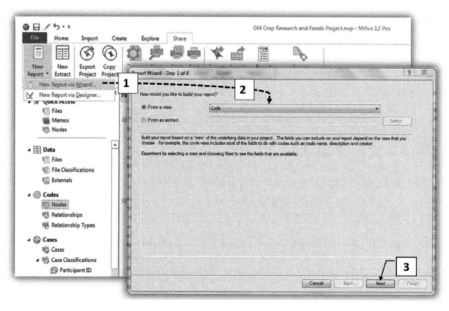

Exhibit 11.51. Setting up the codebook

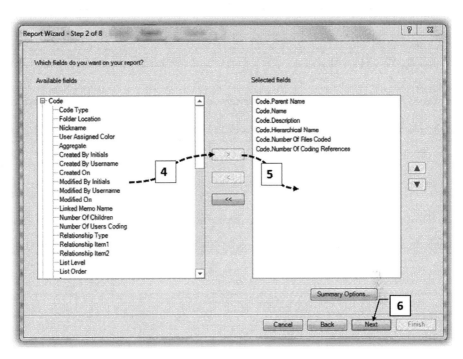

Exhibit 11.52. Selecting the content of the codebook

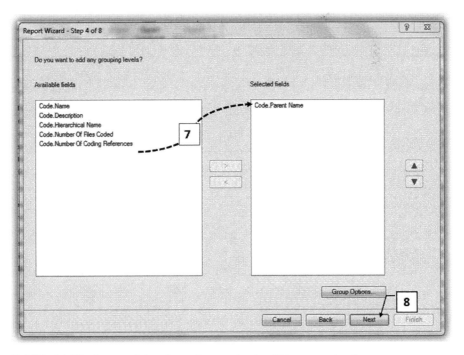

Exhibit 11.53. Determining how the content will be organized

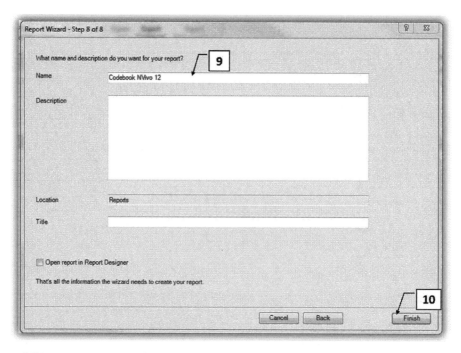

Exhibit 11.54. Naming the codebook

    iv. ***'Hierarchical Name':*** This is a label given to a code, sub-theme or theme reflecting in a subsequent order the parent node(s) it is connected to.

    v. ***'Number Of Files Coded'***: This refers to the number of cases or participants connected to a code, sub-theme or theme.

    vi. ***'Number Of Coding References'***: This is also called counts or frequencies, which represents the number of empirical indicators linked to a code, sub-theme or theme.

5. Click on **'>'** to move them to the ***'Selected fields'***

    ✓ You could arrange them in the order shown in Exhibit 11.52

6. Click on ***'Next'*** in ***'Report Wizard 2 of 8'*** and in ***'Report Wizard 3 of 8'***

7. In ***'Report Wizard 4 of 8'*** in the ***'Available fields'***, select the ***'Parent Name'*** and click on **'>'** to move them to the ***'Selected fields'***

    ✓ ***'Parent Name'*** is selected because I want the codes/themes and their characteristics to be organized by the anchor codes (research questions).

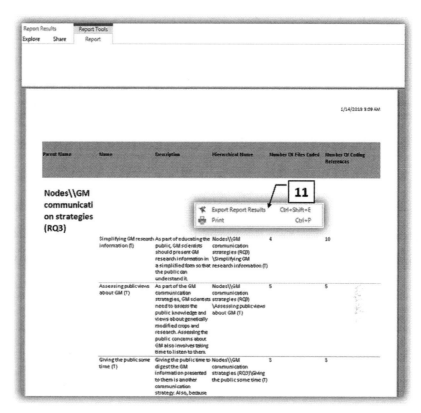

Exhibit 11.55. Exporting the codebook

8. Click on **'Next'** in **'Report Wizard 4 of 8'** and then click on **'Next'** in **'Report Wizard 5 of 8'**, **'Report Wizard 6 of 8'** and **'Report Wizard 7 of 8'**

9. In **'Report Wizard 8 of 8'**, provide a name for the codebook

10. Click on **'Finish'** to create the codebook

11. To export the document, right-click on it and select **'Export Report Results'**

STEP 11.3. EXPORTING SUPPLEMENTARY INFORMATION (MATRICES, CHARTS, PROJECT MAPS, WORD CLOUDS AND WORD TREES)

- All the illustrations produced in NVivo can be exported by right-clicking on them and selecting **'Export...'**

Box 11.1 Qualitative analysis steps using NVivo 12

1. Prepare qualitative data
2. Explore data
3. Code empirical indicators
4. Develop categories/themes
5. Visualize outcomes
6. Export outcomes

CONCLUSION

NVivo (Version 12.1.249; QSR International Pty Ltd, 2018) is a sophisticated and user-friendly qualitative analysis software program. It is endowed with numerous self-explanatory functions, making it easy for qualitative researchers to learn within a short span of time. As demonstrated in this chapter, you can closely work with this software to prepare and explore your data – including importing interview files, creating cases for the files, connecting participants' demographic information to them, and examining the kinds of words they frequently use and the context in which they were used. Another way of utilizing NVivo to engage with the data reduction process is to generate nodes/codes. With this software, you could create nodes for your research questions (called anchor codes), the empirical indicators discovered, and categories/themes built. One of the final stages of the data analysis process is to develop visual representations of the results. NVivo could facilitate the generation of matrices, maps and charts. Finally, you could export all the outcomes including your codebook and illustrations to help to communicate the findings.

REFERENCES

Adu, P. (2015). Conducting qualitative analysis using NVivo: A quick reference [PowerPoint slides]. SlideShare. Retrieved from www.slideshare.net/kontorphilip/conducting-qualitative-analysis-using-nvivo-a-quick-reference

Adu, P. (2016, January 31). Perfecting the art of qualitative coding. Retrieved July 7, 2018, from www.qsrinternational.com/nvivo/nvivo-community/the-nvivo-blog/perfecting-the-art-of-qualitative-coding

Adu, P. (2018). Introduction to NVivo: Making good use of the qualitative software [PowerPoint slides]. SlideShare. Retrieved from www.slideshare.net/kontorphilip/introduction-to-nvivo-making-good-use-of-the-qualitative-software

Baxter, P., & Jack, S. (2008). Qualitative case study methodology: Study design and implementation for novice researchers. *The Qualitative Report, 13*(4), 544–559. Retrieved from https://nsuworks.nova.edu/tqr/vol13/iss4/2/

Bazeley, P., & Jackson, K. (2014). *Qualitative data analysis with NVivo*. Los Angeles, CA: Sage.

Cook, G., & Robbins, P.T. (2005). *Presentation of genetically modified (GM) crop research to non-specialists, 1997–2002: A case study*. [data collection]. UK Data Service. SN: 5069, http://doi.org/10.5255/UKDA-SN-5069-1

NVivo Transcription. (2018). Retrieved October 20, 2018, from www.qsrinternational.com/nvivo/nvivo-products/transcription

QSR International Pty Ltd. (2018). NVivo 12. Version 12.1.249 [Computer software]. Retrieved from www.qsrinternational.com/nvivo/nvivo-products/

Saldaña, J. (2016). *The coding manual for qualitative researchers*. Los Angeles, CA: Sage.

Slavin, R. E. (2007). *Educational research: In an age of accountability*. Boston, MA: Pearson Education, Inc.

12

Using Dedoose to analyze qualitative data

OBJECTIVES

Readers will be able to:

1. Recognize the features and functions of Dedoose
2. Prepare qualitative data for analysis
3. Code qualitative data using Dedoose
4. Drop or merge codes into their respective categories/themes created
5. Retrieve and export outcomes

DEDOOSE SOFTWARE OVERVIEW

Dedoose (Version 8.1.8; SocioCultural Research Consultants LLC, 2018) is a web-based software tool used to analyze qualitative and quantitative data. Since the software is used online, you just need a computer, internet access and a web browser ("Features," n.d.). To access Dedoose, you can go to: www.dedoose.com/. This software includes an additional security option of encrypting data imported into the software and stored remotely (in a cloud server) – making you the sole user of your data. Dedoose makes accessing the imported data a lot easier, not only for a single user but also for multiple users working on a single project. Besides utilizing Dedoose to generate codes to represent selected empirical indicators, you can rate the indicators. As you engage in coding the data, the software concurrently generates and updates the data analysis outputs displayed in the form of matrices and graphs. In addition, if you have quantitative data in a Microsoft Excel spreadsheet, you can import the data into the software and run statistical tests.

For starters, let me present you with an overview of the Dedoose interface – briefly touching on the functions of the main features (see Exhibit 12.1).

Exhibit 12.1. Dedoose interface displaying the main functions

1. **Home:** Clicking on the **'Home'** tab provides an overview of the project in terms of the number of **'Users'**, codes created, project data (i.e. **'Media'**), empirical indicators (i.e. **'Excerpts'**), and charts that reflect participants' demographics (**'Descriptor Ratios'**) and code–demographic relationship (**'Codes x Descriptor'**).

2. **Codes:** Codes are tags assigned to relevant information in the data (Saldaña, 2016). Selecting the **'Codes'** tab displays all the codes created and graphs showing the number of codes connected to each data file (i.e. **'Code Count x Media'**) and the number of codes linked to each demographic group/value (**'Codes x Descriptor'**).

3. **Media:** Media is any kind of qualitative data imported into Dedoose for analysis. Selecting the **'Media'** tab takes you to a list of data files with their associated characteristics such as demographic information (**'Descriptors'**), number of **'Excerpts'** and **'Memos'**.

4. **Excerpts:** Excerpts are empirical indicators extracted from data. In Dedoose, an empirical indicator doesn't have to be coded so as to be named an excerpt. To see all the excerpts selected and associated characteristics such as number of codes and demographic information, you can click on the **'Excerpts'** tab.

5. **Descriptors:** Under the **'Descriptors'** tab, there are **'Descriptor Sets'**, **'Set Fields'** and **'Descriptors In Set'** sections. View a descriptor set as a container that holds characteristics of what you intend to analyze. You could call it a unit of analysis or the source of data. For example, if data collected are from participants, then

Table 12.1 Dedoose terms and their meanings

Dedoose terms	Meaning
Media	Data files (in the form of text, images, audio and/or video) imported into Dedoose for analysis
Excerpts	Relevant segments (empirical indicators) identified in the data
Set fields	Demographic variables
Field type	Level of measurement of a demographic variable
Descriptor	A set of assigned categories or values of variables depicting participants' characteristics

you can create a descriptor set, namely *'Participant Demographics'*. If the data is from organizations, you could create a descriptor set called *'Organization Characteristics'*. Let's discuss another concept, namely a set field. If a descriptor set is a reservoir of participant demographics, a set field is a demographic variable. Therefore, the **'Set Fields'** section contains a list of demographic variables and their level of measurement, which is called **'Type'** in Dedoose (see Table 12.1). For instance, the field type of age and gender would be **'Number'** (i.e. continuous level of measurement) and **'Option List'** (i.e. categorical level of measurement), respectively. Lastly, the **'Descriptors In Set'** section encompasses a list of all participants and their demographic information. A descriptor consists of the demographic characteristics of a participant. For instance, a descriptor of Participant 'A' could be 26 years old, female with a high income and educational level.

6. **Analyze:** Selecting the **'Analyze'** tab will take you to all the outputs generated as a result of the data analysis-related actions taken. There is a countless variety of charts and metrics (related to media, descriptors, excerpts and codes) you could use to help conduct further analysis and/or communicate your results. In addition to analyzing qualitative data, Dedoose has a unique feature that gives you the option to conduct statistical analyses if you have quantitative data. By going to **'Descriptor Number Distribution Plot'**, **'Descriptor Field T-Test'**, **'Descriptor Field Correlation'** and **'Descriptor ANOVA'** under **'Quantitative Charts'**, you will be able to run tests for descriptive statistics such as mean, median, range, standard deviation and variance, and inferential statistics which include correlation, t-test and analysis of variance (ANOVA).

7. **Memos:** To see all the documentation of personal reflections, you can click on the **'Memo'** tab. Hovering over each memo (in the **'Memos'** window) with the cursor displays the codes, excerpts and descriptors connected to it.

8. **Training:** The information shown when you click on the **'Training'** tab is useful for researchers working in a team. This tool helps in training team members to ensure reliability of code application and how they rate the empirical indicators (excerpts).

9. **Security:** Clicking on the **'Security'** tab takes you to the **'Project Active Users and Groups'** window. This window enables members of a research team to have access to the project. It is not only useful for a group of researchers working on a qualitative analysis project but also for a single user who wants to grant access of the project to a reviewer for member-checking purposes (see Chapter 14 for further information about member checking). In the **'Project Active Users and Groups'** window, you have an option to grant users access – ranging from full to no access to some parts of the project. To invite a user to be part of the project:
   ✓ Click on **'Add Group'** on the **'Project Active Users and Groups'** window to open the **'Add User Group'** window
   ✓ In the window, input the title you want to give to the group
   ✓ Select one of the access options and click on **'Submit'** to create the group
   ✓ To add a user to the group, click on **'Add User'** in the **'Project Active Users and Groups'** window; to open, click the **'Add User To Project'** window
   ✓ In the window, select the group created and click on **'Use Selected Group'**
   ✓ In the **'Add User To Project'** prompt, type the user's email address and click on **'Submit'**

10. **Data Set:** Selecting the **'Data Set'** tab takes you to a **'Data Selector'**, which contains a list of excerpts, descriptors, media, users and codes. This tool gives you an option to choose the excerpts, descriptors, media, users and codes you want to run your analysis on.

11. **Projects:** The **'Projects'** tab takes you to all the projects you are working on. Also, you could create a new project by clicking on the **'+'** located on the top right of the **'Select Project'** window.

Functions of Dedoose across qualitative analysis stages

From the perspective of a single user with interview transcripts to analyze, I would group the main functions of Dedoose under the following stages of a qualitative data analysis process: preparing qualitative data, coding empirical indicators, developing categories/themes, and retrieving and exporting outcomes (see Figure 12.1).

The journey of analyzing data with Dedoose (Version 8.1.8; SocioCultural Research Consultants LLC, 2018) starts with data

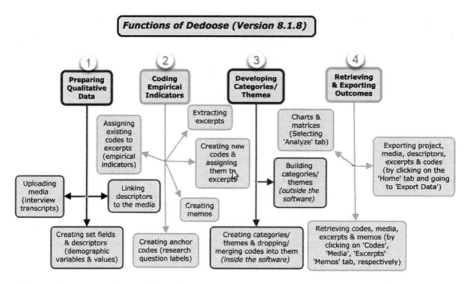

Figure 12.1. Functions of Dedoose across the four stages of data analysis

preparation. Assuming you have interview transcripts, you review them, take out all identifiable information and assign an ID to each of them. The data files are then imported into Dedoose. Within the software, demographic variables (**'Set Fields'**) and participants' demographic characteristics (**'Descriptors'**) are created – making it possible to link descriptors to participants' files (**'Media'**).

After data preparation, the next stage is to go through each of the interview files and select empirical indicators (**'Excerpts'**). But before selecting excerpts and assigning codes to them, you need to first create codes (also known as anchor codes) to represent the research questions. Subsequently, for each excerpt selected, you tag it with the appropriate code(s) created. During the coding process, you don't need to create and assign a code to an excerpt if existing code(s) would best represent the empirical indicator. At this stage, there is an option to document your reflections using the **'Memo'** tool. One of the unique features of Dedoose is the option of rating ('weighting') the excerpts coded – leading to quantitative outcomes complementing the qualitative findings.

When it comes to generating categories/themes based on the codes developed, there are two main steps. The first step is to build categories/themes outside Dedoose using the presumption-focused coding strategy, individual-based sorting strategy or the group-based sorting strategy (see Chapter 8). Second, you transfer the categories/themes to the software – creating them under their respective research questions (anchor codes). The final action under the second step of the categorization process is to drop or merge codes into their associated categories/themes.

The last stage of the data analysis process in Dedoose is to retrieve and export outcomes. To retrieve the outcomes, you could select the

'Media', *'Descriptors'*, *'Excerpts'*, *'Codes'* or *'Analyze'* tab. Clicking on some of the tabs such as *'Media'*, *'Descriptors'* and *'Excerpts'* tab would display tables and options to select the information you want to retrieve and export. You could also retrieve and export a variety of matrices and charts by clicking on the *'Analyze'* tab.

PREPARING QUALITATIVE DATA

As discussed in Chapter 4, data preparation involves compiling the audio file (assuming interviews were conducted and audio-recorded), transcribing the data, removing any identifiable information, reviewing the transcripts and deciding on a qualitative analysis tool or software program to use (see Box 4.1). In this section, I will be showing you how to set up data in Dedoose to make it ready for coding. Let's imagine you have chosen Dedoose (Version 8.1.8; SocioCultural Research Consultants LLC, 2018) and you have ten interview transcripts sampled from a case study project (see Chapter 4). The research project was implemented between 1997 and 2002 with the aim of studying how GM research and crop information are shared with the public (Cook & Robbins, 2005). Similar to the previous study, you plan to address the following research questions:

1. What were the factors contributing to public concerns about GM research and foods in the UK?
2. What were the challenges faced by GM scientists when communicating GM crop research to the public?
3. How should GM crop research be communicated to the public to address their concerns?

Demonstration 12.1

Here are the steps needed to make the interview transcripts ready for analysis:

STEP 12.1. CREATING A PROJECT IN DEDOOSE (SEE EXHIBIT 12.2)

1. *'Sign in'* to open the software
   ✓ To *'Sign up'*, go to the Dedoose website (www.dedoose.com/)
2. Click on the *'Projects'* tab to open the *'Select Project'* window
3. In the window, click on the *'+'* (i.e. *'Add New Project'* icon) to open the *'Create New Project'* window
4. In the window, input the title of the project and provide a brief description of the project in the *'Description'* textbox
5. Click on *'Submit'* to create the project (taking you to the main page)

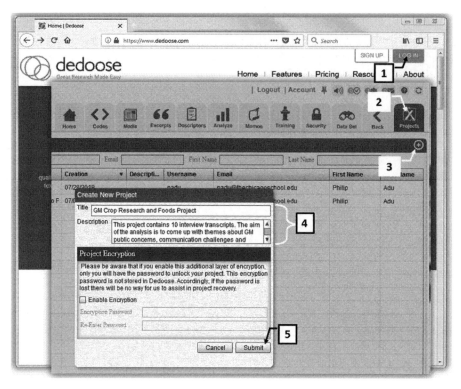

Exhibit 12.2. Creating a project in Dedoose

STEP 12.2. IMPORTING MEDIA (SEE EXHIBIT 12.3)

1. Click on the **'+'** (**'Add/Import Data'** icon) to open the **'Import Data'** window
2. In the window, select **'Import Text'** to locate the interview transcripts
3. Double-click on one of the files to import it into the software under the **'Media'** section on the **'Home'** page
   - ✓ Repeat Actions 1–3 until all the files have been imported
   - ✓ Alternatively, to select and import all files at once, click on the first file, press and hold the **'Shift'** key on the keyboard, click on the last file and click on **'Open'**

STEP 12.3. CREATING SET FIELDS (SEE EXHIBITS 12.4–12.6)

1. Click on the **'Descriptors'** tab to open a workspace containing **'Descriptor Sets'**, **'Set Fields'** and the **'Descriptors in Field'** sections/work areas
2. In the **'Descriptor Sets'** work area, hover the cursor over **'Default, Fields: 0, Descriptors: 0'** and click on the **'Edit'** icon

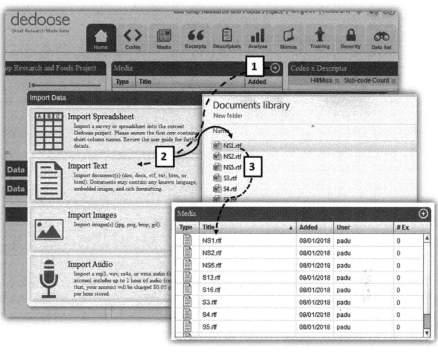

Exhibit 12.3. Importing media into Dedoose

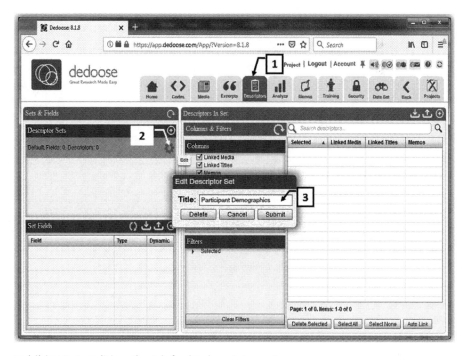

Exhibit 12.4. Editing the 'default' descriptor set

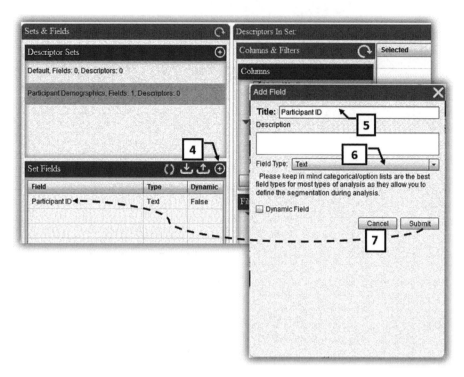

Exhibit 12.5. Creating a 'Participant ID' field

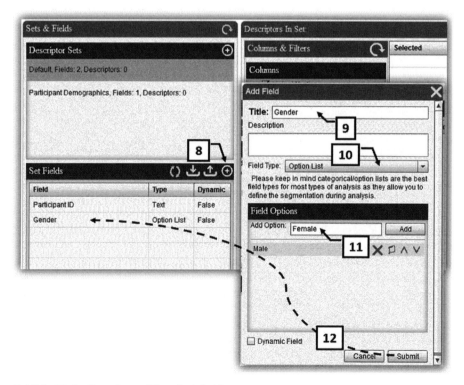

Exhibit 12.6. Creating a 'Gender' field

3. In the **'Edit Descriptor Set'** box, provide a title for participants' demographic information to be entered and click on **'Submit'**
   - ✓ Alternatively, you can delete the default version in the **'Descriptor Sets'** work area and click on the **'+'** icon (**'Add Set'**) in the **'Descriptor Sets'** panel header to create a new descriptor set.
4. In the **'Set Fields'** panel header, click on the **'+'** icon (**'Add Field'**) to open the **'Add Field'** dialog box
5. In the dialog box, type the title of the field (which would be **'Participant ID'**)
   - ✓ You could type the description of the field created in the **'Description'** textbox but this is optional.
6. Select the **'Field Type'** (in this case, **'Text'** is selected)
   - ✓ Since the field is **'Participant ID'**, you can indicate **'Text'** as the field type. This provides the option of typing IDs for participants when creating descriptors for them.
7. Click on **'Submit'** to create the **'Participant ID'** field
8. To create a demographic variable such as **'Gender'** in the **'Set Field'** work area, click on the **'+'** icon (**'Add Field'**) to open the **'Add Field'** dialog box
9. In the dialog box, type the title of the field (which would be **'Gender'**)
10. Select the **'Field Type'** (in this case, **'Option List'** is selected)
11. In the option textbox, type one of the **'Gender'** categories and click on **'Add'**
    - ✓ Repeat this action until all the categories are entered
12. Click on **'Submit'** to create the **'Gender'** field

Note: Repeat Actions 8 to 12 to create an **'Occupation'** field

STEP 12.3. CREATING DESCRIPTORS FOR PARTICIPANTS (SEE EXHIBIT 12.7)

1. To create a descriptor for a participant (in this case, 'NS1') in the **'Descriptors In Set'** work area, click on the **'+'** icon (**'Add New Descriptor'**) to open the **'Add Descriptor'** dialog box
2. In the dialog box, type **'Participant ID'**
3. For each field (variable), select the appropriate variable value/category (in this case, **'Male'** and **'Academic Staff'** are chosen for **'Gender'** and **'Occupation'**, respectively for Participant **'NS1'**)
4. Click on **'Submit'**

Note: Repeat Actions 1–4 until all participants' descriptors are created

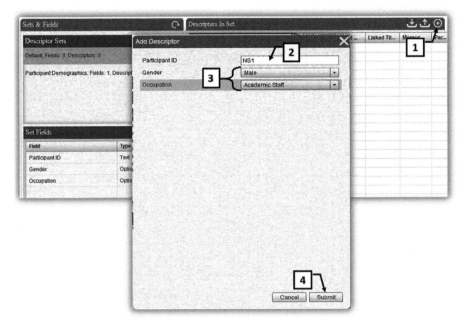

Exhibit 12.7. Creating participants' descriptors

STEP 12.4. LINKING DESCRIPTORS TO MEDIA (SEE EXHIBITS 12.8–12.9)

1. In the **'Descriptors In Set'** work area, click on the first cell in the **'Linked Media'** column (which is the cell for Participant **'NS1'**) to open the **'Linked Media'** window
2. In the window, click on the **'Link'** cell in the **'Linked'** column that belongs to the first participants (**'NS1'**) to connect the participant's descriptor to his/her media (interview file) and close the window

Note: Repeat Actions 1 and 2 until all participants' descriptors are connected to their respective media

Commentary 12.1. As shown in Exhibit 12.9, the number under **'Linked Media'** is one for each participant. This means one file (media) was connected to each participant's descriptor. You could link more than one document to a descriptor if needed. The **'Linked Titles'** column contains the name of files attached to the descriptors. So the question is, why should we connect descriptors to media? By doing so, all the codes assigned to excerpts in the media will automatically be connected to participants' descriptors. This also facilitates the generation of charts and matrices depicting the shared relationships among media, descriptors, excerpts and codes.

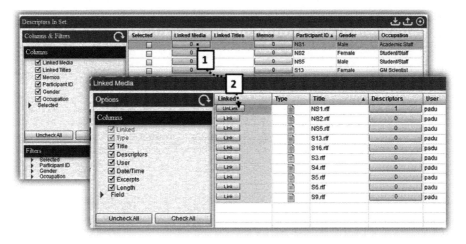

Exhibit 12.8. Linking descriptors to the media

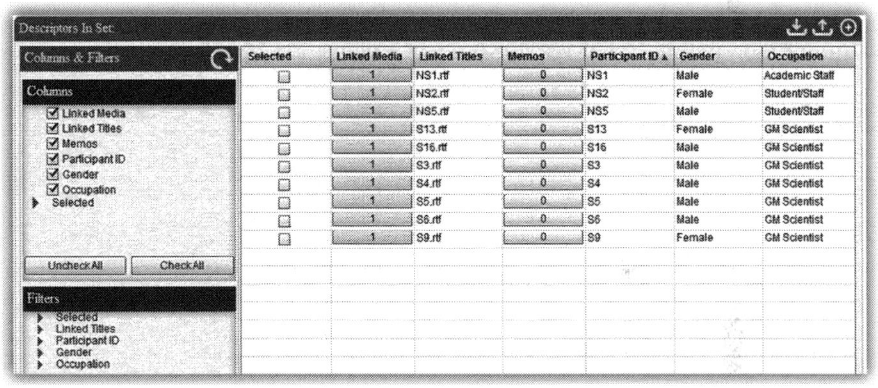

Exhibit 12.9. Participants' descriptors with linked media

CODING EXCERPTS (EMPIRICAL INDICATORS)

Coding involves going through all the media, identifying excerpts and tagging them with words or phrases known as codes. You can use any of the three coding strategies (namely: description-focused, interpretation-focused and presumption-focused coding) discussed in Chapter 3. However, determining an appropriate strategy depends on the features of the research method, purpose, questions and data of the study. After critically examining the above factors, interpretation-focused coding was chosen to help develop codes to represent the empirical indicators and address the research questions (see Chapter 7). You should review Chapters 3 and 7 to learn more about how to generate appropriate codes. The following are the research questions (with their labels) to be addressed:

1. What were the factors contributing to public concerns about GM research and foods in the UK? *(GM concerns factors)*
2. What were the challenges faced by GM scientists when communicating GM crop research to the public? *(GM communication challenges)*
3. How should GM crop research be communicated to the public to address their concerns? *(GM communication strategies)*

Demonstration 12.2

The following demonstrations focus on how to create anchor codes (which are labels for the research questions) and extract excerpts, create and define codes, assign codes to excerpts, create memos, and assign existing codes to excerpts.

STEP 12.1. CREATING AN ANCHOR CODE (RESEARCH QUESTION LABEL) (SEE EXHIBIT 12.10)

1. Click on the *'Codes'* tab to display a workspace containing *'Codes'*, the *'Code Count × Media'* and the *'Codes × Descriptor'* sections/work areas
2. In the panel header of the *'Codes'* work area, click on the *'+'* icon (*'Add Root Code'*) to open the *'Add Code'* window
3. In the window, type the code title, which is the anchor code
4. In the *'Description'* textbox, input what the anchor code represents
5. Click on *'Submit'*

Note: The above actions are repeated for all the research questions

STEP 12.2. EXTRACTING AN EXCERPT (SEE EXHIBITS 12.11–12.12)

1. Click on the *'Media'* tab to display a list of data files
2. Click on the file of interest to open in the *'Media'* workspace
3. To show line numbers in the document, click on the first icon (*'Show Settings Panel'*) under the *'Document'* header panel
   ✓ Action 3 is optional
   ✓ You could edit the document by clicking on the *'Lock/Unlock document editing'* icon
4. Select the excerpt (which is relevant to what you are studying or in addressing any of the research questions)
5. Click on the *'Create Excerpt from Selection'* icon to display the excerpt in the *'Selection Info'* work area

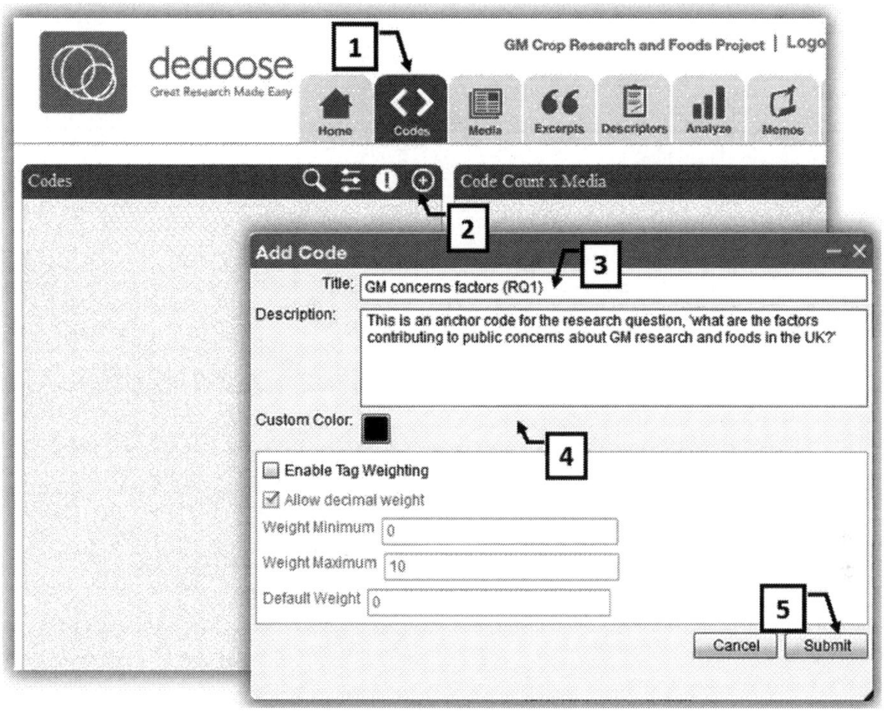

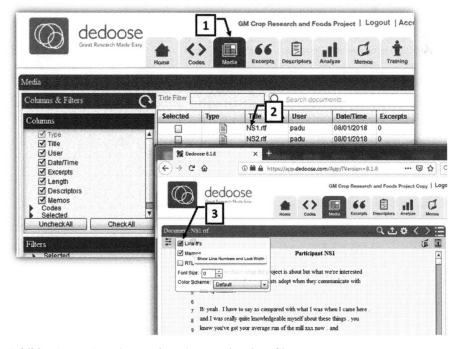

Exhibit 12.10. Creating an anchor code

Exhibit 12.11. Opening and setting up the data file

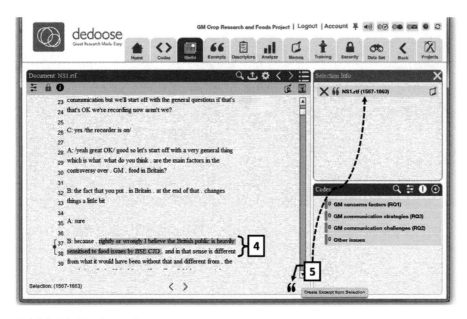

Exhibit 12.12. Extracting an excerpt

STEP 12.3. CREATING A NEW CODE AND ASSIGNING THE CODE TO AN EXCERPT (SEE EXHIBITS 12.13–12.14)

1. Click on the code brace/bracket of the yet-to-be coded excerpt to display it in the **'Selection Info'** work area (if it is not already shown in the work area)
2. After deciding on the appropriate code to represent the excerpt and its associated anchor code, click on the **'+'** icon (**'Add Child Code'**) for the anchor code to open it in the **'Add Code'** window
   ✓ The code being created is termed child code because it is developed under a parent code (which is the anchor code).
3. In the window, type the code title (name)
4. In the **'Description'** textbox, provide what the code represents
5. Click on **'Submit'** to create the code
6. To assign the code to the excerpt, press and hold the code, and drag and drop it into the **'Selection Info'** work area
   ✓ Alternatively, you could just double-click on the code to connect it to the excerpt.

STEP 12.4. ASSIGNING AN EXISTING CODE TO AN EXCERPT (SEE EXHIBIT 12.15)

1. Click on the code brace/bracket of the yet to be coded excerpt to display it in the **'Selection Info'** work area (if it is not already shown in the work area)

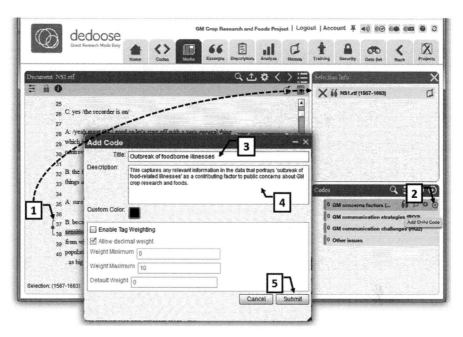

Exhibit 12.13. Creating a new code

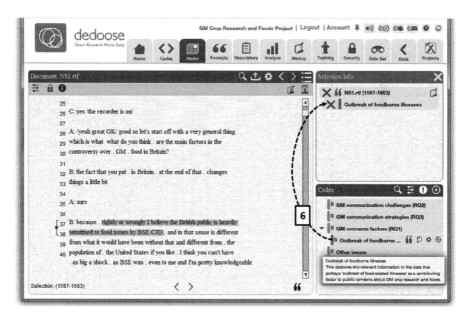

Exhibit 12.14. Assigning a code to an excerpt

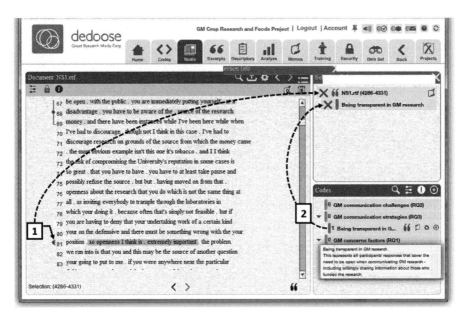

Exhibit 12.15. Assigning an existing code to an excerpt

2. To assign the code to the excerpt, double-click on the code
   ✓ Alternatively, you could select the excerpt and then double-click on the existing code to connect it to the excerpt.

STEP 12.5. CREATING AND LINKING A MEMO TO AN EXCERPT (SEE EXHIBITS 12.16–12.17)

1. In the **'Selection Info'** work area, click on the memo icon for the excerpt to open the **'Link Memo to Excerpt'** window
2. In the window, write your reflections/thoughts
3. Click on **'Save'** and close the window

Commentary 12.2. As shown in Exhibit 12.17, 64 **'Codes'** were created and assigned to 135 **'Excerpts'**. As you can see, the number of **'Excerpts'** is equal to the number of **'Code Applications'** – meaning, all the empirical indicators were coded. Furthermore, the number of **'Codes'** is less than that of the **'Code Applications'** because some of the codes were assigned to more than one excerpt. Tables 12.2–12.4 show all the codes generated under their respective research questions. Each code has a description, the number of excerpts connected to the code, and the number of participants whose responses were linked to it. Codes that didn't fall under any of the three research questions (but are considered relevant to the study) were put under **'Other issues'** (see Table 12.5).

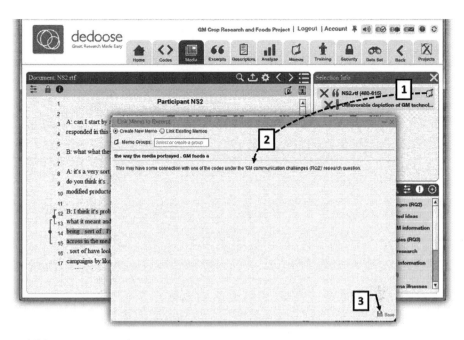

Exhibit 12.16. Creating a memo

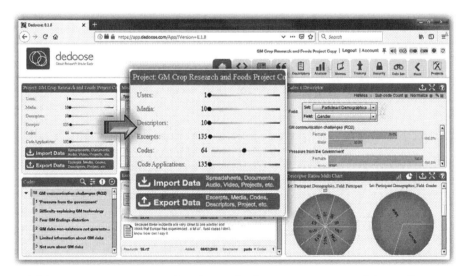

Exhibit 12.17. Home page of Dedoose displaying a summary of the coding outcomes

Tables 12.3–12.5 were generated based on the *'Code Description'*, *'Code Applications'*, and *'Code Presence'* tables exported from Dedoose (Version 8.1.8; SocioCultural Research Consultants LLC, 2018). As the name implies, the *'Code*

Description' table contains codes developed and what they represent. It is exported by clicking on the *'Codes'* tab and subsequently clicking on the *'!'* icon (*'Show Action Panel'*) in the *'Codes'* header panel and selecting *'Export Codes'*. Also, the *'Code Applications'* table shows the number of times a code is assigned to excerpts from a specific media (interview file). The table also includes the total number of excerpts per code. To retrieve the *'Code Applications'* table, you click on the *'Analyze'* tab and in the *'Chart Selector'* section, click on '*Code Application'* under the *'Code Charts'* option. Additionally, under *'Code Charts'*, you can access the *'Code Presence'* table (see Exhibit 12.18). This table shows whether a code is connected to any of the excerpts in a media file. If it is linked to an excerpt, a number *'1'* is indicated in the cell, which is the intersection of the row and column of the media and code, respectively. To get the total number of cases (participants) connected to a code, you tally all the cells showing *'1'* under the code. I would like to point out that I used the *'Code Presence'* table to compute the number of cases/participants for each code because each media (interview file) belongs to a participant. In a situation where you have more than one media file for some of the participants, you could use the *'Descriptor x Code Case Count Table'* under *'Code Charts'* to calculate the cases linked to a code.

Media \ Codes	GM communication challenges	Pressure from the	Difficulty explaining GM	Fear of GM findings distortion	GM risks non-existence	Limited information about	Not sure about GM risks	Pressure from the public	Public pressure for GM	Risk of disclosing	Risk of oversimplifying GM	GM communication strategies	Assessing public views	Assessing public	Listening to the	Giving the public some	Giving the public	Making GM research	Collaborating with	Creating press
S9.rtf			1		1															
S6.rtf								1											1	
S5.rtf			1						1									1		
S4.rtf							1							1						
S3.rtf							1													1
S16.rtf								1												
S13.rtf				1	1	1								1						
NS5.rtf														1				1		
NS2.rtf		1								1							1	1		
NS1.rtf										1	1									

Exhibit 12.18. A table displaying the connection between media and codes

Table 12.2 Codes and their characteristics under *'GM concerns factors (RQ1)'*

Code	Code description	Number of excerpts (counts)	Number of participants (cases)
Belief in GM product side effects	This code covers information on the public belief in the adverse effects of consuming GM products.	5	2
Conflicting views about GM safety	While the government was assuring the public about how safe GM products are, GM scientists are unsure about GM safety.	1	1
Criticism from interest groups	This captures any reference to criticism of interest groups on GM research and foods.	4	3
Disinterested in learning about GM	This focuses on representing the public as not being interested in learning about GM.	1	1
Extensively unexamined GM side effects	This code represents parts of the data which imply that not many studies have been conducted on GM side effects.	1	1
GM scientists' ineffective communication	This represents empirical indicators that imply that GM scientists have poor communication when it comes to helping the public to understand GM.	1	1
GM's proximity to foodborne illnesses	This represents any reference made to the closeness of afoodborne illness outbreak (such as mad cow disease) to the emergence and awareness of GM technology.	3	3
Hesitant to embrace GM technology	This covers the public unwillingness to accept something new.	1	1

(*continued*)

Table 12.2 (Cont.)

Code	Code description	Number of excerpts (counts)	Number of participants (cases)
Hesitant to explain GM research	This covers empirical indicators that portray GM scientists' hesitance in explaining the GM research process to the public.	3	2
Inadequate promotion of GM benefits	This code depicts participants' expression of the poor promotion of GM benefits.	1	1
Irrational 'response to risks'	This code covers all relevant information that makes reference to issues related to unreasonable decisions and reactions of the public about potential GM risks.	2	1
Lack of effective government communication	This covers the lack of communication on the part of the government.	2	1
Limited knowledge about GM research	This represents significant information in the data that explains how limited the public understanding of GM research and foods is.	10	6
'Mistrust of commercial companies'	This covers all references to the public mistrust of GM companies.	3	2
Mistrust of scientists	This covers all references to the public mistrust of scientists.	4	2
Mistrust of the government	This code covers all issues related to the public mistrust of the government in relation to assuring them of GM safety.	2	2
Multiple meanings of GM concepts	This captures explanations of the concept of 'natural' and how the meaning differs between scientists and the public.	2	1

Table 12.2 (Cont.)

Code	Code description	Number of excerpts (counts)	Number of participants (cases)
Objective-driven nature of scientific research	This captures any reference made about the objective nature of conducting scientific study.	1	1
Outbreak of foodborne illnesses	This captures any relevant information in the data that portrays 'outbreak of food-related illnesses' as a contributing factor to public concerns about GM crop research and foods.	3	3
Uncertain about GM research	This covers relevant portions of the data that depict the public sense of uncertainty about GM research and products.	1	1
Unfavorable depiction of GM technology	This code represents the media and interest groups' perceived negative depiction of GM products or distortion of GM research findings.	7	3
Unsatisfactory answer to GM risks	This covers any information in the data that makes reference to the fact that the public was not satisfied with the risks and uncertainty-related answers they received from GM scientists.	3	2

Rating excerpts (empirical indicators)

Although rating excerpts is beyond the scope of this chapter, let me briefly touch on how to rate (weight) empirical indicators in Dedoose (Version 8.1.8; SocioCultural Research Consultants LLC, 2018). In qualitative analysis, you are not required to rate excerpts. However, if you think assigning scores to empirical indicators could add meaningful information to the qualitative findings then it would be appropriate. Concurrently, you could rate excerpts as you are assigning codes to them. But a rating activity is more efficient if it is done after completing the initial coding process. To ensure consistency and credibility in the

Table 12.3 Codes and their characteristics including ratings under *'GM communication challenges (RQ2)'*

Code	Code description	Number of excerpts (counts)	Number of participants (cases)
Difficulty explaining GM technology	This entails reference to having difficulty explaining GM technology to a lay person.	5	2
Fear of GM findings distortion	This code represents relevant portions of the data that portray GM scientists' concern about the misrepresentation of GM crop research findings.	2	1
GM risks non-existence not guaranteed	This code covers the communication challenges related to GM scientists' difficulty in satisfying public interest regarding the assurance of there being no GM innovation-related risks.	2	2
Limited information about GM risks	This code focuses on GM scientists' inability to adequately address the public concerns about GM-related risks due to limited research done.	1	1
Not sure about GM risks	This is about empirical indicators that show expression of GM scientists not being sure about GM risks.	3	3
'Pressure from the government'	This includes statements in the data that indicate government pressure on GM scientists to say that GM research and products are safe.	1	1
Pressure from the public	This represents relevant information that makes reference to public pressure on GM scientists regarding the issue of declaring that GM has no risk.	1	1

Table 12.3 (Cont.)

Code	Code description	Number of excerpts (counts)	Number of participants (cases)
Public pressure for GM safety	This is about GM scientists being pressured by the public to declare that GM products are safe.	1	1
Risk of disclosing protected ideas	This captures information about the dilemma of being open to the public and putting GM scientists' protected ideas at risk of being used by their competitors.	1	1
Risk of oversimplifying GM information	This code is about the challenge of presenting easy-to-understand GM crop research information, and at the same time making sure the information is not oversimplified and/or misleading.	1	1

entire qualitative analysis process, rating significant segments in the data should be done in a systematic manner.

First, you start this process by choosing the excerpts you want to rate. For instance, let's select the second research question (*GM communication challenges*) – focusing on rating the excerpts under this question. The second step is to assess the excerpts and their assigned codes to help determine the appropriate rating scale to use. To review them (see Exhibits 12.18–12.19):

1. Click on the **'Data Set'** tab to open the **'Data Selector'** window
2. In the window, click on **'Codes'**
3. Click on **'Filter None'**
   ✓ Remember to click on **'Filter All'** after completing the analysis related to excerpt rating.
4. Check the codes of interest (in this case, the anchor code, *'GM communication challenges (RQ2)'*, and the codes under it are selected) and close the **'Data Selector'** window
5. Click on the **'Media'** tab and click on one of the files to open it

Table 12.4 Codes and their characteristics under *'GM communication strategies (RQ3)'*

Code	Code description	Number of excerpts (counts)	Number of participants (cases)
Assessing public GM knowledge level	Any participant's expression related to the need to assess the public knowledge level and perceptions about GM innovations will be put under this code.	4	4
Being proactive in GM information-sharing	This is about the need to anticipate the public reactions to GM research and to devise ways of responding to them (including informing them about the source of their research funding).	2	1
Being transparent in GM research	This entails all participants' responses that cover the need to be open when communicating GM research – including willingly sharing information about those who funded the research.	2	1
Collaborating with other departments	This covers parts of the data that suggest the need to work with university departments specializing in helping with presentation of GM content to the public.	1	1
Communicating GM innovation benefits	This code captures ideas in the data which imply the need to put a greater emphasis on the benefits of GM research and foods than the potential risks when making a presentation.	2	2
Creating awareness of GM risks	This is about the fact that the public should be aware of any potential risks related to GM crop research and products.	1	1
Creating press releases	This focuses on reference to creating press releases as one of the communication strategies.	1	1

Table 12.4 (Cont.)

Code	Code description	Number of excerpts (counts)	Number of participants (cases)
Debating with pressure groups	This covers the need for GM scientists to engage in a debate with pressure groups.	1	1
Discussing specific GM case	This focuses on a communication strategy related to discussing in detail a specific GM case, including risks. It also includes discussing both GM benefits and risks.	3	3
Educating the public about GM	This covers the need to go beyond just telling the public what GM is about but teaching them about GM innovations and products.	3	2
Emphasizing crossbreeding/ GM similarities	This covers the need to discuss the similarities between traditional crossbreeding practice and GM technology.	2	2
Emphasizing GM's positive side	This focuses on the need to promote the benefits of GM more than its negative side.	2	1
Giving the public some time	This code represents all information that indicates the need to give the public some time to understand issues related to GM.	3	3
Having conversations about GM risks	This code captures significant information that shows that GM scientists should have a conversation with the public about GM risks in terms of what they are, the extent of the risks, the likelihood that they will occur, and ways to prevent them from happening.	2	2
Having public debate about GM	This covers the need to have public debate about GM – discussing GM risks and benefits.	1	1

(continued)

Table 12.4 (Cont.)

Code	Code description	Number of excerpts (counts)	Number of participants (cases)
Listening to the public concerns	This code represents the need for GM scientists to meet the public and listen to their concerns.	1	1
Making GM research publicly available	This code focuses on the need for GM scientists to make the GM research available for public consumption.	1	1
Making in-depth GM presentations	This focuses on the need to be more detailed when presenting GM information rather than just giving brief information.	4	3
Organizing seminars for the public	This is about the need to organize seminars for the public.	2	2
Presenting GM research rationale	This is about the need to present the reason why GM research should be carried out. In addition, it represents information about why GM foods are needed.	2	2
Presenting GM risks and benefits	This focuses on the need to present a balanced argument when communicating with the public about GM technology – discussing not only the benefits but also talking about the risks.	3	1
Simplifying GM research information	This represents portions of the data that depict the need to present information about GM research and food in a simplified format so that the public can understand it.	3	2
Tailoring GM information	This is about adjusting the GM information being presented based on the audience's GM knowledge level.	2	1

Table 12.5 Codes and their characteristics under *'Other issues'*

Code	Code description	Number of excerpts (counts)	Number of participants (cases)
Difficulty in labeling products	This represents the difficulty of differentiating GM products from non-GM products (especially processed foods) by labeling.	1	1
Finding out GM research sponsor	This code is for any remarks by participants that recommend the need to look for the source of funding when reviewing a GM research article.	1	1
Government funding for GM research	This is part of the recommendations. It calls for the government to sponsor independent research on GM.	2	2
More research on GM risks	This focuses on the need for more research on the potential side effects of GM.	2	2
Single definition of GM concepts	This captures the need to have a single definition of natural crops, health and safety.	2	1

6. In the **'Media'** work area, click on the **'>'** icon (**'Next Excerpt'**) to review the excerpts under the research question of interest (i.e. the *'GM communication challenges (RQ2)'* anchor code) and their assigned codes
   ✓ After reviewing an excerpt and its code(s), click on the **'Next Excerpt'** icon to review the next excerpt
   Note: To review excerpts in the subsequent files, repeat Actions 5 and 6

Third, taking into consideration the content of the excerpts, associated codes and research question to be addressed, decide on an appropriate rating scale. Vagias' (2006) paper, *Likert-Type Scale Response Anchors*, could be a very useful resource to help choose the right scale. After reviewing the empirical indicators under *'GM communication challenges (RQ2)'*, a five-point Likert scale rating based on the "level of difficulty"

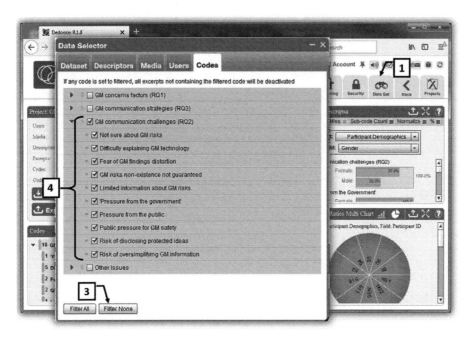

Exhibit 12.19. Selecting an anchor code and its associated codes

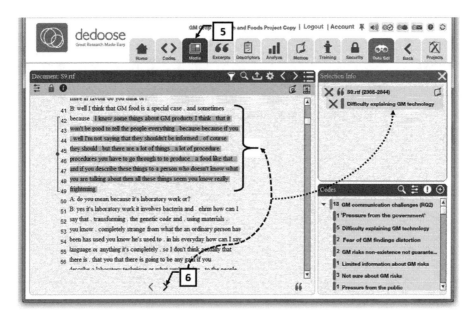

Exhibit 12.20. Reviewing excerpts and their assigned codes to decide on the rating scale

was selected as the suitable measure (Vagias, 2006, p. 2). In other words, each excerpt would be weighted based on how difficult it is to address the challenges expressed by participants. The fifth step is to develop criteria for rating the excerpts. Table 12.6 shows the rating levels for

Table 12.6 Level of difficulty rating criteria

Difficulty	Score/weight	Criteria
Very difficult	5	• Portrays the challenge as from an external source • Seems to portray the challenge as a problem beyond his/her control • Suggests difficulty in addressing the challenge
Difficult	4	• Portrays the challenge as from an external source • Suggests the challenge can be addressed
Neutral	3	• Acknowledges the existence of the challenge but no indication of whether it is difficult or easy
Easy	2	• Portrays the challenge as from an internal source and that it can be easily addressed by taking action internally
Very easy	1	• Portrays the challenge as from an internal source and that it can be fixed without much effort

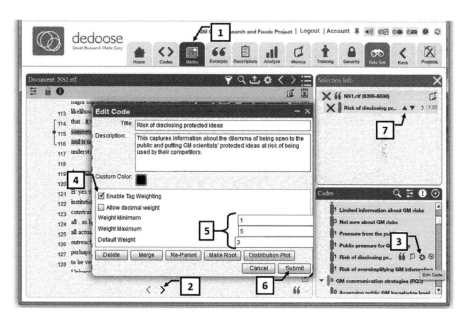

Exhibit 12.21. Weighting excerpts

difficulty and their respective conditions. The final step is to rate the excerpts. Here are the actions under this step (see Exhibit 12.21):

1. Click on the *'Media'* tab and click on one of the files to open it
2. In the *'Media'* work area, click on the *'>'* icon (*'Next Excerpt'*) to display the excerpt

3. Under the *'Codes'* section, click on the *'Edit Code'* icon for the code assigned to the excerpt
4. In the *'Edit Code'* window, check *'Enable Tag Weighting'*
5. Indicate the *'Weight Minimum'*, *'Weight Maximum'* and *'Default Weight'*
   ✓ *'Default weight'* is the value automatically assigned to an excerpt before an actual rate is assigned. In this case, every excerpt will be tagged *'3'* (which is *'Neutral'*) until the final weight is provided.
6. Click on *'Submit'* in the *'Edit Code'* window and close it
7. Under the *'Selection info'* section, indicate the weight for the excerpt
   ✓ After rating the excerpt, click on the *'Next Excerpt'* icon to weight the next excerpt.
   Note: To rate excerpts in the subsequent files, repeat Actions 1–7

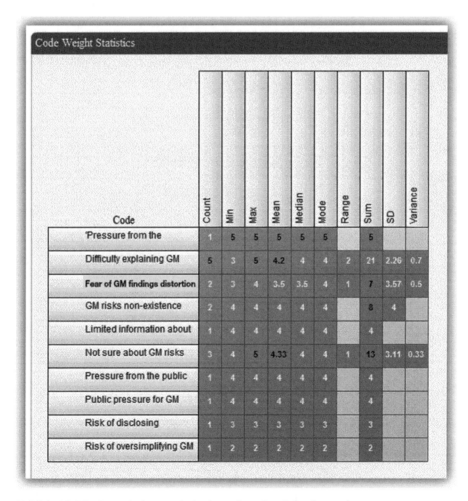

Code Weight Statistics

Code	Count	Min	Max	Mean	Median	Mode	Range	Sum	SD	Variance
'Pressure from the	1	5	5	5	5	5		5		
Difficulty explaining GM	5	3	5	4.2	4	4	2	21	2.26	0.7
Fear of GM findings distortion	2	3	4	3.5	3.5	4	1	7	3.57	0.5
GM risks non-existence	2	4	4	4	4	4		8	4	
Limited information about	1	4	4	4	4	4		4		
Not sure about GM risks	3	4	5	4.33	4	4	1	13	3.11	0.33
Pressure from the public	1	4	4	4	4	4		4		
Public pressure for GM	1	4	4	4	4	4		4		
Risk of disclosing	1	3	3	3	3	3		3		
Risk of oversimplifying GM	1	2	2	2	2	2		2		

Exhibit 12.22. Descriptive statistical results of ratings for codes

Commentary 12.3. As shown in the demonstrations and results, it is possible to rate excerpts. The most important thing is to be meticulous in this process so as to not only arrive at meaningful, but also credible, results. The rating outcome shows that the code *'Pressure from the government'* has the highest level of difficulty (Count = 1; Mean = 5) (see Exhibit 12.22). This implies that one of the challenges that GM scientists face is the pressure from the government to assure the public that GM crops are totally safe. Because this pressure originates externally and more research needs to be done to conclude that the crops are totally safe, it is very difficult to address this problem. Lastly, the code with the lowest rating (in terms of the level of difficulty) was *'Risk of oversimplifying GM information'* (Count = 1; Mean = 2) – meaning, to GM scientists, it is easy to address the problem of oversimplifying information about GM crops and research. When reviewing the **'Code Weight Statistics'** table, more attention should be paid to: the number of excerpts (**'Count'** column), the average weight of excerpts under a code (**'Mean'** column), and the average difference between the weights of individual excerpts and their mean weight (**'SD'** [standard deviation] column).

DEVELOPING CATEGORIES/THEMES

The first step in category/theme development is to transform the codes into categories/themes using one of the following strategies: presumption-focused coding, individual-based sorting or group-based sorting (see Chapter 8). Concerning using the presumption-focused coding and individual-based sorting strategies, you need to use Microsoft Word, specifically its **'New Comment'**, **'Tables'** and **'Shapes'** functions. In addition to having at least ten participants when using the group-based sorting strategy, you need tools such as SPSS and Microsoft Word to help sort the codes into categories/themes. You could creatively use the **'Memo'** function in Dedoose (Version 8.1.8; SocioCultural Research Consultants LLC, 2018) to conduct the categorization of codes with the presumption-focused coding strategy and the individual-based sorting strategy. However, the **'Memo'** function in Dedoose doesn't have the needed functions similar to those found in Microsoft Word– making it challenging and time-consuming to use. Due to this limitation, I recommend you first create the categories/themes outside of the Dedoose software and then transfer them to the software.

Under the first step of code categorization, you could take the following actions:

1. Decide on the appropriate categorization strategy
2. Export the following from Dedoose:

     a. Codebook (a list of codes with their descriptions)
     b. **'Code Applications'** table (a matrix showing the number of excerpts from media and their associated codes)
     c. **'Code Presence'** table (a matrix showing excerpts coded as present or absent in media)
     d. **'Descriptor × Code Case Count Table'** (a matrix displaying which participant (descriptor) a code is connected to)
3. Follow the steps under Demonstration 8.1, 8.2 or 8.3 (in Chapter 8) if presumption-focused coding, individual-based sorting or group-based sorting, respectively, was chosen

For demonstration purposes, I used presumption-focused coding and individual-based sorting in a Microsoft Word document to generate themes under *'GM concerns factors (RQ1)'* and *'GM communication strategies (RQ3)'*, respectively (see Chapter 8). In the following are the themes and their respective codes.

List of themes and their respective codes
for *'GM concerns factors (RQ1)'*

1. GM risks uncertainties
    i. Extensively unexamined GM side effects
    ii. Objective-driven nature of scientific research
    iii. Uncertain about GM research
2. Lack of effective communication
    i. GM scientists' ineffective communication
    ii. Hesitant to explain GM research
    iii. Inadequate promotion of GM benefits
    iv. Lack of effective government communication
    v. Multiple meanings of GM concepts
    vi. Mixed messaging about GM safety
        a. Conflicting views about GM safety
3. Limited knowledge about GM research
    i. Disinterested in learning about GM
    ii. Limited knowledge about GM research
4. Mistrust towards GM stakeholders
    i. 'Mistrust of commercial companies'
    ii. Mistrust of scientists
    iii. Mistrust of the government
5. Misunderstanding of GM risks
    i. GM's proximity to foodborne illnesses
    ii. Irrational 'response to risks'
    iii. Outbreak of foodborne illnesses
    iv. Unsatisfactory answer to GM risks
    v. Perceived existence of GM risks

      a. Belief in GM product side effects
      b. Hesitant to embrace GM technology
      c. Irrational 'response to risks'

6. Unfavorable depiction of GM technology
    i. Criticism from interest groups
    ii. Unfavorable depiction of GM technology

List of themes and their respective codes
for *'GM communication strategies (RQ3)'*

1. Assessing public views about GM
    i. Assessing public GM knowledge level
    ii. Listening to the public concerns
2. Sharing GM risks and benefits
    i. Being transparent in GM research
    ii. Creating awareness of GM risks
    iii. Communicating GM innovation benefits
    iv. Emphasizing GM's positive side
    v. Having conversations about GM risks
    vi. Presenting GM research rationale
    vii. Presenting GM risks and benefits
3. Giving the public some time
    i. Giving the public some time
4. Making GM research publicly available
    i. Creating press releases
    ii. Making GM research publicly available
    iii. Collaborating with other departments
5. Proactively engaging with the public
    i. Debating with pressure groups
    ii. Discussing specific GM case
    iii. Having public debate about GM
    iv. Making in-depth GM presentations
    v. Organizing seminars for the public
    vi. Being proactive in GM information-sharing
6. Simplifying GM research information
    i. Simplifying GM research information
    ii. Tailoring GM information
    iii. Emphasizing crossbreeding/GM similarities
    iv. Educating the public about GM

Demonstration 12.3

The next step is to transfer the themes generated to Dedoose by creating them under their anchor codes (research questions). After creating the themes in Dedoose, you have two options. You could either drop the code into the themes they belong to (i.e. using the *dropping strategy*) or merge the codes into their respective themes (i.e. using the *merging strategy*). Both strategies have strengths and weaknesses. With the merging strategy, the codes linked to the excerpts disappear and are replaced by themes while with the dropping strategy, codes are seen under their themes – becoming child codes of the themes. When utilizing the dropping strategy, it is assumed that all the excerpts connected to a code are also linked to the theme it is associated with. However, matrices that proceed after the analysis such as **'Code Application'**, **'Code Presence'**, **'Descriptor x Code Count Table'** and **'Descriptor x Code Case Count Table'** do not have values in the theme columns. Therefore, you end up having limited information about the shared relationship between themes and descriptors. On the contrary, you will have rich information about the themes and their connections with media and descriptors if you make use of the merging strategy. I recommend you determine what you want from the data analysis outcomes and then decide on which strategy would help get those outputs. Alternatively, you could use both strategies.

Before creating the themes, you could preserve the original project in Dedoose by creating a duplicate of it. In this way, you have the option to work on the duplicate project – creating themes and dropping codes under them. To create a copy of the project (see Exhibit 12.23):

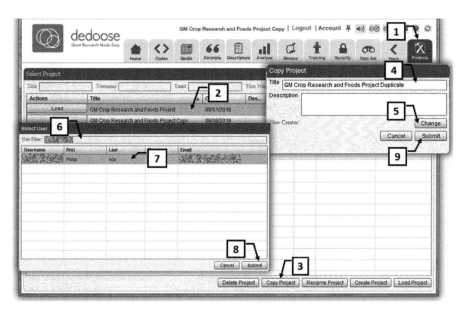

Exhibit 12.23. Creating a copy of the original project

1. Click on the *'Project'* tab to open a window with a list of projects
2. Select the project to be copied by clicking on it
3. Click on *'Copy Project'* to open the *'Copy Project'* window
4. In the window, state the title of the duplicate project
   ✓ Stating a description of the project is optional.
5. In the window, click on *'Change'* to open the *'Select User'* window
6. In the window, state the username of the user of the project (i.e. your username) to display user information
7. Select the user information
8. Click on *'Submit'* to close the *'Select User'* window
9. In the *'Copy Project'* window click on *'Submit'* to create a copy of the original project

STEP 12.1. CREATING THEMES UNDER THE ANCHOR CODE (SEE EXHIBIT 12.24)

1. Click on the *'Codes'* tab to display a workspace containing *'Codes'*, *'Code Count × Media'* and *'Codes × Descriptor'* sections/work areas
2. Click on the *'+'* icon (*'Add Child Code'*) for the anchor code to open the *'Add Code'* window
3. In the window, type the name of the theme and state *'T'* in parentheses to show that it is a theme

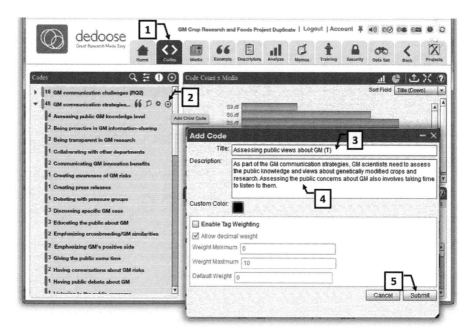

Exhibit 12.24. Creating themes

4. In the **'Description'** text area, input what the theme represents
5. Click on **'Submit'** to create the code
   Note: To create additional themes under the anchor code, repeat Actions 2–5

STEP 12.2. CREATING DUPLICATES OF CODES BELONGING TO MORE THAN ONE THEME (SEE EXHIBITS 12.25–12.27)

✓ Sometimes, after doing presumption-focused coding, you end up with a code or group of codes connected to (supporting) more than one theme (claim). In this case, you need to create copies of codes based on the themes that are associated with them.

1. Click on the **'+'** icon (**'Add Child Code'**) for the anchor code to open the **'Add Code'** window
2. In the window, type the name of the code to be duplicated and state **'D'** in parentheses to show that it is a copy of the original code
3. In the **'Description'** text area, input what the code represents
4. Click on **'Submit'** to create the code
5. Click on the **'View Code Excerpts'** icon (for the original code) to open the **'Chart Selection Reviewer'** window
6. In the window, click on the first excerpt (and wait for the **'Text Excerpt'** window to open)

Exhibit 12.25. Creating a duplicate of a code

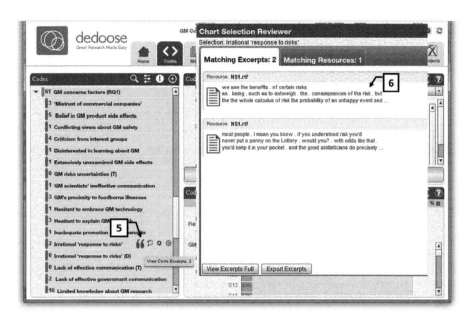

Exhibit 12.26. Opening excerpts linked to the original code

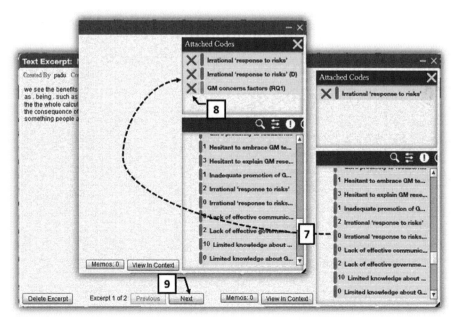

Exhibit 12.27. Connecting a duplicate code to an excerpt

7. In the **'Text Excerpt'** window, double-click on the duplicate code to connect it to the excerpt
   ✓ When you double-click the duplicate code, it will be shown with its anchor code in the **'Attached Codes'** section. The next action is to delete the anchor code in the section since it is not supposed to be there.
8. Click on the **'X'** sign for the anchor code in the **'Attached Codes'** section to remove the anchor code
9. Click on **'Next'** in the **'Text Excerpt'** window to display the next excerpt and repeat Actions 7 and 8

*STEP 12.3A. DROPPING THE CODES INTO THEIR RESPECTIVE THEMES (**USING THE DROPPING STRATEGY**) (SEE EXHIBITS 12.28–12.29)*

1. Select and drag the code of interest
2. Drop it into the theme it belongs to
   Note: The above actions are repeated until all the codes are dropped into their themes

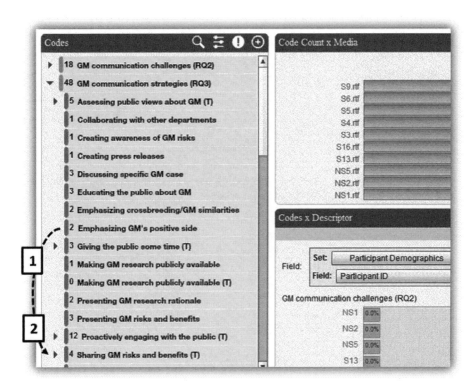

Exhibit 12.28. Dropping a code into the theme it belongs to

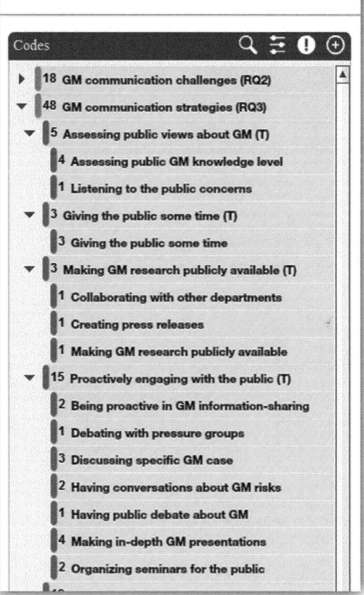

Exhibit 12.29. Extract of the themes and their codes

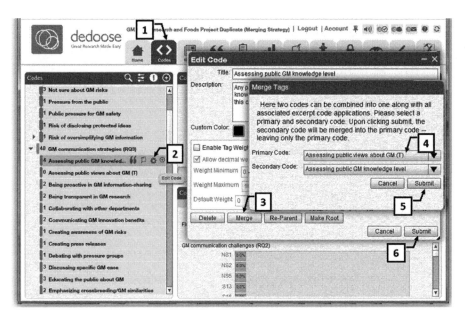

Exhibit 12.30. Merging a code into the theme it belongs to

STEP 12.3B. MERGING CODES INTO THEMES (**USING MERGING STRATEGY**) (SEE EXHIBITS 12.30–12.31)

✓ Before merging codes into the themes, you should follow the actions under Steps 12.1 and 12.2
1. Click on the **'Code'** tab
2. In the **'Codes'** section, click on the **'Edit Code'** icon for the code of interest to open the **'Edit Code'** window
3. In the window, click on **'Merge'** to open the **'Merge Tags'** dialog box
4. In the dialog box in the **'Primary Code'** drop-down menu, select the theme which is connected to the code shown in the **'Secondary Code'** selection box
5. Click on **'Submit'**
6. In the **'Edit Code'** window, click on **'Submit'**
   Note: The above actions are repeated until all the codes are merged into their themes

RETRIEVING AND EXPORTING OUTCOMES

With Dedoose (Version 8.1.8; SocioCultural Research Consultants LLC, 2018), since data analysis projects are saved in the cloud, I recommend you download your completed project and save it on your computer. This can be done by:

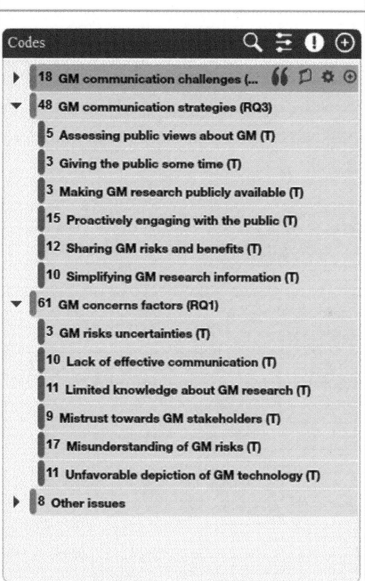

Exhibit 12.31. Outcome of merging codes into their themes

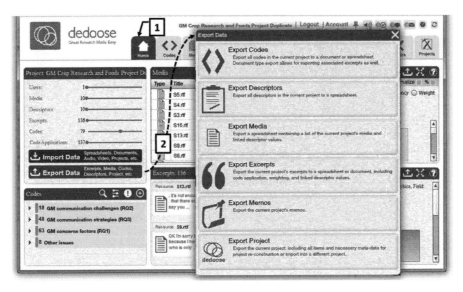

Exhibit 12.32. Exporting project and its outcomes

1. Going to the home page by clicking on the **'Home'** tab
2. Clicking on **'Export Data'** to open the **'Export Data'** selector and clicking on **'Export Project'**

You could follow similar steps to export information related to the media, descriptors, excerpts, codes/categories/themes and memo. There are numerous outputs generated in Dedoose as the result of the data analysis-related steps taken. So, in order to retrieve and export outcomes that are meaningful to you and which could help communicate the findings to your audience, it is essential to ask the following questions: *Why is it important to export a particular outcome?* And *what will it be used for?* Table 12.7 shows a chart and matrices that would be useful for gaining an understanding of the results, creating illustrations and facilitating the presentation of the findings. The **'Code Count x Media'** chart shows how many excerpts were coded under each media type (see Exhibit 12.33). For demonstration purposes, the following illustrations are based on excerpts coded under *'GM concerns factors (RQ1)'* and the *'GM communication strategies (RQ2)'* anchor codes.

What about visualizing how many excerpts are linked to individual codes/themes? A **'Packed Code Cloud'** would be an appropriate illustration to create (see Exhibits 12.34 and 12.38). With this figure, the font size of a code/theme is determined by the number of excerpts it is affiliated with. So the larger the number of excerpts connected to a code/theme, the bigger its font. Another illustration is the **'Descriptor x Code Count**

Table 12.7 Dedoose illustrations and how to access them

What you need	What it is	Where to go	Example
Number of coded excerpts connected to each media	Code Count x Media	1. Click on the **'Analyze'** tab 2. In the **'Chart Selector'** section, click on **'Code Count x Media'** under **'Code Charts'**	Exhibit 12.33
Visual representation of the number of excerpts connected to each code/theme	Packed Code Cloud	1. Click on the **'Analyze'** tab 2. In the **'Chart Selector'** section, click on **'Packed Code Cloud'** under **'Code Charts'** *Note:* Check **'Sub-code Count'** below the **'Packed Code Cloud'** header panel (this is highly recommended if you used the dropping strategy)	Exhibits 12.34 & 12.38
Number of excerpts rated under each code and related average weight	Code Weight Statistics	1. Click on the **'Analyze'** tab 2. In the **'Chart Selector'** section, click on **'Code Weight Statistics'** under **'Code Charts'** *Note:* This table is useful if you rated some (if not all) of the excerpts	Exhibit 12.22
Number of excerpts under each code assigned to each participant (descriptor) Number of excerpts linked to a specific code/theme across descriptor values (categories) of a descriptor field (demographic variable)	Descriptor x Code Count Table	1. Click on the **'Analyze'** tab 2. In the **'Chart Selector'** section, click on **'Descriptor x Code Count Table'** under **'Descriptor Charts'** *Note:* If you applied the dropping strategy, you will not have values in the cells in the theme columns.	Exhibits 12.35 & 12.39
Number of descriptors (participants) linked to a specific code/theme across descriptor values (categories) of a descriptor field (demographic variable)	Descriptor x Code Case Count Table	1. Click on the **'Analyze'** tab 2. In the **'Chart Selector'** section, click on **'Descriptor x Code Case Count Table'** under **'Code Charts'** *Note:* If you applied the dropping strategy, you will not have values in the cells in the theme columns.	Exhibits 12.36 & 12.40

(continued)

Table 12.7 (Cont.)

What you need	What it is	Where to go	Example
Number of excerpts under each media connected to each code Total number of excerpts connected to each code	Code Application	1. Click on the **'Analyze'** tab 2. In the **'Chart Selector'** section, click on **'Code Application'** under **'Code Charts'**	Exhibits 12.37 & 12.41

Note: *To export a chart or matrix, click on the 'Export' icon located in the header panel of the illustration*

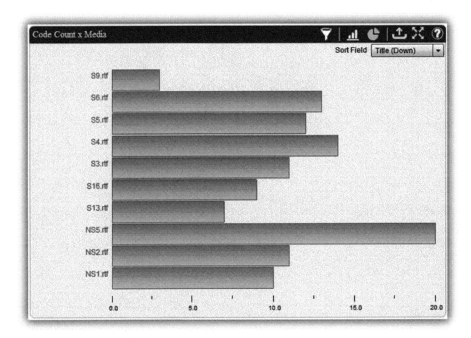

Exhibit 12.33. 'Code Count x Media' chart

Table' (see Exhibits 12.35 and 12.39). This table displays codes/themes with their number of excerpts across individual participants and also groups of participants based on the descriptor fields (demographic variables).

Similar to the **'Descriptor x Code Count Table'**, the **'Descriptor x Code Case Count Table'** shows the relationship between the descriptor fields and codes/themes (see Exhibits 12.35, 12.36, 12.39 and 12.40). The only difference is that the **'Descriptor x Code Case Count Table'**

Exhibit 12.34. 'Packed Code Cloud' (an outcome based on using the dropping strategy)

Descriptor Field \ Codes	GM communication strategies	Assessing public views	Assessing public	Listening to the	Giving the public some	Giving the public	Making GM research	Collaborating with	Creating press	Making GM	Proactively engaging with	Being proactive in	Debating with	Discussing	Having	Having public	Making in-depth
Participant ID: NS1																	
Participant ID: NS2					1		1								1		
Participant ID: NS5				1		1							1	1			1
Participant ID: S13				1					1								
Participant ID: S16																	
Participant ID: S3			1					1									
Participant ID: S4			1									2					2
Participant ID: S5					1									1			
Participant ID: S6						1									1	1	1
Participant ID: S9																	
Occupation: Academic Staff																	
Occupation: GM Scientist			3			1		1	1			2		2	1	1	3
Occupation: Student/Staff			1	1		2							1	1	1		
Gender: Female			1	1		1									1		
Gender: Male			3			2		1	1			2	1	3	1	1	4

Exhibit 12.35. Extract of 'Descriptor x Code Count Table' (an outcome based on using the dropping strategy)

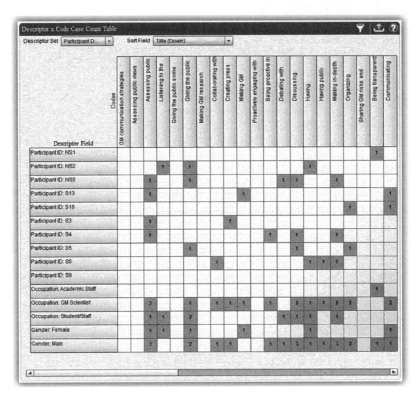

Exhibit 12.36. Extract of 'Descriptor x Code Case Count Table' (an outcome based on using the dropping strategy)

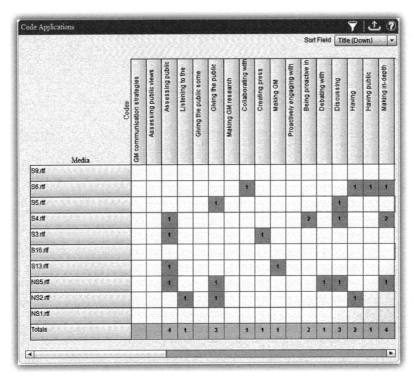

Exhibit 12.37. Extract of 'Code Applications' table (an outcome based on using the dropping strategy)

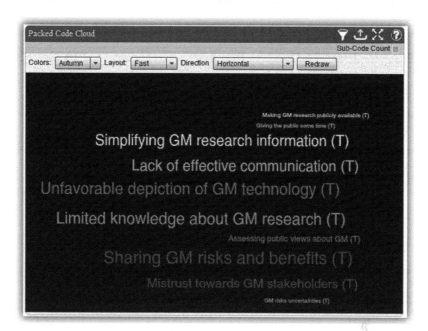

Exhibit 12.38. 'Packed Code Cloud' (an outcome based on using the merging strategy)

Descriptor Field	GM communication strategies	Assessing public views	Giving the public some	Making GM research	Proactively engaging with	Sharing GM risks and	Simplifying GM research	GM concerns factors (RQ1)	GM risks uncertainties (T)	Lack of effective	Limited knowledge about	Mistrust towards GM	Misunderstanding of GM	Unfavorable depiction of
Participant ID: NS1						2	2						4	
Participant ID: NS2		1	1	1	1	1			1		1		2	2
Participant ID: NS5		1	1	3	3					2	5			5
Participant ID: S13		1		1	1				1		1		2	
Participant ID: S16					1	3			1		1		3	
Participant ID: S3		1		1						4		3	1	2
Participant ID: S4		1			5	2	5				1			
Participant ID: S5			1		2					3		5	1	
Participant ID: S6				1	3		2			1	2	1	2	1
Participant ID: S9													2	1
Occupation: Academic Staff						2	2						4	
Occupation: GM Scientist	3	1	3	11	6	7			2	8	5	9	11	4
Occupation: Student/Staff	2	2		4	4	1			1	2	6		2	7
Gender: Female	2	1	1	1	2	1			2		2		6	3
Gender: Male	3	2	2	14	10	9			1	10	9	9	11	8

Exhibit 12.39. 'Descriptor x Code Count Table' (an outcome based on using the merging strategy)

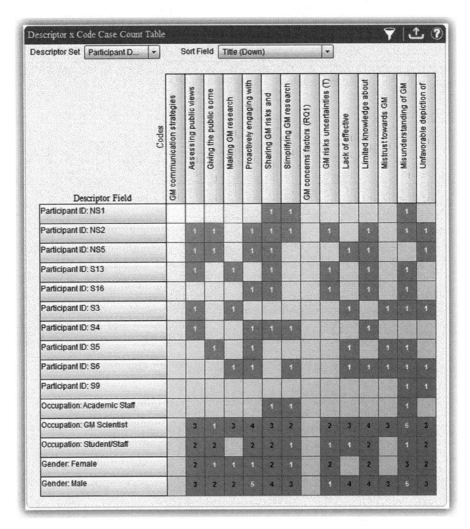

Exhibit 12.40. 'Descriptor x Code Case Count Table' (an outcome based on using the merging strategy)

has (in its cells) the number of participants (case counts) belonging to descriptor values and linked to codes/themes. In other words, the cells contain the number of participants shared between the groups under variables and codes/themes. Lastly, think about the **'Code Applications'** table as an exhibition of the number of excerpts shared between a code/theme and a media type (see Exhibits 12.37 and 12.41). It also shows the total number of excerpts linked to each code/theme.

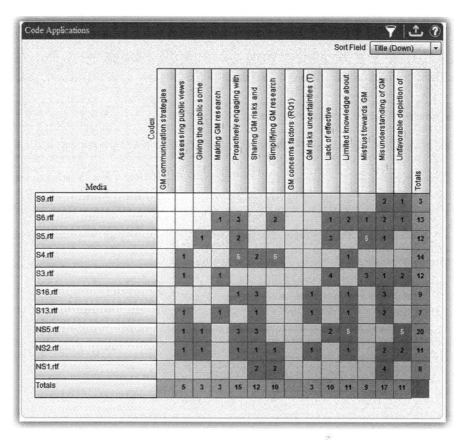

Exhibit 12.41. 'Code Applications' table (an outcome based on using the merging strategy)

Box 12.1 Qualitative analysis steps using Dedoose

1. Prepare qualitative data
2. Code excerpts (empirical indicators)
3. Develop categories/themes
4. Retrieve and export outcomes

CONCLUSION

Dedoose (Version 8.1.8; SocioCultural Research Consultants LLC, 2018) is an online data analysis tool used to help extract relevant text (called excerpts) from data. The software not only assists in creating codes and assigning them to excerpts, but also aids in rating them. Similar to other qualitative data analysis software (QDAS), you can build participants' demographic information (descriptors) in Dedoose and link them to their respective data files (media). By making the connection, codes tagged to the excerpts are automatically linked to the descriptors. During the coding process, you could document your thoughts using the *'Memo'* function in Dedoose. Completion of the initial coding process paves the way for the implementation of code categorization. After choosing one of three categorization strategies, the next step is to build the categories/themes outside of the software. You then create the themes under their respective anchor codes inside Dedoose. At this stage, the initial codes under their anchor codes are then linked to the themes they belong to. This can be done using either the dropping or merging strategy. The final stage of the qualitative analysis process is to retrieve, review and export the outcomes by clicking on the *'Home'*, *'Codes'*, *'Excerpts'*, *'Analyze'* and *'Memo'* tabs.

REFERENCES

Cook, G., & Robbins, P.T. (2005). *Presentation of genetically modified (GM) crop research to non-specialists, 1997–2002: A case study*. [data collection]. UK Data Service. SN: 5069, http://doi.org/10.5255/UKDA-SN-5069-1

Features. (n.d.). Retrieved from www.dedoose.com/home/features

Saldaña, J. (2016). *The coding manual for qualitative researchers*. Los Angeles, CA: Sage.

SocioCultural Research Consultants LLC. (2018). *Dedoose Version 8.1.8* [Web application for managing, analyzing, and presenting qualitative and mixed methods research data]. Los Angeles, CA (www.dedoose.com).

Vagias, W. M. (2006). *Likert-type scale response anchors*. Clemson International Institute for Tourism & Research Development, Department of Parks, Recreation and Tourism Management. Clemson, CA: Clemson University.

13

Presenting qualitative findings

OBJECTIVES

Readers will be able to:

1. Recognize the elements of a good presentation of qualitative findings
2. Choose the best strategy for reporting the findings
3. Write a report on the qualitative findings

INTRODUCTION

There are three things your audience (readers) want to know when you present the findings. They want to know: the kind of data you analyzed, the data analysis process, and data analysis outcomes (Smith, Flowers, & Larkin, 2012). To meet these expectations, you need to extensively analyze the data – extracting the core descriptions and/or meanings from the data and meaningfully presenting them to the readers. Communicating the findings is not just about stating what was found. It is also about being deliberate with your delivery – harnessing your creativity as you shed light on the decisions and actions you took. By so doing, readers will be fully engaged with the results delivery and understand the findings, thus promoting the credibility of the data analysis outcomes (Dey, 1993; Levitt et al., 2018; Stake, 1995).

Qualitative analysis presentations should be more about presenting 'words' than 'numbers'. We limit the efficacy of using narrative ('words') in communicating rich qualitative findings if we overly utilize descriptive statistics ('numbers'). Similar to visual aids, statistics such as the number of words in an empirical indicator (i.e. word counts), number of empirical indicators under a code (i.e. code counts), and number of cases (e.g. participants) connected to a code (i.e. case counts) could play a supporting role in our presentation.

When preparing to report the results, always think about your readers. For instance, as I was working on this chapter of the book, I was thinking about you, my reader. You may be an instructor, professor, student, researcher or practitioner, who is new to qualitative analysis as a whole. Consistent with your expectations, my goal is to help you meet the objectives of this chapter (see above). To achieve this goal, I will first present the elements of a good report about qualitative findings. Second, I will use the findings of the data I have been working on in the previous chapters to demonstrate how qualitative findings could be presented.

ELEMENTS OF A QUALITATIVE FINDINGS REPORT

The journey of presenting the findings to readers begins with giving them an overview of the report. This include stating the purpose of the study and what you will be presenting. Writing in the first person ('I' or 'We') point of view is generally accepted as the best way of presenting qualitative results (Bogdan & Biklen, 2007; Levitt et al., 2018). Writing in the first person aligns with the philosophical assumptions associated with conducting qualitative studies. The belief that there is a close link between the qualitative researcher and what he/she is studying makes it appropriate to share the actions he/she took from the first person viewpoint (Bogdan & Biklen, 2007; Creswell & Poth, 2018). Specifically, when communicating qualitative findings, most readers want to know the action you took to arrive at the results – making the first-person style of writing the suitable choice.

As discussed in Chapter 2, incidence, experience and thoughts do not happen in a vacuum in qualitative research. There is always a connection between a phenomenon (which includes the data) and the context in which it occurred (Creswell & Poth, 2018). Due to this, when presenting the findings, you should communicate the situation and setting in which the phenomenon of study happened and the characteristics of the sources of the data. As a qualitative analyst, your background experience and biases may influence the findings, so you should communicate perspectives, preconceptions and lens (if any) to your readers. You also need to discuss how you bracketed them (see Chapter 5).

Because qualitative data analysis is generally a subjective experience, reporting how data was analyzed is as important as presenting the outcomes of the analysis. To help readers believe what you found, you should describe the data analysis steps (Adu, 2016). The final information to report is the content, which includes the outcomes of the analysis. Being thoughtful about how the findings are presented and following a specified structure promotes understanding and engagement among readers. You should always present the findings with the readers and research questions/purpose in mind. Make sure the results make sense to you before sharing them. As Dey (1993) states, "what you cannot explain to others, you do not understand yourself" (p. 245).

In sum, a good qualitative analysis report should include the following: an overview, information on context, preconceptions, perspectives, lens and expectations disclosure, data analysis steps, content (main findings) and a summary. In the following are detailed explanations and examples of the sections.

Overview

Presenting an overview is about zooming out from a reader's 'lens' – helping them to see the 'big picture' of the main components of the findings report. An overview entails a description of the research purpose, objective(s) of the presentation, and snapshots of what will be presented. It should be creatively and succinctly written with the intention of engaging readers at the early stage of the presentation and sustaining their interest until the end of the presentation.

Example 13.1

Overview

As a qualitative data analyst, I analyzed secondary data about the strategies genetic modification (GM) scientists used to share their GM research and innovations with the public. I obtained ten interview transcripts from a primary data source of a research project conducted between 1997 and 2002 in the UK (Cook & Robbins, 2005). Similar to the original project, the purpose of my research inquiry was to explore some of the UK's public concerns about genetically modified (GM) crops, the challenges GM scientists faced and the strategies used as they communicated their GM research and food technology to the public. After reading this report, you will be able to:

1. Recognize six main factors that contributed to public concerns about GM crops and innovations
2. Identify ten distinct challenges GM scientists encountered when presenting GM-related information to the public
3. Understand six strategic communication steps GM scientists suggested should be taken to address the public concerns

In the presentation of findings, I describe my background and biases, and how I tried to prevent them from having undue influence on the data analysis process. I provide the data sources, their characteristics and setting, and the situation at the time the data was collected. Finally, I detail the data analysis process and the outcomes – addressing the three research questions.

Commentary 13.1. I view the overview as not only introducing readers to the report but also shaping their expectations – especially the portion where I presented the objectives to the readers. By stating what they will gain, you promote their level of engagement with the findings.

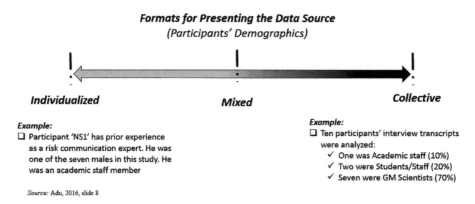

Formats for Presenting the Data Source
(Participants' Demographics)

Individualized   Mixed   Collective

Example:
❑ Participant 'NS1' has prior experience as a risk communication expert. He was one of the seven males in this study. He was an academic staff member

Example:
❑ Ten participants' interview transcripts were analyzed:
  ✓ One was Academic staff (10%)
  ✓ Two were Students/Staff (20%)
  ✓ Seven were GM Scientists (70%)

Source: Adu, 2016, slide 8

Figure 13.1. Formats used in presenting characteristics of participants

Context of the data and findings

In this section, you are expected to describe who you collected the data from (data source), where you collected the data (setting) and the time the data was collected (situation). These elements of contextual information help your readers to better understand the findings, put the results in an appropriate context and enhance proper transfer of the results to a similar situation and location. Presenting the context associated with qualitative data/findings is consistent with the philosophical assumptions linked to qualitative inquiry. It implies that every 'truth' is connected to a context (Creswell & Poth, 2018). However, when describing the context, avoid presenting any identifiable information that could adversely affect the privacy and confidentiality of participants (Adu, 2016).

In terms of describing the data source (such as a group of participants), you could present their demographic information in an individualized manner, collective format or both (Adu, 2016). If there are unique characteristics you want to highlight to your readers, you could present each participant's demographics – thus narrating them in an individualized format (see Figure 13.1). Conversely, if participants don't have distinctive characteristics then you could communicate their demographics in a collective form. Alternatively, you could use a mixture of individualized and collective formats – pointing out distinguishing participants' features as you describe shared characteristics.

Example 13.2

Context of the data and findings

The primary data was collected at a time when the UK public was concerned about food safety, although it was stated, "…no evidence of harm resulting from the consumption of GM foods worldwide" had been reported (Moseley, 2002, p. 129). The GM crop safety concerns were partially influenced by the outbreak of food-related diseases in the UK (Cook & Robbins, 2005). About 30,000 cases of bovine spongiform encephalopathy (BSE) (also known as mad cow disease) were reported in 1997 – a drastic increase from 300 cases in 1991 (Beck, Asenova, & Dickson, 2005). With this epidemic, accompanied with mistrust of the government about food safety, it made the public worried about future food-related outbreaks (Beck et al., 2005; Moseley, 2002). Simultaneously, the growth of genetically modified (GM) crops and research was met with criticism from interest groups. This incident partly fueled public concerns about the GM-related risks (Cook & Robbins, 2005).

As a way of addressing the concerns about GM foods and innovation, GM scientists informed the public about GM research through press releases. However, this communication strategy did not curtail the growing negative perception about GM innovations and products. Between 1997 and 2002, a research project was conducted "to understand the factors governing communication strategies of experts in explaining or justifying controversial technology" (Cook & Robbins, 2005, p. 1). Part of the data collected in the case study project was from interviews with seventeen GM scientists and seven university staff from a public institution in the UK. Out of these, I selected ten participants' interview transcriptions to analyze to help address my research questions. The majority of participants were males (n=7, 70%) and GM scientists (n=7, 70%) (see Table 13.1). In terms of their occupations, two (20%) and one (10%) of the ten participants were students/staff and academic staff, respectively. To ensure that I had good representation of females' perspectives in the findings, I selected all the three females in the original research project for this inquiry. As shown in Table 13.2, two of the three females were GM scientists.

Commentary 13.2. The context section shouldn't be too long. It should be concise – just enough to paint an accurate depiction of the situation, setting and source of data. As you can see from the example, I presented participants' demographics in the collective format (see Example 13.2). Their characteristics are highly homogeneous considering their gender and occupation. Due to this, presenting their demographics in an individualized manner would be repetitive – making communication about participants less engaging to readers. Demographic tables, whether in a collective version (See Table 13.1) or individualized version (See Table 13.2), could be useful for readers in learning about participants' background. An individualized table could be a very valuable resource for readers irrespective of the format you used when writing about the background of participants. With this table, readers can easily review a participant's demographics to make sense of his/her quotes (responses to the interview questions).

Disclosure of preconceptions, perspectives, lens and expectations

You may ask, *why should I disclose my preconceptions, perspectives, lens and expectations to my readers?*. You should do so because human-led qualitative analysis is a subjective process and being transparent (by bringing to light the behind-the-scenes coding strategies and

Table 13.1 Participants' demographics and their percentages (in parentheses)

Characteristic	N (%)
Gender	
Male	7 (70)
Female	3 (30)
Occupation	
GM scientists	7(70)
Students/staff	2 (20)
Academic staff	1 (10)

Table 13.2 Characteristics related to gender and occupation of each participant

Participant ID	Gender	Occupation
NS1	Male	Academic staff
NS2	Female	Student/staff
NS5	Male	Student/staff
S13	Female	GM scientist
S16	Male	GM scientist
S3	Male	GM scientist
S4	Male	GM scientist
S5	Male	GM scientist
S6	Male	GM scientist
S9	Female	GM scientist

analytical procedures) makes readers believe the findings. As discussed in Chapter 5, most readers want to know about the person who analyzed the data in terms of: conclusions he/she has made about the phenomenon of study before the analysis (i.e. preconceptions), how he/she viewed the phenomenon (i.e. perspectives), the specific perspective he/she used to analyze the data (i.e. lens) and what kind of findings did he/she expect to see (i.e. expectations). In Example 13.3, I present my preconceptions, perspectives and expectations. Since I didn't utilize a particular perspective, the following narrative doesn't have information about a lens. It is a reductive form of what I wrote in Chapter 5.

Example 13.3

Disclosure of preconceptions, perspectives and expectations

As a pragmatist, I embrace technological innovations that alleviate the problems we face and improve our lives. Before analyzing the data, I believed that genetically modified organism (GMO) innovations had a place in our modern world. From my understanding, I thought the development of GMOs had enormous benefits to mankind. However, I knew that supplying genetically modified (GM) seeds to farmers could create a sense of dependence among them, especially in developing countries. Moreover, in my view, having lower-price GM food products puts small-scale farmers who use non-GM seeds at a disadvantage – they are competing with 'affordable' GM foods produced by big corporations.

Although based on my past knowledge, I haven't heard of any food safety issues directly linked to GMOs, I was concerned about the long-term health-related effects of consuming GM foods. I thought more studies should be done to determine the long-term effects of GM foods on our health. Also, I was in favor of labeling all food products with regards to whether or not they have traces of GMOs, as required in EU countries.

Considering the focus of the study and the research questions, I expected to find that GM scientists were mindful of the public concerns about GM foods and the potential misinterpretation of GM research findings. I also assumed they were also aware of the difficulty of making sure that their press releases about the findings did not ignite controversy. Besides this, I view GM scientists as accepting the need to do more to lessen public concerns.

Commentary 13.3. When presenting your preconceptions, perspectives, lens and expectations, focus on only the issues related to the phenomenon of study and the data you analyzed. Your narrative should not be too long – making sure you provide adequate information to assist readers to understand your opinions and the biases you had before conducting the analysis. Although you might have bracketed most (if not all) of your views, biases and expectations, making them known to readers promotes openness in the data analysis process and the credibility of the findings.

Data analysis process

This section is about describing specific main actions taken to prepare the data (e.g. participants' interview transcripts) for the analysis. The level of detail of the account of the data analysis process depends on the goals of your presentation, requirements of the type of research report, journal article, thesis or dissertation you are working on and expectations of your audience. Besides these factors, make sure the data analysis steps are clearly presented in a chronological fashion and can be easily followed by researchers interested in using your data analysis strategies (Levitt et al., 2018). Moreover, qualitative analysis is mostly a subjective experience and the best way to make readers believe what you found is to show them how you arrived at the findings.

Based on the example below, let's assume that:

- Secondary data of ten interview transcripts were analyzed
- The transcripts were manually coded with the assistance of Microsoft Word tools

- The interpretation-focused coding strategy was used to code the data (see Chapter 7)
- At the category/theme development stage (see Chapter 8)
    - The presumption-focused coding strategy was used to generate themes under research question 1 *('GM concerns factors')*
    - The individualized-based sorting strategy was used to generate themes under research question 3 *('GM communication strategies')*

Example 13.4

Data analysis process

I started the data analysis process by preparing the ten interview transcripts selected from existing data for the analysis (see Figure 13.2). This process involved assigning IDs to the transcripts and making sure there was no identifiable information, reviewing the transcripts to gain an overall understanding of the data and determining what qualitative analysis tools to use (Adu, 2018). Exhibit 13.1 shows an excerpt of the verbatim transcript of Participant 'S6'. In deciding on the data analysis tool, I chose to conduct manual coding with the assistance of Microsoft Word tools.

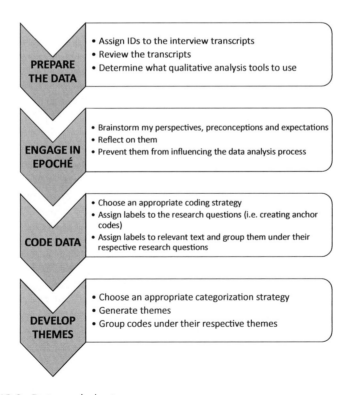

Figure 13.2. Data analysis steps

Participant S6	**PA** Participant ID
A: OK . it's it's working	**PA** Interviewer's label
B: there's nothing worse than when you get to the end and find there's nothing .	**PA** Interviewee's label
A: can I place this [the microphone] closer to you actually?	
B: yes wherever you want to . can I feel intimidated by it now?	**PA** Non-verbal behavior
A: no [both laugh] . ehm . the interview is actually . well we're studying . the way . science is communicated controversial science and so research on genetic modification . is communicated from experts to non-experts . and so we are interviewing scientists from this University . but we are also interviewing other interested . parties outside the University like Greenpeace GeneWatch . and then	**PA** Conversional filter **PA** Pause
B: are you interviewing any other scientists outside this University?	
A: yes because we are interviewing some industries as well so . people from Monsanto and Syngenta and they . often have a . background a scientific background	**PA** Pause
B: but no . publicly-funded . scientists other than effectively what's in the University	
A: yeah because it's a case study . of Reading University	
B: ah I see . oh OK I'm with you	
A: so the others are sort of informants . but they are not being studied . by us [laughs]	**PA** Non-verbal behavior
B: I'm with you I'm with you	

Exhibit 13.1. Participant 'S6' transcript excerpt showing some elements of a verbatim transcript

Data preparation goes beyond making the data ready for the analysis. It also involves making the mind ready for the task. I mentally prepared myself by engaging in epoché, which is simply bringing to consciousness my perspectives, preconceptions and expectations, and setting them aside (Moustakas, 1994; Patton, 2015). The three main epoché steps I followed were: brainstorming my perspectives, preconceptions and expectations, reflecting on them and preventing them from influencing the code and theme development process (see Figure 13.2). I engaged in epoché whenever I returned to the data after taking a break.

Coding data

The next step was to select an appropriate coding strategy to help me identify relevant information called empirical indicators and assign labels (called codes)

to them (Strauss, 1989). After critically examining the research approach used in the original study (which was a case study), the research purpose and questions I wanted to address, and the kind of data I had, I concluded that the interpretation-focused coding technique was the most suitable coding technique. Interpretation-focused coding is used to create codes which portray the meaning an analyst derives from the significant information identified in the data. For organizational purposes, before using this strategy, I first labeled each of my three research questions. These tags are called anchor codes. Below are the research questions and their anchor codes:

1. What were the factors contributing to public concerns about GM research and foods in the UK? *(GM concerns factors)*
2. What were the challenges faced by GM scientists when communicating GM crop research to the public? *(GM communication challenges)*
3. How should GM crop research be communicated to the public to address their concerns? *(GM communication strategies)*

Using the interpretation-focused coding strategy, I was able to examine each empirical indicator – gaining an understanding and constructing a brief response to address the indicator's associated research question. The answer to the question was then transformed, creating a phrase (not more than five words' long) called a code to represent the empirical indicator selected (see Exhibit 13.2 for an excerpt of the analytical memo table created).

Chronologically, for each interview transcript, I read through the data, selecting relevant information (empirical indicator). I then transferred the empirical indicator to the analytical memo to help generate a code to represent the excerpt. I came back to the transcript and used the *'New Comment'* function under the *'Review'* tab

Anchor code	Empirical indicator	Empirical indicator meaning	Research question answer	Code	Code description
GM concerns factors (RQ1)	"...rightly or wrongly I believe the British public is heavily sensitised to food issues by BSE CJD ." *(NS1, lines 39-40)*	The public have become concerned about food safety in general due to the outbreak of mad cow disease and related illness – making them hesitant to trust GM foods.	The outbreak of mad cow disease and related illnesses has contributed to the public concerns about GM foods.	*Outbreak of foodborne illnesses*	This captures any relevant information in the data that portrays 'outbreak of food-related illnesses' as a contributing factor to public concerns about GM crop research and foods.
GM research communication challenges (RQ2)	"...rather than focussing on on . on risk communication given that risks are not assessed . at the moment . and may take . years and years and years . to be able to do that ..." *(S13, lines 34-37)*	Because not much research has been done about GM-related risks, it is challenging for GM scientists to adequately address the public concerns about GM potential or perceived risks.	Since there is limited research on the potential risks of GM products, GM scientists may not have extensive response to public concerns about potential GM-associated risks.	*Limited information about GM risks*	This code focuses on the challenge of inability for GM scientists to adequately address the public concerns about GM-related risks due to limited research done.
GM research communication strategies (RQ3)	"...you can't expect that all lay members of the public will have those things . and that's when . you have possibly to simplify the statements you would make ." *(NS1, lines 89-90)*	The need to consider the public level of knowledge and perceptions about GM crop research and foods and present the information at the level they can understand – leading to addressing their concerns.	Information about GM crop research and foods should be presented in such a way they the public can easily understand it.	*Simplifying GM research information*	This represents portions of the data that depict the need to present GM research and food information in a simplified format so that the public can understand it.

Exhibit 13.2. Excerpt of an analytical memo table displaying the steps of developing codes

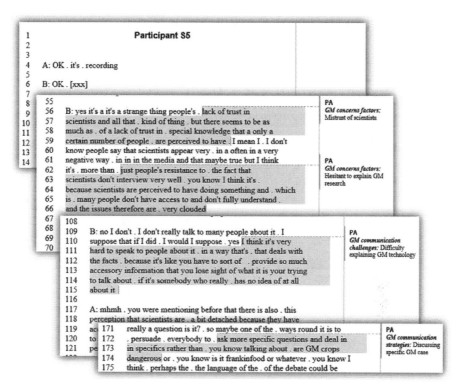

Exhibit 13.3. Excerpts from Participant 'S5' coded transcript

(in Microsoft Word) to assign the code to the empirical indicator. Before I inputted the code into the comment box, I indicated the anchor code linked to the code (see Exhibit 13.3). Besides creating analytical memos, I also developed initial memos to document my thoughts about some of the empirical indicators and their assigned codes (Birks, Chapman, & Francis, 2008; Charmaz, 2014; Strauss, 1989). Similar code development related actions were taken until I completed coding all the interview transcripts. I want to emphasize that:

- A new code was created when the existing codes wouldn't best represent an empirical indicator
- Each new code created had a description in terms of what it represented (see Exhibit 13.2)
- Any code which I considered relevant but which didn't belong to any of the three anchor codes was put under *'Other issues'*

After compiling all the codes under their respective anchor codes and tallying the number of times each code was assigned to the empirical indicators found, 22, 10, 23 and 5 codes were created under *'GM concerns factors (RQ1)'*, *'GM communication challenges (RQ2)'* and *'GM communication strategies (RQ3)'* and *'Other issues'*, respectively. The following charts show the number of participants (cases) and the number of empirical indicators (counts) associated with each code (see Figures 13.3–13.6).

Developing themes

I began the development of themes by selecting the presumption-focused coding strategy and individual-based strategy for the generation of themes for *'GM concerns factors (RQ1)'* and 'GM communication strategies (RQ3)', respectively. However, I did not create themes under the *'GM communication challenges (RQ2)'* anchor code. This is due to my plan of maintaining the uniqueness of each code under the anchor code as they independently address the second research question.

Presumption-focused coding, in the code development phase, involves generating claims based initially on the review of the data, and selecting evidence (empirical indicators) from the data to back the claims. At the theme development phase, it entails creating claims (i.e. initial themes) and choosing the codes (i.e. evidence) under the anchor code to support the claims. The confirmed claims become themes. Applying the presumption-focused coding strategy, I followed the steps below to create themes for the anchor code, *'GM concerns factors (RQ1)'*:

1. Compiled all the codes under the research question
2. Reviewed the codebook which contains the features of each code
3. Created initial claims (themes) and tagged them to codes (which were considered to be evidence supporting the themes)
4. Compared confirmed claims to determine the main themes and sub-themes

At the end, six themes and two sub-themes were created (see Figures 13.7–13.12). They were:

1. Unfavorable depiction of GM technology
2. Limited knowledge about GM research
3. GM risks uncertainties
4. Mistrust towards GM stakeholders
5. Lack of effective communication
   a. Mixed messaging about GM safety
6. Misunderstanding of GM risks
   a. Perceived existence of GM risks

The second categorization strategy I utilized was the individual-based sorting strategy. With this strategy, I grouped codes for *'GM communication strategies (RQ3)'* into six clusters. I started by reviewing and comparing the characteristics of the codes – determining what they have in common and considering the research question I wanted to address. Specifically, I first created a table with six columns (representing six proposed clusters). I then put the dominant code (which was the code with the highest number of cases and counts) into the first column (i.e. Cluster 1). The dominant code was *'Assessing public GM knowledge level'*. Each of the remaining codes was compared with the dominant code to see if they had a shared relationship. If they did, they were dropped into the cluster with the dominant code. A code was dropped into the next cluster if it did not have a shared relationship with the members of the existing clusters. After sorting all the codes into clusters (themes), I labeled the clusters based on the characteristics of their members (i.e. assigned codes). Lastly, to compute the total counts for each cluster,

Codes under *'GM concerns factors (RQ1)'*

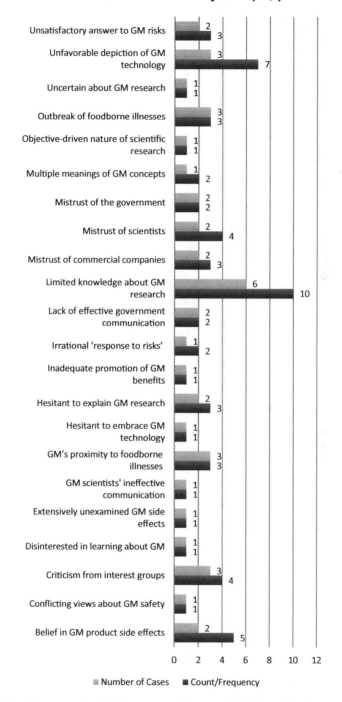

Figure 13.3. Codes under 'GM concerns factors (RQ1)' and their cases and counts

Codes under *'GM communication challenges (RQ2)'*

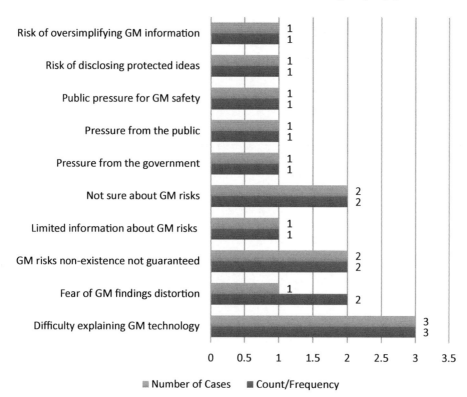

Figure 13.4. Codes under 'GM communication challenges (RQ2)' and their cases and counts

I summed up the counts for the codes (cluster members). Here are the clusters (themes) and their associated codes and counts:

- **Cluster 1:** Assessing public views about GM *(5 counts)*
  - a. Assessing public GM knowledge level *(4 counts)*
  - b. Listening to the public concerns *(1 count)*
- **Cluster 2:** Sharing GM risks and benefits *(14 counts)*
  - a. Being transparent in GM research *(2 counts)*
  - b. Creating awareness of GM risks *(1 count)*
  - c. Communicating GM innovation benefits *(2 counts)*
  - d. Emphasizing GM's positive side *(2 counts)*
  - e. Having conversations about GM risks *(2 counts)*
  - f. Presenting GM research rationale *(2 counts)*
  - g. Presenting GM risks and benefits *(3 counts)*
- **Cluster 3:** Giving the public some time *(3 counts)*
  - a. Giving the public some time *(3 counts)*

Codes under *'GM communication strategies (RQ3)'*

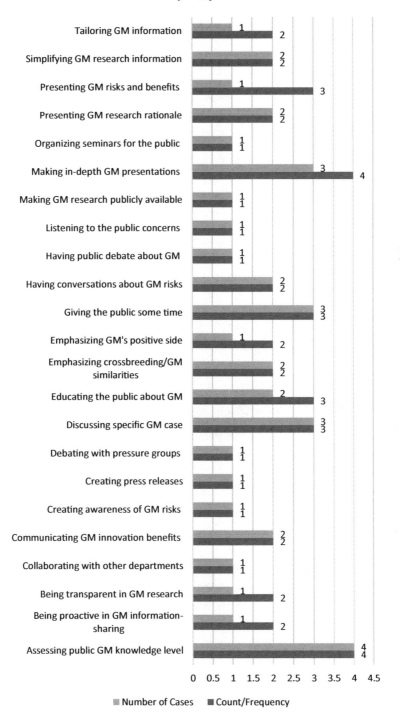

Figure 13.5. Codes under 'GM communication strategies (RQ3)' and their cases and counts

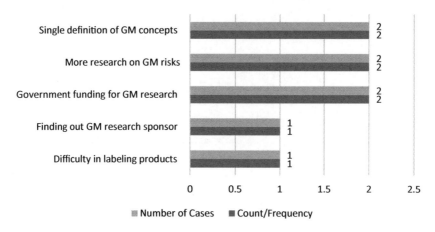

Figure 13.6. Codes under 'Other issues' and their cases and counts

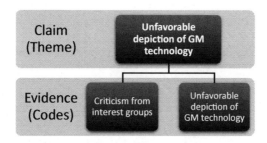

Figure 13.7. The theme 'Unfavorable depiction of GM technology' and its supporting codes

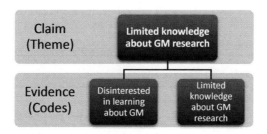

Figure 13.8. The theme 'Limited knowledge about GM research' and its supporting codes

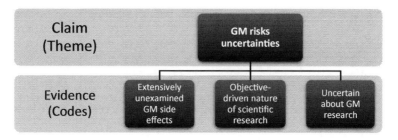

Figure 13.9. The theme 'GM risks uncertainties' and its supporting codes

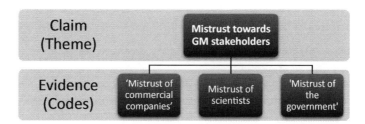

Figure 13.10. The theme 'Mistrust towards GM stakeholders' and its supporting codes

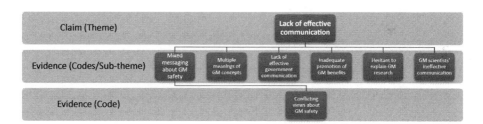

Figure 13.11. The theme 'Lack of effective communication' and its sub-theme and supporting codes

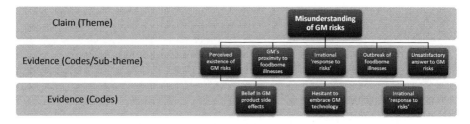

Figure 13.12. The theme 'Misunderstanding of GM risks' and its sub-theme and supporting codes

- **Cluster 4:** Making GM research publicly available *(3 counts)*
  a. Creating press releases *(1 count)*
  b. Making GM research publicly available *(1 count)*
  c. Collaborating with other departments *(1 count)*
- **Cluster 5:** Proactively engaging with the public *(12 counts)*
  a. Debating with pressure groups *(1 count)*
  b. Discussing specific GM case *(3 counts)*
  c. Having public debate about GM *(1 count)*
  d. Making in-depth GM presentations *(4 counts)*
  e. Organizing seminars for the public *(1 count)*
  f. Being proactive in GM information-sharing *(2 counts)*
- **Cluster 6:** Simplifying GM research information *(9 counts)*
  a. Simplifying GM research information *(2 counts)*
  b. Tailoring GM information *(2 counts)*
  c. Emphasizing crossbreeding/GM similarities *(2 counts)*
  d. Educating the public about GM *(3 counts)*

Presenting the main findings

Readers expect to see a well-organized presentation of the findings, where little or no effort is needed to ascertain how the results address the research questions or meet the purpose of the study. Your role is to present the findings in such a way that the reader may understand and be engaged. In other words, you are writing the findings with the readers' expectations in mind (Guest, MacQueen, & Namey, 2012):

- Reminding them about the research questions or purpose you want to address
- Describing the themes/cases including what they stand for and their characteristics
- Smoothly transitioning from what the themes/cases mean to what has been said/mentioned about them in the data
- Systematically synthesizing the themes/cases when needed
- Using meaningful illustrations to complement the text about the results

Findings presentation structures

There are many ways of presenting qualitative findings. One way is to organize the report around the themes and their features (including evidence from the data). This *theme-driven format* is characterized by communicating (in the written form) the categories/themes in relation to what or who you are studying. For instance, let's say you are studying factors that contribute to substance abuse among young people in community X. With this example, the phenomenon you are concerned with is the *'contributing factors of substance abuse'* and the unit of analysis (case of interest) is *'young people in community X'*. After analyzing the data and generating themes representing the substance abuse contributing factors, an appropriate way of presenting the findings is to follow the theme-driven format. To put it differently, you could report each contributing factor – including synthesized participants' information (related to the factor) as supporting evidence (see Figure 13.13).

Another way, which is also in a *case-driven format*, is to present cases as they relate to the themes. Cases could be individual participants or participants grouped by their demographics such as gender and geographic location. They could be organizations,

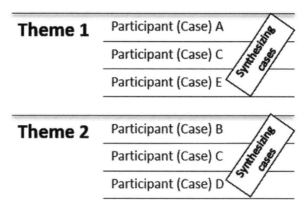

Figure 13.13. Theme-driven format

Participant (Case) A	Theme 2	
	Theme 4	
	Theme 5	

Participant (Case) B	Theme 1	
	Theme 3	
	Theme 5	

Figure 13.14. Case-driven format

groups of people, communities or countries. Back to the example, if your focus is to depict the unique contributing factors of substance abuse of each participant, then an appropriate presentation structure could be the case-driven format. This is where each participant's substance abuse related characteristics are individually presented, including touching on associated themes (see Figure 13.14). This reporting structure is not simply organizing themes under each case but thoughtfully and creatively synthesizing them.

There are two kinds of case-driven formats: distinctive case-driven and comparative case-driven formats (see Figure 13.15). With the distinctive format, your focus is to organize individual features of a case or group of cases with the aim of sharing their uniqueness to readers, and at the same time addressing the research purpose or question(s). However, if the purpose of the study or research question requires comparing and/or contrasting cases, then presenting the findings in a comparative case-driven format will be applicable. This kind of format is about presenting the differences and similarities of themes among cases.

The theme-driven format includes individualized and synthesized structures (see Figure 13.15). If you have standalone themes which can be independently used to address the research purpose or question(s) then the individualized theme-driven format

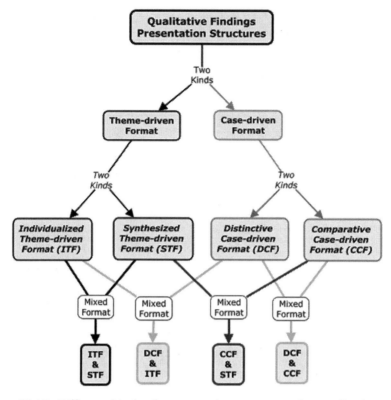

Figure 13.15. Different kinds of presentation structures for qualitative findings

Note: This figure was created using 'CmapTools' (Version 6.03; IHMC, 2018).

will be a suitable presentation structure. With this format, you present the themes one by one – describing their uniqueness as you answer the research question(s). Let's take a look at the themes developed under the research question, *'What were the factors contributing to public concerns about GM research and foods in the UK?'* **(GM concerns factors RQ1)**:

1. Unfavorable depiction of GM technology
2. Limited knowledge about GM research
3. GM risks uncertainties
4. Mistrust towards GM stakeholders
5. Lack of effective communication
6. Misunderstanding of GM risks

Since each of the themes are considered a contributing factor to public concerns about GM, you could individually use them to address the research question without considering the potential relationship among them. Therefore, the individualized theme-driven format could be the most suitable presentation format for reporting the findings under the above research question.

Let's look at another example. Examining the themes (as stated below) for the research question, *'How should GM crop research be communicated to the public to address their concerns?'* **(GM communication strategies RQ3)**, I concluded that the synthetized theme-driven format would best fit the way I should present the findings.

- Assessing public views about GM
- Sharing GM risks and benefits
- Giving the public some time
- Making GM research publicly available
- Proactively engaging with the public
- Simplifying GM research information

Due to the interconnectedness of the themes, the research question cannot be adequately answered without making reference to the chronological, concurrent, embedded, explanatory, and overlapping relationship among them (see Chapter 9). For instance, the theme, *'Simplifying GM research information'* follows *'Assessing public views about GM'* – implying they have a chronological relationship (Dey, 1993). In this case, the synthetized theme-driven format will be the appropriate way of organizing the presentation of the themes. This form of presentation exhibits a meaningful interweaving of themes, structured to sufficiently meet the purpose of a study or to address the research question.

To keep your creative writing and innovative ideas at work, you could present your findings in a mixed format – harmoniously combining two kinds of presentation formats to communicate data analysis outcomes to your readers (Greckhamer & Cilesiz, 2014) (see Figure 13.15). For instance, you could first present the meaning and features of each theme (using the individualized theme-driven format [ITF]) and end with a written and/or visual depiction of the fusion of the themes (using the synthesized theme-driven format [STF]). As you can see from Figure 13.15, there are endless writing formats. The most important thing is to help your readers to 'see' what you want to communicate. Baldwin (1984) put it perfectly during his interview with the *Paris Review*, he said "...I'm still learning how to write. I don't know what technique is. All I know is that you have to make the reader see it. This I learned from Dostoyevsky, from Balzac." I suggest you select the writing format that you think would assist you to share your findings to your audience, and at the same time show how the findings address the research purpose or question(s).

Example 13.5a (Individualized theme-driven format)

Presentation of the main findings

The outcomes of the data analysis show that there are six main factors contributing to public concerns about GM research and foods in the UK: the unfavorable depiction of GM technology, limited knowledge about GM research, GM risks uncertainties, mistrust towards GM stakeholders, lack of effective communication, and misunderstanding of GM risks (see Table 13.3).

Unfavorable depiction of GM technology

Participants were concerned about the unfair characterization of GM technology and products by interest groups and the media. To them, the media has misrepresented the implications of the growth of GM research and crops – overstating GM side

Table 13.3 Themes and their features under 'GM concerns factors (RQ1)'

Theme	Description (what it represents)	Cases (no. of participants)	Counts (no. of empirical indicators)	Empirical indicator (evidence)
Unfavorable depiction of GM technology	This is about the media exaggeration of the side effects of GM technology and the interest groups' strategy of unfairly criticizing GM research findings – fueling public attitudes towards GM food.	5	11	"...people like Greenpeace . actually promoting the the bad sides of GM..." (NS5)
Limited knowledge about GM research	This represents the notion that the public has limited understanding of the meaning of genetic modification, what it involves, its benefits and potential risks.	6	11	"...I think there's a lack of information . and a lack of understanding . by the public..." (NS5)
GM risks uncertainties	This depicts the public sense of uncertainty about the GM research and products including a lack of definitive response from GM scientists on whether GM foods have side effects.	3	3	"[It is about] perceived uncertainty of . possible potential future outcomes..." (S13)
Mistrust towards GM stakeholders	This theme encompasses all issues related to the public mistrust of the government, GM companies and GM scientists in relation to assuring them of GM safety.	3	9	"...lack of trust in scientists... but there seems to be as much as . of a lack of trust in . special knowledge that a only a certain number of people . are perceived to have..." (S5)

Theme		Count	Quote
Lack of effective communication	This represents GM scientists' ineffective communication and, in some situations, their reluctance in helping the public to understand GM research and technology. It also entails mixed messaging about GM safety on the part of GM scientists and the government.	4	10	"…I say I think our . communication of science's 's s been very poor" (S6)
Misunderstanding of GM risks	This portrays the public's lack of full understanding of the risks associated with GM technology and products. In addition, it represents the public's inability to objectively evaluate GM potential side effects.	8	19	"… the whole calculus of risk the probability of an unhappy event and the consequence of the character of that event if it occurs is something people are . not well adjusted to making…" (NS1)

effects which have not been scientifically proven. In addition, negative labeling of GM foods such as 'Frankenstein foods' adversely contributed to the public negative perception about GM research and innovations. As Participant 'NS2', a student/staff said:

…the way the media portrayed. GM foods as being. sort of. Frankenstein foods or whatever. the way it was put across in the media. and people just react to that and don't actually. sort of have looked into it. any deeper…

In the same way, they mentioned the interest groups' relentless campaign against GM research and foods. Greenpeace was mentioned several times as a pressure group skilled in swaying public opinion about GM crop research and foods. As a GM scientist (Participant 'S3') put it:

…when Greenpeace have been attacking. they've been doing it for publicity. purposes . and therefore. they've told the media. and they've informed them. and they're taking their own videos… and they've given the videos to the media. a-as a form of publicity…

Greenpeace fought against GM innovations using media platforms – making their message easily available and accessible to a targeted group of people. Examining the

Figure 13.16. Word Cloud for empirical indicators under the 'Unfavorable depiction of GM technology' theme
Note: This figure was created in NVivo 12 (Version 12.1.249; QSR International Pty Ltd, 2018).

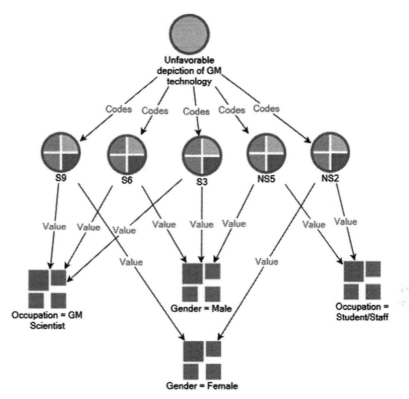

Figure 13.17. Project Map displaying participants connected to the
'Unfavorable depiction of GM technology' theme
Note: This figure was created in NVivo 12 (Version 12.1.249; QSR International
Pty Ltd, 2018).

significant excerpts that were coded under the theme, *'Unfavorable depiction of GM technology'*, I found that the words *'Greenpeace'* and *'media'* were among the words with the highest frequency (see Figure 13.16). Five participants, constituting three GM scientists and two student/staff, made reference to the two words when asked about what promoted the public reservations about GM crops (see Figure 13.17).

Limited knowledge about GM research

The findings show that the public did not have much knowledge about genetic modification – contributing to their fears about GM foods. They were not clear about scientific concepts related to GM. Some were confused in terms of the process of editing a crop DNA to attain desired characteristics. They did not understand the possibility of taking DNA from one organism and inserting it into another. Others were completely aware of the risks associated with the growth of GM technology. However, they did not comprehend the likelihood of the risks occurring – feeding into speculation about the potential risks without scientific proof. Evidently, as shown in Figure 13.18, participants frequently used words such as *'lack'*, *'understanding'*, and *'knowledge'* to voice their concerns about the public knowledge level about GM. Specifically, the Word

Figure 13.18. Word Cloud for empirical indicators under the 'Limited knowledge about GM research' theme
Note: This figure was created in Microsoft Word using 'Pro Word Cloud' (Version 1.0.0.3; Orpheus Technology Ltd, 2014).

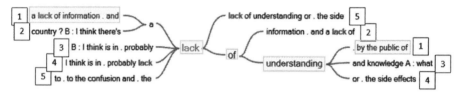

Figure 13.19. Word Tree for empirical indicators under the 'Limited knowledge about GM research' theme
Note: This figure was created in NVivo 12 (Version 12.1.249; QSR International Pty Ltd, 2018).

Tree showing the words participants used before and after the word *'lack'* depicts the public misunderstanding and limited knowledge about GM (see Figure 13.19). Similarly, Participant 'NS5' asserted *"...if you say GMO. they won't know actually what you're talking about. so there's so the the depth of knowledge isn't really great..."* and suggested *"...so we should be doing something about it"*. In sum, the public concerns about GM could partly be explained by a lack of understanding of the GM concept, GM process and the probability of GM risks occurring.

GM risks uncertainties

Similar to any technological innovation such as the production of self-driving vehicles, GM research and products have potential risks. The findings show that the public wanted an assurance from GM scientists that there were no side effects associated with GM technology and crops. To them, the scientists should be certain about the risks involved before making them available for consumption. However, according to one GM scientist ('S16'), not many studies have been conducted about GM side effects – making it challenging to completely promise safe GM technology outcomes. Moreover, due to the nature of scientific inquiry, they could not guarantee that GM foods are totally safe although there has not been any evidence proving otherwise. As a student/staff ('NS2') asserted, GM scientists could not assure the public that there was no risk due to the nature of scientific studies. In effect, this lack of assurance from GM scientists about GM safety and related uncertainties influenced the public negative attitude towards GM research and crops.

Mistrust towards GM stakeholders

Mistrust of GM scientists, commercial companies and the government emerged as part of the contributing factors to the public GM concerns. The public believed that scientific knowledge was limited to a specific group of people and that it was the responsibility of GM scientists to assure them (the public) that scientific research outcomes were safe. So, not getting a definite answer when asked about whether or not GM products were safe made them think that GM scientists were not being truthful to them. As described by a GM scientist ('S6'):

...it feels I think to the public as though therefore you're hiding something or you're trying to make a clever statement which fools them into whereas in fact that's what science is. it's you know you try and base everything on factual. statements...

The mistrust of the commercial companies was based on the public's past experience of food and drug safety issues. To them, the companies were concerned about making profit without equally considering that some of their products could be detrimental to public health. In support of this observation, Participant 'S3' who was a GM scientist expressed that:

...it also goes back to Thalidomide as well. in my opinion. though that. what's the phrase. evidence in other words that commercial companies can't always be trusted. to to bear in mind the public good. over- overriding commercial. whatever. commercial imperatives...

In a similar situation, during the BSE (mad cow disease) crisis (between 1986 and 1998), the way the government initially handled the epidemic adversely affected UK public trust in politicians and government agencies (Beck et al., 2005). Due to the public's previous experience with the government with regard to withholding 'sensitive' information from the public and softening the severity of a crisis, they did not trust what it said about GM safety. When asked about why the public had apprehension about GM research and crops, Participant 'S5' responded:

...I think also there's a deeper. deeper resistance to. the way in which. society works in the UK to some extent I think. there's a perception that. what was MAFF [Minister of State for Agriculture, Fisheries and Food]. wasn't very open wasn't very clear had it's own agenda it was on the side of agriculture if you like not. what not thinking necessarily in the public interest. I think those

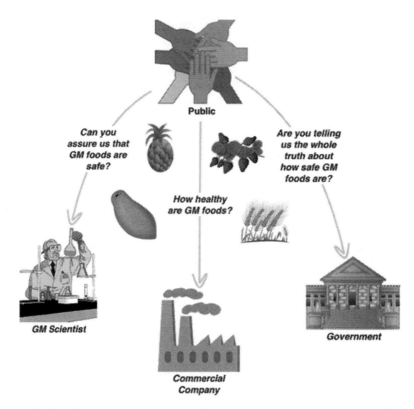

Figure 13.20. Diagram portraying the kind of questions the public may have asked GM stakeholders

are really the. things that. make people. nervous or made people nervous about GM.

Based on my interpretation of the evidence found in the data, I created a diagram to depict GM-related questions the public may have asked – voicing their concerns to GM stakeholders (see Figure 13.20).

Lack of effective communication

GM scientists saw their primary responsibility as conducting research and presenting the findings to the scientific community. In effect, less time, effort and resources were allotted to engage the public in making sense of the trends, benefits and risks of GM innovations. Participant 'NS5' described it this way: *"… there's really there's been a very poor job done. of actually promoting the benefits of GM. that's why I think the public are against it at the moment…"*. Also, some of the participants interviewed uttered a sense of hesitance about having a conversion with the public about GM research and crops. As Participant 'S5' explained, it was challenging to break down their research for the lay person to understand – concluding that *"…if I had a choice I wouldn't talk to them about it…"* (see Table 13.4).

Table 13.4 Sub-theme and codes with their associated characteristics under the 'Lack of effective communication' theme

Sub-theme and code	Frequency/ count	Participant	Empirical indicator
Mixed messaging about GM safety (Sub-theme)	1	S3	"…the fact that that . well it wasn't scientists so much . it was ministers who said . that . that . that the beef was safe . now sadly we know . well we don't actually know . because it's not completely proven . but it seems very highly probable…"
GM scientists' ineffective communication (Code)	1	S6	"…I say I think our . communication of science's 's s been very poor"
Hesitant to explain GM research (Code)	3	S3; S5	"…it's quite difficult I wouldn't really try and talk to anybody about that . if I had a choice I wouldn't talk to them about it . I mean I might . I'd even try and resist talking to other . food scientists or . animal scientists about it because you . it's just not a . a useful form of com-of communication…"
Inadequate promotion of GM benefits (Code)	1	NS5	"…there's really there's been a very poor job done . of actually promoting the benefits of GM . that's why I think the public are against it at the moment…"
Lack of effective government communication (Code)	2	NS5; S5	"…government I think had failed to . deal effectively with . communication of uncertainty because . they tried to they have tried to . respond to the public's wish for a black and white answer by giving them a black and white answer…"
Multiple meanings of GM concepts (Code)	2	S3	"…most things that you talk about . whether it's fruits . I mean especially the fruits . I mean most of the foods that we eat . are not natural . if you . if you mean . not being . influenced or bred by men . so . I mean . that's one of the words you might look at . what do people understand by the word natural…"

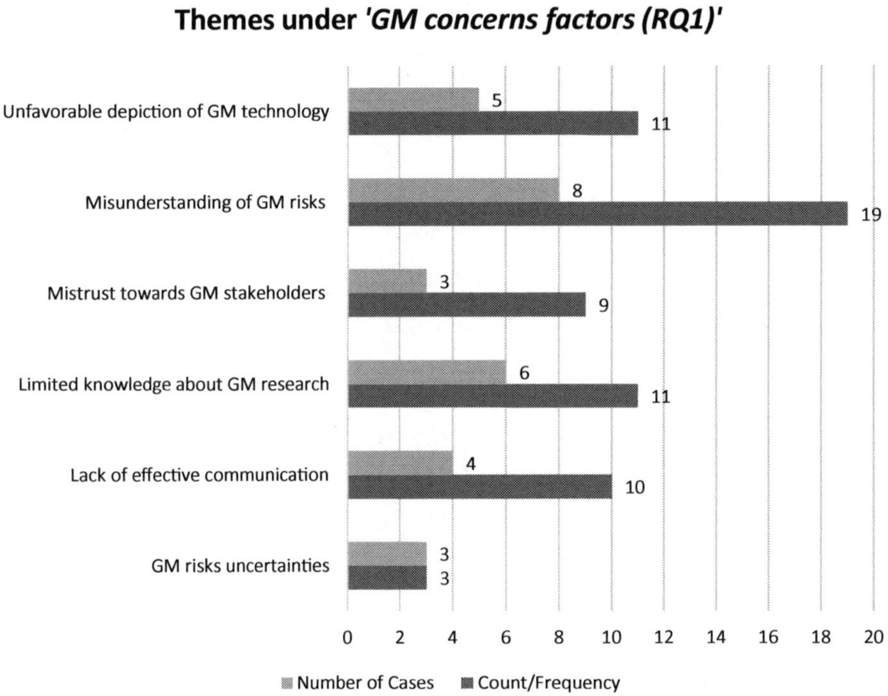

Themes under *'GM concerns factors (RQ1)'*

Figure 13.21. Codes under *'GM concerns factors (RQ1)'* and their cases and counts

Another factor that made it difficult to discuss GM-related issues with the public was that GM scientists and the public were not on the same page with respect to the meaning of some scientific terms. For example, what the public termed as natural food was different from that of the GM scientists. As said by Participant 'S3', most of the crops the public consume are not natural because they have been modified or domesticated for thousands of years.

I also found that the public's GM concerns can partly be attributed to mixed messaging about GM safety received from the government and GM scientists. While the government was assuring the public about how safe GM products were, GM scientists' communication fell short of making a definite claim about GM safety. A similar situation happened during the BSE crisis in the UK. As Participant 'S3' narrated, *"...it was ministers [government agencies] who said. that . that . that the beef was safe. now sadly we know. well we don't actually know. because it's not completely proven..."*

Misunderstanding of GM risks

'Misunderstanding of GM risks' was the most talked about of all the themes under *'GM concerns factors (RQ1)'*. Out of ten participants interviewed, eight of them (80%) made reference to this theme. It also has the highest count of empirical indicators – specifically, 19 empirical indicators (see Figure 13.21). As a result, I consider the public inability to completely make sense of GM technology and crop risks as the core contributing factor to their GM concerns.

Most participants thought the public had difficulty in accurately conceptualizing risks associated with the growth and consumption of GM crops. They attested how human beings are prone to make unreasonable decisions in life – making the UK public reaction to potential GM risks not an exception. They were not skilled in evaluating the severity of the dangers and their tendency of occurrence. As noted by Participant 'NS1':

> …most people. I mean you know. if you understood risk you'd never put a penny on the Lottery. would you?. with odds like that. you'd keep it in your pocket. and the good statisticians do precisely that but the human being isn't rational. so . we don't really behave in response to risks in a rational way…

To the public, there are risks involved in consuming GM foods but they were not sure when the adverse effects might occur and their extent of occurrence. This fear of the unknown led to the public search for answers. GM scientists' unsatisfactory responses to their quest for answers about GM risks related questions added to their misunderstanding of the risks. In addressing this issue, one GM scientist ('S13') suggested that *"…it's not enough to say. we cannot prove. that there are risks so there are no risks. you have to say you don't know. whether there are any. risks…"* Likewise, another scientist ('S5') commented:

> …people feel they have to say one way or the other. you know. genes either definitely cannot escape from plants into the environment or they can. and the the answer is that that. maybe under some circumstances they can. but . we don't know. need to we don't know enough about it.

The UK public were very concerned about food safety in general due to what they experienced during the mad cow disease crises. This has made them more skeptical about GM technology in terms of safety (as explained by Participants 'NS1', 'S3', 'S6'). Also, the proximity of the crises to GM innovation emergence and awareness influenced their anxieties about GM foods. As Participant 'S6' said, *"…I think the unfortunate timing with ehm. with other things like. BSE . and what have you and the. supposed . role of scientific advice. in that. did not. help the matter at all…"*

Commentary 13.4. After completing writing about the themes under *'GM concerns factors (RQ1)'*, I have gained a fresh appreciation of writing memos and defining codes when analyzing data. They were extremely beneficial to me. I adapted some information from the memos and code descriptions to write up the findings. Before writing about a theme, I reviewed the codes and their descriptions under the theme, went through the empirical indicators connected to it, and looked at associated memos.

When presenting your findings, make sure you support your claims, interpretations or observations with the evidence in the data. You could quote participants, present a table with sampled empirical indicators, or even visualize the evidence to back up what you found. As you can see, I used block quotations for participants' quotes with 40 or more words (McAdoo, 2013). You could choose to clean up the quotes obtained from a verbatim transcription. However, if you want to maintain the authenticity of what participants said, I recommend you present unfiltered quotes (see Mero-Jaffe, 2011). Another recommendation is to avoid flooding your presentation with a lot of quotes. As Koch, Niesz, and McCarthy (2014) suggest, "quotations should be judiciously interwoven throughout the text to illustrate findings that emerged in the data analysis" (p. 140).

To ensure a smooth transition from the claim/interpretation and evidence, you sometimes need to introduce a brief context as I did under the section 'Mistrust towards GM stakeholders' (see the last paragraph). As you are explaining the themes, make sure you connect them to the research question you are addressing. In other words, as you are describing what the theme is about, you are at the same time demonstrating how it addresses the research question.

The goal of creating a visual representation is to aid readers to have a clear understanding about what you are communicating. Depending on the qualitative analysis tool you are using, you could create meaningful visuals to complement the written information. Besides this, you could explore available visual tools to design creative pieces to help tell your story (Adu, 2016). The last illustration I suggest is that you create a table, especially if you are presenting the results in an individualized theme-driven format. It should contain all the themes presented including the following features.

- Description of the themes
- The number of participants connected to each theme (i.e. cases)
- The number of empirical indicators connected to each theme (i.e. counts)
- Example brief quotes from participants to support the themes

With this table, readers can easily refer to and review the themes and their characteristics (Saldaña, 2016).

Example 13.5b (Synthesized theme-driven format)

Presentation of the main findings

To adequately address the research question, *'How should GM crop research be communicated to the public to address their concerns?'*, I further analyzed the six themes generated to establish data-driven relationships among them. I started

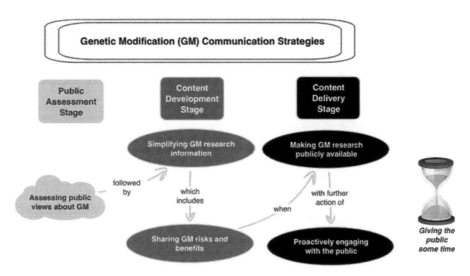

Figure 13.22. GM communication strategies and the connections between them

the process by practicing epoché – with the aim of bracketing my background experience, past knowledge and biases (Moustakas, 1994; Patton, 2015). I then examined the characteristics of each theme and compared them to determine whether potential relationships existed. In effect, I found five potential relationships. To confirm the relationships among the themes, I compared the data. Charmaz (2014) labels this practice as the "constant comparative method" (p. 181). At the end, four out of five possible relationships were confirmed. Table 13.5 shows a list of confirmed relationships and their respective types, together with supporting evidence.

Here is the data-driven answer to the research question about GM communication strategies: Participants' suggestions on how GM crop research should be communicated to the public were grouped into three stages: public assessment, content development and content delivery stages. As evident in the data, across these stages is interwoven an interdependence of five communication techniques, namely: *'Assessing public views about GM'*, *'Simplifying GM research information'*, *'Sharing GM risks and benefits'*, *'Making GM research publicly available'* and *'Proactively engaging with the public'* (see Figure 13.22). However, some of the participants ('NS2', 'NS5' and 'S5') recommended *'Giving the public some time'* as an appropriate standalone strategy. As Participant 'NS2' projected, *"...I think after a while people would begin to accept them. and I think a lot of the initial fears and stuff have already died down..."*

In terms of how GM scientists should communicate the GM crop research to the public, the first and most important step is to assess the public views about GM crops, research and innovations. The outcome of this assessment would help them in the content development stage. This stage of the GM communication process comprises simplifying GM research information, tailoring it to address UK public concerns about GM technology. In addition, the content of the communication should include not only the GM benefits but also its risks, creating an atmosphere of honest and balanced conversation about GM technology. In the content delivery stage, as GM scientists make available the information, they should proactively engage with the public in discussion and debate. By so doing, the fears

Table 13.5 Confirmed relationship and their types and empirical indicators under 'GM communication strategies (RQ3)'

Confirmed relationship	Type of relationship	Empirical indicator (Evidence)
1. **'Assessing public views about GM'** is followed by **'Simplifying GM research information'**	Chronological relationship	"…in that sense we don't I mean because we want their views we're not . providing a lot of information . except for the very basic . you know . what they call biotechnology and . you know that genetic modification can be used to do . one of two things just just to . sort of introduce . the topic to them but . we don't want to give too much information because we want to see . how much they know and what kind of . attitudes they have…" (S13) "…if we assume to begin with that an article in a scientific journal captures . 100% of what the scientist was doing wanted to say . that itself actually is not always the case . but if we make that assumption when that work gets translated into an article in my weekend newspaper . there will have been made . inevitably . simplifications . roundings up roundings down . fillings out all kinds . of things will have happened to the . pristine information to make it fit the . public format …" (NS1)
2. **'Making GM research publicly available'** and **'Proactively engaging with the public'** could concurrently be done after **'Assessing public views about GM'**	Concurrent and chronological relationship	"…in that sense we don't I mean because we want their views we're not . providing a lot of information . except for the very basic . you know . what they call biotechnology and . you know that genetic modification can be used to do . one of two things just just to . sort of introduce . the topic to them but . we don't want to give too much information because we want to see . how much they know and what kind of . attitudes they have…" (S13) "…they should find a way of of communicating this you know . as as they go along . doing their research the results they . they . they get . not only publish them in academic journals but ma-- make them probably a bit . you know . available to the wider public…" (S13) "…there should be much more public debate and much more information . for public so that . when decisions are made . they may or not be . absolutely what people want but they can see why they're made . and I think the same's true with GM…" (S6)

3. 'Sharing GM risks and benefits' is part of 'Making GM research publicly available' and 'Proactively engaging with the public'	Embedded relationship	"I think if we look at most of the literature that's been . published . most of it is . on the disadvantages of of GM and there has been very little publicity on . on the benefits and there always needs to be a balanced argument . and the public need to know all the facts..." (NS5) "...they should find a way of of communicating this you know . as as they go along . doing their research the results they . they . they get . not only publish them in academic journals but ma- . make them probably a bit . you know . available to the wider public..." (S13) "...there should be much more public debate and much more information . for public so that . when decisions are made . they may or not be . absolutely what people want but they can see why they're made . and I think the same's true with GM..." (S6)
4. 'Simplifying GM research information' and 'Sharing GM risks and benefits' have a shared idea of simplifying and balancing the GM information being communicated	Overlapping relationship	"...if we assume to begin with that an article in a scientific journal captures . 100% of what the scientist was doing wanted to say . that itself actually is not always the case . but if we make that assumption when that work gets translated into an article in my weekend newspaper . there will have been made . inevitably . simplifications . roundings up roundings down . fillings out all kinds . of things will have happened to the . pristine information to make it fit the . public format..." (NS1) "I think if we look at most of the literature that's been . published . most of it is . on the disadvantages of of GM and there has been very little publicity on . on the benefits and there always needs to be a balanced argument . and the public need to know all the facts..." (NS5)

and misunderstanding about GM crops and research would subside (if not dissipate) (see Figure 13.22).

Commentary 13.5. When presenting your findings in a synthesized theme-driven format, it is important to describe how you arrived at the confirmed relationship among themes. To enhance readers' understanding of the theme synthetization process and outcomes, I presented a table with evidence supporting the relationships (see Table 13.5). The information presented under Example 13.5b is a revised version of what I provided in Chapter 9.

Summary

The last section of a presentation of the findings report is the summary. It contains snapshots of what was written under the overview, context, preconceptions, perspectives, lens and expectations disclosure, data analysis steps, and main findings sections. The question you could think about is, if you have been asked to provide brief information (in one to three sentences) about each of the four sections, what would you write? Let's assume I have presented the findings to address all three research questions; here is an example of the summary of findings report:

Example 13.6

Summary

The goal of the analysis was to address the research questions related to genetic modification (GM) concerns factors, GM communication challenges and GM communication strategies. I analyzed secondary data from a case study conducted at a time in the UK where the public were generally concerned about GM innovations and products. I created codes for all the research questions and themes for *'GM concerns factors (RQ1)'* and *'GM communication strategies (RQ3)'*. I further examined the themes under the third research question to build and confirm connections among them. The findings show that the main contributing factor to the public GM concerns was inadequate understanding of the concept and implications of genetic modification. The core communication-related challenge faced by GM scientists is that they have difficulty explaining GM technology to the public. Lastly, the first and most important step in addressing the public concerns suggested by participants was to assess their level of knowledge. By so doing, GM scientists would be able to effectively tailor, and simplify, GM information for sharing.

Box 13.1 Findings reporting steps

1. Provide an overview of the report
2. Describe the context
3. Write preconceptions, perspectives, lens and expectations disclosure

---

4. Describe the data analysis process
5. Decide on an appropriate findings presentation format
6. Present the findings
7. Write a summary

CONCLUSION

Presentation of the findings starts with providing an overview of what you plan to communicate to your readers. It contains brief information about the purpose of the study, the goal of the presentation, and very concise information on what you will be sharing. Since in qualitative study the context of the data/findings is as important as the content of the presentation, you are expected to describe the data collection source, setting and situation. You also need to disclose your preconceptions, perspectives, lens and expectations, and how you were able to bracket them. Further, you then report how you analyzed the data – from describing how codes were generated to the way themes were developed. Based on the nature of the research purpose or question(s), you may need to further examine the themes to confirm relationships among them. At the end, make sure the data analysis outcomes can adequately meet the purpose of the study or address the research questions. The next task is to present the findings after selecting an appropriate presentation format. Complement your presentation with quotes, illustrations, tables and charts. This supporting information should be used meaningfully and judiciously. You end the presentation with a summary, briefly touching on the main issues you want readers to take into consideration.

REFERENCES

Adu, P. (2016). Presenting qualitative findings using NVivo output to tell the story. [PowerPoint slides]. SlideShare. Retrieved from www.slideshare.net/kontorphilip/presenting-qualitative-findings-using-nvivo-output-to-tell-the-story

Adu, P. (2018). What to do with your data: Qualitative research [PowerPoint slides]. SlideShare. Retrieved from www.slideshare.net/kontorphilip/what-to-do-with-your-data-qualitative-research

Baldwin, J. (1984). *The Art of Fiction No. 78*. (Interview by J. Elgrably). *Paris Review*, Issue 91. Retrieved September 12, 2018, from www.theparisreview.org/interviews/2994/james-baldwin-the-art-of-fiction-no-78-james-baldwin.

Beck, M., Asenova, D., & Dickson, G. (2005). Public administration, science, and risk assessment: A case study of the U.K. bovine spongiform encephalopathy crisis. *Public Administration Review*, 65(4), 396–408. doi:10.1111/j.1540-6210.2005.00467.x

Birks, M., Chapman, Y., & Francis, K. (2008). Memoing in qualitative research: Probing data and processes. *Journal of Research in Nursing, 13*(1), 68–75. doi:10.1177/ 1744987107081254

Bogdan, R., & Biklen, S. K. (2007). *Qualitative research for education: An introduction to theories and methods* (5th ed.). Boston, MA: Allyn & Bacon.

Charmaz, K. (2014). *Constructing grounded theory*. London, England: Sage.

Cook, G., & Robbins, P. T. (2005). *Presentation of genetically modified (GM) crop research to non-specialists, 1997–2002: A case study*. [data collection]. UK Data Service. SN: 5069, http://doi.org/10.5255/UKDA-SN-5069-1

Creswell, J. W., & Poth, C. N. (2018). *Qualitative inquiry & research design: Choosing among five approaches*. Los Angeles, CA: Sage.

Dey, I. (1993). *Qualitative data analysis: A user-friendly guide for social scientists*. London, England: Routledge.

Greckhamer, T., & Cilesiz, S. (2014). Rigor, transparency, evidence, and representation in discourse analysis: Challenges and recommendations. *International Journal of Qualitative Methods, 13*(1), 422–443. doi:10.1177/ 160940691401300123

Guest, G., MacQueen, K. M., & Namey, E. E. (2012). *Applied thematic analysis*. Los Angeles, CA: Sage.

IHMC. (2018). CmapTools. Version 6.03 [Computer software]. Retrieved from https://cmap.ihmc.us/products/

Inspiration Software, Inc. (2018). Inspiration Maps. Version 3.0 [Mobile app]

Koch, L. C., Niesz, T., & McCarthy, H. (2014). Understanding and reporting qualitative research. *Rehabilitation Counseling Bulletin, 57*(3), 131–143. doi:10.1177/0034355213502549

Levitt, H. M., Bamberg, M., Creswell, J. W., Frost, D. M., Josselson, R., & Suárez-Orozco, C. (2018). Journal article reporting standards for qualitative primary, qualitative meta-analytic, and mixed methods research in psychology: The APA Publications and Communications Board task force report. *American Psychologist, 73*(1), 26–46. doi:10.1037/amp0000151

McAdoo, T. (2013, June 14). Block quotations in APA style. Retrieved September 19, 2018, from http://blog.apastyle.org/apastyle/2013/06/block-quotations-in-apa-style.html

Mero-Jaffe, I. (2011). 'Is that what I said?' Interview transcript approval by participants: An aspect of ethics in qualitative research. *International Journal of Qualitative Methods, 10*(3), 231–247. doi:10.1177/160940691101000304

Moseley, B. E. (2002). Safety assessment and public concern for genetically modified food products: The European view. *Toxicologic Pathology, 30*(1), 129–131. doi:10.1080/01926230252824824

Moustakas, C. (1994). *Phenomenological research methods*. Thousand Oaks, CA: Sage.

Orpheus Technology Ltd. (2014). *Pro Word Cloud*. Version 1.0.0.3 [Computer software]. Oxford, England.

Patton, M. Q. (2015). *Qualitative research & evaluation methods: Integrating theory and practice*. Los Angeles, CA: Sage.

QSR International Pty Ltd. (2018). NVivo 12. Version 12.1.249 [Computer software]. Retrieved from www.qsrinternational.com/nvivo/products

Saldaña, J. (2016). *The coding manual for qualitative researchers*. Los Angeles, CA: Sage.

Smith, J. A., Flowers, P., & Larkin, M. (2012). *Interpretative phenomenological analysis: Theory, method and research*. London, England: Sage.

Stake, R. E. (1995). *The art of case study research*. Thousand Oaks, CA: Sage.

Strauss, A. L. (1989). *Qualitative analysis for social scientists*. Cambridge, England: Cambridge University Press.

14

Ensuring the credibility of the analysis process and findings

OBJECTIVES

Readers will be able to:

1. Conduct a qualitative analysis which promotes transparency
2. Develop strategies for improving the credibility of findings

THE CONCEPT OF CREDIBILITY

As qualitative researchers, we want our audience or consumers of our research report to believe what we have found. So what makes our findings credible? A qualitative analysis outcome is credible if it is directly drawn from data. Promoting credibility is about systematically drawing your findings from appropriately collected data, and presenting them with supporting evidence from the data (Cho & Trent, 2006). Limiting our discussion to the data analysis process and presentation of the findings, what can we do to ensure credibility? Here are some of the strategies that are necessary to help boost the credibility of your findings: ensuring consistency, being systematic and promoting transparency.

Ensuring consistency

Ensuring consistency involves taking actions and making decisions about data analysis that are in line with the philosophical paradigm, associated assumptions and research method you have chosen (Greckhamer & Cilesiz, 2014). Choosing a qualitative approach as your research method comes with assumptions and the belief that there is an existence of multiple realities, these realities are influenced by the characteristics of our experiences, and our knowledge is based on time and context (see Chapter 1). As a qualitative researcher, you are expected to work within the boundaries of these assumptions – making consistent decisions from choosing a suitable research method to selecting the right findings and presentation structure (see Table 14.1).

Being systematic

The qualitative data analysis process could be a complex and chaotic process if a well-thought-out process is not followed. During the data analysis planning stage, you need to decide on the specific steps you will follow. The data analysis steps should be consistent with your research method. You then choose a data analysis tool that will help you to carry out the steps (Adu, 2018). During the data analysis implementation stage, you clean, review and import the data into software (if you are not coding the data manually). Based on the coding and categorization strategy you use, you develop your codes and categories/themes. Based on the kind of research purpose or question you have, you could further develop connections among the themes. The final stage is the delivery stage – where you present the findings. All these carefully planned steps will not only yield data-driven outcomes but aid in trusting the results.

Promoting transparency

Transparency focuses on bringing to light your private and subjective experience of the qualitative analysis process (Greckhamer & Cilesiz, 2014). It starts with accurately documenting all the actions you took during the analysis and presenting them to your audience. In addition to recording your actions, it is important to write memos about your reflections, analytical procedures and the rationale behind your decisions – ready to be shared when the need be. Sharing all these behind-the-scenes documentations "…enables readers to evaluate a study's rigor and the trustworthiness of its results" (Greckhamer & Cilesiz, 2014, p. 426). It also helps future researchers to use some of your best practices.

AUXILIARY CREDIBILITY STRATEGIES

Besides making use of the essential credibility-related strategies discussed above, there are other techniques you could choose from and incorporate in your data analysis process. They are: implementing member checking, using theoretical sampling, actively involving participants and having a data analysis team.

Implementing member checking

Member checking is a process of sending data collected and/or findings to participants for their reactions – with the aim of using their feedback to improve the authenticity of data and/or accuracy of findings (Birt, Scott, Cavers, Campbell, & Walter, 2016; Caretta, 2015; Cho & Trent,

Table 14.1 Qualitative research methods and their respective purpose, data analysis goal, coding strategy, categorization strategy and presentation structure

Research method (see Chapter 2)	Main purpose of the method (see Chapter 2)	Main goal of the data analysis (see Chapter 2)	Potential coding strategy (see Chapter 3)	Potential categorization strategy (see Chapter 8)	Primary presentation of findings structure (see Chapter 13)
Phenomenological approach	Examine participants' experience and/ or thoughts about a phenomenon experienced	Develop themes or concepts which represent participants' experience	Description-focused and interpretation-focused coding	Individual-based sorting strategy	Theme-driven format
Hermeneutic phenomenological approach	Examine and interpret written texts to capture their underlying meaning (i.e. making sense of texts)	Determine what the texts mean in a condensed form	Interpretation-focused coding	Individual-based sorting strategy	Theme-driven format
Interpretative phenomenological analysis	Explore how participants make sense of their experience	Assess participants' perspectives of their experience and interpret their views	Interpretation-focused coding	Presumption-focused coding strategy or individual-based sorting strategy	Theme-driven format
Transcendental phenomenological approach	Examine participants' experience and make sense of the experience from a bias-free perspective	In a bias-free state, develop themes which reflect participants' experience and determine the essence of the experience	Description-focused coding	Individual-based sorting strategy	Individualized theme-driven and synthesized theme-driven format

Ethnography	Explore a phenomenon or an event as it happened in its natural setting	Develop themes to describe or generate a theory to explain a process, phenomenon or happening which occurred in its natural environment	Description-focused and interpretation-focused coding	Presumption-focused coding strategy or individual-based sorting strategy	Theme-driven and/or case-driven format
Narrative approach	Gather participants' stories with the aim of restating those stories	Combine participants' stories and narrate them in a chronological order and/or specified themes	Description-focused coding	Individual-based sorting strategy	Theme-driven and/or case-driven format
Case study	Understand a case or bring to light a unique case – collecting multiple kinds of data	Develop themes, a model or theory to explain a case or describe a unique case	Description-focused, interpretation-focused and/or presumption-focused coding	Presumption-focused coding strategy or individual-based sorting strategy	Case-driven and/or theme-driven format
Grounded theory	Explain a process, behavior, event or phenomenon	Develop a statement, model or theory to explain a process, behavior, event or phenomenon	Interpretation-focused and presumption-focused coding	Presumption-focused coding strategy or individual-based sorting strategy	Theme-driven format (specifically, synthesized theme-driven format)

2006; Mero-Jaffe, 2011). Member checking is not just a task to complete and check off your data preparation and analysis to-do-list (Birt et al., 2016). It is, however, a well-planned series of actions with a well-defined rationale and goal (Greckhamer & Cilesiz, 2014). Questions you need to ask yourself are: what do I want to gain from conducting member checking? How would the activity promote the credibility of the findings? Before carrying out the member checking task, you need to also access its implications for participants. Some participants may feel discomfort when their transcripts are sent to them for review (Mero-Jaffe, 2011). It is the responsibility of the researcher to put a support system in place to help participants deal with potential discomfort that could occur while participating in member checking.

During the data analysis stage, there are a couple of steps you could take regarding member checking to build the credibility of the findings. One way is to send each participant the codes generated from their transcripts for their feedback. This approach is suitable for codes generated using the description-focused coding strategy. With this coding strategy, the focus is on describing the empirical indicators in the data and developing labels (codes) based on the description. It is more focused on summarizing without interpreting the data. Therefore, codes generated are seen as a summary of the data. You send the reduced form of data to each participant to find out whether the codes best represent the information they provided to you during the interview. The codes are accompanied with their definitions (in terms of what they represent) and examples of the empirical indicators. Here are the steps you could take:

1. Contact participants to find out whether they are willing to be a part of the member checking activity
2. Schedule a meeting with each participant
3. During the meeting, explain to the participant the purpose of the study, the essence of the activity and what it is expected of him/her
4. Provide the codes generated based on his/her transcript, the description of the codes, and some of the empirical indicators connected to the codes
5. Go through with him/her the codes and what they represent
6. Ask him/her the following questions:
   a. Do you think the codes represent what you said in the interview?
   b. Which of the codes do you want to remove or adjust?
   c. What information (you have provided in the interview) did you think the codes did not capture?
   d. Is there any additional information you want to add?
7. Document the conversation for further analysis
8. Make the necessary adjustments to the initial codes

If you are using either interpretation-focused or presumption-focused coding, the best way of conducting member checking is to do it in a group setting. Birt et al. (2016) call this strategy "Synthesized Member Checking" (p. 1803). This is about organizing focus groups and seeking their reactions to condensed data analysis outcomes, developed based on the interpretations made or conclusions drawn from the data. "Focus groups are a recognized way of exploring the opinions, beliefs, and attitudes of a group of people and of enabling people to respond and interact together" (Birt et al., 2016, p. 1805). Just like a jury in a court-room, the focus groups are presented with the data analysis process and outcomes and asked for their views. Here are the steps you could take:

1. Contact participants willing to be a part of the focus group for the member checking activity
2. Schedule a meeting for the focus group
3. During the meeting, provide the group with the purpose of the study, the essence of the activity and what it is expected of them
4. Provide the data analysis process and outcomes to the group
5. Go through the codes/categories/themes with the group and address any questions they may have
6. Facilitate a discussion about the following:
   a. Whether the codes/categories/themes meaningfully represent the empirical indicators considering the coding strategy used
   b. Reactions to the codes/categories/themes developed
   c. Any other relevant information
7. Document the conversation for further analysis
8. Analyze data collected

Utilizing theoretical sampling

Theoretical sampling is typically used at the data analysis stage in a grounded theory study (Adu, 2017a; Charmaz, 2014; Strauss, 1989). This sampling technique could also be utilized if your research purpose or question requires exploring the connections among categories/themes. Theoretical sampling is a process of purposefully selecting participants who may have data to help adjust or confirm the initial theory or model which was created based on original data (Charmaz, 2014; Draucker, Martsolf, Ross, & Rusk, 2007). As a credibility strategy, theoretical sampling could be a first step in critic-ally comparing yet to be confirmed relationships among themes with new data. Instead of relying on the initial data to confirm proposed links among categories/themes (which may not be adequate), you collect new data to further examine the suggested relationships. Similar to what Charmaz (2014) recommends, here are the theoretical sampling related actions:

1. During data analysis, document questions surrounding the proposed relationships among the categories/themes developed

2. Determine who you want to collect data from to help adjust and/ or confirm the proposed relationships
3. Recruit participants for interview – addressing questions related to the proposed connections among categories/themes
4. Compare the proposed relationship among categories/themes with the new data
5. Make the necessary modifications of the relationships – leading to confirmation of the connections

Actively involving participants

Besides collecting data from participants, they can play an active role in the data analysis process, especially when conducting action research or program evaluation. The main focus of action research is to conduct research to ultimately address specific problems directly or indirectly faced by participants (Adu, 2017b; Craig, 2009). One way of actively involving participants in this type of study is to work with them to analyze the data. Besides gaining a sense of empowerment in solving their problem, it gives participants the chance to participate in making sense of the data, which promotes the credibility of the results. Similarly, program stakeholders are more likely to use the evaluation outcomes if they are actively involved in the evaluation process including data analysis (Adu, 2017c; Alkin & Vo, 2018; Kettner, Moroney, & Martin, 2017; Patton, 2012). Also, engaging them positively affects the trustworthiness of the evaluation findings.

To have a fruitful collaboration with participants in analyzing data, you need to know the specific data analysis role they can effectively play. One way is to have a discussion with those who are interested – talking about what the data analysis entails and agreeing on what they will be doing. Next, you remind them about the research purpose and questions you want to address and lead them in practicing epoché (Charmaz, 2014; Moustakas, 1994). As a facilitator, you go through each transcript with them, seeking empirical indicators to code. When significant information is identified in the data, they discuss what it stands for and its meaning or implication depending on the coding strategy you are using. The next step is to give participants the chance to suggest a code that best reflects the empirical indicator. The coding process is similar to the steps provided in Chapter 7.

You could also involve them in the sorting of the codes – developing categories/themes following steps similar to the individual-based sorting strategy. Going further, if you need to establish relationships among themes, you could work with them to complete this task. The most important thing is that involving participants in the data analysis process should be well-planned, systematic and transparent.

Having a data analysis team

Working with a team to analyze qualitative data "…is an arduous process. Simply because something that is collaborative gives no guarantee that its results are more significant, thoughtful or enriched than those gleaned by an individual researcher" (Bresler, Wasser, Hertzog, & Lemons,1996, p. 24). However, if it is done systematically with transparency and adherence to qualitative research related assumptions, it can promote credibility of the findings (Davidson, Thompson, & Harris, 2017). If you are working with a team, before analyzing the data, you should have a meeting with the team to discussion the following:

- Research purpose or question(s) you intend to address
- Each member's perspectives, preconceptions, lens and expectations
- When and how to engage in epoché
- Individual members' expertise in qualitative data analysis
- Roles and expectations of each member

Each member could be assigned with a specific data analysis related task such as identifying empirical indicators and assigning codes to them. Another member could be a reviewer of the codes generated – determining whether they best represent their respective empirical indicators. In addition, there should be a person supervising and coordinating the tasks (Bresler et al., 1996). After all the transcripts have been coded, another meeting could be organized to work on the codes to generate categories and themes. Alternatively, if you have no fewer than ten members in the team, you could use a group-based sorting strategy (see Chapter 8).

CONCLUSION

Whether you are analyzing the data yourself or involving others, your data analysis related actions and decisions should be consistent with the three essential strategies of attaining credibility: ensuring consistency, being systematic and promoting transparency. The successful execution of each of the auxiliary credibility strategies depends on a complete implementation of the essential credibility strategies (Birt et al., 2016).

REFERENCES

Adu, P. (2017a). Using grounded theory approach: From start to finish [PowerPoint slides]. SlideShare. Retrieved from www.slideshare.net/kontorphilip/using-grounded-theory-approach-from-start-to-finish

Adu, P. (2017b). Action research dissertation: What to think about [PowerPoint slides]. SlideShare. Retrieved from www.slideshare.net/kontorphilip/action-research-dissertation-what-to-think-about

Adu, P. (2017c). Program evaluation: Simplifying the program evaluation process [PowerPoint slides]. SlideShare. Retrieved from www.slideshare.net/kontorphilip/program-evaluation-simplifying-the-program-evaluation-process

Adu, P. (2018). What to do with your data: Qualitative research [PowerPoint slides]. SlideShare. Retrieved from www.slideshare.net/kontorphilip/what-to-do-with-your-data-qualitative-research

Alkin, M. C., & Vo, A. T. (2018). *Evaluation essentials from A to Z*. New York, NY: Guilford Press.

Birt, L., Scott, S., Cavers, D., Campbell, C., & Walter, F. (2016). Member checking: A tool to enhance trustworthiness or merely a nod to validation? *Qualitative Health Research*, *26*(13), 1802–1811. doi:10.1177/1049732316654870

Bresler, L., Wasser, J. D., Hertzog, N. B., & Lemons, M. (1996). Beyond the lone ranger researcher: Team work in qualitative research. *Research Studies in Music Education*, *7*(1), 13–27. https://doi.org/10.1177/1321103X9600700102

Caretta, M. A. (2015). Member checking: A feminist participatory analysis of the use of preliminary results pamphlets in cross-cultural, cross-language research. *Qualitative Research*, *16*(3), 305–318. doi:10.1177/1468794115606495

Charmaz, K. (2014). *Constructing grounded theory*. London, England: Sage.

Cho, J., & Trent, A. (2006). Validity in qualitative research revisited. *Qualitative Research*, *6*(3), 319–340. doi:10.1177/1468794106065006

Craig, D. V. (2009). *Action research essentials*. San Francisco, CA: Jossey-Bass.

Davidson, J., Thompson, S., & Harris, A. (2017). Qualitative data analysis software practices in complex research teams: Troubling the assumptions about transparency and portability. *Qualitative Inquiry*, *23*(10), 779–788. https://doi.org/10.1177/1077800417731082

Draucker, C. B., Martsolf, D. S., Ross, R., & Rusk, T. B. (2007). Theoretical sampling and category development in grounded theory. *Qualitative Health Research*, *17*(8), 1137–1148. doi:10.1177/1049732307308450

Greckhamer, T., & Cilesiz, S. (2014). Rigor, transparency, evidence, and representation in discourse analysis: Challenges and recommendations. *International Journal of Qualitative Methods*, *13*(1), 422–443. doi:10.1177/160940691401300123

Kettner, P. M., Moroney, R. M., & Martin, L. L. (2017). *Designing and managing programs: An effectiveness-based approach*. Los Angeles, CA: Sage.

Mero-Jaffe, I. (2011). 'Is that what I said?' Interview transcript approval by participants: An aspect of ethics in qualitative research. *International Journal of Qualitative Methods*, *10*(3), 231–247. doi:10.1177/160940691101000304

Moustakas, C. (1994). *Phenomenological research methods*. Thousand Oaks, CA: Sage.

Patton, M. Q. (2012). *Essentials of utilization-focused evaluation*. Los Angeles, CA: Sage.

Strauss, A. L. (1989). *Qualitative analysis for social scientists*. Cambridge, England: Cambridge University Press.

Appendix A

Table A.1 Analytical memo displaying the five main steps of developing codes when using interpretation-focused coding

Anchor code	Empirical indicator	Empirical indicator meaning	Research question answer	Code	Code description
GM concerns (RQ1)	"…rightly or wrongly I believe the British public is heavily sensitised to food issues by BSE CJD…" (NS1, lines 39–40)	The public have become concerned about food safety in general due to the outbreak of mad cow disease and related illnesses – making them hesitant to trust GM foods.	The outbreak of mad cow disease and related illnesses has contributed to public concerns about GM foods.	**Outbreak of foodborne illnesses**	This captures any relevant information in the data that portrays 'outbreak of food-related illnesses' as a contributing factor to public concerns about GM crop research and foods.
GM concerns (RQ1)	"I do think the BSE. crisis deepened everything in this area it's rather like the way the Japanese are so sensitive to anything nuclear. you have a couple of nuclear bombs on you and it changes your perception of nuclear" (NS1, lines 52–55)	One of the contributing factors of the public GM concerns is the close proximity of the mad cow disease outbreak and GM technology. The closer these two incidences are, the higher the sensitivity towards GM crop research and foods.	The proximity of the mad cow disease outbreak to GM innovation may have influenced their concerns about GM crop research and foods.	**GM's proximity to foodborne illnesses**	This represents any reference made to the closeness of a foodborne illness outbreak (such as mad cow disease) to the emergence and awareness of GM technology.

GM communication strategies (RQ3)	"if you cannot be open. with the public. you are immediately putting yourself. at a disadvantage. you have to be aware of the source of the research money." (NS1, lines 68–71)	Being open about the GM research process and sponsors of the research contributes to building public trust and addressing their concerns.	When communicating GM crop research, scientists should be open – discussing the research process and sponsors of the research project.	**Being transparent about GM research**	This entails all participants' responses that cover the need to be open when communicating GM research – including willingly sharing those who funded the research.
GM communication strategies (RQ3)	"…you can't expect that all lay members of the public will have those things. and that's when. you have possibly to simplify the statements you would make." (NS1, lines 89–90)	The need to consider the public level of knowledge and perceptions about GM crop research and foods, and present the information at a level they can understand – leading to addressing their concerns.	Information about GM crop research and foods should be presented in such a way that the public can easily understand it.	**Simplifying GM research information**	This represents portions of the data that depict the need to present GM research and food information in a simplified format so that the public can understand it.

(continued)

Table A.1 (Cont.)

Anchor code	Empirical indicator	Empirical indicator meaning	Research question answer	Code	Code description
GM communication challenges (RQ2)	"it wouldn't be reasonable I think not to. the the idea that someone might pinch your ideas is always there in science and and and is not improper actually. in the way science is conducted." (NS1, lines 116–118)	In order to build trust and address public concerns, GM scientists should be open about the GM research process and findings. However, they face the risk of disclosing information that may give their competitors the upper hand.	The effort of promoting transparency could lead to the risk of disclosing information which is initially protected from being used by their competitors.	***Risk of disclosing protected ideas***	This captures information about the dilemma of being open to the public and putting GM scientists' protected ideas at risk of being used by their competitors.
GM communication challenges (RQ2)	"it will be open to challenge on the grounds that. you have over simplified it. or you have disguised some risk. and it's impossible. wholly to refute those criticisms because they are inherent in the. translation which will have occurred from the scientifically	In the manner in which they help the public to easily digest the GM crop research process and findings, and minimize (if not alleviate) the controversies, GM scientists run into the risk of oversimplifying the research. In effect, the demystified GM information could lead	As GM scientists are working on making the GM research presentation easy to understand, there is the tendency to oversimplify the information.	***Risk of oversimplifying GM information***	This code is about the challenge of presenting easy-to-understand GM crop research information, and at the same time making sure the information is not oversimplified and/or misleading.

accurate. to the publicly. useful . and . one of the techniques for example regularly used in that context is analogy. analogy is. desperately dangerous. and yet you know all of us. find it useful" (NS1, lines 223–230)

to misinformation – fueling the controversies they were trying to address in the first place.

| **GM concerns (RQ1)** | "…most people. I mean you know. if you understood risk you'd never put a penny on the Lottery. would you?. with odds like that. you'd keep it in your pocket. and the good statisticians do precisely that but the human being isn't rational. so . we don't really behave in response to risks in a rational way." (NS1, lines 245–249) | We are generally inclined not to make rational decisions in relation to risks. In other words, the decision to take or not to take a certain risk is not based on thoughtful and critical analysis of what it involves and its consequences. This assertion partly explains the concerns the public have about GM crop research and foods. | The tendency of the public to make irrational responses to GM foods related risks partly explains the concerns about GM foods. | **Irrational 'response to risks'** | This code covers all relevant information that makes reference to issues related to unreasonable decisions and reactions of the public about potential GM risks. |

(continued)

Table A.1 (Cont.)

Anchor code	Empirical indicator	Empirical indicator meaning	Research question answer	Code	Code description
GM concerns (RQ1)	"because there are so many. ways of talking about. the issue and. biotechnology is different from genetic modification and that's different from. other . other terms. and so I think that that somehow adds to. to the confusion and. the lack of understanding and knowledge" (S13, lines 23–27)	The public don't fully understand concepts about genetic modification and the mechanisms involved.	Lack of understanding of GM-related information has contributed to their concerns.	***Limited knowledge about GM research***	This represents significant information in the data that explains how limited the public understanding of GM research and foods is.
GM concerns (RQ1)	" perceived uncertainty of. possible potential future outcomes that. it's not people are not. able to control so it is lack of control lack of knowledge. uncertainty about. potential. you know." (S13, lines 7–10)	The public are concerned about GM research and foods because they don't know their implications. They are not sure about the long-term effects of the GM foods on their health and the consequences of GM materials being produced.	The public feel uncertain about the implications of GM crop research and foods – contributing to their concerns.	***Uncertain about GM research***	This covers relevant portions of the data that depict the public's sense of uncertainty about the GM research and products.

GM communication challenges (RQ2)	"...rather than focusing on on. on risk communication given that risks are not assessed. at the moment. and may take. years and years and years. to be able to do that ..." (S13, lines 34–37)	Because not much research has been done on GM-related risks, it is challenging for GM scientists to adequately address the public concerns about GM's potential or perceived risks.	Limited information about GM risks	Since there is limited research on the potential risks of GM products, GM scientists may not have extensive responses to public concerns about potential GM-associated risks.	This code focuses on GM scientists' inability to adequately address the public concerns about GM-related risks due to limited research done.
GM communication strategies (RQ3)	"if people see. trade-offs between accepting something that is new and to some extent. unknown . and . benefits there are quite tangible like perhaps. health benefits. if you know if. products are developed that can. can be either either. functional . type of foods or or can can give. you know. specific benefits then that may be an idea otherwise." (S13, lines 39–43)	When presenting GM research and related implications, it is important to focus more on the benefits than the potential risks (which could take time to know whether they exist).	Communicating GM innovation benefits	Communicating more of the GM research and foods' benefits and less on the potential risks which are uncertain.	This code captures ideas in the data which imply the need to put a greater emphasis on the benefits of GM research and foods than the potential risks when making a presentation.

(continued)

Table A.1 (Cont.)

Anchor code	Empirical indicator	Empirical indicator meaning	Research question answer	Code	Code description
GM communication strategies (RQ3)	"the way we approach consumers at the moment is through something. it is through a data collection. instrument . it's a questionnaire. so . in that sense we don't I mean because we want their views we're not. providing a lot of information. except for the very basic. you know. what they call biotechnology and. you know that genetic modification can be used to do. one of two things just just to. sort of introduce. the topic to them but. we don't want to give too much information because we want to see. how much they know and what kind of. attitudes they have" *(S13, lines 56–64)*	Before sharing GM research with the public, GM scientists need to know their level of knowledge and perceptions about GM innovations. This is done by collecting data on the public's GM knowledge and perspectives.	Examining the GM knowledge level and perceptions of the public before communicating GM research to them.	***Assessing public GM knowledge level***	Any participant's expression related to the need to assess the public knowledge level and perceptions about GM innovations will be put under this code.

Theme	Quote			Code	Description
GM communication challenges (RQ2)	"we cannot prove. that there are risks so there are no risks. you have to say you don't know. whether there are any. risks ." (S13, lines 73–75)	There is hesitance by GM scientists to make a claim or assure the public about GM risks. To them, they are not sure because it has not been scientifically proven that GM risks exist.	The public want assurance that there are no GM-related risks but since their existence has not been proven, the only conclusion they can make is that they don't know GM-related risks for now.	**GM risks' non-existence not guaranteed**	This code covers the communication challenges related to GM scientists' difficulty in satisfying the public interest in the assurance of there being no GM innovation-related risks.
GM communication challenges (RQ2)	"perhaps find a way which is difficult because if you know the newspapers get hold of. of information and then. it's . you know it it. may not. be conveyed the in in an objective and right way to to. to the wider public." (S13, lines 77–80)	There is a concern that the media may misrepresent GM research findings when sharing them with the public.	GM scientists fear that the findings may be distorted when they are presented to the public.	**Fear of GM findings distortion**	This code represents relevant portions of the data that portray GM scientists' concern about the misrepresentation of GM crop research findings.

Appendix B

Table B.1 Memos with their cases and codes retrieved from QDA Miner Lite

Comment/Memo	Case	Code
1. This may have some connection with one of the codes under the 'GM communication challenges (RQ2)' research question.	NS2	Unfavorable depiction of GM technology
2. This is more about being proactive in sharing information about GM research and foods by teaching the public using documentaries and movies. Also, using social media to share GM information would help.	NS2	Educating the public about GM
3. I think the public are potential consumers of GM products and they have the right to know the rationale behind GM research and the process through which GM foods are produced. But how much information about GM should be provided to satisfy their quest for answers, since GM scientists and companies don't want to provide information that may help their competitors?	NS2	Presenting GM research rationale
4. Due to the objective nature of science, GM scientists can't just assure the public that there is no risk associated with GM research and foods when there is currently no evidence to support or refute this assertion.	NS2	Objective-driven nature of scientific research
5. I was thinking that if the government sponsors GM research, wouldn't GM scientists be pressured to produce favorable results, especially on issues about GM risks?	NS2	Government funding for GM research
6. This code may come under the 'communicating GM innovation benefits' code. Emphasizing the positive side makes sense since they are not certain about the potential side effects of GM. At the same time they need to be open to the public – having a conversation about the people's concerns.	S16	Emphasizing GM's positive side

(continued)

Table B.1 (Cont.)

Comment/Memo	Case	Code
7. I coded this empirical indicator as 'Belief in GM product side effects' although I used this code to label an indicator previously. This is because, in this case, the 'side effects' were being discussed in a different context under a different interview question.	S16	Belief in GM product side effects
8. This supports the assertion that GM scientists are not in the position to emphatically assure the general public because (1) it takes time to know the effects and (2) not much research has been done on the risk.	S16	Not sure about GM risks
9. Because GM risks have not been extensively studied, GM scientists can't fully guarantee the potential side effects of GM. There is a possible connection of this code to 'Inability to guarantee GM risks non-existence'.	S16	Extensively unexamined GM side effects
10. This is a great opportunity for the public to know the GM research process and findings and how GM seeds are produced. It will be an avenue for the GM scientists to address their concerns.	S16	Organizing seminars for the public
11. Since GM is a new innovation, the public needs time to understand and get comfortable with it.	S16	Giving the public some time
12. What the public terms as natural food is different from that of the GM scientists. According to them, most of the crops we consume are not natural because they have been modified or domesticated for thousands of years.	S3	Multiple meanings of GM concepts
13. I think that to GM scientists, their role is to do research and publish it. To them, having a discussion with the public about their research is not their responsibility. It is challenging to explain their research for the lay person to understand. They might think that their inability to clearly explain GM-related issues may cause further controversies. Most of the scientists are buying time hoping the controversies surrounding GM crop research and food fades away.	S3	Hesitant to explain GM research

14. These interest groups are skilled in swaying public opinion about GM crop research and foods. They know the best way to phrase a narrative that will win people over to their side, and use social media to make their message easily available and accessible to a targeted group of people._	S3	Criticism from interest groups
15. The need to first present the history of crop domestication and how it is similar to GM innovation.	S4	Making in-depth GM presentations
16. It is interesting that some people have strong opinions about GM but lack basic understanding of GM technology.	S6	Disinterested in learning about GM
17. They may be hesitant because they thought something bad may happen and they are not sure when and the extent to which the adverse effects may occur. This fear of the unknown may have caused some of them to search for answers – leading to an unsatisfied quest for information, and mistrust of the scientists, government and food corporations.	S9	Hesitant to embrace GM technology

Table B.2 Empirical indicators and their respective codes and cases retrieved from QDA Miner Lite

Code	Case	Text/Empirical indicator
GM communication challenges (RQ2)		
Risk of oversimplifying GM information	NS1	"it will be open to challenge on the grounds that. you have over simplified it. or you have disguised some risk. and it's impossible. wholly to refute those criticisms because they are inherent in the. translation which will have occurred from the scientifically accurate. to the publicly. useful . and . one of the techniques for example regularly used in that context is analogy. analogy is. desperately dangerous. and yet you know all of us. find it useful"
Risk of disclosing protected ideas	NS1	"it wouldn't be reasonable I think not to. the the idea that someone might pinch your ideas is always there in science and and and is not improper actually. in the way science is conducted."
Public pressure for GM safety	NS2	"I think also the public want to hear that as well"
'Pressure from the government'	NS2	"I think there is pressure from the government on scientists. to make sure that they can make it safe and that they can. say that it's safe."
Limited information about GM risks	S13	"rather than focussing on on. on risk communication given that risks are not assessed. at the moment. and may take. years and years and years. to be able to do that."
Fear of GM findings distortion	S13	"there is a risk of of. of misleading the public or not communicating properly or something like that some people argue that. you know scientists are just scientists like with their heads in a box."
GM risks non-existence not guaranteed	S13	"we cannot prove. that there are risks so there are no risks. you have to say you don't know. whether there are any. risks . "
Fear of GM findings distortion	S13	"perhaps find a way which is difficult because if you know the newspapers get hold of. of information and then. it's . you know it it. may not. be conveyed the in in an objective and right way to to. to the wider public."

Not sure about GM risks	S16	"those side effects I am not I'm. not very sure of what exactly side effects it had it's always speculating but I think there should be some side effects"
Not sure about GM risks	S4	"I have to saat the moment there is. none of transgene that I am aware of which. are any problem at all. but . that's not to say that sort of 20 years down the line or 30 years down the line somebody might. accidentally put one out which. does have an effect."
Not sure about GM risks	S5	"I don't know. because . if you say you're not sure about something it just seems that you don't know. well I suppose you don't know do you?"
Difficulty explaining GM technology	S5	"I think it's quite hard to see. you can involve people in a sort of general way. but any. it seems to me that any. you know idea of consulting with people. on these. issues things like. what's the best way to go about generating a GM plant or. I mean or you know I suppose if it's if they're ethical things you can have that. consultation and that's fine people just do that. but when it's on the technical issues about. how you know what's the. best method to do the transformation or or maybe that's what people want. not what people want to know about. but I think there're. you can talk in general terms about it. and about the ethical implications"
Difficulty explaining GM technology	S5	"I think it's very hard to speak to people about it. in a way that's. that deals with the facts. because it's like you have to sort of. provide so much accessory information that you lose sight of what it is your trying to talk about. if it's somebody who really. has no idea of at all about it"
Difficulty explaining GM technology	S5	"isn't it so that this that or the other you know they they they have opinions about it themselves it's hard to deal with that because. it's it's almost worse than somebody who has. absolutely no interest or information about it because they. they often say things which are. which sound true. or sound like they could be true. they sound like they. they have the. sound of reason to them."

(continued)

Table B.2 (Cont.)

Code	Case	Text/Empirical indicator
Pressure from the public	S6	"B: you you do feel that there's a certain amount of pressure. from people wanting you to say this A: from the public? B: yes. yes . yes and people who. want you to say that to the public. as well"
Difficulty explaining GM technology	S9	"I know some things about GM products I think. that it won't be good to tell the people everything. because because if you. well I'm not saying that they shouldn't be informed. of course they should. but there are a lot of things. a lot of procedure procedures you have to go through to to produce. a food like that. and if you describe these things to a person who doesn't know what you are talking about then all these things seem you know really frightening"
GM risks non-existence not guaranteed	S9	"I think that these people they need the reassurance that it's not bad for them. and unfortunately scientists. responsible scientists they can't say something like that because they don't know"
Difficulty explaining GM technology	S9	"OK I'm sorry but first of all I think that it's very difficult because I have tried that. to communicate with a person who is only whose only source of information is the media. of course I'm not experienced in something like that in communicating with people like that but I think that. what they would like to see is a simple way to explain. what exactly the product is. without . going into technical information too much. and . try to make it as as as simple as possible and as harmless as possible. not by saying lies. but telling the truth telling what exactly what is exactly happening. during the procedure of producing a a food product like that. so what I would like to see is simplicity. in in the argument and. I don't know reassurance that. you know. nothing's they are not bad nothing which is used. in the procedure. will make. will be bad for someone"

GM communication strategies (RQ3)

Simplifying GM research information	NS1	"you can't expect that all lay members of the public will have those things. and that's when. you have possibly to simplify the statements you would make"
Being transparent in GM research	NS1	"so openness I think is. extremely important"
Simplifying GM research information	NS1	"if we assume to begin with that an article in a scientific journal captures. 100% of what the scientist was doing wanted to say. that itself actually is not always the case. but if we make that assumption when that work gets translated into an article in my weekend newspaper. there will have been made. inevitably . simplifications . roundings up roundings down. fillings out all kinds. of things will have happened to the. pristine information to make it fit the. public format."
Being transparent in GM research	NS1	"if you cannot be open. with the public. you are immediately putting yourself. at a disadvantage. you have to be aware of the. source of the research money."
Educating the public about GM	NS2	"I think more education would help."
Giving the public some time	NS2	"I think after a while people would begin to accept them. and I think a lot of the initial fears and stuff have already died down."
Having conversations about GM risks	NS2	"people need to be really clear about. how realistic it is that that happens and when it happens and how you can prevent it happening things like that. and also I think people are worried about the health effects. so . that needs to be clearly communicated. about what effect if any there are on eating. GM foods and that kind of thing"
Presenting GM research rationale	NS2	"I think. you need to. communicate what the main aims of doing it are. because a lot of the time people don't really know. why it was done in the first place. so the sort of background to the research and the use of GM foods"

(continued)

Table B.2 (Cont.)

Code	Case	Text/Empirical indicator
Listening to the public concerns	NS2	"I think there are a lot of reasons why. people . have genuine concerns about it it's just a question of. being able to. hear those in a sensible way rather than. just being reactionary about it"
Assessing public GM knowledge level	NS5	"have a give a clear understanding to the consumer what's involved"
Giving the public some time	NS5	"I think it will take quite a long time. and I don't think it's going to happen overnight"
Debating with pressure groups	NS5	"well I know we've mentioned Greenpeace quite a lot but. people like Greenpeace I think need to. actually enter into a debate. rather than. kind of standing away from the crowd and shouting at everyone I think they need to come into the. to the group. and just talk in an open manner. and to the consumer about. what . GM actually is and how it's going to affect. kind of farming and our countryside and biodiversity"
Discussing specific GM case	NS5	"there'd have to be a free and open debate about GM. I think people would have to put aside. kind of what they. believe politically and. and just try and. talk about it rationally"
Presenting GM risks and benefits	NS5	"it's important that people understand that if we have GM we can. pretty much cut out. so so many of the chemicals that we have to put on the crop. it's obviously going to provide. environmental benefits in that way. but then the disadvantage of that it may affect actual biodiversity. and we need to look at kind of both of those things. and decide what's what which way we want to go basically"
Making in-depth GM presentations	NS5	"I think people need to understand a lot more. about the whole. the whole way. farming's run"

Presenting GM risks and benefits	NS5	"we can also combine that with looking at. at things like organic farming. kind of the benefits and disadvantage of that and then a series people might gradually. grow an understanding of the whole area rather than. just concentrating on GM"
Presenting GM risks and benefits	NS5	"I think if we look at most of the literature that's been. published . most of it is. on the disadvantages of of GM and there has been very little publicity on. on the benefits and there always needs to be a balanced argument. and the public need to know all the facts."
Assessing public GM knowledge level	S13	"the way we approach consumers at the moment is through something. it is through a data collection. instrument . it's a questionnaire. so . in that sense we don't I mean because we want their views we're not. providing a lot of information. except for the very basic. you know. what they call biotechnology and. you know that genetic modification can be used to do. one of two things just just to. sort of introduce. the topic to them but. we don't want to give too much information because we want to see. how much they know and what kind of. attitudes they have"
Making GM research publicly available	S13	"they should find a way of of communicating this you know. as as they go along. doing their research the results they. they . they get. not only publish them in academic journals but ma-. make them probably a bit. you know. available to the wider public."
Communicating GM innovation benefits	S13	"if people see. trade-offs between accepting something that is new and to some extent. unknown . and . benefits there are quite tangible like perhaps. health benefits. if you know if. products are developed that can. can be either either. functional . type of foods or or can can give. you know. specific benefits then that may be an idea otherwise."
Organizing seminars for the public	S16	"are seminars for. the staff and students or even outsiders they come those are inter-departmental seminars"

(continued)

Table B.2 (Cont.)

Code	Case	Text/Empirical indicator
Emphasizing GM's positive side	S16	"so they I think these scientists that have been trying to promote. GM they have looked and concentrated more on the. good part of it. I can give an example of. but I wouldn't like to mention someone"
Giving the public some time	S16	"are seminars for. the staff and students or even outsiders they come those are inter-departmental seminars"
Emphasizing GM's positive side	S16	"more or to concentrate on the both the. the good part of it and the side effects of it. but it's like they have been highlighting more on the. the good part of. GM . than the bad part of it"
Communicating GM innovation benefits	S16	"yeah advertising and showing the good parts of. GM"
Assessing public GM knowledge level	S3	"what do you understand by the word natural. and then ask them. how would you distinguish between. a natural food. and a GM food."
Creating press releases	S3	"that's that's another thing for you to look at. the . what's on the web. is archieved. in terms of press releases. so if I just. if I just find one of the pages for you."
Tailoring GM information	S4	"some cases it's only. possible to be. superficial and. just to build a bit. because it's. you you want it to be. a broad subject. and in in other cases you can be quite detailed but not cover. as much. breadth . it depends on the. /audience/"
Making in-depth GM presentations	S4	"I would say. there's . several scopes for different sorts of documentaries I mean. the history of GM. and putting GM in context I think is quite important. especially in context of the Green Revolution. and in the impact that that has had. I think. so in other words the. reason for doing. GM . I think is important to do. I think it's also important to. look at each of the. areas of risk. separately . so . I think. you need to look at. health issues. human health in terms of. how that it's assessed and. what what the likely. procedure is going to be for that. I think. for the environmental impact"

Being proactive in GM information-sharing	S4	"it's likely to be cause of. media attract media attention. then we will. probably . approach the university's. information office. and but also those at the BBSRC and NERC. because we have to inform the people that we. are funded by. not that we would change what we are going to say. but it's important that people are aware. of what we are going to say."
Educating the public about GM	S4	"I think it's it's it's a matter of slowly building up. the knowledge base so that. not so that you take away the fears because I. I think. you have to be. you have to acknowledge that there are risks. but so that you can focus. on the ones that are real. and . not the phantoms"
Assessing public GM knowledge level	S4	"you've really got to think. in every case though. it's a matter of. identifying . what you. perceive . the lack of information. knowledge base. of the audience is and address that. so ."
Emphasizing crossbreeding/GM similarities	S4	"GM technology it's been around for quite some time. I . believe . that it is not. it is fundamentally different. from . simply making crosses. it is in some ways far more targetted but. it's a bit of an oversimplified-cation just to say. it is. very different and it's against gardeners. blah blah blah blah. however . it it does represent the next stage on. from some of the things that I have been doing we have been working on. various means of. of getting small amounts of DNA across. for the last 15–20 years other than GM. and I think that work will also continue"
Tailoring GM information	S4	"I'll give. in broad terms. how we go about. trying to quantify those risks. for a. an audience which is. fairly well. tuned into GM. and GM technology. again it depends on what the audience is. for instance if I talked to an audience which. is . very much informed on. how the technology works. I'll probably concentrate on the areas which I feel they will be weaker. on . which will be. perhaps on the areas of agriculture and. ecology . on the other hand if I am talking to. a . room full of ecologists. I'll probably spend more time talking about. technology . how gene interactions. work and how. the transformation technology works. and what our. capabilities are . and then. bring in the ecology so"

Table B.2 (Cont.)

Code	Case	Text/Empirical indicator
Presenting GM research rationale	S4	"so when I talk to a lay audience what I start off with is the basis of the technology"
Being proactive in GM information-sharing	S4	"if we are going to say something which. people are. are aware is going to cause. some amount of controversies about it all. so we do that"
Creating awareness of GM risks	S4	"I mean in a positive way. I think. it's a good thing. to . be aware of possible. risks and hazards. but you've not got to be hypocritical with that. you've got to accept. that . there are risks. and hazards in. several areas. associated . with . the environment in general"
Making in-depth GM presentations	S4	"we need. more in-depth. coverage . and less. headline . coverage . I think we need more. documentaries and less news items for instance."
Educating the public about GM	S4	"in order to communicate it effectively I think. some people. would say that it's a softly softly approach I wouldn't say that I would say. that it's it. it's far more. seeking to provide information. so that people become. more able to. be rational in the. areas that they are worried about. and . and become more relaxed in the areas that are really frankly. nothing to worry about"
Discussing specific GM case	S4	"I. outlying what the major areas are perceived as. and I give a. a detailed either a detailed case study"
Discussing specific GM case	S5	"ask more specific questions and deal in in specifics rather than. you know talking about. are GM crops dangerous"
Giving the public some time	S5	"GM products being available I think in a long term. it will become. you know accepted as. but in the short term it seems. hard to imagine"
Organizing seminars for the public	S5	"given seminars and things to. for instance the students who do. you know MSc in horticulture or amenity things and they don't really know very much about. genetic modification"

Collaborating with other departments	S6	"did it in collaboration with the. do you know I can't remember what they're. called but anyway one of the groups in Oxford. which . does quite a lot of liaison work and the typography department. and so they. sort of rescreened what we said and how we presented things. and that. was very successful it was in the Exhibition Centre but in the public area bit"
Emphasizing crossbreeding/ GM similarities	S6	"what they would term traditional. breeding . and . what we would call manipulation. but we wouldn't any more because it gets misinterpreted what what's already been done by breeders. in terms of crossing different species of introducing. genes from different places but by. what people regard as quite happily. as traditional means of. crossing and what have you. and the fact that we've manipulated. the genotypes. that we. call food. for a long time"
Simplifying GM research information	S6	"there is also a need for people to have an understanding of the. of the basics of of of what DNA is and what it does and how it operates"
Having public debate about GM	S6	"there should be much more public debate and much more information. for public so that. when decisions are made. they may or not be. absolutely what people want but they can see why they're made. and I think the same's true with GM"
Making in-depth GM presentations	S6	"GM you have to have people. knowing what's happening in. genetics what's happening in biology what's happening with the food position what. you know what does nutr- nutrition means etcetera. I mean when you get. and I had a a a lady from a magazine ring me up about genetic manipulation and said their readers were worried and they were worried about this fact that they were eating DNA."
Having conversations about GM risks	S6	"you can't put your hand on your heart as a scientist and say there is no risk. you have to say well our experiments have not shown anything that we need to be worried about"

(continued)

Table B.2 (Cont.)

Code	Case	Text/Empirical indicator
GM concerns factors (RQ1)		
Irrational 'response to risks'	NS1	"we see the benefits. of certain risks as. being . such as to outweigh. the . consequences of the risk. but the the whole calculus of risk the probability of an unhappy event and the consequence of the character of that event if it occurs is something people are. not well adjusted to making."
Irrational 'response to risks'	NS1	"most people. I mean you know. if you understood risk you'd never put a penny on the Lottery. would you?. with odds like that. you'd keep it in your pocket. and the good statisticians do precisely that but the human being isn't rational. so . we don't really behave in response to risks in a rational way."
GM's proximity to foodborne illnesses	NS1	"I do think the BSE. crisis deepened everything in this area it's rather like the way the Japanese are so sensitive to anything nuclear. you have a couple of nuclear bombs on you and it changes your perception of nuclear."
Outbreak of foodborne illnesses	NS1	"rightly or wrongly I believe the British public is heavily sensitised to food issues by BSE CJD"
Belief in GM product side effects	NS2	"I think a little bit about the actual scientific effects of. genetically modified foods and how it will affect. the rest of agriculture and so on and. things like cross fertilization and those kind of things."
Belief in GM product side effects	NS2	"also I think people are worried about the health effects."
Limited knowledge about GM research	NS2	"I think it's probably due to. people not knowing enough about. what it meant and that."

Unfavorable depiction of GM technology	NS2	"the way the media portrayed. GM foods as being. sort of. Frankenstein foods or whatever. the way it was put across in the media."
Unfavorable depiction of GM technology	NS2	"because there was campaigns by like. people like Greenpeace to. wreck GM crops and stuff like that so"
Objective-driven nature of scientific research	NS2	"it's very nature it's like. very technical and it's not about. being . subjective it's about being objective so"
Criticism from interest groups	NS5	". people like Greenpeace. actually promoting the the bad sides of GM."
Limited knowledge about GM research	NS5	"I've had a few conversations with friends about GM. but I. I think most of my friends don't have a real. deep understanding of what GM's about."
Unfavorable depiction of GM technology	NS5	"there is obviously the science behind it but. the way it's which is being portrayed in the media certainly. it's much easier to kind of write a sensationalist article about something that. an action group have done rather than about. the scientific issues. because no-one will read it."
Unfavorable depiction of GM technology	NS5	"The Mirror. the really. influential papers across the country if they weren't so sensationalist. and they considered more. what GM might do. that would affect the public attitude I think. quite dramatically. but they're the basis of public opinion. unfortunately"
Limited knowledge about GM research	NS5	"If you say GMO. they won't know actually what you're talking about. so there's so the the depth of knowledge isn't really great. so we should be doing something about it"
Limited knowledge about GM research	NS5	"I think there's a lack of information. and a lack of understanding. by the public of what GM actually really entails. partly through."
Limited knowledge about GM research	NS5	"I'm not saying that I'm in favour of it. but I just think people don't understand it very well"

(continued)

Table B.2 (Cont.)

Code	Case	Text/Empirical indicator
Inadequate promotion of GM benefits	NS5	"there's really there's been a very poor job done. of actually promoting the benefits of GM. that's why I think the public are against it at the moment"
Lack of effective government communication	NS5	"lack of Government's. communication"
Unfavorable depiction of GM technology	NS5	"I think it's a lot of spinning on. the part of. some of the. organizations who don't really like GM."
Limited knowledge about GM research	NS5	"the other side wasn't put and people understand alright this is a. a risk that actually may occur. but . people then aren't told what the actual risk is."
Unfavorable depiction of GM technology	NS5	.I know GM. made a big issue sorry Greenpeace made a big issue of promoting that. gene transfer through soil. could actually happen but the chances are one in a billion.
Limited knowledge about GM research	S13	"because there are so many. ways of talking about. the issue and. biotechnology is different from genetic modification and that's different from. other . other terms. and so I think that that somehow adds to. to the confusion and. the lack of understanding and knowledge"
Unsatisfactory answer to GM risks	S13	"you can't you can't just say you know we don't have. we don't have results yet but. you know we termed that it it's. it's good for you because we cannot tell you that it's bad. I don't think that people accept that."
Unsatisfactory answer to GM risks	S13	"it's not enough to say. we cannot prove. that there are risks so there are no risks. you have to say you don't know. whether there are any. risks . "

Uncertain about GM research	S13	"perceived uncertainty of. possible potential future outcomes that. it's not people are not. able to control so it is lack of control lack of knowledge. uncertainty about. potential . you know."
Belief in GM product side effects	S16	"they believe it has some side effects"
Belief in GM product side effects	S16	"people think it will take long for the side effects to show up"
Extensively unexamined GM side effects	S16	"it might be doing well. as crops but it probably. the side effect area I think it hasn't been exploited [=explored?] fully"
Extensively unexamined GM side effects	S16	"so they I think these scientists that have been trying to promote. GM they have looked and concentrated more on the. good part of it. I can give an example of. but I wouldn't like to mention someone"
Belief in GM product side effects	S16	"even when you. genetically modified genes it's when you're cha- changing the genes so people think if you're changing genes. then it will have some side effects probably in the human body when you eat it."
Limited knowledge about GM research	S16	"I think is in. probably lack lack of understanding"
Criticism from interest groups	S3	"as it were the debate has been won by the lobbyists. and . you know I mean I mean. obviously I mean Greenpeace and people like that."
Multiple meanings of GM concepts	S3	"most things that you talk about. whether it's fruits. I mean especially the fruits. I mean most of the foods that we eat. are not natural. if you. if you mean. not being. influenced or bred by men. so . I mean. that's one of the words you might look at. what do people understand by the word natural."
Outbreak of foodborne illnesses	S3	"the reason why GM foods. have been so so . so problematic in this country. compared to say the United States of America. is because of the backg-. because of the problem of BSE. in the last fifteen and sixteen years."

(continued)

Table B.2 (Cont.)

Code	Case	Text/Empirical indicator
Conflicting views about GM safety	S3	"the fact that that. well it wasn't scientists so much. it was ministers who said. that . that . that the beef was safe. now sadly we know. well we don't actually know. because it's not completely proven. but it seems very highly probable. that . that . what is it?"
'Mistrust of commercial companies'	S3	"there might be a problem. so the. the sort of mistrust of GM foods isn't just BSE. but it also goes back to Thalidimite as well. in my opinion. though that. what's the phrase. evidence in other words that commercial companies can't always be trusted. to to bear in mind the public good."
Hesitant to explain GM research	S3	"they saw no reason why they should explain to other people what we were doing. and . so they managed to. what's the word"
Mistrust of the government	S3	"and the government? what do you think? people maybe. some people may not trust the government's judgement as well. not just companies. but also B: yeah. oh yeah. I mean I think. well over BSE it was the government that was not trusted. but also. the . what's. only become clear. to the general public in recent years."
Multiple meanings of GM concepts	S3	"I mean they wouldn't be. so most of what you look at in terms of crop production. is not natural. but . and and people are redefining the word natural. to mean. something they're happy with"
'Mistrust of commercial companies'	S3	"a mistrust of commercial companies in safety cases."
Criticism from interest groups	S3	"there're being different groups. doing things. and . I mean I am now guessing. ok?. when Greenpeace have been attacking. they've been doing it for publicity. purposes . and therefore. they've told the media. and they've informed them. and they're taking their own videos"

Limited knowledge about GM research	S4	"so so that in in that sense. a little knowledge or or no knowledge. you're more likely to be. generically against the technology than when you have got a lot of knowledge. in which case you are likely to be quite focussed. in your in your fears or. objections against technology"
Unsatisfactory answer to GM risks	S5	"people feel they have to say one way or the other. you know. genes either definitely cannot escape from plants into the environment or they can. and the the answer is that that. maybe under some circumstances they can. but . we don't know. need to we don't know enough about it"
'Mistrust of commercial companies'	S5	"mistrust. I think. of .(5) organizations"
Lack of effective government communication	S5	"government I think had failed to. deal effectively with. communication of uncertainty because. they tried to they have tried to. respond to the public's wish for a black and white answer by giving them a black and white answer"
Hesitant to explain GM research	S5	"it's quite difficult I wouldn't really try and talk to anybody about that. if I had a choice I wouldn't talk to them about it. I mean I might. I'd even try and resist talking to other. food scientists or. animal scientists about it because you. it's just not a. a useful form of com–of communication"
Mistrust of scientists	S5	"what's happened with this is that. for a number of reasons people have decided that they they're not going to believe that. so . whether you can regain it I don't know"
Hesitant to explain GM research	S5	"just people's resistance to. the fact that scientists don't interview very well. you know I think it's. because scientists are perceived to have doing something and. which is. many people don't have access to and don't fully understand. and the issues therefore are. very clouded"

(continued)

Table B.2 (Cont.)

Code	Case	Text/Empirical indicator
Mistrust of scientists	S5	"lack of trust in scientists and all that. kind of thing. but there seems to be as much as. of a lack of trust in. special knowledge that a only a certain number of people. are perceived to have."
Mistrust of the government	S5	"people who are. seen to be. in authority"
Mistrust of scientists	S5	"a position of special knowledge. and I think it's. stems from. a number of. origins . A: mhmh. in the field of. in the. related field of food. scares or B: well I think yes I think."
GM scientists' ineffective communication	S6	"I say I think our. communication of science's 's s been very poor"
Disinterested in learning about GM	S6	"we had to advertise in the newspaper. everything like that we did that we didn't get a single person. come to the meeting. from the general public they were just not interested. in it and that was in."
Limited knowledge about GM research	S6	"I think as scientists we have not. given people enough information in the past. it's not something you can switch the tap on and off. so it's not. our communication on genetic modification so much as our communication on science and the advances of science and what's happening and. general communication with the with the public"
Mistrust of scientists	S6	"it feels I think to the public as though therefore your hiding something or your trying to make a clever statement which fools them into whereas in fact that's what science is. it's you know you try and base everything on factual. statements"
GM's proximity to foodborne illnesses	S6	"yes I think the unfortunate timing with ehm. with other things like. BSE . and what have you and the. supposed . role of scientific advice. in that. did not. help the matter at all."

Unfavorable depiction of GM technology	S6	"the particularly things like the tabloid press to simple scare. tactics . I mean it's very very easy. to make claims. which are completely unsubstantiated."
Outbreak of foodborne illnesses	S6	"a general antagonism towards. GM increasing. but in this country I think it made people particularly sensitive to. to this and to the views of scientists"
Criticism from interest groups	S9	"the media started to campaign against. GM products so. in general I think the media has a very. high impact on public opinion"
Hesitant to embrace GM technology	S9	"people are afraid of new things. you can see that all through. the time you know at first they were afraid of the car they thought that it was something bad well. it turned out to be something bad but anyway. they were they are afraid of new things. they are reluctant to try something completely new. different from what they know"
GM's proximity to foodborne illnesses	S9	"because these incidents are very close to one another and I think that Europe has experienced. a lot of. food cases I don't know how can I say it"
Other issues		
Finding out GM research sponsor	NS2	"if I was to look at any research I would always find out who paid for it. and then that would affect."
More research on GM risks	NS2	"I think if there could be more research and it could and it could be clearly. proved that there's no health risk or anything that I don't think"
Government funding for GM research	NS2	"I think it would be good if the Government could pay for some research. and some independent research as well"
Single definition of GM concepts	S3	"I mean saf- again safe is not a word. what's your definition of safe. I mean safe is another word. that it actually involves. I mean. a statistician's answer to that questions. would be very different to a lay person's."

(continued)

Table B.2 (Cont.)

Code	Case	Text/Empirical indicator
Single definition of GM concepts	S3	"see work out what how people define natural"
Difficulty in labeling products	S4	"I think the only real- rational way. about really is. is to be very tight. prior . to release. I think. I think the labeling. is . very very complex. very complex and very difficult"
More research on GM risks	S4	"there's. there's risks in not doing anything. and not using the technology as well as using the technology. but if you just. blindly accept. the technology and you say well we are going to use all of it. it's inevitable that there will be some. areas of the technology which. will pose an unacceptable risk. for some."
Government funding for GM research	S5	"I think a bit of industry funding's fine. there has to be. money that comes from. non-industry sources A: the Government or B: yes I suppose. so that. I mean the Research Council money I think is. even though they are closer to industry than they used to be. it doesn't. seem yet to have got so bad that. that one is dictated to. although I think research is a bit more focused than it used to. you have to sort of talk in the grant proposals about. you know what are the."

Index

Note: Page numbers in *italic* denote figures and exhibits, and in **bold** indicate tables.

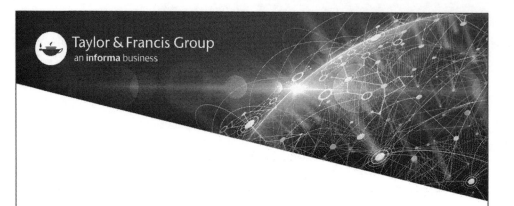